ASCENDENCIES ENCOMPASSING

ASCENDENCIES ENCOMPASSING

Travis Wallenfang

atmosphere press

Table of Contents

Introduction

This book has been dedicated to acknowledging and bringing awareness to issues of sovereignty. Sovereignty can be defined as supreme power, especially over a body politic.[1] It can also be stated as supreme political authority; paramount control of the constitution and frame of government and its administration; the self-sufficient source of political power, from which all specific political powers are derived; the international independence of a state, combined with the right and power of regulating its internal affairs without foreign dictation; also a political society, or state, which is sovereign and independent. This all can be more clearly defined in footnote: Chisholm v. Georgia, 2 Dall. 455, 1 L. Ed. 440: Union Bank v. Hill, 3 Cold. (Tenn.) 325; Moore v. Shaw, 17 Cal. 218, 79 Am. Dec. 123. "The freedom of the nation has its correlate in the sovereignty of the nation. Political sovereignty is the assertion of the self-determinate will of the organic people, and in this, there is the manifestation of its freedom. It is in and through the determination of its sovereignty that the order of the nation is constituted and maintained." Mulford, Nation, p. 129.[2]

The acronyms contained in this book are defined in this book, so help clarify the many acronyms used. This book reflects how tribes have enacted in the past while attempting to enforce Indian/Native Employment Preference Law, which is grounded in the inherent sovereign status of the Nation's First Peoples. This legal doctrine is the most basic principle of Indian law and is supported by a host of Supreme Court decisions. This book will also bring the blatant nepotism and

---

1. https://www.merriam-webster.com/dictionary/sovereignty

2. What is SOVEREIGNTY? https://thelawdictionary.org/sovereignty/

corruption within all agencies and how they are currently applied. It will show the attempts at the state of stalling individuals, making false accusations, and saying there was little or no information when it was currently available because this was a current and active project in which the requests for information were submitted to the state. It is clear to understand the Tribes all possess the right to which Inherent sovereign powers derive from the principle that certain powers do not necessarily come from delegated powers granted by express acts of Congress but are inherent powers of a limited sovereign that have never been taken away. Tribes have a basic relationship with the federal government as sovereign powers. This is recognized in both treaties and federal statutes. The sovereignty of tribes has been limited from time to time by treaties and federal legislation; however, what has not been expressly limited remains within tribal sovereignty.[3]

TERO and IP law is grounded in its inherent sovereign status and has Supreme Courts because of the recognition recognized in both treaties and federal statutes for hundreds of years. The reason for this information is to show the applicability of not just the Federally Recognized Tribes of Wisconsin, but all the Tribes across the Nation and their working relationships with other entities. These relationships are generally with agencies and entities from other Tribes, Federal and State, or County and Municipalities agencies. The reason for these working relationships is because of things like the Construction of highways or bridgework, utilities, and public works, just to name a few.

So the next time you're riding past projects where there are many people on these projects, located on or near Federally Recognized Tribes of Wisconsin which are composed of: Lac Du Flambeau (LDF), Ho-Chunk Nation (HCN) and Lac Courte Oreilles Band of Lake Superior Chippewa (LCO), Red Cliff Band of Lake Superior Chippewa (RC), Forest County Potawatomi

---

3. What is the Legal Basis for TERO? https://cter-tero.org/tero-faq/

(FCP), Sokaogon Chippewa Community Mole Lake Band of Lake Superior Chippewa (SCC), Menominee Indian Tribe of Wisconsin (MITW), Stockbridge-Munsee Band of Mohican Indians (SMBM), Bad River Band of Lake Superior Chippewa (BRB), Oneida Nation of Wisconsin (ONW), and St. Croix Chippewa Indians of Wisconsin (SCCIW) will be referred to as (TRIBES). These projects take a great deal of time and money, along with the immense amount of time invested in coordinating everyone from the Wisconsin Department of Transportation (WisDOT), Federal Highways Administration (FHWA), Construction Unions (CU) Construction Industry (CI), Department of Workforce Development (DWD) and TRIBES. These projects take immense oversight from Field Engineers, Project Managers, and Project leaders and require the oversight to make sure the contractors are adhering to these specifications. The CI holds many requirements that the construction contractors are expected to adhere to. These documents are generally contained in a manual that is provided by the bidders who have been awarded the project. A good example of a manual like the one presented is generally referred to as a Construction and Materials Manual (CMM). The manuals are generally specific to the type of work being done as this manual is composed of the general practices related to the specific type of work, such as Heavy Construction, Residential Construction, or Transportation Construction work.

The CMM referenced is provided by the WisDOT as a standard for projects like the 441 Mega Projects mentioned. As a Field Engineer, I have the responsibility of having a firm understanding of the specifications and codes required by the WisDOT, contained in the WisDOT CMM. The manual presents general or common industry practices for transportation construction work by the clarification of contracts referencing requirements through communicating WisDOT policies, practices, and expectations for consultants, contractors, and other construction industry partners.[4]

Through the analysis of the WisDOT CMM, we can scrutinize one specific important section contained in the manual. This section is identified as Section 2-24 *Labor Compliance*, more specifically in Section 2 titled: "Native American Hiring Provision" (NAHP). In examining everything encompassing the NAHP, we must ask why this was implemented instead of the Indian Preference laws (IP) or Tribal Employment Rights Ordinances (TERO). Next, we will look at the history of the NAHP, the series of events or meetings from as far back as 2002 and 2004 – leading until early 2018 through 2019. Next, we must look at the development of these provisions in 2009 to understand what influences led to the suspension of the Native American Hiring provision.

We will also look at all surrounding issues encountered in establishing the provision, the parties or people associated with the creation of this provision, the development process through records of the meeting minutes, and any other influences associated with the provision. Although the Wisconsin Department of Transportation (DOT) and the Wisconsin Transportation Builders Association (WTBA) assisted in establishing the Native American Hiring Provision, which has constrained TRIBES from utilizing Indian Preference Laws (IP) or Tribal Employment Rights Ordinances (TERO), nevertheless, exposing the overreaching which transpired though the application of the provision as it impeded on TRIBES employment opportunities should bring about changes because of the influences exerted by WTBA's pressure on WisDOT pushing to rescind the provision only to show these same entities' influences. These same entities also helped establish a budget for the WisDOT, as many of the affiliated people are also board members within the WTBA, which is directly associated with owners of these Construction Companies being awarded these projects.

---

4. WisDOT Construction and Materials Manual (CMM) https://wisconsindot.gov/rdwy/cmm/cm-00-10.pdf

Through analysis, the influences encompassing the development process were mainly presented by the following: DWD, CU, CI, WisDOT, FHWA, WTBA and the TRIBES. All the associated parties participated in the development of the NAHP directly or indirectly influencing the establishment and implementation of the NAHP processes to set in place an outline for rquirements and policy procedures necessary for the promotion and encouragement of Native American economic and employment opportunities on any construction projects located on, partially on, near and adjacent to tribal lands within the state of Wisconsin. The Wisconsin Department of Transportation Tribal Affairs (WisDOT TA) has made numerous statements the NAHP was developed with direct consultation with the TRIBES. This was established in response to the statutory limitations expressed by the WisDOT's inability to enforce TERO. The NAHP was established as a tool designed and implemented by the Tribal Labor Advisory Committee (TLAC) and the Statewide Native American Labor Initiative. These groups established other tools and resources designed to promote labor opportunities that extend beyond project-by-project hiring. The provision intends to stimulate early meaningful dialog between contractors doing business on, partially on, and within a commutable distance of tribal communities and tribal workforce development programs with the intent of the NAHP to encourage Native American hiring opportunities through enhanced communications and establishing reporting mechanisms.[5]

Included below is the chronology of all the meetings and provisions, Partnership Agreements (PA), and Executive Orders (EO), along with the meeting minutes and place where these meetings took place, directly reflecting on how the formation of the NAHP was established and the restraining of the TRIBES to implement their own TERO or IP on their projects.

---

5. http://wisdottribaltaskforce.org/wp-content/uploads/2017/12/Native-American-Hiring-Provision.pdf

Below is a set of chronological events that transpired as they relate to the establishment of the NAHP. The information released is captions of the actual minutes from the meetings established by the WisDOT TL and delegated to the TLAC Coordinator to set up and coordinate these events. (*It is also important to note that all this information presented has been removed from the TLAC website[6] by the new TLAC Coordinator as of March 2019 as it related to the NAHP*): *FOR THE ORIGINAL TIMELINE OF MEETING MINUTES PLEASE GO TO PAGE 329 IN THE APPENDIX*

---

6. Tribal Labor Advisory Committee website: https://www.wisdottlac.org/

Chapter 1

Have you ever noticed when reading documents relating to the government-to-government relationships related to Federally Recognized Tribes there is a common theme in these working relationships and these agreements as the common language inserted into documents like the ones for the state of Wisconsin like the: PA,[7] MOU,[8] MOA,[9] EO#39,[10] NAHP,[11] and Tribal Initiatives?[12] Through the examination of these documents, you will notice the mention of the language between all of these documents between Federal, Tribal, State, Municipalities, and other agencies, the reoccurring clauses stating to the TRIBES which is: "Respecting Tribal Sovereignty and Self Determination Rights" and "Respecting the TRIBES' Rights to Self-Government." This language is present in every document. The TRIBES are currently working with numerous agencies, but are these just words on paper? In this book, you will notice the actions of the agencies are quite different from the words on the papers. This will be seen through the actions presented, as much of this information has been documented through communications and meeting minutes over the past

---

7. Partnership Agreement 2010 https://wisdottribaltaskforce.org/wp-content/uploads/2015/05/2010-Partnership-Agreement.pdf

8. Memorandum of Understanding https://dpi.wi.gov/amind/mou

9. Memorandum of Agreements http://wisdottribaltaskforce.org/wp-content/uploads/2015/05/PartnershipAgreement.pdf

10. Executive Order http://wisdottribaltaskforce.org/wp-content/uploads/2015/05/Executive-Order-39.pdf

11. WisDOT Tribal Affairs Initiative https://www.wisdottlac.org/

12. WisDOT Tribal Affairs Initiative https://wisconsindot.gov/Pages/doing-bus/civil-rights/tribalaffairs/default.aspx

ten (10) years. One might be inclined to ask if these governmental agencies truly know and understand the meaning of: "Tribal Sovereignty and Self-Determination Rights."

A "tribes' sovereignty" is the power to make and enforce laws and establish courts, which is another forum for resolving disputes. This is the same as the tribe's power to regulate and implement Indian Preference Laws (IP) and Tribal Employment Rights Ordinances (TERO). IP is defined as a unique legal right that tribal members have that entitles them to first consideration at all employment, training, contracting, subcontracting, and business opportunities that exist on, and in some cases, near reservations. There are no federal laws that prohibit IP. Tribes are exempt from Title VII of the Civil Rights Act and several other employment laws. Numerous court cases have upheld this exemption. Court rulings have held that IP is a political preference, not a racial preference, and as such, does not violate the dictates of federal employment law.[13] TERO requires that all employers who are engaged in operating a business on reservations give preference to qualified Indians in all aspects of employment, contracting, and other business activities. TERO Offices were established and empowered to monitor and enforce the requirements of TERO. They are ratified within the authority to administer an Indian/Native employment preference as long as laws or ordinances are grounded in the TRIBE's inherent sovereign status. This premise is the most rudimentary principle of Indian law and is reinforced by a host of Supreme Court decisions. Inherent sovereign powers originate from the principle that undeniable powers do not come from entrusted powers conceded by express acts of Congress but are natural powers of a limited sovereign that have never been taken away. This is recognized in both treaties and federal statutes. The sovereignty of tribes has been limited time and time again by treaties and federal legislation; however, what has not been expressly limited remains within

---

13. What is Indian Preference Law: https://www.bia.gov/jobs/Indian_Preference

a TRIBE'S sovereignty.[14]

Tribes Self Determination means: "The Indigenous Peoples, by virtue of that right, freely determine their political status and freely pursue their economic, social, and cultural development," according to Article 3 of the U.N. Declaration of the Rights of Indigenous People.[15]

Indigenous peoples, in exercising their right to self-determination, have the right to autonomy or self-government in matters relating to their internal and local affairs, as well as ways and means for financing their autonomous functions, according to Article 4 of the U.N. Declaration on the Rights of Indigenous People.[16]

The most protected and sacred right of all peoples is the right to govern their affairs and make decisions without being coerced by other governments. This is an inherent right of people that has existed since time immemorial.[17]

The current issues presented directly are rudimentary principles to IP and TERO resulting from the lack of knowledge relevant to the subject, leading to only speculative assumptions, and thereby perpetuating the creation of ambiguous language or statements when it can be simply stated that as long as IP and TERO are grounded in the inherent sovereign status, they are reinforced by a host of Supreme Court decisions. As we address this issue, we can ask why the TRIBES were opposed to the removal of the application of IP or TERO "on," "near," or within a commutable distance of Indian roadways, Indian country, Indian trust lands, fee lands, and reservations.

14. What is the legal basis for TERO? https://cter-tero.org/tero-faq/#1

15. Source: NNHRC Human Rights Issues for the Navajo Nation, self-determination http://www.nnhrc.navajo-nsn.gov/selfDetermination.html

16. Source: NNHRC Human Rights Issues for the Navajo Nation, self-determination http://www.nnhrc.navajo-nsn.gov/selfDetermination.html

17. Source: NNHRC Human Rights Issues for the Navajo Nation, self-determination http://www.nnhrc.navajo-nsn.gov/selfDetermination.html

First, we shall begin with a review of the information at the foundation of IP and TERO. This is because without understanding the history, it is easy to get dissuaded by inaccurate information. This is a key point; as you begin your journey through these readings, you will be able to view one person's interpretation of language presented in these documents and the monumental impact affecting many tribes in a region. These impacts have already been felt in communities located "on," "near," and within a "commutable distance," and can also have a detrimental effect to be felt across the nation if they are not resolved by all tribes, including both federally and non-federally recognized tribes. It is with the greatest importance that this journey begins by stressing that all tribes work together in a conducive manner while respecting each other's laws, rights, constitutions, sovereignty, and inherent rights to self-government.

Now beginning, we focus on a more specific region in the Midwest and on a group of Tribes located within the state of Wisconsin known as the Eleven Federally Recognized Tribes of Wisconsin, which will be referred to as TRIBES. This group is composed of the following TRIBES: Bad River Band of Lake Superior Chippewa Indians, Forest County Potawatomi Community, Ho-Chunk Nation, Lac Courte Oreilles Band of Lake Superior Chippewa Indians, Lac Du Flambeau Band of Lake Superior Chippewa Indians, Menominee Indian Nation of Wisconsin, Oneida Nation of Wisconsin, Red Cliff Band of Lake Superior Chippewa Indians, Sokaogon Chippewa Community, St. Croix Band of Chippewa Indians, and Stockbridge-Munsee Band of Mohican Indians. Many of these tribes were here long before the state of Wisconsin was established on May 29, 1848.[18]

The reason this is brought forward is that the TRIBES have embarked on numerous adventures related to Indian Preference Employment on Federal-Aid Highway State projects on and

---

18. Wisconsin was established in 1848 https://www.history.com/topics/us-states/wisconsin

near Indian reservations which can be traced back as far as through meeting minutes, memorandums, correspondence, and emails as far back as March 15, 1993, document Titled: "IP employment on Federal-Aid Highway State projects 'on' and 'near' Indian reservations." You will notice this document was from the Federal Highways Administration (FHWA), which states its purpose: *"To consolidate all previous guidance for FHWA field officials, State Highway Agencies, and their sub-recipients and contractors regarding the allowance for Indian preference in employment on projects on and near Indian reservations."*[19] Then proceeds to call out the specific process for the consideration and applicability of TERO and IP on Indian IRR, but are located near the boundaries of reservations and other Indian lands. Near can be defined as: "Roads 'Near' an Indian reservation are those within a reasonable commuting distance from the reservation."

This document then calls out a specific process of establishing an IP goal, which is developed during the development process as the Tribal and State representatives are to confer to make determinations regarding Indian Employment Goals for contractors' workforce who are other than core work crews. In setting reasonable Indian Employment (IE) goals, consideration should be given to the availability of skilled and unskilled Indian workers, the type of work being performed, and contractors' requirements regarding projects near reservations. Once this has been established, the only time the goals can be changed by the State is after consultation with the Indian tribal government representative or TERO and the contractor, but only after considering the good faith efforts to meet the goal and work to be performed. It is at this time the contractor was to consider all qualified job applicants referred by TERO or the designated Tribal labor representative.

After the Indian employment goal has been inserted into the contract, the state will follow normal contract compliance

---

19. IP in employment on Federal Aid Highway Projects on and near Indian Reservations https://www.fhwa.dot.gov/legsregs/directives/notices/n4720-7.cfm

or contract administration oversight procedures. At this time, the state can elect to invite the Tribal labor representatives to assist efforts in monitoring the compliance process. The state then reviews the employment practices of the contractors when a goal is not reached after the consideration of the effort's taking in good faith.

This document then concludes with the "TERO Tax," stating the TRIBE's ability to impose a tax on reservations, but in off-reservation situations, the TRIBES can bill contractors at agreed-upon rates for services rendered (i.e., recruitment, employee referral, and related supportive services). This document recommends where the use of these funds should be utilized in a statement: "*It has been FHWA's longstanding policy to participate in State and local taxes which do not discriminate against or otherwise single out Federal-aid highway construction contracts for special or different tax treatment. Therefore, if the TERO tax rate on highway construction contracts is the same as that which is imposed on other contracts on the reservation, such costs are eligible for Federal-aid reimbursement.*"[20] Finally, it concluded with the purpose of the FHWA and who the intended audience is: "State, Local, Tribal, governments, and TERO representatives and contractors."

The next information provided by WisDOT moves forward to 2002 when the FHWA released a report showing the Wisconsin Department of Transportation (WisDOT) places a Native American Hiring Preference in Federal Aid projects on or near Indian reservations and titled: "*Outreach to Native Americans, A Comprehensive Look at Wisconsin's Efforts.*"[21] This was established with the WisDOT and Wisconsin Division of the FHWA who partnered together, including Native American Businesses, Individuals, Two Native American Community Colleges, and the TRIBES on a government-to-government basis:

---

20. IP in employment on Federal Aid Highway Projects on and near Indian Reservations https://www.fhwa.dot.gov/legsregs/directives/notices/n4720-7.cfm

21. Outreach to Native Americans, A Comprehensive Look at Wisconsin's Efforts https://www.fhwa.dot.gov/tribal/state/oct31_03.htm

- *Lac Courte Oreilles Ojibwa Community College (LCOOCC).*

- *College of the Menominee Nation (CMN).*

The goals put in place by the FHWA were established to proactively seek out ways to increase employment of Native Americans and increase participation of Native American Businesses to contract for, or to bid on the contract for the Transportation infrastructures, development, and increased participation of the TRIBES in the FHWA program. These colleges have worked with the WisDOT and FHWA since 1995 after the staff visited the college in September 1995, signing a PA between the LCOOCC, WisDOT, and FHWA stating: "Key elements of the action plan and partnering charter include a commitment to work together as partners to plan, develop, and foster careers and business development for Native Americans in Wisconsin's transportation industry; to make the College aware of grant money which may become available and assist the College in obtaining the money; to offer surplus furniture and equipment, including computers to the College as a priority; and to provide the College with any technical assistance they may request, such as program-specific information about FHWA, WisDOT, the DBE program, and other state agencies and programs."[22] To help with the establishment of an associate's degree program in Business Administration with an emphasis on Entrepreneurship and the establishment of the Disadvantaged Business Enterprises (DBE) workshops through 2003 with the following transportation-related activities:

- *LCO/Sawyer County Transit System – LCOOCC faculty, staff, and students participated in developing and implementing a mass transportation system for the Lac Courte Oreilles Community.*

- *Faculty/Professional Development Activities and Domestic Travel – Students learned the fundamentals of transportation location*

---

22. Outreach to Native Americans, A Comprehensive Look at Wisconsin's Efforts, partnering: Sharing of Resources, https://www.fhwa.dot.gov/tribal/state/oct31_03.htm

referencing systems, specifically the WisDOT linear location referencing system, as well as basic spatial and non-spatial GIS operations necessary for transportation operations.

- *GIS Lab Transportation Apprenticeship Opportunities – These positions give students opportunities to work on transportation-related
projects for the Lac Courte Oreilles Reservation while pursuing their
college degrees. Students have helped GIS Lab staff on the following
transportation-related projects over the past year: 1) Development
of route schedules and maps and a website for the Sawyer County
and Lac Courte Oreilles (LCO) Transit System; 2) Updating the
inventory of pavement conditions for LCO's road system; and 3)
Compilation of conference materials, survey results, web page material and database information needed to develop a working group
of tribal GIS and transportation managers, FHWA, TTAP, BIA, and
WisDOT staff involved in other regional transportation initiatives.*

This inspired other Partnering initiatives such as:

- *Dwight David Eisenhower Transportation Fellowship Program
(DDETFP) – Objectives are to attract the United States' bright-
est minds to the field of transportation, to enhance the careers of
transportation professionals by encouraging them to seek advanced
degrees, and to retain top talent in the US transportation community. The DDETFP encompasses all areas of transportation and
has six award categories, including the Eisenhower Tribal Colleges
Initiatives, which identifies transportation activities at tribal colleges to provide Native American students and faculty fellowships.*

- *National Summer Transportation Institute for Secondary School
Students – The program features four weeks of instruction, including life management seminars, field trips, and student projects,
which stimulated interest in engineering, science, transportation,
and technology careers. Another objective of the program is to attract
minority and low-income youths into the transportation industry.*

- *Partnering for Indian Employment in Highway Construction –
The LCOOCC hosted a 1998 workshop designed to increase the*

employment and retention of Indians in highway construction. The two-day workshop, held on the college campus, was arranged in cooperation with the National Highway Institute, the Tribal Technical Assistance Program at the Michigan Technological University, and the WisDOT's Office of DBE Programs. Speakers from the Council for Tribal Employment Rights (CTER) presented the course.

- *Native American Hiring Preference – The WisDOT places a Native American hiring preference in federal aid projects on or near Indian lands. The special provision requires that the contractor(s) shall make aggressive, concerted efforts to employ Native Americans on the projects. The provision also applies to all subcontractors who will perform work on the project for more than five working days. It is the intent of the provision that the contractor(s) and subcontractor(s) new hires for the project, independent of the permanent core crew, shall be composed of Native Americans. The permanent core crew is composed of those full-time employed individuals necessary to satisfy his/her reasonable needs for supervisory or especially experienced personnel to ensure the efficient execution of the contract work. This special provision was written to comply with 23 USC 140, as amended by section 1026(c) of the 1991 Intermodal Surface Transportation Efficiency Act (ISTEA).*

- *Tribes have one week of the placement of a job order by the contractor to provide enough qualified or non-qualified applicants to meet the employment goal. The contractor, ensuring non-discrimination and providing equal employment opportunity, may employ persons living off the reservation. The contractor shall consider all qualified applicants referred by the tribe. Under this provision, the contractor is not required to employ any applicants who, in the contractor's opinion, are not qualified to perform the classification of work required.*

- *Contractors may request reasonable exemptions from and modifications to this provision upon grounds of undue hardship, inequity, and when special circumstances in the public interest or local or area-wide employment situations so require. Exemptions or modifications, with justification, are directed to the WisDOT District*

Office, where the project is located. Exemptions, if granted, are made after consideration of the good faith efforts of the contractor together with the ability of the Tribal government to refer workers in enough numbers and in time for the contractor to meet the goal and perform the work.

- *AASHTO (American Association of State Highway and Transportation Officials)/Transportation Activities Research Center (TRAC) Program – is a hands-on program that allows middle and high school students to use math and science to solve real-world problems in transportation and civil engineering. The program opens young minds to new ways of learning. Wisconsin currently has 33 schools participating in the program.*

There was no information for 2003, but as we hop forward into 2004, on 27th February, Wisconsin Executive Order #39 (EO#39) was established. This document states the state of Wisconsin recognizes the sovereignty of the TRIBES governments and the unique government-to-government relationship that exists between the state and the TRIBES. This resulted from the State-Tribal Consultation Initiative being created as nearly all the agencies in the Governor's Cabinet drafted policies establishing the framework for interaction with TRIBES. These policies were drafted with input from the TRIBES representatives. The goal of this Initiative will be greatly improved communications, allowing for any potential issues to be corrected early on or avoided entirely on both sides. Through the Initiative, valuable state and tribal resources are put to more effective use, delivering government services in a more streamlined, coordinated, and economically efficient manner.[23] The following agencies established State Tribal Consultation policies:

- *Department of Administration (DOA).*

- *Department of Agriculture, Trade and Consumer Protection.*

---

23. State-Tribal Consultation Initiative http://witribes.wi.gov/section.asp?linkid=28 3andlocid=57

- *Department of Children and Families.*

- *Department of Commerce.*

- *Department of Corrections.*

- *Department of Financial Institutions.*

- *Department of Health Services.*

- *Wisconsin Housing and Economic Development Authority.*

- *Wisconsin Office of Justice Assistance.*

- *Department of Natural Resources.*

- *Department of Revenue.*

- *Department of Tourism.*

- *Department of Workforce Development (DWD).*

- *The WisDOT has signed a state-tribal consultation agreement with each TRIBE'S government.*

The Department of Public Instruction, the Public Service Commission, and the Department of Justice are not a part of the Governor's Cabinet. It is important to mention this because if there is no defining language from the Department of Instruction, then the Public Service Commission will not act on any issues that are not specifically called out. If the presence, or the lack of enforcement by the Department of Justice, then there is no one to enforce any laws or violations if they are all not part of the Governor's Cabinet.

Through examination of EO#39, when you take a look at the third "WHEREAS," which states: "*WHEREAS the State of Wisconsin, a sovereign state within the United States recognizes the unique status of Indian Tribes and their right to existence, self-government and self-determination*"[24] This was signed by the Governor at the

24. WisDOT Executive Order #39 http://witribes.wi.gov/docview.asp?docid=23379 andlocid=57

time, Jim Doyle, but it is important to note the language which states the state of Wisconsin recognizes the "unique status of TRIBES, their right to existence, self-government and self-determination." Self-government is defined as the self-control, self-command government of a country by its people, especially after having been a colony.[25] Self-determination is defined as all peoples having the right freely to determine, without external interference, their political status and to pursue their economic, social, and cultural development, and every State must respect this right without external compulsion. This can include choices regarding the exercise of sovereignty and independent external relations (external self-determination), or it can refer to the selection of forms of government (internal self-determination).[26] "Indigenous Peoples have the right to self-determination. Under that right they freely determine their political status and freely pursue their economic, social, and cultural development," according to Article 3 of the U.N. Declaration of the Rights of Indigenous People. "Indigenous peoples, in exercising their right to self-determination, have the right to autonomy or self-government in matters relating to their internal and local affairs, as well as ways and means for financing their autonomous functions," according to Article 4 of the U.N. Declaration on the Rights of Indigenous People. "The most protected and sacred right of all peoples is the right to govern their affairs and make decisions without being coerced by other governments. This is an inherent right of peoples, and for the Navajo people it has existed since time immemorial. However, Navajo law states that the Navajo Nation must still obtain it; the 'Ultimate goal of the Navajo Nation is self-determination.' 10 N.N.C. § 124 (A) (2002). The commission recommends that the Navajo government, instead, recognize that the Navajo people's right to

---

25. Definition of Self Government https://www.merriam-webster.com/dictionary/self-government

26. Definition of Self Determination Page 54 https://pesd.princeton.edu/?q=node/266

self-determination has been absolute since time immemorial and is not an aspiration as stated in Title 10 of the Navajo Nation Code. Moreover, "Navajo written law must recognize the Navajo people's right to self-determination comes from the Holy People."

Chapter 2

2005–2008

This led to the creation of one document called the: "Partnership Agreement" (PA), established on May 25th, 2005. This document was created as a result of Governor James Doyle's EO#39, "*Relating to an affirmation of the government-to-government relationship between the State of Wisconsin and Indian tribal governments located within the State of Wisconsin.*" The purpose of this document is to define a process by which WisDOT and FHWA work in collaboration with the TRIBES. In this document, it is also noted: "*This agreement is designed to acknowledge and support the government-to-government relationship between Tribes and State and Federal Agencies and to support American Indian sovereignty.*" Sovereignty is defined as the status, dominion, rule, or power of a sovereign. Tribes have the power to make and enforce laws for their tribe and reservation, and to establish courts and other forums for the resolution of disputes.[27] The PA document was established to begin building and sustaining a true government-to-government relationship between the TRIBES, Wisconsin division FHWA, and the WisDOT. The goal of such a relationship is to move beyond the Agency mindset of simply consulting with TRIBES as a legal requirement, but instead, working with TRIBES as equal partners focused on people, economics, and natural and human environments to improve the quality of life for all people.

On June 28th, 2005, The Wisconsin Governor and the

---

27. Definition Sovereignty https://www.epa.gov/sites/production/files/2015-03/documents/ips-consultation-guide_0.pdf

TRIBES signed The State of Wisconsin Department of Administration policy regarding consultation with Wisconsin Tribes, which also states that each of the federally recognized sovereign Tribes in the State of Wisconsin is recognized by the state for its unique status and its right to self-government and self-determination and the Department of Administration (DOA) respects the fundamental principles that establish and maintain the relationship between TRIBES and the DOA and accord Tribal governments the same respect accorded to other governments.[28]

After this document was signed, there was little documentation for the next almost 3 years until May 08, 2008. This communication had been sent from the Office of Civil Rights, consulting suspension and debarment, which is an FHWA representative, and it was sent to the WisDOT OGC email from FHWA WisDOT OGC and stating in this email was looking to collaborate on a scheduling date between the FHWA and the WisDOT OGC. A date was confirmed for May 22, 2008, but there was no information regarding the meeting that had transpired. But there is an important statement of language as stated in the documents within the FHWA, Civil Rights, Consulting, Suspension, and Debarment departments, which states: "*Federal law provides authority to use a TERO clause in federal-aid contracts. But does not mandate it. A State DOT has the discretion to implement their own overall program promoting employment among less advantaged populations, consistent with State law and with their other efforts (such as TRANS in Wisconsin).*" This is an inaccurate statement, and it is important to comprehend and address this misinterpretation, which came from the level of the FHWA. This is only a fragment of the statement that was inaccurately portrayed, as it lacked the complete information to be provided before this statement. The federal law provides authority to use a TERO clause in Federal Aid Contractors but does not mandate it is only partially true. If any work is within the boundaries of a reservation, this may not be the case unless

---

28. State of Wis DOA: https://doa.wi.gov/Pages/home.aspx

this is spelled out as stated in federal processes. This would only come from an act of Congress to make a statement like this, meaning Congress can intercede on these actions if not clearly defined. The second part states that state DOT has discretions to implement its own program promoting employment among less advantaged populations, consistent with the state law. This is an inaccurate statement because the state lacks jurisdiction within a reservation. After all, TRIBES are a sovereign nation as this has been set in place by treaties and case law in the past.

On May 16, 2008, an email was sent from the WisDOT OGC to Communications Manager, SE Freeways Program/SE Region tribal liaison and the subject matter of this email was: *"No WisDOT Authority to Mandate or Require or Participate in TERO."*[29] This was reiterated by WisDOT OGC who stated TERO provisions of federal law are permissive as shown in FHWA guidance, law [23USC 140] and regulations [23 CFR 635.117 and 25 CFR 170 .912]. WisDOT OGC makes the direct statement that if state laws allow, then the federal government U.S. DOT FHWA may participate in the cost whatever TERO provisions the state may implement. TERO provisions are "not" required in WisDOT contracts to obtain federal funds. One thing overlooked was this is not based on state laws allowing to implementation of TERO or because if this is within the boundaries of a reservation, then the State lacks jurisdiction to make any statement relevant to projects located within the boundaries of a reservation as the TRIBES are sovereign nations and it is based at the foundation of their inherent rights and sovereignty of TRIBES to implement TERO or IP, because of being domestic dependent nations. This information is relevant to the case stated, where it was concluded: "The Wisconsin Supreme Court ruled WisDOT exceeded its statutory authority." The court rejected DOT's reliance on two federal statutes.

Mitton v. Wisconsin Dept of Transp.184 Wis.2d 738 (Wis.

---

29. What is TERO: https://cter-tero.org/tero-faq/#1

1994). This was because the state was trying to take control of lands located within the boundaries of TRIBES. (This will be explained in more depth in the February 2012 legal opinion from WisDOT OGC.)

In a WisDOT OGC Chief Council Jim Thiel stated: "*I found no express or implied authority for WisDOT to require TERO provisions in its contractors or enter into TERO agreements, or expend amounts of money for Express Purposes,*" this is all once again dependent on the locations of the projects, as stated earlier, if it is within the boundaries of the reservation, then IP and TERO are mandated by the TRIBES. If near or within commutable distances of the Indian lands or IRR, then the agreements are negotiated with the TRIBES in the as stated March 15, 1993, documents following this process and by WisDOT trying to confer by Wisconsin state statutes is moot which does not reflect or incorporate the Tribal laws and judicial structures to reflect their inherent rights to self-govern. It is difficult to understand the purpose of a cost-benefit analysis related to services, as this is not pertinent to the employment of a tribe within the boundaries of their reservation.

In June 2008, a formal request was submitted to the WisDOT OGC for a formal legal opinion and to develop a plan for creating job opportunities for tribes. It wasn't until two months later, and the response was then placed in the Correspondence Memorandum. This was dated back to August 04, 2008, when it was addressed when there were two questions asked:

- *Is WisDOT Participation in a TERO program required by the FHWA?*

- *Do Wisconsin State Statutes Authorize the WisDOT to implement a TERO Program of Hiring Preferences or Payment of TERO Taxes in WisDOT Let Highway Contracts?*

This document is concerning because the questions asked were not the proper questions needed to be asked. The first question asks, "*Is WisDOT participation in a TERO program required by the FHWA?"* This question neglected to address the relevant question because it is not the WisDOT's participation in a TERO program required by the FHWA. The question that should have been asked is: "Does WisDOT have the ability to dictate to TRIBES that WisDOT is NOT allowed to implement TERO or IP when these projects come on, near or within commutable distances of reservations?" This question would exemplify how the relations between TRIBES and States are to work together cohesively when working on projects located near or within a commutable distance, as this would be a prequel to the projects located on the reservations. This clarification would assist the State, contractors CI, etc., in understanding when these entities have work to be done on the reservations, it is not the states who have jurisdiction, but it is the TRIBE's inherent jurisdiction as sovereign nations, and the TERO and IP are not permissive, but the Ordinances or Laws are mandatory. It is the time when projects are near or within a commutable distance the negotiation process begins to work towards the drafting of a possible provision implementation of IP or TERO.

Where the FHWA may not require state transportation agencies to comply with TERO as a condition of federal funding, this does not change the fact that the only entities who can determine how laws are implemented within the boundaries of a reservation are the TRIBES or an act by congress, and until there is an act by congress, then it is the responsibility of the TRIBES to make sure the States are implementing their IP and TERO within the boundaries of the reservations. This is a rather reciprocal response to the taxing or fees process as well. In March 1993, it is clear the document was a spelled-out definitive process, but it is apparent that without the education or knowledge of the processes, which are currently being circumvented to allow contractors to do the work within the boundaries of the reservations. The IP, or TERO, states all contractors must adhere to the IP and TERO processes and fails to mention unless the projects are State funded projects. This has never been a question in the application of these processes.

In the arguments made relating to the *City of Appleton v. Transportation Commissioner, 116 Wis. 2d 352, 342 N.W.2d 68 (Ct. App. 1983); American Brass v. Wisconsin State Board of Health. 245 Wis. 440, 15 N.W.2d 27 (1944); Mitton v. Wisconsin Department of Transportation. 184 Wis. 2d 738 (Wis 1994); Milwaukee County Pavers Assoc. v. Fiedler, 731 F. Supp. 1395, 1415-1416 (1990), affirmed by 7th Circuit 922 F.2d 419 (1991), Certiorari denied by US Supreme Court, 500 US 954 (1991)* and all other relative arguments made by WisDOT OGC's arguments are deliberated later in the February 22, 2012, Legal Opinion which was sent to the TRIBES and distributed in a TLAC meeting was a pretty extensive response while not only articulating WisDOT OGC's argument but also to invalidating any arguments made by WisDOT OGC as it related to the application of TERO and IP.

Chapter 3

2009

In March 2009, there was a presentation and discussion, at the TRANC-AC about the NAHP, with the Office of Civil Rights and Labor Opportunities in a WisDOT Contracting meeting with Tribal Government representatives to begin working on new spec language. This language developed a point of contact for the Tribe's Labor Representatives and established a tracking form.[30] This was later documented in a December 08, 2011, meeting with a PowerPoint presentation by the WisDOT TA representative, as there were no other available communications related to these meetings or dates.

The official beginning of the NAHP was in 2009, as was documented by the DBE U.S. 41 Labor Development Committee in May 2009. This was hosted by WisDOT, the WisDOT representative from DBE, and at the end of the meeting minutes it is posted in the next Agenda Items: "Native American Special Provision." This was scheduled for the next meeting on July 21, 2009, but there are no meeting minutes available for this meeting. In July 2009, the Wisconsin Native American Tracking Form, the DT2405, was created by the WisDOT representative from Government Administration, Regulation and Administration of Transportation Programs, General Government (GARA) and (TPGG). Sometime in September, communications between a construction contractor and a Tribal labor representative stressed the need for labor report information as

---

30. Please see March 2009. This was documented in the December 08, 2011, presentation by a WisDOT TA Representative.

one of the TRIBES did not receive the information. It has been noted this was dated back as far as sometime in 2009, reflecting how far back requests for the labor report information had initially been requested. The reason this information was never presented was because of the attempts to stall information or release inaccurate information or minimal information until sometime in mid-2017-2018. These charts reflect information presented and used to count people numerous times (EX.) 1. Women are labeled as a minority, and 2. They are documented as a female when they are documented on the CRCS quarterly and annual reports.

When the information was finally received and compiled to present in the context of annual reports (and will be presented later), it is important to remember this information was not available until 2017-2018. It is also important to mention this information was inaccurate because the information presented was from all projects across the state of Wisconsin and not just the NALHP projects. This information was then presented to the TRIBES, the CI, and other agencies involved with the Transportation industry in Wisconsin. These numbers used presented higher numbers on reports than the actual TSTW numbers, which had been presented at annual conferences and meetings of TRIBES. (*Please see Appendix B: Chapter 3.1 Chart 2009 Regional Report*)

The Annual Labor Reports (ALR) for 2009 is the true baseline of information that should have been presented. This information, which was presented, was from all of the regional reports from all construction projects across the state of Wisconsin. These regions are North Central, Northeast, Northwest, Southeast, and Southwest, encompassing Wisconsin. This information is provided quarterly and presented by the WisDOT Regional Tribal Liaisons. It is important to mention this was all the information that was reported to contractors by the method of self-reporting. This means the TSTW is the one who reports they are Native American. In 2009, in the regional report presented, there was a total of 1.43% TSTW on all projects across

Wisconsin, and they attained about 1.66% of the hours available.

Above is the 2009 WisDOT Minority Analysis Report (MAR) information obtained from the WisDOT Labor Compliance representative from the CRCS system. This document reported there was a total of 1.29% of TSTW on all projects, and they attained about 1.66% of the hour's averages for each person. All of this information will be presented in a graph later on when it is finally received. The reason this was shown is because of the inaccuracy of information from two different times the information was requested. This is the information received from the WisDOT Labor Compliance representative.

In 2010, with the establishment of the DBE, the quarterly WisDOT DBE reporter in January, is when the 41 Mega Project began. The information reported reflected the minority reports available for the US41 Corridor Expansion project, including Brown and Winnebago counties. The report shows there was a 9.97% participation of minority hours worked with no percentages available for the classifications of minorities broken down or even gender. The Annual Minority Reports (AMR) was requested in 2017 of the WisDOT Labor Compliance, and they responded with the included information, which shows that for all of the projects across Wisconsin, the TSTW attained 1.61% opportunities and 1.31% of the hours on these projects for 2010. Later on, a WisDOT MAR presented a different set of numbers, which stated in 2010 the TSTW were able to attain 1.51% of the opportunities and 1.31% of the hours on these projects. This directly shows the opportunities are inaccurate numbers and shows, even more, the need for enhanced communication with these discrepancies because this information is presented by the WisDOT Officers, which is then presented to the TRIBES and FHWA. As of September, the Winter DBE reporter mentions the U.S. 41 Corridor Expansion Project, located in Brown and Winnebago Counties, the I-94 CTH N Badger Interchange, located in Dane County, and the

2009 WisDOT Annual Minority Analysis Report

Caucasian		African		Hispanic		Asian		Native american		Total Participation	Native American
Male	Female	Male	Female	Male	Female	Male	Female	Male	Female		Particiaption
Head Count 2009											
4,529.00	157.00	244.00	17.00	457.00	6.00	24.00	5.00	66.00	5.00	5,510.00	1.29%
								1.20%	0.09%		
Hours Worked 2009											
Male	Female	Male	Female	Male	Female	Male	Female	Male	Female	Hours Worked	
784,155.40	25,838.10	38,449.20	4,052.50	84,813.90	841.50	2,633.80	246.00	14,871.90	1,001.50	956,903.80	1.66%
								1.55%	0.10%		

I-94 North-South Freeway project, located in Milwaukee, Racine, and Kenosha Counties. The Volume 1 issue of the DBE reporters mentions the total hours worked on projects, total minority hours worked, and the total female hours worked as well. The DBE reporter was established with the intent to reflect all workers on the projects and the number of hours available to work with an annual total of workers on the projects. This is the second document to show that after looking at the regional reports, their participation numbers and percentages are not adding up, and some may be inflated or misconstrued, showing inaccurate numbers.

Chapter 4

2010

In 2010, the DBE established the quarterly WisDOT DBE reporter. In January, these reporters discussed many reports related to the mega projects across Wisconsin. In these reporters, when the 41 Mega Project had begun, the information reported was only the minority reports available for the US41 Corridor Expansion project, which included Brown and Winnebago counties. This is where it was shown there was a 9.97% participation of minority hours worked. There were no percentages available for the minorities broken down or even gender. The Annual Minority Reports (AMR) were requested in 2017 of the WisDOT Labor Compliance, and they responded with the included information, which shows that for all of the projects across Wisconsin, the TSTW attained 1.61% opportunities and 1.31% of the hours on these projects for 2010. Later, a WisDOT MAR presented a different set of numbers, which state in 2010, the TSTW was able to attain 1.51% of the opportunities and 1.31% of the hours on these projects. This clearly shows that the opportunities are not accurate once again; and shows, even more, the need for enhanced communication with these discrepancies. As of September, the Winter DBE reporter mentions the U.S. 41 Corridor Expansion Project, located in Brown and Winnebago Counties, the I-94 CTH Badger Interchange, located in Dane County, and the I-94 North-South Freeway project, located in Milwaukee, Racine, and Kenosha Counties. The Volume 1 issue of the DBE Reporters mentions the total hours worked on projects, total minority hours worked, and the total female hours worked as well. I would like to mention that the DBE Reporter mentions the total number of workers on the projects was:

Annual DBE Report as of September 30, 2010

Spring

- *I-94 North-South Freeway Project (Milwaukee, Racine, and Kenosha Counties)*

  Work Hours as of March 2010
  Total Hours Worked 519,138.2
  Total Minority Hours Worked 88,118.1
  Total Female Hours Worked 23,474.6

- *I-94 CTH Badger Interchange Project (Dane County)*

  Work Hours as of March 2010
  No information available for this project

- *US 41 Corridor Expansion Project (Brown and Winnebago Counties)*

  Work Hours as of March 2010
  Total Hours Worked 107,311
  Total Minority Hours Worked 10,699.1
  Total Female Hours Worked 6,128.9

Summer

- *I-94 North-South Freeway Project (Milwaukee, Racine, and Kenosha Counties)*

  Work Hours as of June 30, 2010
  Total Hours Worked 193,614.70
  Total Minority Hours Worked 8,468.70
  Total Female Hours Worked 6,967.10

- *I-94 CTH Badger Interchange Project (Dane County)*

  Work Hours as of June 30, 2010
  Total Hours Worked 598,647.80

Total Minority Hours Worked 97,729.70
Total Female Hours Worked 19,214.20

- **US 41 Corridor Expansion Project (Brown and Winnebago Counties)**

    Work Hours as of June 30, 2010
    No information available for this project

Winter

- **I-94 North-South Freeway Project (Milwaukee, Racine, and Kenosha Counties)**

    Work Hours as of September 30, 2010
    Total Hours Worked 401,240
    Total Minority Hours Worked 98,752
    Total Female Hours Worked 9,146

- **I-94 CTH Badger Interchange Project (Dane County)**

    Work Hours as of September 30, 2010
    Total Hours Worked 193,614.70
    Total Minority Hours Worked 8,468.70
    Total Female Hours Worked 6,967.10

- **US 41 Corridor Expansion Project (Brown and Winnebago Counties)**

    Work Hours as of September 30, 2010
    Total Hours Worked 313,948
    Total Minority Hours Worked 15,169
    Total Female Hours 10,531

- **I-94 North-South Freeway Project (Milwaukee, Racine, and Kenosha Counties)**

    Work Hours as of September 30, 2010
    Total Hours Worked 1,113,992.90
    Total Minority Hours Worked 195,338.80
    Total Female Hours Worked 16,113.10

- **I-94 CTH Badger Interchange Project (Dane County)**

    Work Hours as of September 30, 2010
    Total Hours Worked 792,262.50

Total Minority Hours Worked 106,198.40
Total Female Hours Worked 26,181.30

- **US 41 Corridor Expansion Project (Brown and Winnebago Counties)**

Work Hours as of September 30, 2010
Total Hours Worked 421,259.00
Total Minority Hours Worked 15,169.00
Total Female Hours 16,659.90

- **All Projects across Wisconsin Annually**

Work Hours as of September 30, 2010
Total Hours Worked 1,325,445
Total Minority Hours Worked 924,642
Total Female Hours 453,088

All WisDOT projects across Wisconsin for 2010:
Total hours 2,703,175

In October of 2,010, the PA wasn't revisited after five (5) years, and the PA was amended. The language was still contained in the PA, which stated: "*The federal government recognizes the right of self-determination for Indian tribal governments and the obligation to work with Indian tribal governments in a government-to-government relationship. As an executive agency, the US Department of Transportation has a responsibility and is committed to working with Indian tribal governments in this unique relationship, respecting tribal sovereignty and self-determination.*"[31] This PA still had much of the same language as it states that: "Its purpose is to continue to create and define the processes by which the WisDOT and the Wisconsin Division-FHWA will work in collaboration with the TRIBES. This agreement is designed to acknowledge and support the government-to-government relationship and support American Indian sovereignty. This emphasized for all of the entities, including the TRIBES, as

---

31. 2010 Partnership Agreement https://wisconsindot.gov/Documents/doing-bus/civil-rights/tribalaffairs/pa2010.pdf

stated in the section key reference terms: Consultation and Coordination with Indian Tribal Governments: *This is the title of Executive Order 13084, signed by the President on May 14, 1998, that requires federal agencies to respect tribal self-government and sovereignty, tribal rights, and tribal responsibilities whenever they formulate policies that affect Indian tribal governments in a unique and significant way.*[32] This explained the need for constant communication between all TRIBES because if there was one issue with one tribe, they could all bring it to the table together versus a tribe doing this on their own to make sure the TRIBES' self-government sovereignty and tribal rights are all being respected.

For the 2010 ALR reports for Wisconsin, were only recently able to be obtained after numerous Public Records Requests from 2015 to 2018, when the WisDOT Labor Compliance and CRCS representatives provided this information. This document is the information presented for all projects across the state of Wisconsin, not for the NAHP-specific Projects, and only reflects from the Skilled Trades Workers, including TSTW, who are listed because they are from those who have self-reported. To self-report is to give details about something yourself rather than having them reported by someone else. *(Please see Appendix B: Chapter 4.1 Chart 2010 Regional Report)*

The Total Regional Report drafted from the information presented was a little different in reporting because this information does not match up with any of the other information presented. The WisDOT MAR from 2010 presented reflects variances in the percentages of participation of TRIBES TSTW. The variances between the two documents are 10% from the headcounts. Yet, the hours are still the same percentages which may be concerning because of the information reported from the WisDOT labor compliance CRCS program. Still, this information shows two different results. Please see below. *(Please see Appendix B: Chapter 4.1 Chart 2010 Regional Report)*

---

32. 2010 Partnership Agreement https://wisconsindot.gov/Documents/doing-bus/civil-rights/tribalaffairs/pa2010.pdf

Chapter 5

2011

In 2011, the WisDOT Labor Compliance representative provided WisDOT MAR information from the CRCS system. In this document it was reported there was a total of 1.51% of TSTW on all projects, and they attained about 1.31% of the hour's averages for each person. All of this information will be presented in a graph later on when it is finally received. The reason this was shown is because of the inaccuracy of information from two different times the information was requested. This is the information received from the WisDOT Labor Compliance representatives.

Mid-July 2011 is when the TRANS-AC Meeting was scheduled, and the following representatives from WisDOT attended: 1 representative each from TA, OBOC, FHWA, Serendipity Communications, Prism Technical, DTSD, 2 from WTBA, 4 each from NAMC and AACC, and 9 from DBE. The topic of this meeting was the discussion of the NAHP. As representatives, we were concerned about TERO in Wisconsin as it had caught the Governor's attention. It was mentioned that the communication had been continuous since 2008 with the TRIBES regarding an alternative plan to increase Native American employment. This was mentioned by WisDOT TA of the determination by WisDOT's OGC stating Wisconsin's inability to implement TERO. This resulted in the development of the NAHP, as this provision encourages and promotes hiring Native Americans on transportation projects on or near Indian reservations. The only drawback was the NAHP

WisDOT Annual Minority Analysis Report 2011

Caucasian		African		Hispanic		Asian		Native american		Total Participation	Native American Particiaption
Male	Female	Male	Female	Male	Female	Male	Female	Male	Female		
Head Count 2010											
Male	Female	Male	Female	Male	Female	Male	Female	Male	Female	Head Count	
8,432.00	245.00	384.00	19.00	757.00	13.00	37.00	9.00	143.00	9.00	10,048.00	1.51%
								1.42%	0.09%		
Hours Worked 2010											
Male	Female	Male	Female	Male	Female	Male	Female	Male	Female	Hours Worked	
2,185,057.10	58,055.30	96,397.90	4,646.30	260,693.30	4,274.50	10,696.30	325.80	32,345.80	2,472.30	2,654,964.60	1.31%
								1.22%	0.09%		

was not mandatory for the CI to hire TSTW on these projects. During this time is when the DT2405 form was also presented as it was used to track and evaluate Native American labor development activities across the state. This form required the contractors and tribal labor representatives to fill out and send to WisDOT TA. While this was going on, there were joint partnerships and training events to help increase TSTW participation. The WisDOT OGC is currently working on a written opinion that will be available for public distribution. The need to further discuss the NAHP was mentioned, but at this time it was stated to include the TRIBES representatives.

In August 2011, a copy of the NAHP had been presented when it was requested if there were any meeting minutes from TRANS-AC Meeting. This request was made to the WTBA, who is one of the representatives, and this was presented:

08112011
Native American Employment.

The department promotes and encourages Native American employment on transportation projects on or near reservations. This contract is choosing an item. Enter name of reservation. Enter NAE1 and press F3 only if project is on, or partially on, the reservation. If project is NOT on nor partially on the reservation, delete this line. When the contract work is on or partially on the reservation, the contractor, prior to submitting a bid for this proposal, contacts the individual below to determine all tribal requirements for working on the reservation:

- *Name: Enter Name*
  - *Title: Enter Title*
  - *Tribe: Enter Tribe*
  - *Address: Enter Address*
  - *Phone: Enter Phone*

- **Email:** *Enter Email*

- **FAX:** *Enter FAX*

The contractor is advised to work with the tribal government(s) to utilize Native American labor in performing the contract work and contact each individual listed in this article for Native American employment opportunities under this contract:

- **Name:** *Enter tribal government contact(s) based on the "Native American Hiring Provision – Counties and Contacts" matrix found at HCCI website http://roadwaystandards.dot.wi.gov/hcci/*

  - **Title:** *Enter Title*

  - **Tribe:** *Enter Tribe*

  - **Address:** *Enter Address*

  - **Phone:** *Enter Phone*

  - **Email:** *Enter Email*

  - **FAX:** *Enter FAX*

If the contractor or subcontractor does not live up to the spirit of this article, the department will address these issues with the contractor and/or subcontractor and the Tribal contact person. If the tribe requests it, the contractor shall meet with the Tribal contact person to discuss Native American employment issues.

Submit the Native American Hiring Tracking form (DT2405) to the department's Division of Transportation System Development Tribal Affairs team, at XXXXX@dot.wi.gov, 30 days after work is substantially complete. The engineer may withhold monies due the contractor if the contractor fails to submit this form. On the form, identify the tribal government(s) contacted by the contractor or any subcontractor under this contract, whether individuals were hired or not. If hired by the contractor or any subcontractor, list all individuals who were referred and hired for this project through one of the federally recognized tribes in Wisconsin.

If the contractor deems that an employee referred by the Tribal

Contact person is in danger of being suspended or terminated, the con-
tractor shall notify the Tribal Contact person for assistance in resolv-
ing the problem. Nothing in this article will be construed to interfere
with the contractor's ability to dismiss any employee for cause includ-
ing, but not limited to, lack of adequate skills or training, inability to
perform by virtue of state or federal law, or breach of the contractor's
standards of conduct.

This article does not replace the existing equal employment
opportunity requirements contained Elsewhere in this contract. Direct
questions, other than tribal employment questions, to the person(s)
named above or to the WisDOT Tribal Liaison at (xxx) xxx-xxxx or
(xxx) xxx-xxxx.

107-200 (20110615)

This is the same document that had been questioned at
the TRANS-AC meeting. The NAHP had warranted further
discussion by the "Focus Group," and on August 16, 2011, an
email was sent to the TRIBES introducing the new WisDOT
Office of Business Outreach and Compliance (OBOC) representative. It was at this time the WisDOT OBOC expounds in
communications stating WisDOT recently has been asked to
revisit the WisDOT NAHP, a provision that encourages Native
American labor opportunities on WisDOT projects that are
located on or near reservations. The department will be hosting a focus group meeting which will consist of various stakeholders, including tribes, to:

1. Review and propose provision language that communicates
clear instructions to contractors.

2. Clarify tracking and enforcement components of the provision.

3. Develop an education and outreach plan to inform.

It was not until this time all the TRIBES had been formally invited to participate in the "Focus Group" meetings.

It is rather interesting the TRIBES have not been requested to participate in the prior discussion, which directly impacts their communities. WisDOT has been attempting to establish the NAHP since roughly about 2002, when there was a comprehensive outreach to Native Americans in establishing steps to building the bridges and forging relationships with Federal, State, Local, Municipalities & Construction Industries. This was all a direct result of the *"Native American Initiative,"* this all took place in 2002; what has transpired since 2002 because there was little or lack of communication and more of a delegation to the TRIBES back in May 2008 – *"WisDOT OGC makes position that there is No WisDOT authority to mandate or require to participate in TERO."* It seems WisDOT's joint partnerships and working cooperatively have deteriorated over time. This can be shown by the scheduling of meetings with WisDOT and other representatives from the TRANS-AC meetings prior. This included DBE, TA, OBOC, DTSD, WTBA, NAMC, and AACC, FHWA, Serendipity Communications, and Prism Technical. They were all discussing a NAHP, which only affects them, requiring them to work with the TRIBES as it relates to IP and TERO. The WisDOT OGC has only made the statements that *"WisDOT does not have statutory authority to impose and enforce TERO and other hiring preferences on WisDOT contracts."* This neglects to mention what the TRIBES' rights are as it relates to any work that transpires within the boundaries of reservations. These actions present the current conflicting issues as it relates to the statements made by the agencies stating:

- *"The federal government recognizes the right of self-determination for Indian tribal-governments and the obligation to work with Indian tribal governments in a government-to-government relationship. As an executive agency, the US Department of Transportation has a responsibility and is committed to working with Indian tribal governments in this unique relationship, respecting tribal sovereignty and self- determination."*[33]

---

33. 2010 Partnership Agreement https://wisconsindot.gov/Documents/doing-bus/

- *This is the title of Executive Order 13084, signed by the President on May 14, 1998, that requires federal agencies to respect tribal self-government and sovereignty, tribal rights, and tribal responsibilities whenever they formulate policies that affect Indian tribal governments in a unique and significant way.*[34]

Without any communications to the TRIBES during this whole process, all communications have been between all the other agencies behind closed doors, looking at ways to:

> *1. Make sure the IP or TERO is not implemented on projects located on, near or within a commutable distance of the TRIBES.*

> *2. Implement the NAHP, thereby circumventing the IP and TERO processes, executing the WisDOT influenced NAHP, which states it is not mandatory for contractors to employ the TRIBES TSTW on the projects located "on," "near," or "within a commutable distance" of their reservations.*

This all can be understood by reviewing these meeting minutes from the meetings presented because there is a record of attendance showing who was present at these meetings. With the TRIBES not having an equal seat at the table, it is difficult to have the TRIBES all communicate as it is in the best interests of the WisDOT and the CI for the TRIBES to lack communication.

In September 2011, a document was submitted with the concerns of representatives present at the WisDOT NAHP Focus Group meeting. Present were the following representatives: 7-WisDOT, 2-WTBA, 2-Union, 1-AICCW, 1-FHWA, and 1-Tribe. There were only 3 TRIBES invited to this meeting to discuss the concerns regarding the NAHP, which resulted in the following recommendations:

civil-rights/tribalaffairs/pa2010.pdf

34. 2010 Partnership Agreementhttps://wisconsindot.gov/Documents/doing-bus/civil-rights/tribalaffairs/pa2010.pdf

- *Come up with something that is more consistent and efficient, and less of a workload on contractors.*

- *Willing to work with TRIBES during the off-season to do some education and tracking.*

- *Have requirements for doing work on tribal land to be "flagged" as a special provision for projects that are located on or partially on the reservation.*

- *See NAHP suspended until a plan is created and implemented.*

There was also a document of meeting minutes which entailed a copy of the concerns brought forward by the WTBA and NAMC, as their concerns were in the following areas:

WisDOT Native American Hiring Provision Date: 8-Sep-11

- *Training and Outreach*

  - *WTBA (Concerns): Not involved with the language development process and vetting of the provision. Would like more education and outreach regarding NAHP implementation?*

- *Applicability*

  - *WTBA (Concerns): The provision is being included in contracts all across the state (as a result of the "on" or "near" boundaries), whereas they were under the impression that it would only apply to contracts that are "on" or "partially on" the reservation.*

  - *NAMC (Concerns): Does the provision apply to subcontractors?*

- *Provision Language*

  - *WTBA (Concerns): Would like to know what "spirit" of the provision means. Who decides? What are the criteria?*

  - *Concerned with this provision statement – "if the tribe requests, the contractor shall meet with the Tribal Contact person to discuss Native American employment issues" – because of the additional burden, negative perception, and legal issues it lays on contractors.*

- *Concern with statement that "engineer may withhold monies due the contractor if the contractor fails to submit this form."*

- **Tracking and Monitoring**

  - *WTBA (Concerns): The submission of the DT2405 tracking form is due 30 days after the work is substantially complete, which they feel is too subjective and conveys a negative message. Contractors are fearful of discrimination lawsuits if they do not hire recommended Native Americans that they believe are unqualified or hire from the union bench.*

- **General Concerns**

  - *WTBA (Concerns): Overall, WTBA cautioned that NAHP is communicating the wrong message to contractors and are receiving several questions from their members' representative from NAMC also asked about the inclusion of subcontractors in the provision language and would like clarification as to whether the provision also applies to them.*

  - *WTBA (Concerns):There is not a lot of hiring going on at this time; concerns were raised about perceptions that contractors are just not hiring Native Americans, and with the potential conflicts with the impacts of contractors' union obligations.*

Many of these questions were asked at the "Focus Group" meeting as well as addressing concerns covering topics like:

- *Can WisDOT enforce NAHP on tribal lands? What is the recourse?*

- *Can the state enter into individual agreements with each tribe that addresses NAHP?*

- *What does "desired skill set" mean (on the tracking form)? A contractor can make the skill set as difficult as they want it to be.*

- *Union currently has about 200 Native Americans on their rosters; can contractors request Native Americans specifically?*

- *Does the union agreement become exempt when the work is on the reservation?*

- *Can Indian Reservation Roads (IRR) definitions be used to assist with defining "near"?*

- *Agency or WisDOT OGC's opinion that WisDOT does not have the authority to enforce TERO is also implying that the TRIBES don't have the authority either.*

- *How do we go forward with the provision in its current form?*

- *Develop action plans under these 3 topics:*

  - *Labor development.*

  - *Best ways to collect hiring data.*

  - *Project level hiring opportunities.*

Three (3) days later, another Focus Group NAHP was established, and the following WisDOT representatives were present: 1 from TA, OBOC, OGC, DBE Program Manager, DTSD Operations Director, TA Lead, TA Analyst, AICCW, NAMC, 2 from Local 139 Union, and WTBA, and only one of the TRIBES was present at this meeting. In this meeting was discussed the definition of *"within a commutable distance,"* IRR Definition of *"roads that provide access to reservations,"* and *"The PA definition of Indian Country."* The entities at the table wanted to create a *"one-stop shop or clearing house"* encompassing a statewide rule for *"near"* that is used when a project is located *"on or partially on"* the reservation for the application of TSTW on projects. This was all done because the CI representatives stated they would like to:

- *Come up with something that is more consistent and efficient, and less of a workload on contractors.*

- *Work with tribes during the off-season to do some education and tracking.*

- *Have requirements for doing work on tribal land to be "flagged" as a special provision for projects that are located on or partially on the reservation.*

These were the current recommendations for the current NAHP:

- *Tribal affairs will work with BPD/Bill McNary to identify which projects will be included in the November let to determine whether any of these would include NAHP and may potentially be located on or partially on a reservation.*

- *Approach tribal leaders at the September 19th consultation regarding the recommendations to gain input on the application of the current NAHP.*

- *Examine current NAHP tracking forms that have been collected.*

- *Contact contractors that have used NAHP and obtain feedback on implementation, concerns, etc.*

The WisDOT Annual Consultation meeting took place with DTSD Administrator, WisDOT Secretary of Transportation, TA, Tribal Affairs Analyst (TAA), and seven (7) TRIBES present and in the summary action steps for all tribes, there was a mention as it related to looking into legal issues regarding the application of tribal laws or hiring preference, especially state versus tribal laws. These were the listed action items from the TRIBES present.

October 2011 An email was sent to one of the TRIBES Leadership regarding specific issues surrounding the NAHP and construction on the U.S. 41 Corridor located: "On" and "Near" the confines of a reservation. Some concerns presented where is relevant to one of the initiatives completed was a NAHP for Indian Workers when they're on or near the reservation since the construction had moved up to their area. There was a concern that since the construction has moved closer to a TRIBE's reservation when TSTW are to be utilized on these projects, the TSTW are laid off shortly after. The concern is the current NAHP doesn't have anything to enforce the provision if the TRIBE doesn't contact DOT, who's supporting the provision and the Indian subcommittee.

In November 2011, a letter from WisDOT OBOEC was sent to the TRIBES requesting their presence to participate in the WisDOT Tribal Labor Advisory Committee (TLAC), as the purpose for creating this committee is to explore mechanisms to enhance TSTW opportunities while also amending the WisDOT statewide NAHP to address TSTW opportunities on WisDOT projects located "on" or "near" reservations. WisDOT OBOEC sent email invitations to the TRIBES: The following word document contains the invitation language for reference. The official notice to TRIBES issuing the suspension of the NAAP was issued in November 2011 by the WisDOT TA, the same message at the 2011 Great Lakes Intertribal Committee (GLITC) Meeting and the annual Secretary's Consultation. As a result, WisDOT convened two focus group meetings with various stakeholders, which included a tribal representative, WisDOT staff, and CI. The two major outcomes of these focus group meetings were to:

1) Suspend the current NAHP from future lets until revisions could be made; and

2) Establish the WisDOT TLAC.

This first official TLAC meeting was scheduled for December 2011 as the following WisDOT representatives were present: 1 representative from OBOC, OGC, DWD, DBE Program Manager, DTSD Operations Director, TA Lead, TAA, and FHWA 2-Local 139 Union, AICCW, NAMC, 2 from WTBA, 16-tribal members from 8 TRIBES. The committee developed strategies to enhance Native American Labor opportunities on state and federal projects. A PowerPoint was established to walk through the history of NAHP and TERO. A set of eight recommendations were developed by TLAC over the course of the first year.

The final recommendations document was approved by committee resolution on July 26, 2012, and endorsed and supported by the WisDOT Secretary on September 17, 2012. The next steps of this effort were to establish five work teams to develop implementation plans that allocate the needed tasks, responsibilities, resources, budget, and timeline to carry the recommendations forward. The work teams met at least three times throughout the months of September through November 2012. (This is also the conduit that was used to finalize the TLAC work plan and encourage the authorization of a $190,000 allocation of state aid to implement the plan.)

This was all concluded with a PowerPoint of the history of the NAHP. The letter was sent by the WisDOT OBOC in November, and the official TLAC meeting commenced as there was a presentation for the NAHP covering the following categories:

- *"On" or "near" the reservation goal: Reach a resolution on the focus of labor opportunities "on" versus "near" the reservation.*

- *Recruitment and referral goal: Identify approaches to recruit and refer tribal members for construction employment opportunities.*

- *Maintain information goal: Identify mechanisms to maintain information regarding tribal members and their skill sets.*

- *Training and professional development goal: Identify mechanisms to promote career development in the transportation industry, such as TRANS, union membership, apprenticeship programs, and other skills and career development opportunities.*

This opened the door to a whole laundry list of items like: CI involvement and the application of the language of "on" or "near" given the fact they work all over the state, CI Signatories to the unions and other topics like training, youth engagement, barriers/challenges to employment, tracking and monitoring, communication between the CI and TRIBES. The DBE was also a component as the FHWA stated WisDOT cannot have a quota program; only a goal may be established. Possible incentives for contractors hiring on or near reservations was also mentioned.

The presentation contained information that there is no dialog available to obtain. The map also contained "on" or "near" was referenced, a timeline from October 2002 – when FHWA released a report WisDOT placed NAHP in federal aid for projects "on" or "near" Indian lands. This required contractors at all tiers to make an aggressive concerted effort to employ TSTW on these projects.

This PowerPoint had some dates referenced, but public records requests had to be filed in order to obtain this information. It also showed the WisDOT Native American tracking form, the concerns from the CI and other entities, concluding with a goal to:

- *Reach a resolution on the focus of labor opportunities "on" versus "near" the reservation.*

- *Identify approaches to recruit and refer tribal members for construction employment opportunities.*

- *Identify mechanisms to promote career development in the transportation industry, such as TRANS, Union membership, apprenticeship programs, and other skills and career development opportunities.*

- *Identify mechanisms to maintain information regarding tribal members and their skill sets.*

After these few meetings, it is clear to see the importance of the participation from the TRIBES and how they conduct communications to emphasize the detrimental effect it can have on the TRIBES. They need to continue to work in a cohesive manner for their communities, with the purpose of analyzing and interpreting the hiring provision. The WisDOT created the NAHP, as its original intent is to help enhance the economic opportunities much the same way IP or TERO is implemented, but it is not mandatory for the CI to hire TSTW on these projects. The application of NAHP is clouded by the perceived undue influence of outside agencies as the NAHP has been in place for the past 10 years for the TRIBES since 2009. The NAHP indicates when the provision's application should be included in projects. Currently, this provision would apply to projects located on or partially on lands held under the ownership and jurisdiction of the tribes.[35] *(Please see Appendix B: Chapter 5.1 Chart 2011 Regional Report)*

In ALR for 2011 is the true baseline of information that should have been presented. This information was presented from all the regional reports from all construction projects across the state of Wisconsin. These regions are North Central, Northeast,

Northwest, Southeast, and Southwest regions and encompass all of Wisconsin. This information is provided quarterly and presented by the WisDOT Regional TL. It is important to mention that all information was reported to contractors by the method of self-reporting; this means the TSTW is the one who reports they are Native American.

In 2009, in the regional report presented, there was a total of 1.86% TSTW on all projects across Wisconsin, and they attained about 1.97% of the hours available.

Above is the annual 2011 WisDOT MAR information obtained from the WisDOT Labor Compliance representative from the CRCS system. Also in this document, it had reported there was a total of 1.85% of TSTW on all projects, and they attained about 1.64% of the hour's averages for each person. All this information will be presented in a graph later when it is finally received. The reason this was shown is because of the

---

35. NAHP Applicability https://wisconsindot.gov/Documents/doing-bus/civil-rights/tribalaffairs/stspd-final-hiring-provision-adopted2-17-14.pdf

inaccuracy of information from two different times the information was requested. This is the information received from the WisDOT Labor Compliance Representative.

**** There is no information available for the DBE Reporter or quarterly reports 2011[36] ****
The link has been submitted in the referenced citations.

---

36. Newsletter – DBE reporter updates and information on contracting issues and projects https://wisconsindot.gov/Pages/doing-bus/civil-rights/dbe/newsletter.aspx

2011 WisDOT Annual Minority Analysis Report

Caucasian		African		Hispanic		Asian		Native american		Total Participation	Native American
Male	Female	Male	Female	Male	Female	Male	Female	Male	Female		Particiaption
Head Count 2011											
Male	Female	Male	Female	Male	Female	Male	Female	Male	Female	Head Count	
11,016.00	364.00	384.00	20.00	774.00	9.00	36.00	2.00	217.00	21.00	12,843.00	1.85%
								1.69%	0.16%		
Hours Worked 2011											
Male	Female	Male	Female	Male	Female	Male	Female	Male	Female	Hours Worked	
4,238,610.10	114,950.40	1,111,766.10	6,573.30	270,251.90	2,293.10	15,539.50	735.30	88,256.00	7,637.80	5,856,613.50	1.64%
								1.51%	0.13%		

Chapter 6

2012

January 2012 started quickly with communications from WisDOT TA Analyst to the newly formed TLAC recommending scheduling out for the TLAC and Subcommittee meetings. These meetings began as soon as the end of January. The following representatives were present: 1 from WisDOT TA, Local #139 UNION, WisDOT and TRANS, 2 from WTBA, and 8-tribal members from the TRIBES. The meeting discussed networking, requirements of Unions for TSTW, reaching out to the CI, establish avenues for TSTW to be able to obtain employment within the CI (Union, Non-union, TRANS, etc.). There were continued discussions of the definitions of "on" or "near" concerns as was stated:

- *TRIBES feel that DOT should acknowledge that tribal law prevails on tribal lands.*

- *The committee does not believe that "on" should be addressed by the subcommittee, but rather should be addressed between the agency and the TRIBES.*

- *Hiring on a project-by-project basis is difficult.*

This meeting concluded with an action item stating to provide a copy of the federal equal employment coals by county.

February 2012 presented the long-awaited "legal opinion" from WisDOT OGC, which states: *"Does the State of WisDOT have the legal authority to include and enforce TERO requirements as a WisDOT contractual requirement on any Federal-Aid Highway Program highway* projects?" The WisDOT OGC's response is: "*No. In brief, federal permission does not grant WisDOT legal authority to require such TERO preferences on federally funded projects. There is no Wisconsin state statutory grant of authority to WisDOT to require TERO preferences. The rule of law in Wisconsin is that State agencies like WisDOT must find legal authority for a proposed action within the express or necessarily implied language of a statute. Any doubt is resolved in favor of the lack of legal authority, which was followed up by a 5-page analysis.*"[37] With the NAHP being relatively new and only utilized for such a short time in 2009-2011 and through 2013, as the WTBA states, it continues to be implemented on projects across Wisconsin throughout the revisions. This language presents a lack of any requirements or special provisions. A good example of this is the 441 Mega Projects. The 441 Mega Projects were a 10-year project that started in 2009 and carried on through 2018 when it was tentatively completed. A WisDOT DBE representative in 2018 stated regarding these mega projects: "*These projects weren't selected for the application of the NAHP.*"[38] The immediate response to this from the TRIBES should have been that WisDOT does not have the authority to "*Select a project*" as the authority is left with the tribes, as stated in the NAHP.

The NAHP addressee's applicability thus, "Reference a map and reference tool to determine when this provision will be included in projects. Currently, this provision would apply to projects located on or partially on lands held under the ownership and jurisdiction of the tribes."[39]

This is duly noted because NAHP had not been implemented on these projects as this was stated by the WisDOT

---

37. Memo; February 27, 2012, OGCWISDOT Jim Thiel response to Secretary Gotlibb regarding TERO Preferences.

38. Native American Hiring Provision https://static1.squarespace.com/static/5c96658a523958f5d18c4d1a/t/5ca5fea124a694e7e328e41b/1554382497607/Native+American+Hiring+Provision.pdf

48. Native American Hiring https://static1.squarespace.com/static/5c96658a523958f5d18c4d1a/t/5ca5fea124a694e7e328e41b/1554382497607/Native+American+Hiring+Provision.pdf

Labor Compliance DBE representative; this was at the discretion of the WisDOT. The 441-Corridor Mega Projects from roughly 2009 to 2019, a "ten-year" project involving approximately $907 million, of which approximately over $500 million was federally funded. This project is also located "on," "near," or within a commutable distance of Indian roadways, Indian country, Indian trust lands, fee lands, and reservations, and the TRIBES were excluded from the NAHP participation for their TSTW on these projects because the WisDOT DBE did not "SELECT" this project. It wasn't until after communications with one of the consulting firms contracted to do work from 2009 to 2013 on the Highway 441-Corridor Mega Project that this information was determined and was backed up and verified that the application of the NAHP had not been applied. A few days passed until we received correspondence from the consultant firm, which stated: "There *was no application of anything relevant to any special provision,*" "amendments in the 2009-2013 WisDOT specifications books for IP, TERO, or NAHP." A copy of the WisDOT State specification books can be located at Standard specification archives on the public website at: https://wisconsindot.gov/Pages/doing-bus/eng-consultants/cnslt-rsrces/rdwy/ss-archive.aspx

This communication then incited more questions to be asked:

1) Why has the IP or TERO been removed?

2) Why was the NAHP put in its place?

3) Why does the WisDOT "select" or include the NAHP on projects located "on" or "near" or within a commutable distance of Indian roadways, Indian country, Indian trust lands, fee lands, and reservations in the state of Wisconsin?

4) How are we able to track labor reports of how many tribal members we have on the projects?

This led to many of these questions being answered as we return to 2011 when the first NAHP was suspended because of the direct influence of the 1 representative from WTBA, CI, DWD, Unions, AAIC, WisDOT, and FHWA. All these questions point to the responses from WisDOT OGC, which were given in early 2012. Through the analysis of these meeting minutes and emails, the messages were inconsistent as they related to the WisDOT OGC. There were two different responses given, and they are not succinct responses documented and preserved in meeting minutes, which have all been removed from the TLAC meeting minutes. It is essential to mention the second message, which defines the WisDOT OGC legal opinion presented, as we analyze all this information and be sure to scrutinize every part.

OGC/WisDOT 2 Responses

The responses given by WisDOT OGC presented why the NAHP that had been established had constrained TRIBE's ability to implement IP or TERO. Because of this, it is of great importance to the preservation of all relevant communications and information, including meeting minutes preserved from TLAC meeting minutes on February 27, 2012.

The documented responses sent by the WisDOT's OGC had given two answers addressing the TRIBES, explaining why the IP and TERO will no longer be implemented any further. It was then clarified by WisDOT OGC that the NAHP had been in place from 2009 through 2011 until it had been suspended from 2011 to 2013. During this time, the only statements or legal opinions made were by WisDOT OGC reflecting the two responses, because the responses were not identical regardless of both being released on the same day. The first response, which was only presented to the WisDOT Secretary but was stated this would be later disbursed to the TRIBES, said:

Legal Opinion (Response 2) *(WisDOT Secretary Correspondence)*

Presented by WisDOT OGC[40] distributed to the TLAC committee in February 2012, which was a more formal legal opinion that asserted:

> *CORRESPONDENCE MEMORANDUM, WisDOT*
> *Date: February 24, 2012*
> *To: Secretary of Transportation*
> *From: WisDOT OGC*
> *Subject: TERO Ordinances and WisDOT Highway Contracts*
>
> *This legal opinion is prepared to distribute to the TLAC on Monday, February 27, 2012. The Opinion States:*
>
> > *It supplements my previous legal opinion that came to the same conclusion dated August 4, 2008. The TLAC was established in 2011 to explore mechanisms to enhance Native American labor opportunities to more suitably address Native American labor opportunities on WisDOT highway-related transportation projects. The committee consists of TRIBES, industry representatives, unions, WisDOT staff representatives from the DWD, and other Native American interest groups.*
> >
> > ***QUESTION:*** *Does the WisDOT have the legal authority to include and enforce TERO requirements as a WisDOT contractual requirement on any Federal-Aid Highway Program highway projects?*
> >
> > ***ANSWER:*** *No. In brief, federal permission does not grant WisDOT legal authority to require such TERO 1 preferences on federally funded projects. There is no Wisconsin state statutory grant of authority to WisDOT to require TERO preferences. The rule of law in Wisconsin is that State agencies like WisDOT must find legal authority for a proposed action within the express or necessarily implied language of a statute. Any doubt is resolved in favor of the lack of legal authority.*

---

40. All the meeting minutes from the Tribal Labor Advisor Committee website were archived and copied in January 2019, but all the archived information has been removed from the new website. https://wisdottribaltaskforce.org/

ANALYSIS: *23 U.S.C. 140(d) addresses Indian employment preferences in Federal Highway Administration ("FHWA") funded programs. It reads:*

> *"(d) Indian employment. – Consistent with section 703(i) of the Civil Rights Act of 1964 (42 U.S.C. 2000e-2(i)),* **nothing in this section shall preclude the preferential employment of Indians living on or near a reservation on projects and contracts on Indian reservation roads.** *3 States* **may** *implement a preference for the employment of Indians on projects carried out under this title near Indian reservations. The Secretary shall cooperate with Indian tribal governments and the States to implement this subsection." [Emphasis added.]*

The section referred to is 23 U.S.C. 140, which requires WisDOT to assure FHWA that employment in connection with proposed federally funded projects will be provided without regard to race, color, creed, national origin, or sex. This federal statute creates an exception to these required assurances that allow but do not mandate, as a condition of the allocated federal funds, that States implement a preference for the employment of Indians on projects carried out under this title near Indian reservations.

Federal regulations implementing this federal statute include 23 CFR 635.117(d) and 25 CFR 170.912(a) as follows:

- *23 CFR 117(d) "(d) Pursuant to 23 U.S.C. 140(d), it is* **permissible** *for STD's [State Transportation Departments] to implement procedures or requirements which will extend preferential employment to Indians living on or near a reservation on eligible projects as defined in paragraph (e)4 of this section. Indian preference shall be applied without regard to tribal affiliation or place of enrolment. In no instance should a contractor be compelled to lay off or terminate a permanent core-crew employee to meet a preference goal." [Emphasis added.]*

- *25 CFR 170.912(a) "(a) Tribal, State, and local governments* **may** *provide an Indian employment preference for Indians living on or*

near a reservation on projects and contracts that meet the definition of an Indian Reservation Road. (See 23 U.S.C. 101(a)(12) and
140(d), and 23 CFR 635.117(d).)" (Emphasis added.)

In 1993, FHWA issued a Notice entitled "IP in Employment on
Federal-aid Highway Projects on and Near Indian Reservations."
**"This Notice, implementing regulations, and subsequent legal guid-
ance have all been consistent in the approach that the 23 U.S.C.
140(d) Indian employment preference is permissive, not mandatory."**
Richard O. Jones, Indian Transportation Law, Selected Studies in
Transportation Law, 3-85 (2007) (emphasis added). "[T]he [FHWA]
has never required a state to follow Indian employment preference"
to obtain federal funds. /d. The Alaska Supreme Court held that such
a "hiring preference violates the Alaska Constitution's guarantee of
equal protection because the borough lacks a legitimate governmental
interest to enact a hiring preference favoring one class of citizens at
the expense of others and because the preference enacted is not closely
tailored to meet its goals." /d. at 3-86 (quoting Malabed v. North
Slope Borough, 70 P.3d 416, 427-28 (Alaska 2003)).

Thus, although 23 U.S.C. 140(d) is permissive, permissive federal
statutes and regulations do not authorize WisDOT to act.

"Administrative agencies have only such powers as are expressly
granted to them or necessarily implied, and any such power sought to
be exercised must be found within the four corners of the statute under
which the agency proceeds."

American Brass Co. v. Wisconsin State Bd. of Health, 245 Wis.
440, 448, 15 N.W.2d 27, 30 (1944). Therefore, "[t]he nature and scope
of an agency's authority is a matter of statutory interpretation or
construction." City of Appleton v. Transp. Com'n of Wisconsin, 116
Wis. 2d 352, 357, 342 N.W.2d 68, 71 (Ct. App. 1983).

No Wisconsin statute authorizes WisDOT to implement the
characteristics of a TERO, which include an Indian employment preference, exclusive or preferential use of Indian enterprises or services, or
payment of TERO-imposed taxes.

Mitton v. WisDOT illustrates the principles that define the scope
of an administrative agency's authority when considering permissive

federal statutes. In Mitton, WisDOT attempted to condemn several acres of land beyond what was needed to construct a portion of US Highway 29. Mitton v. WisDOT 184 Wis. 2d 738, 742, 516 N.W.2d 709, 711 (1994). Wisconsin Stat.s. 84.01 (15), 84.015, and 84.03 require WisDOT to expend federal highway funds in accordance with acts of Congress relating to such funds. Thus, WisDOT argued that the additional condemnation would fulfill the requirements of federal regulations precluding the disturbance of historical sites without prior approval from the FHWA. /d. However, the Wisconsin Court held that the federal statutes that WisDOT alleged provided it with the authority to condemn the additional land did not mandate such specific action, but rather only required that WisDOT "do whatever planning possible to minimize the harm done ...."/d. at 714. Therefore, WisDOT had exceeded its authority under the state condemnation statute. Another set of federal statutes worth analyzing in the TERO context is those comprising the federal DBE program.

Although state statutes authorize WisDOT to implement the federal DBE program, these statutes do not authorize the implementation of an Indian employment preference or any other TERO characteristic. Wis. Stat. s. 84.072(8) states:

84.072(8) "[t]his section does not apply if federal law does not require, as a condition of using federal funds, this state to establish goals for the participation of disadvantaged business or the employment of disadvantaged individuals in projects using federal funds." Wis. Stat. s. 84.072(8) (Emphasis added).

Similarly, Wis. Stat. 84.076(5) sunsets the disadvantaged business demonstration and training program when no longer required as a condition of federal funding:

84.076(5) "Sunset. This section does not apply after the latter of the following:

(a) September 30, 1997.

(b) The date on which federal law does not require, as a condition of using federal funds, that this state establish goals for the

participation of disadvantaged businesses or the employment of disadvantaged individuals in projects using federal funds."

49 CFR 26.21 (a)(1) mandates a DBE program, but it does not mandate the implementation of Indian employment preference:

"All FHWA recipients receiving funds authorized by a statute to which this part applies ..." who "let [US]DOT-assisted contracts, [...] must have a DBE program." This regulation does not mandate the implementation of an Indian employment preference.

The federal DBE program also prohibits targeting any individual minority or gender groups. For instance, 49 CFR 26.7(a) provides that those to whom the program applies may not "exclude any person from participation in, deny any person the benefits of, or otherwise discriminate against anyone in connection with the award and performance of any contract covered by this part based on race, color, sex, or national origin."

To allow for an Indian employment preference in the administration of a federal DBE program would discriminate against those certified DBEs who do not meet the statutory definition of "Native American." Further, 49 CFR 26.7(b) provides that any federal DBE program may not "use criteria or methods of administration that have the effect of defeating or substantially impairing accomplishment of the objectives of the program with respect.to individuals of a particular race, color, sex, or national origin." 49 CFR 26.7(b).

In any event, *Milwaukee County Pavers Assoc. v. Fiedler* has, nevertheless, prohibited WisDOT from participating in any federal DBE program unless conditionally required for federal funding. There, the court stated that "[w]hat is important to a determination of constitutionality is not the source of the funds, but the source of the state's authority for spending the funds." *Milwaukee County Pavers Assoc. v. Fiedler* (*Milwaukee County Pavers Ill*), 731 F. Supp. 1395, 1412 O/V.D. Wis. 1990). *Fiedler* held that "when the state provides race-conscious relief that bears no relationship to meeting its overall goal under the [federal DBE program], it is acting on its own and must base its action on state findings of prior discrimination." /d.

Milwaukee County Pavers Assn's v. Fiedler (Milwaukee County Pavers 1), 707 F. Supp. 1016 (WD WI 1989).
Milwaukee County Pavers Assn's v. Fiedler (Milwaukee County Pavers II), 710 F. Supp. 1532 (WD WI 1989).
Milwaukee County Pavers Assn's v. Fiedler (Milwaukee County Pavers Ill), 731 F. Supp. 1395 (WD Wl1990).
Milwaukee County Pavers Assn's v. Fiedler (Milwaukee County Pavers Affirmed), 922 F.2d 419 (7th Cir.1991).
Milwaukee County Pavers Assn's v. Fiedler (Milwaukee County Pavers Cert. Denied), 114 L.Ed.2d 714, 111S.Ct. 2261 (1991).

The permanent injunction is in Milwaukee Pavers Ill that was upheld by 7th Circ. Cert. Denied by U.S. Supreme Court. Milwaukee County Pavers Assn's v. Fiedler 731 F.Supp. 1395, 1415-1416 (W.D. Wis. 1990):

"FURTHER IT IS ORDERED that defendants are enjoined permanently from implementing the following aspects of their disadvantaged business enterprise preferences:

(1) The setting of goals for disadvantaged business subcontractor participation on exclusively state-funded projects.

(2) The provision in Wis. Stat.§ 84.076(3)(b) setting goals for disadvantaged business subcontractor participation on projects led to disadvantaged prime contractors under the state's set aside program.

(3) Any goals for disadvantaged business subcontractor participation on individual projects or any set-asides under Wis. Stat. § 84.076 past the date that the disadvantaged business enterprise program in the Surface Transportation Uniform Relocation and Assistance Act of 1987 is authorized."

Further, as noted in the Milwaukee Pavers Ill decision, WisDOT never applied the minority program under Wis. Stat. 84.075 to highway contracting. That statute is dormant and remains dormant for the highway program because it is unconstitutional on its face if it sets a fixed minority goal, or would be unconstitutional as applied without a valid availability and disparity study:

"It is undisputed that the Wisconsin Department of Transportation has never implemented the 5% minority business goal in Wis. Stat.§ 84.075 and the portion of Wis. Stat.§ 84.076(2)(a) that requires that 75% of the $4 million set-aside be allocated to minority businesses. Plaintiffs have presented no evidence to suggest that their business interests have been harmed or impaired in any way by threatened enforcement of these minority business statutes. Therefore, because plaintiffs fail to allege an actual case or controversy with respect to these statutes, I decline to exercise jurisdiction over challenges to their constitutionality." Milwaukee County Pavers Ass'n v. Fiedler, 731 F.Supp. 1395, 1407 (W.D. Wis.1990).

If the Wisconsin Legislature enacted a true race and gender-neutral small business set-aside program, WisDOT would NOT violate the injunction or the DBE statutory limitations or the US or Wisconsin Constitutions. Link: http://www.trb.org/Main/Blurbs/165 240. aspx

Here is the Q and A on the USDOT small business initiative regulation: https://www.transportation.gov/content/office-small-and-disadvantaged-business-utilization#26.39

This is from the executive summary of the synthesis:

"As a group, supportive services and training measures ranked among the most effective in the survey. The strategy ranking the very highest, however, was an administrative support strategy 'limiting certain small contracts to proposals by small firms only,' which was rated effective by 91% of those who had used it."[41]

A few days after the first communications sent by the WisDOT OGC to the WisDOT Secretary, a TLAC meeting had taken place. The TLAC meeting transpired in February 2012

---

41. Memo; February 27, 2012, OGCWISDOT Jim Thiel response to Secretary Gotlibb regarding TERO Preferences.

because, as the meeting minutes state, the following WisDOT representatives were present: 1 representative from OGC, TA, TAA, Laborers, NACCW, Serendipity, DTSD, NMAC, and AICCW, 2 from TL, DBE, TRANS, 3 from Local #139, UNION, and WTBA, and 7-tribal members of 6-Tribes. These meeting minutes from the TLAC meeting reflect the following recommendations and action items:

- *Request for the total hours and total contract dollar amounts for each project cited in the NAHP data.*

- *Recommendation to provide more education to the committee on the EO#39 and the WisDOT PA.*

- *Request for a copy of the 1854 treaty that addresses the transportation alliance.*

- *Recommendation to take the PA to the Inter-tribal Task Force (ITTF) to revise and strengthen the document.*

- *Request for the agency to look at set-asides, for example, those under the Department of Defense (DOD).*

- *Request for information on how the amount of federal dollars allocated to WisDOT projects.*

- *Recommendation to elect a Tribal government representative on TRANS-AC.*

- *Charter a separate task force to work directly with TRIBES and internal WisDOT staff to explore a policy that addresses projects that are "on" or "partially on" Tribal lands.*

This opinion was finally presented by WisDOT OGC in person at the TLAC meetings in February 2012. This was documented through the meeting minutes, which were collected from the meeting. WisDOT OGC conveyed his legal opinion, which asserted to the TRIBES as this was the WisDOT OGC TERO legal opinion:

> *WisDOT does not have statutory authority, and the federal government doesn't require the enforcement of hiring preference. **That does***

not mean that the TRIBES cannot require it. They can require it on their reservations and lands in trust for the benefit of their members. If DOT has a contract that requires being on Tribal land, it cannot go on Tribal land without their permission and compliance. You must comply in that instance, but it's not WisDOT that's requiring it, but the Tribe. This has been the same decision for the past 20 years. Transportation alliance in the treaties indicates that some state trunk highways on reservation/Tribal lands belong to the state for transportation purposes, and thus TRIBES would not be able to apply hiring preference in those instances. Request for a copy of the 1854 treaty that addresses the transportation alliance.

The legal opinion was presented at the first TLAC meeting in mid-February 2012, which documented the message presented by WisDOT's OGC asserted his legal opinion to the TRIBES: "WisDOT does not have the statutory authority, and the federal government doesn't require the enforcement of hiring preference but does not mean TRIBES cannot make this a requirement on projects located within their reservations, including trust lands for communities. When contracts require to be on tribal lands, WisDOT cannot trespass on Tribal lands without first obtaining the TRIBE'S consent, which has been a requirement of the TRIBES.

With the abundance of projects located both "on," "near," and within a commutable distance of Indian roadways, Indian country, Indian trust lands, fee lands, and reservations over the past 10 years (from 2008 to 2019), it is bewildering, because of the lack of a presence of TSTW on these projects while the NAHP had been established in 2009 and after two short years this led to the suspension of the NAHP in 2011. From 2008, and until 2012, this had shown the participation had risen until the suspension of the NAHP, when the TSTW began to decline.

In March 2012, a TLAC meeting had convened with the following WisDOT representatives: 1 from TA, TAA, CRCS Representative, Senior Labor Development Specialist, 2 from

Local#139, 3 from WTBA, and 6 from TRIBES. This was The TLAC Capacity Subcommittee Meeting scheduled to demonstrate the Civil Rights and Compliance Systems (CRCS), and it was also used to help identify a standardized qualification system for referrals based on the skill sets and standards of the industry. This was followed up by another meeting in April, where the TLAC group would have the WisDOT TA release a solicitation for representation on the task force to redraft a policy for projects located on or partially on tribal lands. There was also a request for more education on the PA and EO#39. It was also noted that there was a request to appoint a Tribal government representative to participate in the TRANS-AC. The TRANS-AC focuses on construction and is an advisory group to the Secretary of DBE Construction. These members mostly consist of construction associations, including the WTBS, AICCW, and NAMC. A request for an overview of the Civil Rights and Compliance Systems (CRCS). It was here that it was stated by the FDHWA that the agency lacks the ability to solicit to the contractor establishing requirements who will be hired, whether local or Native American workforce. A question was made to the entities on the validity of the reported number of hires on the U.S. 41 corridor project. There was also a final mention regarding the monitoring and tracking processes.

In April 2012, the initial release of the solicitation for representation on the task force to redraft a policy for projects located "on" or "partially on" Tribal lands was announced. This has been released by the WisDOT TA as the meeting concluded with the TRIBES requesting more literature and education for the Partnership Agreement and Executive Order #39.

In May, the next TLAC subcommittee session helped to establish the task items like an establishment of the criteria or prerequisites to begin building a database that can Track the information provided by TRIBES, TSTW, and contractors. This information was then collected by the WisDOT. If TLAC were to host a focus group with Native American employees with experience working in the construction industry, what information do you think would be beneficial to gather? This is the question that was asked to help identify the challenges faced by all entities, including:

- *Examples of the pathways to initial entry into the industry.*

- *Examples of barriers to entry.*

- *Include Native American Disadvantaged Business Enterprises (NADBEs) perspective as an employer.*

- *Barriers to maintaining a job (e.g., family, finances, etc.).*

- *Cultural sensitivity/both ways of awareness.*

- *What are their areas of expertise?*

- *What are the needs of the industry?*

- *What training is needed to get the jobs?*

- *Benefits of working in the construction industry.*

- *Resources that are available to assist with the barriers that applicants may have.*

- *Just ask the Tribal Skilled Workers about their hardships working in the Construction Labor workforce in reference to prompt discussion about their lives.*

- *Potential earnings in these trades (see the white wage sheet that is included in every contract).*

The next TLAC meeting scheduled was for July 2012, as this was the time to review the committees and recommendations to enhance the Native American labor opportunities on state and federal projects, which is interesting because this did not emphasize the NAHP projects at the time. One thing to note was the establishment of the original eight (8) recommendations, which had been established to help enhance Native American labor opportunities on state and federal projects. The 8-recommendations included the following information and emphasized the relevance to the NAHP:

This was proceeding with the FINAL implementation plan of the TLAC, which outlined the 8-recommendations approved in July 2012 and a fully detailed document reflecting:

2.0 TLAC Recommendations

RECOMMENDATION 1 | STATEWIDE NATIVE AMERICAN LABOR INITIATIVE

> **Goal 1:** *Develop an initiative administered by the tribe*
> **Objective A:** *Establish the scope of work*
> **Objective B:** *Solicit interest and select a tribe*

RECOMMENDATION 2 | STATEWIDE NATIVE AMERICAN LABOR DATABASE

> **Goal 1:** *Capacity to maintain info*
> **Objective A:** *Peer exchange*

> **Goal 2:** Create a statewide labor database
> **Objective A:** *Work team to develop a database concept*
> **Objective B:** *Create a database system*

RECOMMENDATION 3 | STANDARDIZED RECRUITMENT and REFERRAL

> **Goal 1:** Establish a process
> **Objective A:** *Survey tribal employment offices and contractors*
> **Objective B:** *Utilize survey data to develop a process*

RECOMMENDATION 4 | MONITORING, REPORTING and ASSESSMENT

> **Goal 1:** *Monitoring and reporting of data*
> **Objective A:** *Report regularly (existing and new formats)*

Objective B: Annual assessment
Objective C: Regularly report to stakeholders

RECOMMENDATION 5 | PARTNERSHIP BUILDING and COMMUNICATION

Goal 1: Increase cultural awareness
    Objective A: Annual cross-training

Goal 2: Institutionalize formal communication and coordination
    Objective A: Formal advisory committee

Goal 3: Regular communication
    Objective A: Direct 1:1 contact between tribal employment offices and contractors
    Objective B: Broad-based outreach between tribes and construction industry contractors, unions, and other WisDOT

Goal 4: Project-specific outreach
    Objective A: Project forecasting
    Objective B: Pre-bid, construction, and face-to-face meetings
    Objective C: Job classifications

RECOMMENDATION 6 | EDUCATION RESOURCES, PREPAREDNESS and CAREER DEVELOPMENT

Goal 1: Equitable access to training opportunities
    Objective A: Expand TRANS services to tribal communities
    Objective B: Establish tribal tailored recruitment strategy to participate in TRANS and other construction training opportunities
    Objective C: Identify resources and funding to increase participation and programming offered to tribal communities

Goal 2: Utilize placement strategies employed by successful TRANS programs
    Objective A: Survey TRANS providers to identify successful strategies (e.g., curriculum, recruitment, marketing, placement, etc.)

Goal 3: *Increase hiring and long-term employment outcomes*
    Objective A: *Host a focus group with Native Americans who have experience working in the construction industry*
    Objective B: *Create and offer pre-training to prospective construction employees based on industry expectations and qualifications*
    Objective C: *Annual PFEWs and statewide networking*

Goal 4: *Utilize non-DOT training services*
    Objective A: *Apprenticeship and training programs offered by tribal employment offices, DWD, unions, and non-unions*

Goal 5: *Education materials to enhance tribal participation in construction industry training programs and services*
    Objective A: *Create educational materials (brochures, videos, website, etc.)*
    Objective B: *Flow chart on construction industry entry*
    Objective C: *Regular ongoing communication between tribal employment offices, candidates, unions, and other training entities*

RECOMMENDATION 7 | CONSTRUCTION INDUSTRY INCENTIVES FOR NATIVE AMERICAN HIRING

Goal 1: *Increase incentives*
    Objective A: *Establish a work group to examine existing incentives and develop recommendations to create hiring incentives utilizing state, federal, and tribal sources*
    Objective B: *Implement recommendations that are feasible and authorized*
    Objective C: *Annual awards program to recognize contractors*

RECOMMENDATION 8 | NATIVE AMERICAN HIRING PROVISION FOR ON OR PARTIALLY ON TRIBAL LANDS

Goal 1: *Support the government-to-government relationship between the state/tribes and enhance tribal labor opportunities on tribal lands*

Objective A: Work team to redraft NAHP
Objective B: Create a statewide rollout

This meeting concluded with the following outstanding issues that warranted additional information or issues presented by the work teams, which will require further discussion or determination by TLAC or WisDOT Administrations. The Statewide Native American Labor Initiative's outstanding issues were related to the budgets, as the questions asked were:

- *What funding sources will be allocated towards this initiative, and what will be the final budget?*

- *How will funds be allocated to the deliverables?*

- *Will the budget submittal be part of this proposal?*

This was also the same time the DBE Summer Reporter had been released with the information from the following projects: I-94 North-South Freeway Project Update (*Milwaukee, Racine, and Kenosha Counties*), Verona Road Project Update (*Dane County*), and U.S. 41 Corridor Expansion Project Update (*Brown County and Winnebago County*) and followed up with the Fall DBE reports in October. This information showed the total hours worked and the amounts of minority and female workers. This helps to have another number to check through the hours against any other reports obtained.

In August, communications had been sent to the TRIBES from the Secretary of WisDOT stating: "TLAC was charged with developing strategies to enhance Native American labor opportunities on WisDOT state and federal projects. As a result, a request was made to revise the NAHP for projects located 'on' or 'partially on' tribal or reservation lands." It was stated by the WisDOT, "*We are committed to convening a working team of WisDOT staff and tribal representatives to assist with redrafting and revisions of the NAHP by November 2012.*"

Another meeting had been scheduled for September as the

following representatives were present from WisDOT: 1 representative from TA, TAA, OBOC, DTSD, FHWA, and 6-tribal members of 4 TRIBES. In this meeting, WisDOT TA provided an overview of the concerns raised by the CI, WisDOT, and other agencies involved with Transportation Construction. The TRIBES then spoke on their concerns and the development of the implementation process of the NAHP from the "focus group" meetings. The work team agreed that examining other state agency provisions and MOUs would be useful in the redrafting process for the NAHP. The inquiry as to what extent can the provisions require or mandate hiring and preference? WisDOT OGC's GC legal opinion indicates that the agency cannot legally enforce hiring mandates on projects. WisDOT can, however, use alternative tools that enhance communication, recruitment, and build capacity. Discussion recommended the possible implementation and consideration of Native American DBEs and tribal government construction entities (public works programs) as part of the hiring provision currently being redrafted. It was further recommended that a general provision be considered and adopted for all state/federal contracts and use the statewide Native American labor database currently under development. This provision would be more general and informational, while the NAHP for projects located "on or partially on tribal lands" contains specific conditions that require communication and outreach when working within tribal communities.

Although WisDOT policy is to let construction agreements through a competitive bidding process, under special circumstances the department may negotiate directly with local governments for the performance of construction work. FHWA examines the eligibility of tribal governments in the Labor for America (LFA) program. This led to the scheduling of another meeting for some time in October; there is no agenda or meeting minutes relating to this meeting available. The language removed any accountability or authority established for contractors to step foot on the reservations on projects located on or now partially on Indian lands or reservations. It also states this NAHP is mainly informational and general, which is not the same process and does not set in place a pre-mandatory process for contractors for projects located on or partially on tribal lands.

At the annual Wisconsin Tribal Transportation Conferences (WTTC), which began in 2012, is where you began to hear WisDOT TA and TA analysis reference this particular statement: *"American Indians and Alaska Natives as having the highest unemployment rates in Wisconsin and across the nation."*[42] This statement is interesting because the information presented shows that WisDOT and its influences are also equally responsible for this issue within Wisconsin, partially due to the application of the NAHP and removal of TERO and IP. The original intent of the provision is to help establish economic opportunities for the TSTW on WisDOT projects, but it has had negative effects within the TRIBES communities, as noted since the suspension of the NAHP in 2011. You can see in the DBE Reporters, ALR, and the WisDOT MAR's that all will reflect these drops in participation of TSTW across Wisconsin. The next time you attend the WTTC, listen for similar comments mentioned by WisDOT representatives disseminating to the TRIBES they still have the highest unemployment rates across the nation. When the provision was originally drafted and suspended, in many of the meetings, the TRIBES did not have an equal seat at the table, or an opportunity to voice their concerns at the same time with all the other entities at the table for discussion, because the meetings were held by WisDOT in private focus group meetings showing the TRIBES were not invited, directly resulting in direct impacts in Tribal communities of TSTW hindering employment opportunities on projects across the state of Wisconsin for them.

51. Labor force characteristics by race and ethnicity, 2017: BLS Reports https://www.bls.gov/opub/reports/race-and-ethnicity/2017/home.htm

This transpired while current, active projects directly excluded the NAHP on the projects located "on" or "partially on" tribal or reservation lands. The projects reports reflect the suspension of the NAHP for eleven months now. This meeting reflected many recommendations relevant to the NAHP and warranted requests by WisDOT, CI, and other entities involved with the concerns or issues related to their need to amend the NAHP since August 2011. These concerns and issues all directly impacted TRIBES communities. This can be shown through the 2012 DBE Reporters, 2012 regional reports, and the MAR.

2012 DBE Reporter

Spring

- *I-94 North-South Freeway Project (Milwaukee, Racine, and Kenosha Counties)*

  Work Hours as of March 2012
  The DBE Reporter spring quarterly reports there is no information available for this year of 2012

- *I-94 CTH Badger Interchange Project (Dane County)*

  Work Hours as of March 2012
  ****

- *US 41 Corridor Expansion Project (Brown and Winnebago Counties)*

  Work Hours as of March 2012
  ****

Summer

- *I-94 North-South Freeway Project (Milwaukee, Racine, and Kenosha Counties)*

  Work Hours as of June 30, 2012
  Total Hours Worked 2,139,375

Total Minority Hours Worked 394,752
Total Female Hours Worked 53,564

- **I-94 CTH Badger Interchange Project (Dane County)**

  Work Hours as of June 30, 2012

  **

- *US 41 Corridor Expansion Project (Brown and Winnebago Counties)*

  Work Hours as of June 30, 2012
  Total Hours Worked 1,306,253
  Total Minority Hours Worked 69,426
  Total Female Hours Worked 32,109

Winter

- *I-94 North-South Freeway Project (Milwaukee, Racine, and Kenosha Counties)*

  Work Hours as of September 30, 2012
  Total Hours Worked 2,307,256
  Total Minority Hours Worked 426,164
  Total Female Hours Worked 57,906

- **I-94 CTH Badger Interchange Project (Dane County)**

  Work Hours as of September 30, 2012
  **

- *US 41 Corridor Expansion Project (Brown and Winnebago Counties)*

  Work Hours as of September 30, 2012
  Total Hours Worked 1,590,894
  Total Minority Hours Worked 88,492
  Total Female Hours 38,306

Annual DBE Report as of September 30, 2012

- *I-94 North-South Freeway Project (Milwaukee, Racine, and Kenosha Counties)*

Work Hours as of September 30, 2012
Total Hours Worked 4,446,631
Total Minority Hours Worked 820,916
Total Female Hours Worked 111,470

- *I-94 CTH Badger Interchange Project (Dane County)*

Work Hours as of September 30, 2012

**

- *US 41 Corridor Expansion Project (Brown and Winnebago Counties)*

Work Hours as of September 30, 2012
Total Hours Worked 2,897,147
Total Minority Hours Worked 157,918
Total Female Hours 70,415

- *All Projects across Wisconsin Annually*

Work Hours as of September 30, 2012
Total Hours Worked 2,327,514.40
Total Minority Hours Worked 316,706.20
Total Female Hours 58,954.30

All WisDOT projects across Wisconsin for 2012:
Total hours – 8,504,497

The DBE Reporter is used to represent the total number of hours worked, the total amount of hours available for "minorities," and the total female hours worked. This is then referenced when reviewing the regional reports established from the public records requests later on. This helps to identify the variances between things like the total hours worked and the minorities or females worked. If these numbers are inaccurate, then we begin to look for variances. (*Please see Appendix B: Chapter 6.1 Chart 2012 Regional Report*)

The 2012 DBE and ALR Analysis Reports reflect that women are counted twice: once as a "female" and once as a "minority." This means the same issues with the double reporting of individuals. This will throw off the reports. Looking at the two charts to see the totals of workers and the hours are not matching up, there is almost double the numbers listed in the DBE reports versus the regional reports for Wisconsin. This warrants another document to compare to the second public records request. The TRIBES can identify this information as a baseline of the qualitative information presented. The information presented is from all the regional reports from all construction projects across the state of Wisconsin. This complies with the following regions: North Central, Northeast, Northwest, Southeast, and Southwest regions and encompasses all of Wisconsin. The information is provided quarterly, which is then presented at every quarterly TLAC meeting by the WisDOT Regional TL. This information is misreported to contractors by the method of self-reporting. This means the TSTW is the one who reports they are Native American. In 2012, in the regional report presented, there was a total of 1.56% TSTW on all projects across Wisconsin, and they obtained about 1.73% of the hours available.

After reviewing the DBE Reporter and the ALR, we now must analyze the Annual WisDOT MAR to show the variances as presented. Scrutinizing the information, it is clear the regional report and the WisDOT MRA, when looking at the percentage for participation of TSTW, is .04% variance for Native American participation. When looking at the hours worked, these numbers are about .06% variance. Now, reviewing the ALR, the hard numbers for the participants of Native Americans are 743 males and 79 females.

In the MRA, it states the Native American was 187 for males and 23 for women. The variance between them is for the males is rather close for the headcount and the hours worked. But when you look at the numbers identified 556 males and 56 females. We need to now look at the Native American hours for ALR, which is 76224.60 for males and 9400.40 for females. In the MAR it is 73,244.20 for males, and for females it is 9400. These are rather close, but it is interesting because of the difference of 556 males and 56 females totaling over 2000 hours is the difference, but this opens the door to begin asking these questions because this information provided is from two different points, but it was the same information requested and from the same WisDOT Labor Compliance representative and the same WisDOT CRCS program, but still reflected these variances.

2012 WisDOT Annual Minority Analysis Report

Caucasian		African		Hispanic		Asian		Native american		Total Participation	Native American
Male	Female	Male	Female	Male	Female	Male	Female	Male	Female		Particiaption
Head Count 2012											
Male	Female	Male	Female	Male	Female	Male	Female	Male	Female	Head Count	
11,411.00	342.00	342.00	14.00	731.00	8.00	44.00	3.00	187.00	23.00	13,105.00	1.60%
								1.43%	0.18%		
Hours Worked 2012											
Male	Female	Male	Female	Male	Female	Male	Female	Male	Female	Hours Worked	
4,345,260.40	112,854.70	104,034.90	5,189.00	266,632.90	2,231.80	19,406.00	1,828.80	73,224.20	9,400.00	4,940,062.70	1.67%
								1.48%	0.19%		

Chapter 7

2013

Meetings in 2013 began in February with an NAHP redrafting session with the following WisDOT representatives present: 1 representative from OBOEC, TA, TAA, FHWA, 9 from tribal members of the 6 TRIBES. There was a recommendation for a statewide contract provision that ties into the Statewide Native American labor database from the TLAC group. There was a recommendation for the NAHP to serve as a separate government-to-government relationship between the agency and TRIBES. This warranted the need for the establishment due to the suspension of the original NAHP to develop recommendations to enhance labor and connect tribes with the key construction industry stakeholders that do the actual hiring on projects. The TLAC meeting was scheduled for a discussion of the proper procedures to enhance Native American labor opportunities on projects located on or partially on tribal lands. The DWD endorsed the State-wide labor database to explore other partnerships or data sharing and funding opportunities. The process of reviewing the TLAC's Draft implementation plans, including the topics of Establishment of development of a partnership with the DWD for a database for the TRIBES. This resulted in the recommendation from WisDOT TA for the database to be maintained by WisDOT, but there were concerns that the cost would have significantly been larger. A TRIBE did not support the placement in an inter-tribal organization, as the concerns seemed to be surrounded by confidentiality. As this discussion took place at the second

TLAC preparation meeting in February, it is important to note that rather than having the WisDOT control the database; it was mentioned that it should be housed within the Great Lakes Inter-tribal Committee (GLITC). The need for these two critical components to be recognized was also mentioned:

- *A contractual special provision which is underdevelopment; and*

- *The need for a MOU indicating the WisDOT policy needs and Tribal commitments to ensure these efforts are successful.*

The next meeting was in March, labeled as the WisDOT NAHP Redraft Session. The following WisDOT representatives were present: 1 representative from TA and OBOEC and 6 from Tribal members from 5 TRIBES. This meeting began with referencing items like the requests of the application of TRIBES members should be considered for hiring on projects "on" or "near" TRIBES lands. The TRIBES also expressed concern over the exclusion of projects that are adjacent to or had the potential to impact tribal communities (access, etc.). The recommendation was the applicability of the provision to explore options for inclusion in contracts in those counties that contain tribal lands or sustain a significant Native American population. Someone mentioned to also explore methods during the collection and input of data into Statewide databases, identifying Tribal Affiliations, Tribal Members, and Descendancy to allow for more precise reporting to TRIBES moving forwards, thus eliminating the need for identification of "Native American" while recognizing the unique sovereign status of the TRIBES. This statement relates directly to the Civil Rights exception language provided, Tribal preference is not a violation of civil rights act for actions and companies owned and operated on Indian lands. The unions expressed their concerns with hiring minorities and tribal members rather than union members and suggested including in the provision to advocate for the ability to hire Native Americans on state and federal projects. This was also recommended to be brought forward in the next TLAC meeting.

The TLAC meeting took place the next day in March, and at this meeting, the following WisDOT representatives were present: 1 representative from OBOEC, TA, DWD, BL, Serendipity, Bureau of Indian Affairs (BIA), Southwest (SW) TL, and Business Liaisons, 2 from DOA, WTBA, and Local #139, and 9 from Tribal members of the 6 TRIBES. This meeting discussed a need for a three-tiered component with TRIBES for creating a skills database, establishing a statewide inter-tribal database creating an inter-tribal and contractor interface. With this came the recommendations for the need for monitoring, reporting, and assessments. This is to be provided quarterly with the presentation of reports providing a baseline and annual assessments while forecasting the WisDOT six-year plan to develop scopes of work, secure available funding, finalize the scopes of work, advertise, select, and award the contracts all of which derive from the 8-recommendations.

A few weeks later, a meeting was scheduled for the NAHP redrafting session with the mention of the NAHP on a project located within the boundaries of a TRIBE'S Indian lands with the only exemption being the Statewide Native American Database had not been created yet. The NAHP draft was submitted to the TRIBES' leaders, and the next step was for the draft to be presented to the TLAC group. The NAHP was adopted in March 2013, and the release of an Inter-Governmental Agreement (IGA) for tribal governments and tribal colleges was released in March 2013 and must be post marked on February 20, 2014. Once awarded, this establishes available funds for the following areas:

- *WisDOT Statewide Native American Labor Initiative (NALI) consisted of $190,000 in funds available established in 2011, and whoever was awarded this was charged with developing strategies to enhance Native American Labor Opportunities on State and Federal* projects. This included coordination and development of standardized recruitment and referral processes, monitoring and reporting labor data and developing/delivering training programs, which will all be analyzed and distributed at outreach meetings.

- *WisDOT ITTF administration funds $250,000 available for the group to provide guidance to WisDOT on programs, policies, and projects which affect tribal communities through the implementation of the annual work plan, which was appropriated in 2014 to include the coordination of the ITTF Meetings, creating and implementing the ITTF annual work plan including: joint safety initiatives, economic development programs, labor and business development, cultural resource programs, training, technical assistance which benefits the Tribal Transportation systems and WisDOT's government-to-government relations.*

The WisDOT IGA Funding Opportunity solicitation Timeline has been established, which looks like this:

- *January 29, 2014 – Notification of IGA opportunities to Tribal leadership and tribal colleges.*

- *February 3-7, 2014 – Host informal meeting on February 06 in Lac du Flambeau.*

- *February 10-20, 2014 –*

    - *Host TLAC meeting (in Madison) on February 17 (with additional information meeting/Question and Answer to immediately follow).*

    - *Letter of interest deadline: Thursday, February 20.*

    - *Provide proposal instructions to tribes that submitted letters of interest.*

- *February 24-28, 2014, Proposal deadline: Friday, February 28.*

- *March 3-7, 2014 –*

    - *Committee review, selection, and notification.*

    - *Negotiate contract.*

- *March 31, 2014 – Fully executed contract.*

The Important deadlines were noted in a letter of interest deadline, which was 02/2014 and the proposal deadline, which was 02/2014. This information was to be submitted to the member of the same tribe who was also working as the WisDOT TA to review this information. This was then concluded with the contact information of the WisDOT TA for the submissions to be sent to before February 2014 for submitting the letter of interest deadline and February 2014 for the Proposal deadline.

There is no further information available for any other meetings related to the NAHP or TLAC meetings, etc., for 2013 other than the DBE Reporters, Annual Labor Reports (ALR) and the Minority Annual Reports (MAR).

In 2013, there were 3 DBE Reporters: Spring, Summer, and Winter. This had been transpiring while these projects were currently active and ongoing, without a NAHP on the projects located "on" or "partially on" tribal or reservation lands. These reports reflect the projects showing the suspension of the NAHP for about eleven months now. This meeting reflected many recommendations relevant to the NAHP and warranted requests by WisDOT, CI and other entities involved with the concerns or issues related to their need to amend the NAHP since August 2013. These concerns and issues all had directly impacted on TRIBES communities. This can be shown through the 2013 DBE Reporters, 2013 regional reports, and the MAR.

2013 DBE Reporter

Spring

- *I-94 North-South Freeway Project (Milwaukee, Racine, and Kenosha Counties)*

    Work Hours as of March 2013
    Total Hours Worked 2,540,297

Total Minority Hours Worked 465,947
Total Female Hours Worked 62,838

- **I-94 CTH Badger Interchange Project (Dane County)**

  Work Hours as of March 2013

  The DBE Reporter spring quarterly reports there is no information available for this year of 2013

- **US 41 Corridor Expansion Project (Brown and Winnebago Counties)**

  Work Hours as of March 2013
  Total Hours Worked 2,040,676
  Total Minority Hours Worked 122,423
  Total Female Hours Worked 48,596

Summer

- **I-94 North-South Freeway Project (Milwaukee, Racine, and Kenosha Counties)**

  Work Hours as of June 30, 2013
  Total Hours Worked 2,731,301
  Total Minority Hours Worked 497,012
  Total Female Hours Worked 69,675

- **I-94 CTH Badger Interchange Project (Dane County)**

  Work Hours as of June 30, 2013
  **

- **US 41 Corridor Expansion Project (Brown and Winnebago Counties)**

  Work Hours as of June 30, 2013
  Total Hours Worked 2,119,029
  Total Minority Hours Worked 127,436
  Total Female Hours Worked 50,236

Winter

- **I-94 North-South Freeway Project (Milwaukee, Racine, and Kenosha Counties)**

  Work Hours as of September 30, 2013

Total Hours Worked 2,507,906
Total Minority Hours Worked 462,097
Total Female Hours Worked 62,583

- *I-94 CTH Badger Interchange Project (Dane County)*

  Work Hours as of September 30, 2013
  ****

- *US 41 Corridor Expansion Project (Brown and Winnebago Counties)*

  Work Hours as of September 30, 2013
  Total Hours Worked 1,949,333
  Total Minority Hours Worked 114,268
  Total Female Hours 47,515

Annual DBE Report as of September 30, 2013

- *I-94 North-South Freeway Project (Milwaukee, Racine, and Kenosha Counties)*

  Work Hours as of September 30, 2013
  Total Hours Worked 7,779,504
  Total Minority Hours Worked 1,425,056
  Total Female Hours Worked 195,096

- *I-94 CTH Badger Interchange Project (Dane County)*

  Work Hours as of September 30, 2013
  ****

- *US 41 Corridor Expansion Project (Brown and Winnebago Counties)*

  Work Hours as of September 30, 2013
  Total Hours Worked 6,109,038
  Total Minority Hours Worked 364,127
  Total Female Hours 146,347

- **All Projects across Wisconsin Annually**

  Work Hours as of September 30, 2013
  Total Hours Worked 13,888,542
  Total Minority Hours Worked 1,789,183
  Total Female Hours 341,443

All WisDOT projects across Wisconsin for 2013:
Total hours – 16,019,168.00

The DBE Reporter is used to represent the identification of the total number of hours worked, the total amount of hours available for "minorities," total female hours worked, and establishing an annual total along with the complete total of hours. This is then referenced when reviewing the regional reports established from the public records requests later. This helps to identify the variances between things like the total hours worked and the minorities or females worked. If these numbers are inaccurate, then we move forward to begin to look for variances. *(Please see Appendix B: Chapter 7.1 Chart 2013 Regional Report)*

In analyzing the information in the DBE Reporters and the ALR for 2013, one important cat is to notice that women are counted twice: once as a "female" and once as a "minority." This is an important fact to know as well because this can throw off the reports or inflate the numbers. Looking at these two charts, it is important to see the totals of workers and the hours are not matching up. There are almost double the numbers listed in the DBE reports versus the regional reports for Wisconsin. This now presents questions and prompts the need for another document to compare, and this led to the second public records request. This is the closest the TRIBES can identify this information as a baseline of qualitative information presented. This information, which was presented, is from all the regional reports from all construction projects across the state of Wisconsin. These regions are North Central, Northeast, Northwest, Southeast, and Southwest regions and encompassing all of Wisconsin. This information is provided quarterly and presented by the WisDOT Regional TL. It is important to mention this information was all information that was reported to contractors by the method of self-reporting. This means the TSTW is the one who reports they are Native American.

In 2013, in the regional report presented, there was a total of 1.68% TSTW on all projects across Wisconsin, and they attained about 1.87% of the hours available.

After reviewing the DBE Reporter and the ALR, we now must analyze the Annual WisDOT MAR to show the variances as presented. Scrutinizing the information, it is clear the regional report and the WisDOT MRA, when looking at the percent for the participation of TSTW, is .11% variance for Native American participation. When looking at the hours worked, these numbers are about 1.53% variance. Now, reviewing the ALR, the hard numbers for the participants of Native Americans are 748 males and 77 females. In the MRA, it states the Native American is 209 for males and 20 for women. The variance between them is for the males is rather close for the headcount and the hours worked. But when you look at the numbers identified 539 males and 57 females. We need to now look at the Native American hours for ALR, which is 77442.60 for males and 7260.20 for females. In the MAR it is 7742.20 for males, and for females it is 7259.80. These are rather close, but it is interesting because of the difference of 539 males and 57 females totaling over 69,700 hours is the difference, but this opens the door to begin asking these questions because this information provided is from two different points, but it was the same information requested and from the same WisDOT Labor Compliance representative and the same WisDOT CRCS program, but still reflected these variances.

2013 WisDOT Annual Minority Analysis Report

Caucasian		African		Hispanic		Asian		Native american		Total Participation	Native American Particiaption
Male	Female	Male	Female	Male	Female	Male	Female	Male	Female		
Head Count 2013											
Male	Female	Male	Female	Male	Female	Male	Female	Male	Female	Head Count	
10,985.00	358.00	403.00	19.00	723.00	6.00	40.00	4.00	209.00	20.00	12,767.00	1.79%
								1.64%	0.16%		
Hours Worked 2013											
Male	Female	Male	Female	Male	Female	Male	Female	Male	Female	Hours Worked	
3,921,300.60	119,265.70	99,546.00	5,968.40	258,007.40	3,429.80	16,392.50	2,146.30	7,742.20	7,259.80	4,441,058.70	0.34%
								0.17%	0.16%		

Chapter 8

2014

In early February 2014, the TLAC meeting began with the Adoption of the NAHP as the revisions were adopted by WisDOT and TRIBES. This was a one-day event scheduled only for revisions. Other items discussed were related to the action items set in previous meetings to address the following topics:

- *Overview of the TLAC implementation plan.*

- *Review of the Statewide Native American Labor Database.*

- *Review of the Native American Hiring Provision.*

- *WisDOT Funding Appropriation of $190,000 state funding appropriated for 2014.*

- *Inter-governmental Agreement.*

- *Interagency Exploratory meetings with the various departments:*
  - *Department of Administration.*
  - *Department of Workforce Development.*
  - *Bureau of Indian Affairs.*
  - *Local 139 Operating Engineers.*
  - *Wisconsin Transportation Builders Association.*

Through these many topics, there was a duly noted extensive amount of moving parts in this meeting. At times there were discussions about the potential funding sources available, development of the NAHP, Networking and Training opportunities, Union membership and training, the establishment of the database along with the potential risks associated with it, pre-training/apprenticeships available, and concluding with the overview of the pilot project for one of the TRIBES. This is also the same tribe as the WisDOT TA representative, where the pilot project has transpired.

There was a revision to the title of the pre-tribal construction meeting. The removal of the DT form but still requiring the reporting between tribes and contractors. A short time after this, the NAHP was approved, which looked like this:

Native American Hiring

Pre-Bid

Before bid submittal, contact the (insert specific tribe who will serve as the labor contact) to provide information on hiring procedures and future employment opportunities and gather information on the tribal workforce. Tribes labor office contact information: (insert specific contact information) Example: (tribal labor contact, name, and title)

- *(Address)*

- *Office:*

- *Cell:*

- *Email:*

Maintain documentation of all efforts made to communicate with (insert specific tribe who will serve as a contact). Pre-bid, present documentation in conjunction with the DT1633 form. The Eligible Bidders list will not be updated until after this documentation is received. Include the following information in the documentation:

- *Proposal number/route number/termini/county*

- *Person(s) contacted*

- *Method of communication (phone, email, written, in person)*

- *Information exchanged (hiring procedures, available positions, referrals received, employee performance, etc.)*

After Execution

At a minimum of 3 days before the tribal coordination meeting, contact the (insert specific tribe who will serve as a contact) to provide the following information regarding available employment opportunities for prime and subcontractors:

- Job classification/trade

- Job qualifications and required skills

- Employment period

- Wage

- Copy of job application

The (insert specific tribal labor contract) shall provide employment referrals within 2 business days. If no qualified referrals are received, use other recruitment sources to obtain qualified referrals. Document all efforts made to communicate job opportunities and the results of hiring activities throughout the life of the contract. At any time during the life of the contract, provide Lac du Flambeau communication documentation within 5 business days of request by the department.

Tribal Coordination Meeting

Between the execution of the contract and the project preconstruction conference, conduct a meeting with the Tribal officials and leaders at (insert tribe). Prime contractor and all subcontractors shall be present. Discuss available employment opportunities and other tribal areas of interest, such as scope of work, Tribal regulations, borrow sites, waste sites, and available aggregate.

Project Completion

As a part of the document submittals required under standard spec 109.7, submit documentation summarizing communications regarding job opportunities throughout the life of the contract. Provide a final report to the tribe and Statewide Tribal Affairs compiling the results of hiring activities for the prime contractor as well as for subcontractors at all tiers.

USER GUIDANCE

Applicability:

Reference a map and reference tool to determine when this provision will be included in projects. Currently, this provision would apply to projects located on or partially on lands held under the ownership and jurisdiction of the tribes.

Suggested wording for advertising:

This contract requires pre-bid contact with the Tribe whose lands the project resides on, and additional documentation will be submitted with the DT1633 form. See special provisions and contact (insert project manager and contract information) for information on this requirement.

Suggested policy considerations:

Any time this provision is included within a contract, the regional tribal liaison should be included. A pre-advertising meeting between the regional project manager, regional tribal liaison, statewide tribal liaison, and the tribal labor contact should be arranged. WisDOT shall provide a timeline, basic scope of work, and all relevant online links to project plans, bidding, and advertising procedures and assist with outreach expectations and recommendations for tribal coordination meeting agenda and identify any other tribal project coordination needs or requirements. This is also an opportunity to discuss the DBE goals set and outreach processes required as part of ASP 3.

Suggested addition for Notes to Construction:

For the Native American Hiring provision – request documentation of communication with the tribal labor office from the contractor at least twice during the project. Once within a couple of weeks of the preconstruction meeting and again when the project is substantially complete. This documentation does not have to be in any set format. See special provisions for the type of information to expect as documentation. This is to gather information on the process. Forward documentation to the WisDOT regional tribal liaison and Statewide Tribal Affairs.

__Suggested information for PM (Project Manager) for pre-bid inquiries:__
This is a standard special provision. This is where we would likely reference where to find the supportive language regarding the provision. Purpose, background, etc. For further information on the future of statewide hiring provisions, contact WisDOT TA
__Phone: 608-XXX-XXXX__

__*Documentation:*__
There is no standard format for this documentation. Include all pertinent information as outlined in the specials. Documentation needs to be submitted pre-bid with DT1633. Additional communication with the tribal employment labor office should be documented throughout the project. The department will request documentation after the execution of the project, and the contractor will have 5 business days to submit documentation to date.

__*Statewide Native American Labor Database:*__
Currently, this resource is not available. Statewide Tribal Affairs is working with DWD to enlist a tribal component into the Job Centers program. This will be included in the provision but is not available at this time.

The NAHP was finally adopted by WisDOT and the TRIBES in February 2014, and soon after the approval of the provision, the TLAC meeting was also scheduled in February. No meeting minutes showed WisDOT or TRIBES representatives who were present. The discussion at this meeting consisted of the Statewide Native American Labor Database (SNALDB), the NAHP, and Trans Update. WisDOT TA was to meet with various agencies (all at the table): WDOA, DWD, BIA, Local#139 EO#39, WTBA, WisDOT, TRIBES, FHWA, CRCS, etc. The next topic mentioned reflected the amendments of the NAHP. This varied from important things like the removal of the DT2405 Native American Tracking form, thereby removing reporting requirements for CI Contractors to submit this information to the WisDOT TA. A few other changes were the change of the process Preconstruction meeting name and amended to the Pre-Tribal Coordination Meeting. Another important item to note is the NAHP would only be applied to projects adjacent to tribal lands, but there was no mention of projects located within the boundaries of the reservations.

A few months later, in May 2014, the Memorandum of Understanding (MOU) was signed by one of the TRIBES. This is the same Tribe that also obtained a pilot project for the NAHP, the same TRIBE that also had released the RFP for the Inter-Governmental Agreement (IGA) released it in 2013, as this TRIBE is the same TRIBE's person who is WisDOT TA representative. The TRIBE was awarded the allotted amount of $190,000 in funding for the term of one year, beginning in May 2014 and ending in April 2015, and the two-year funding, beginning in May 2015 and ending in April 2016, has also been awarded the pilot projects and the set a MOU with the State of Wisconsin, all while they have the WisDOT TA Representative also from that tribe. This presents a series of questions if there is a perception of a conflict of interests. This is because of the concerns over the violations of the Federal Procurement processes because, if there is even one dollar associated with Federal funds, then this is a violation of this process. The TRIBE who received the IGA and a Tribal member who is also employed as the WisDOT TA representative has awarded this agreement, allocating the funder to their TRIBE not to exceed $380,000. This document was signed and approved in mid-May 2014.

Soon after this, upon looking into the Standardized Special Provisions (STSP) 107-200, it was noticed in June 2014 when the Native American Hiring Provision had been finally implemented for projects. The STSP is archived in a WisDOT public website.[43] Before this, there was no documentation of the NAHP since June 2011, and in June 2016 the NAHP had already

---

43. Standardized Special Provisions (STSP) for engineering design https://wisconsin dot.gov/Pages/doing-bus/eng-consultants/cnslt-rsrces/tools/stsp.aspx

been deleted once again.

A few months later, in October, through searching online in public records, a document was located with the title: Transportation Administrative Manual Directive Div. 102. The subject states Title VI/ Nondiscrimination Complaint Intake Procedure. The purpose of this document is:

> *"As a recipient of federal funds through US DOT, WisDOT has been delegated the responsibility for investigating external complaints of discrimination by the Federal Highway Administration, Federal Aviation Administration, Federal Motor Carrier Safety Administration, Federal Railroad Administration, Federal Transit Administration, and the National Highway Traffic Safety Administration."*

This is based on the scope, which also states:

> *"WisDOT receives federal funding for many of its programs, and so Title VI applies to all WisDOT services. Any person who believes that, in the course of business with a WisDOT program or service, he or she or any specific class of persons or business entity has been subject to discrimination or retaliation prohibited by any of the federal or state Civil Rights statutes or common law principles, based upon race, color, national origin, sex, age or disability may file a complaint. The complaint may be filed by the affected individuals or a representative and should be reduced to writing when possible."*

The Procedures consisted of:

> *Complaints shall be in writing and signed by the person(s) or representative and include the complainant's name, address, and telephone number. Complainants should use the Title VI Complaint Form where possible. Allegations of discrimination received by fax or e-mail will be acknowledged and processed.*
>
> *A complaint must be filed no later than 180 days after the following:*
>
> - *The date of the alleged act of discrimination; or*

- *The date when the person(s) became aware of the alleged discrimination; or*

- *Where there has been a continuing violation, the latest instance of prohibited conduct.*

Acceptance of a complaint will be determined by 1) whether the complaint is timely filed; 2) whether the allegations involve a covered basis such as race, color, national origin, sex, age, disability, or retaliation; and 3) whether the allegations involve a program or activity of a Federal-aid recipient, sub-recipient, or contractor.

If the initial complaint does not meet the threshold for discrimination, the complaint can be refused by the Title VI Program Officer. If the complaint is refused by the Title VI Program Officer, the complainant has the option to go to FHWA or FTA for appeal.

This document is important because remembering what has been mentioned earlier, the statement: "*Native Americans are not a minority, they are of a political classification, that of dual citizenship which entails: one a TRIBES member and second as a United States Citizen.*" When looking at the definition of a DBE and the application of the DBE processes. It is stated: "WisDOT shall not discriminate based on race, color, national origin, or sex in the award and performance of any USDOT assisted contract or the administration of its DBE program or the requirements 49CFR part 26. Wisconsin DOT is committed to the DBE Program Objectives for all contracts that contain U.S.-DOT-Assistance or federal funding. This is important to reiterate that if a tribe is not able to be based on race, color, national origin, or sex. It is important to note that Indians are members of certain political groups towards which the federal government has assumed responsibilities (Cohen's Handbook of Federal Indian Law Ch.1, p. 5). The term Indian Preference has been the subject of the U.S. Supreme Court cases concerning discrimination and due process. One of the most notarized cases is Morton v. Mancari,[44] which has upheld the hiring provision of Indian Preference and enforced by the United States Department of Interior, Bureau of Indian Affairs as the U.S. Supreme Court characterized the term Indian as a political and not racial classification. The Court's all-encompassing title of the US Code (Title 25-Indians) inconceivably would have been excluded by Congress if Indians were defined as a racial classification, and it was also refuted by the state of California and its interpretation of whether Indian is a political classification rather than being racial or national origin classifications and went on further to conclude: *"the federal courts of appeal have concluded that employment preferences are a viable part of federal Indian policy. The Ninth Circuit has upheld both the Indian Self-Determination and Education Assistance Act (25 US C. § 458(e)(b)) employment and contracting preferences in Alaska. In Preston v. Heckler (734 F.2d 1359 (9th Cir. 1984)), the court noted that "Congress [clearly] considers Indian [hiring] preferences to be an important element of federal Indian Policy."*[45]

In more recent case law, in Yashenko v. Harrah's NC Casino Co.,[46] the Fourth Circuit of the United States Court of Appeals alleged that the Indian Preference policy enforced by the subcontractor for the Cherokee Tribe of North Carolina violated his rights pursuant to 42 U.S.C.A §1981, prohibiting discrimination on the basis of race while employed. Later, the courts found the exemptions for Indian Preference contained 42 U.S.C.A. §2000e(b) and §2000e-2(I). Indian Preference has been implemented throughout history and has been a part of the United States Federal Codes. This can be shown as far back as 1834 when the enactment of Congress "25USC§45 instilling the requirement of" for the benefit of Indians, a preference shall be given to those of Indian Descent,

---

44. 417 U.S. 535 (1974).

45. 28 Seattle U. L. Rev. 403,416 (2005).

46. 446 F.3d 541 (2006).

who are properly qualified for the completion of the duties.[47] The Indian Reorganization Act, Sec. 12, in 1934, required the Secretary of the Interior to utilize and implement Indian preference in hiring administrations of services to Indians. In 1950, the Navajo-Hopi Rehabilitation Act, which was enacted by Congress, provided Navajo and Hopi "preference in employment on all projects undertaken pursuant to this subchapter, and, given employment on such projects without regard to the provisions of the civil-service and classification laws."[48] The Civil Rights Act was enacted by Congress in 1964, exempting preferential employment of Indians and by tribes or industries located on or near Indian Lands.[49] In 1972, the Indians were given preference in Government programs for the training and education of teachers for Indian Children, which was a requirement by Congress.[50] This was also the same time the Morton v. Mancari case ruling presented that IP governs in the US Bureau of Indian Affairs as they are permissible under the EEO Act of 1972. This was done because the preferences are not based racially, as they are "reasonably designed to emphasize the right of Indian self-government.[51] The Indian Preference Self-Determination Act from 1975 supports IP to provide tribal employment laws or TEROs approved by TRIBES that will govern the administration of Self-Determination in contrast with the TRIBES.

This is because of the application of IP in hiring for Federal Highway Projects as a notice was provided by the FHWA N4720.7 consolidating guidance for field offices from FHWA and State highway agencies and contractors as it related to the application of the IP for employment on projects located on

---

47. 25 USC§ 46 (1882), § 44 (1894), and § 47 (1908).

48. 25 USC§ 633.

49. 42 USC§§ 2000e(b) and 2000e-2(I).

50. 20 USC§§ 887c(a) and (d), and § 1119a.

51. 417 U.S. 535, 554 (1974).

and near Indian lands, but also providing technical assistance to help assist with the application of IP for state contracting.

The EEOC Chair in June 2002 reaffirmed the partnership with more than 60 TRIBES TERO offices securing IP agreements from employers operating on projects located on or near reservations. This is relevant because the Ninth Circuit case Malabed v. North Slope Borough, 7 (9th Cir. 2003),[52] was brought forward because Alaskan tribes and villages lacked sovereign authority over their lands, making this case irrelevant based on their constitutions. The reason all this information is brought forward is that another state DOT had been asked if they were violating state law[53] by allowing TERO in its contracting for projects "near" Indian lands.

This proposition prohibits the state from granting: "preferential treatment to any individual or group based on race, sex, color, ethnicity, or national origin in the operation of public employment, public education, or public contracting."[54] For the violation of the proposition, the Department shall assist the enforcement of TERO in contracting and must show TERO in contracting constitutes preferential treatment of a TRIBE or TRIBES based on race, ethnicity, or national origin. Preferential treatment alone does not constitute a violation of this state's constitution as this must be on the bases enumerated, but the legal opinion asserts TERO's are based on racial or national origin bases lacking evidence to support their assertion. It is important to first iterate that TERO is designed to decrease unemployment among Indians which in turn reduces alcoholism, drug abuse, poverty, and economic dependency. The TRIBES TERO should be reviewed by the state to determine if they have a legitimate governmental interest to enforce the hiring preference that benefits TRIBES. The US Constitution's commerce clause and treaty power

---

52. Malabed v. North Slope Borough, 335 F.3d 864,

53. California State Law Propositions 209.

54. Art. 1, sec. 31(a), California Constitution.

clause are foundational to the trust relationship between the federal government and the tribes. Morton v. Mancari held the challenge to an Indian preference hiring law does not require scrutiny because Indians constitute a political class, not a racial classification. The state's DOT Legal Division's Legal opinion is in error stating tribal preference in hiring is deemed unconstitutional. These assertions of TERO generally state they are based on racial or national origin classifications. While these presumptions TRIBES lack regulatory authority over non-Indians on non-Indian owned fee land within Indian lands (which included proven state rights of way), there are 2 very well-known and exercised exceptions to the rule as stated in the Montana Test:

> *The US Supreme Court recognizes two exceptions to the main rule:*
>
> *Tribes retain inherent sovereign power to exercise some forms of civil jurisdiction over non-Indians on their reservations, even on non-Indian fee lands. [First, a] tribe may regulate, through taxation, licensing, or other means, the activities of nonmembers who enter consensual relationships with the tribe or its members, through commercial dealing, contracts, leases, or other arrangements. [Second, a] tribe may also retain inherent power to exercise civil authority over the conduct of non-Indians on fee lands within its reservation when that conduct threatens or has some direct effect on the political integrity, the economic security, or the health or welfare of the tribe. 450 US at 565-66.[55]*

It is also important to take notice of the WisDOT/Transportation Administrative Manual, Directive DIV 102 Title VI/Nondiscrimination Complaint Intake Procedure[56] from the WisDOT OBOEC.

---

55. This holding was crucial to the decision in FMC v. Shoshone Bannock Tribes, 905 F. 2d 1311 (9th'" Cir. 1990) (denied cert., 499 U.S. 943 (1991)) which held FMC (a non-Indian company doing business on non-Indian owned fee lands) was subject to the tribal TERO and was liable for damages for violation of the Shoshone Bannock Tribes TERO.

56. Title VI Nondiscrimination Plan & assuranceshttps://wisconsindot.gov/Pages/global-footer/formdocs/default.aspx

The purpose of this is as a recipient of federal funds through the US DOT, WisDOT has been delegated the responsibility for investigating external complaints of discrimination, by the FHWA, Federal Aviation Administration (FAA), Federal Motor Carrier Safety Administration (FMCSA), Federal Railroad Administration (FRA), Federal Transit Administration (FTA), and the National Highway Traffic Safety Administration (NHTSA). This is because WisDOT receives federal funding for many of its programs, and so Title VI applies to all WisDOT services. Any person who believes that, in the course of business with a WisDOT program or service, he or she or any specific class of persons or business entity has been subject to discrimination or retaliation prohibited by any of the federal or state Civil Rights statutes or common law principles, based upon race, color, national origin, sex, age or disability may file a complaint.

The reason this is brought forward is because of how this is worded and has been used in the past to say there can be no discrimination if there is a TRIBE is not defined as "*based upon race, color, national origin,*" in the past was a means to dismiss these cases. It is important to identify that:

Under federal constitutional law, classifications based on a person's membership in an Indian tribe are generally not seen as being based on race or national origin. Because an Indian tribe is not just an ethnic group but a political one, the Court has viewed "preference[s]" for "members of federally recognized tribes" as "political rather than racial in nature." [Citing Mancari, 417 US at 553 n. 24.] This makes sense. The government sorts us by political allegiance in various ways: it sometimes distinguishes US citizens from aliens, and Californians from out-of-state citizens. An Indian tribe is likewise a different sovereign. Tribal Indians, unlike other Californians, belong to a political group that's specifically recognized by federal law and the US Constitution, not merely to an ethnic group that has no independent legal standing. [57]

---

57. No07-304 March 08, 2010, State of California v. Edmund G Brown; Pages 12-15.

It was then stated:

"The California Department of Transportation Legal Division is in error in its assertion that TEROs, generally, are based on racial or national origin classes. This finding can only be done on a case-by-case basis. Since some tribes may have reason to legislate only for their own members, it is possible that they possess tribal preference in hiring provisions or they may be using 'Indian' and 'tribal' interchangeably. If the provision contains a severability clause, the remainder of the TERO remains in effect. If not, the TERO could be rejected. It would be to the benefit of the Department and the tribes to work together on a case-by-case basis to tailor the TEROs to more general Indian preference language."

The next time the TLAC Group convened was in October 2014 and the following representatives were present from WisDOT: 1 representative from TA, TAA, OBOEC, TL, SWTL, TLAC Coord. FHWA, ITTF, 2 from DWD, 3 WTBA, Serendipity Communications, and 6 tribal members for 5 TRIBES. The meeting consisted of discussion relating to the WisDOT entering into the IGA with a TRIBE to implement the TLAC 8-recommendations consisting of the following topics: The Database Work Team, Standard Processes for recruitment and referrals, Monitoring and Reporting, Cultural Awareness and Understanding, Project Forecasting Report, Coordination of Native American Laborers focus groups, NAHP, and TRANS Programs.

The database work team was based on establishing a work team to establish the content and recruitment of their members. It was also mentioned that contractors are not allowed to request information specific to tribal members because of the political status of the TRIBES. They are also not able to obtain demographic specifics based on regional or locational information.

The next topic was the standard process for recruitment referrals, this was stated the TLAC Coordinator would be distributing a survey to gather information from contractors requesting their recruitment and referral practices, including the AICCW, WTBA, and CI contractors who work on WisDOT projects. This will develop a directory of CI contractors, and TERO employment offices across the state of Wisconsin. Next was the monitoring and reporting and the process needed to establish the mechanisms needed to adequately report this information, when to report this information, and establish annual baseline assessments while integrating the implementation of this database as well.

Cultural awareness and understanding are the next topics established to help develop curriculum and training for contractors. The inquiries by the contractors were because of this conditional language, which identified that they may have to work with TRIBES and tribal businesses. This was concluded with the project forecasting part where the WisDOT established a list of upcoming projects to which the NAHP would be applied. This meeting led to the NAHP update as it was stated by the WisDOT TA and TAA the NAHP has been fully implemented on WisDOT and Bureau of Aeronautic (BOA) projects. They then went into the review of upcoming projects for 2015 and 2016, which will have the NAHP applied to them. WISDOT TA and TAA stated they will coordinate training for the WisDOT staff as it relates to the NAHP. And there was a formal request for the definition of "near" as it relates to the NAHP.

The TRANS Program also noted that TLAC has an amount of $40,000 to allocate for additional TRANS Training and would like TLAC to recommend additional training based on upcoming projects.

For the DBE Reporters for 2014 there were 3 DBE Reporters in Spring, Summer, and Winter. This had been transpiring while these projects were currently active and ongoing, without a NAHP on the projects located "on" or "partially on" tribal or reservation lands. The reports from these projects reflect the suspension of the NAHP for about eleven months now.

This meeting reflected many recommendations relevant to the NAHP and warranted requests by WisDOT, CI, and other entities involved with the concerns or issues related to their need to amend the NAHP since August 2014. These concerns and issues all directly impacted TRIBES communities. This can be shown through the 2014 DBE Reporters, 2014 regional reports, and the MAR.

2014 DBE Reporter

Spring

- *I-94 North-South Freeway Project (Milwaukee, Racine, and Kenosha Counties)*

  Work Hours as of March 2014
  Total Hours Worked 2,886,806
  Total Minority Hours Worked 525,825
  Total Female Hours Worked 75,126

- *I-94 CTH Badger Interchange Project (Dane County)*

  Work Hours as of March 2014
  Total Hours Worked 62,326
  Total Minority Hours Worked 3,642
  Total Female Hours Worked 2,199

- *US 41 Corridor Expansion Project (Brown and Winnebago Counties)*

  Work Hours as of March 2014
  Total Hours Worked 2,590,349
  Total Minority Hours Worked 164,255
  Total Female Hours Worked 60,472

- *I-39/90 Expansion Project*

  Work Hours as of March 2014
  Total Hours Worked 65,712
  Total Minority Hours Worked 3,784
  Total Female Hours Worked 1,136

- *Zoo Interchange*

> **Work Hours as of March 2014**
> Total Hours Worked 566,309
> Total Minority Hours Worked 11,386
> Total Female Hours Worked 16,242

Summer

- *I-94 North-South Freeway Project (Milwaukee, Racine, and Kenosha Counties)*

> **Work Hours as of June2014**
> Total Hours Worked 145,817
> Total Minority Hours Worked 8,007
> Total Female Hours Worked 4,122

- **I-94 CTH Badger Interchange Project (Dane County)**

> **Work Hours as of June 2014**
> **The DBE Reporter spring quarterly reports there is no information available for this year of 2012**

- *US 41 Corridor Expansion Project (Brown and Winnebago Counties)*

> **Work Hours as of June 2014**
> Total Hours Worked 2,894,730
> Total Minority Hours Worked 180,831
> Total Female Hours Worked 66,140

- *I-39/90 Expansion Project*

> **Work Hours as of June 2014**
> Total Hours Worked 109,464
> Total Minority Hours Worked 6,909
> Total Female Hours Worked 2,360

- *Zoo Interchange*

> **Work Hours as of June2014**
> Total Hours Worked 858,676
> Total Minority Hours Worked 159,306
> Total Female Hours Worked 28,126

Winter

- *I-94 North-South Freeway Project (Milwaukee, Racine, and Kenosha Counties)*

  Work Hours as of September 2014
  Total Hours Worked 135,223
  Total Minority Hours Worked 8,767
  Total Female Hours Worked 4,206

- *I-94 CTH Badger Interchange Project (Dane County)*

  Work Hours as of September 2014
  **

- *US 41 Corridor Expansion Project (Brown and Winnebago Counties)*

  Work Hours as of September 2014
  Total Hours Worked 3,140,499
  Total Minority Hours Worked 195,655
  Total Female Hours Worked 73,099

- *I-39/90 Expansion Project*

  Work Hours as of September 2014
  Total Hours Worked 117,037
  Total Minority Hours Worked 6,326
  Total Female Hours Worked 3,027

- *Zoo Interchange*

  Work Hours as of September 2014
  Total Hours Worked 1,022,588
  Total Minority Hours Worked 190,184
  Total Female Hours Worked 33,313

Annual DBE Report as of September 30, 2014

- *I-94 North-South Freeway Project (Milwaukee, Racine, and Kenosha Counties)*

  Work Hours as of September 30, 2014
  Total Hours Worked 3,167,846

Total Minority Hours Worked 542,599
Total Female Hours Worked 83,454

- **I-94 CTH Badger Interchange Project (Dane County)**

  Work Hours as of September 30, 2014
  Total Hours Worked 62,326
  Total Minority Hours Worked 3,642
  Total Female Hours Worked 2,199

- **US 41 Corridor Expansion Project (Brown and Winnebago Counties)**

  Work Hours as of September 30, 2014
  Total Hours Worked 8,625,578
  Total Minority Hours Worked 540,741
  Total Female Hours 199,711

- **I-39/90 Expansion Project**

  Work Hours as of September 2014
  Total Hours Worked 292,213
  Total Minority Hours Worked 17,019
  Total Female Hours Worked 6,523

- **Zoo Interchange**

  Work Hours as of September 2014
  Total Hours Worked 2,447,573
  Total Minority Hours Worked 360,876
  Total Female Hours Worked 77,680.80

- **All Projects across Wisconsin Annually**

  Work Hours as of September 30, 2014
  Total Hours Worked 14,595,536
  Total Minority Hours Worked 1,464,877
  Total Female Hours 369,567.80

All WisDOT projects across Wisconsin for 2014:
Total hours – 16,019,168.80

The DBE Reporter is used to represent the identification of the total number of hours worked, the total amount of hours available for "minorities," total female hours worked, and establishing an annual total along with the complete total of hours. This is then referenced when reviewing the regional reports established from the public records requests later. This helps to identify the variances between things like the total hours worked and the minorities or females worked. If these numbers are inaccurate, then we move forward to begin to look for variances. *(Please see Appendix B: Chapter 8.1 Chart 2014 Regional Report)*

In analyzing the information of the DBE Reporters and the ALR for 2014, one important cat is to notice that women are counted twice, once as a "female" and once as a "minority." This is an important fact to know as well because this can throw off the reports or inflate the number. Looking at these two charts it is important to see the totals of workers and the hours are not matching up, there are almost double the numbers listed in the DBE reports versus the regional reports for Wisconsin. This now presents questions and prompts the need for another document to compare and this led to the second public records request. This is the closest the TRIBES can identify this information as a baseline of qualitative information presented. This information which was presented is from all the regional reports from all construction projects across the state of Wisconsin. These regions are North Central, Northeast, Northwest, Southeast, and Southwest regions and encompass all of Wisconsin. This information is provided quarterly and presented by the WisDOT Regional TL. It is important to mention this information was all information that was reported to contractors by the method of self-reporting, this means the TSTW is the one who reports they are Native American. In 2014 in the regional report presented there was a total of 1.40% TSTW on all projects across Wisconsin and they attained about 1.47% of the hours available.

2014 WisDOT Annual Minority Analysis Report

Caucasian		African		Hispanic		Asian		Native american		Total Participation		Particiaption
Head Count 2014												
Male	Female	Male	Female	Male	Female	Male	Female	Male	Female	Head Count		
11,422.00	378.00	518.00	31.00	760.00	15.00	38.00	4.00	185.00	19.00	13,370.00		1.53%
								1.38%	0.14%			
Hours Worked 2014												
Male	Female	Male	Female	Male	Female	Male	Female	Male	Female	Hours Worked		
4,610,025.00	132,248.60	171,806.20	9,317.40	330,169.00	6,769.60	14,966.80	2,951.30	72,976.00	8,359.80	5,359,589.70		1.52%

After reviewing the DBE Reporter, and the ALR, we now must analyze the Annual WisDOT MAR to show the variances as presented. Scrutinizing the information, it is clear the regional report and the WisDOT MRA, when taking a look at the percentage for participation of TSTW is .13% variance for Native American participation. When looking at the hours worked these numbers are .05% variance. Now reviewing the ALR the hard numbers for the participants of Native Americans as 711 males and 59 females. In the MRA, it states that Native Americans are 185 for males and 19 for women. The variance between them for the males is rather close for the headcount and the hours worked, but when you look at the numbers identified, there is a difference of 526 males and 40 females. We need to now look at the Native American hours for ALR, which is 73,058.70 for males and 8,360.10 for females. In the MAR, it is 72,976 for males and for females it is 8,359.80. These are rather close, but it is interesting because the difference of 526 males and 40 females totaling over 81 hours is the difference. This opens the door to asking these questions because this information provided is from two different points, but it was the same information requested from the same WisDOT Labor Compliance representative and the same WisDOT CRCS program but still reflected these variances. In addressing these variances, it is important to notice the fact that these percentages are rather close regardless of the amount of 770 male and female TSTW and their hours are missing because there is only a difference on only 81 hours. This was the conclusion of the minority reports because after this time there were no minority reports. This is because the questions that have begun to be asked based on just this information have been overall the inconsistencies in these charts provided. This information has all been provided by the WisDOT from the same department and from the same person over 4 years. Below are the results provided which contain the Annual Regional reports from 2009-2014.

Chapter 9

Summary 2009-2014

Annual Regional Reports

(Please see Appendix B: Chapter 9.1 Chart 2009-2014 Regional Report)

The information provided from the 2009-2014 Annual Regional Reports. This is done to show the numbers reflect the amount of participation of the TSTWs and also how many hours were attained over the five years totaling the average percentages of male and female workers and the same of hours they have worked as well on the projects across Wisconsin. This also shows in 2009 where the baseline was at 1.37% for males and .06% for Females TSTW averaging out to about 1.43% of TSTW on all projects across Wisconsin. This information was presented from the self-reporting of the TSTW. If you analyze this information, you can notice that the participation of the TSTW begins to rise until 2012 and then continues to decline. It is important to mention from 2011 to 2013 the NAHP was suspended as well, but this also reflected the highest percentages of TSTW on the projects. Over these five years, you will be able to see that the TSTW had attained about 1.62% of opportunities on these projects and this equates to about 1.67% of the hours available as well. This is consecutive for all projects across Wisconsin beginning in 2009 and continuing up until 2014 and provided by the Labor Compliance CRCS self-reporting information. Next, we have a copy of the WisDOT Minority Report from 2009 to 2014 as well. What this means is that in a review of a tentative 32-week construction season, each of the TSTWs attains only 109.05 hours annually which averages out to about only 2.73 weeks annually.

Minority Annual Reports
(Please see Appendix B: Chapter 9.2 Chart WisDOT **MAR** *2009-2014)*

In the review of the WisDOT Minority Annual Reports from 2009 to 2014, it is important to note this information is a little bit different. An interesting fact is this information was requested the same way both times, but the information given is different as it shows for the participation of TSTW on all projects across Wisconsin that they attained about 1.52% of the opportunities on these projects and attained about 1.34% of the hours on these projects as well. This equates to a total of 1,104 TSTW with about 325,547.30 TSTW hours self-reported on all projects from 2009-2014 in Wisconsin. In looking at it, there is a tentative 32-week construction season, give or take 4-5 weeks, which equals out to about 294.88 hours per person equaling 9.21 hours per week of work for both male and female TSTW.

Looking at the total amount of TSTW on the projects from the two documents in the 2009-2014 Regional Reports for Wisconsin shows that during this time, there was 3,969 TSTW vs. the WisDOT Annual Report which reflects 1,104 TSTW and this shows there is a variance of 2,865 TSTW. In the TSTW hours worked there were 432,833.50 hours available for the Regional Reports for Wisconsin and the WisDOT Annual Report reflects 325,547.30 leaving a variance of 107,286.2 hours. Now analyzing this information, it is clear to see the variances are significant, showing:

- *2,865 TSTW variance hours.*

- *107,286.2 variance hours available.*

Then after this, if we also look at the DBE Reporter information. There was a total of 43,656,820.70 available hours on projects across Wisconsin. It is easy to see the total hours worked on the project are double the amount as the WisDOT annual reports and the amount from the Regional Reports 51,814,510.10.

Total hours available on all projects across Wisconsin on WisDOT Projects:

- *The WisDOT DBE 2009-2014 Reporter project hours:* **43,656,820.70**

- *The WisDOT 2009-2014 Annual Regional Reports:* **51,814,510.10**

- *And the WisDOT 2009-2014 Minority Report Analysis:* **24,209,193**

All three of these numbers are different and the variances go to show that when this information is requested numerous times, the information is not as accurate as the variance shows. This is concerning because when you report this information you should be sure to account for any variances. This information has been reported to the TRIBES 2009-2014, but the lack of accurate information when it has been requested numerous times makes it difficult to present accurate information or even for the agencies to present this information to any of these entities.

Chapter 10

2015

It was not until January 2015 when the majority of the NAHP Minority reports of TSTW requests had begun as there was no information available when originally requested. This began the NAHP database management, as stated in the 8-recommendations. This was number two of the 8-recommendations. This meeting was mainly establishing the functions and information needed to develop this database. It was also for the training needed as well to learn the database. There was a discussion of the Tribal Labor Peer Exchange, TRANS Training, the integration of CRCS (WisDOT Labor and Wage Compliance System, Microsoft Platforms/As400, and Bird Dog Department of Laborer-Bear Tracking software). This would hold information like Company and Tribal Labor Reports, the classification of positions like laborers, operators, truck drivers, certifications, projects, locations, employment (long-term or short-term), and the functionality of the primary functions of the DWD Database.

The TLAC meeting took place at the end of January with the following WisDOT representatives present: 1 representative from FHWA, TA, TAA, OBOEC, Project Development Section (PDS), National Environmental Policy Act (NEPA) Southeast Region, DBE/Serendipity, 2 from DWD, and WTBA, 4 from TL, and 8 from tribal members of 7 TRIBES. In this meeting was the discussion of the TRANS Program in which there are reimbursements of $5.00 an hour with a threshold of 2,000 hours, following the TRANS Graduate from WisDOT projects will be on a case-by-case stance. The discussion went on to further discuss the upcoming projects and the needed training for projects coming soon. The Statewide Native American database needed to have access to information and review the regional business and labor reports. The DWD business requirements called for the need for collaboration. The 41-corridor Mega Project had a small portion of the NAHP applied to the HWY-29 project, while in the past 41-corridor Mega Projects were not chosen by the state for the applicability of the NAHP on projects. There was a presentation of the database from the DWD to identify 3 specific areas for possible recommendations for a more advanced TRIBES program to be considered.

The DWD presentation brought forward the need for a definitive time established for the design of the DWD database to meet the needs of the TLAC Group. This was done to establish this proposal and estimate the costs and a timeline for how long it would take to develop the database. This Database was warranted with the capabilities of must-have real-time updateable job skills, with job seekers and employers connecting bridges. The DWD identified the establishment of the database needs for three main topics:

Topic 1: Tribal Identification – Who provides that information?

1. Would be based upon self-identification. The system will currently allow job seekers to identify as a tribal member, but not by tribal affiliation. Additional questions for consideration: Who would verify this information? Should this be verified by the tribal employment office?

2. Need to articulate why tribal identification information is important for individuals signing up.

Topic 2: Skills matching –

The system uses a 5-star rating system, with 5 stars indicating the best match. DWD needs to verify: Does the current system of matching meet the needs of matching job seekers and employers?

Topic 3: Reporting/Frequency of Reporting –

The intent would be for tribal administrators to query that information directly. Monthly and quarterly would be of benefit to the tribes.

The Youth Build presentation mainly focuses on carpentry and pellet furnace installations, distribution, and propane. This primary focus was on ages 16-24 for students at risk. This is paid training as this program matches $10.00 an hour for 6-9 months and can provide tools and equipment from the construction industry. The presenter is also associated with the WisDOT TA Representative because they are both from the same TRIBE.

The next meeting was scheduled in April and the following representatives from WisDOT were present: 1 representative from TA, TAA, OBOEC, DTSD SWTL, Labor Development Specialist (LDS), Serendipity, FHWA, 2 from DWD, Forward Services (FS), and CI/WTBA, and 4 from tribal members from 4 TRIBES. The DWD Native American Labor Database was the main topic. Also mentioned in this meeting was an inquiry as to whether WisDOT maintains copies of all TRIBES TERO/IP Ordinances, as this request was maybe to obtain copies of all known TERO/IP to be released for the next TLAC meeting.

The Database update was given by the DWD explaining the functionalities of the database will roll out soon for phase two. The following questions were asked:

- *When an individual identifies as a Native American, can they also identify as a specific tribal member?*

- *What level of access would the Tribes like to have, if given "administrative," or staff-level, access to the information exchange system?*

- *Would TLAC be interested in providing meta-data to trigger that the utilization of this system by contractors is for DOT projects?*

This concluded with the DWD being charged with establishing a timeline for the specific functionalities and estimates to be presented at the July 2015 meeting. The next section discussed the year one overview as it has been completed. The discussion of the second year for the IGA's remaining deliverables was presented. There were recommendations for the baseline assessment to be established and for the TLAC Coordinator to work with the TRIBES employment offices to establish the useful information to be used for the Baseline Assessment creating a series of questions relevant to workforce and unemployment rates.

The Cultural Awareness Training consisted of the development of training for tribal employment offices and the CI Contractors. There was a recommendation for the TLAC website to include WisDOT Projects Forecasted out a minimum of six years. Doing this would help establish a premise for the scope of training needed based on the upcoming work on projects. The WisDOT TAA stated the NAHP has been applied to the BOA projects from 2014, which consisted of 5 project totals. The final Action item was for the next meeting to provide an overview of the services offered by the Michigan Tribal Technical Assistance Program (MTTAP) including the training provided.

The next meeting was scheduled for August 2015 and in this meeting, the following representatives were present from WisDOT: 1 representative from OBOEC, TA, TAA, Northeast (NETL), SWTL, North Central TL (NCTL), DOA, TLAC Coord, FHWA, DBE, Serendipity, and TLAC Consultant, 2 from Northwest Tribal Liaison (NWTL), 3 from WTBA, and LDF Education, and 7 from tribal members from 5 TRIBES and DWD. This meeting began with the collection of the TRIBES TERO/IP, while the WTBA's representative noted that some contractors are not following the NAHP. The Recruitment and Referral Survey was completed and was to be sent to the WTBA, and DBE offices along with contractors. This Baseline Assessment was established to capture Native American Labor in the state of Wisconsin. The WisDOT TA noted the limited data currently and this will begin to provide a point of reference to annual assessments on smaller scopes. These Assessments are no longer available to the public.

The Statewide Native American Database provided by the DWD will have a series of phased rollouts ending the third enhancement in the Spring of 2016. This meeting concluded with the TRIBES DWD representative to revisit the language in the NAHP to be revised to include "on or near" tribal lands. The WTBA representative also noted that the name of the NAHP should be changed, noting it is difficult for WTBA CI.

The next meeting took place in October 2015 with the following representatives from WisDOT: 1 representative from OBOEC, TA, TAA, NCTL, DBE, Local #139, TLAC Consultant, TLAC Coord., 2 from DWD and TBA, 14 tribal members from 8 TRIBES. The meeting discussion began with the previous comment from the WTBA Representative to be removed. This continued to the discussion of the contract with the MTTAP for training opportunities. The development of the DWD Database for the identification of Native Americans and the Memorandum of Understating (MOU) was also completed. A final review of the Recruitment and Referral survey was completed. It was suggested a computer be available at the WTTC and Business networking sessions for individuals to complete the survey. The following questions were contained in the survey:

TLAC Recruitment and Referral Survey:

The purpose of this survey is to gather data that will assist the Tribal Labor Advisory Committee (TLAC) in creating awareness and increasing the understanding of construction industry hiring practices and standards.

Information we are seeking includes – your application process, your recruitment periods, your recruitment methods, qualifications/ skills needed for your jobs, your lead time for hiring, the availability of entry-level positions each year, and how the amount of those entry-level positions is determined.

Your input is vital, and I thank you in advance for your participation!

1. *Do you have an application process? If yes, please explain your process.*

2. *Do you have a specific recruitment period? If yes, please explain how your recruitment period is determined.*

3. *Do you utilize any special or typical recruitment methods (posting on the Job Center, advertising in local newspapers, etc.)? If so, what methods do you use?*

4. *Do you seek any specific skills or qualifications needed for your open positions? If so, please explain the process used to determine what positions need what qualifications and skills.*

5. *Do you have a certain or pre-determined lead time for hiring – from the application process until someone is hired? If so, please explain your process from start to finish.*

6. *Do you typically have a certain number of entry-level positions available each season?*

7. *When do you typically call back your layoffs?*

8. *When do you start building off your original teams/crews?*

9. *Does your business accept referrals for possible employment?*

The Consultant Firm Bowman Performance Consulting (BPC) was selected to establish the Baseline Assessment, but it was not made clear who sent out the RFP or released for bid on the services needed. The next topic then went into the Statewide Native American Labor Database as it was stated in the presentations from DWD that the total costs for the DWD Database would be $45,900. The discussion was established to address possible additional funding and the development of a work team to complete the details and enhancements. The discussion then continued into the note of the self-identification process, and how they should not classify Native Americans as minorities because of their Political Classifications and dual citizenship: United States Citizens and TRIBES Members. This passed with unanimous consent from the TRIBES.

In December 2015 there was a need to understand the WTBA, thereby identifying the establishment and the history of this group. It was decided in December 2015 for research to begin to investigate the WTBA, because evidence has been brought forward, through the series of meeting minutes from the Focus group meetings, directly presenting the influence of the WTBA for the suspension of the NAHP. The WTBA and other agencies were also responsible for the removal of the application of the TERO and IP Laws within the boundaries of the TRIBES. After this was done a list of the board of directors for the WTBA was compiled and as it was shown, many of these board of directors for the WTBA are also comprised of executives established in WTBA and the owners of CI Companies. These WTBA Board of Executives/Owners of Construction Industry companies are also the same contractors who have been bidding for and awarded projects located within Wisconsin. Soon after this information was discovered this predicated the formal request for this information which was presented to the WisDOT TA representative requesting the following information:

This was the first time the requested information was released, and the responses from the WisDOT Representative were included and are italicized after each question:

> *"I would like to request any documentation relevant to all the questions below."*

- *Please include the explanation of why the NAHP was rescinded in 2011 as I have heard multiple stories.*

- *Were the Tribes saying this NAHP was rescinded due to invalid contact information for Tribal Labor Representatives/or Tribal Contact in general when contractors were trying to contact them and let them know there was work available on a project? No. However, during the revisions process concerns were raised regarding the capacity of tribes to respond. In the original version of the provision, no tracking mechanism was included to indicate the results of tribal contact except for the DT2405 form which was revised in 2010 to include a list of tribes. Contractors*

- *would check a box to indicate which tribes they had contacted; however it did not indicate whether that contact was successful. Before 2010 the form did not list the tribal contacts.*

- *Was it the WisDOT perspective that because of concerns from the industry were voiced that the NAHP was rescinded or needed a complete overhaul on inclusivity? Yes, the industry was represented at TRANS-AC, the first Focus Group meetings, and TLAC. See the NAHP Issues for 9-8-11 document provided above under the September 8, 2011, meeting materials section. This is a comprehensive list of the WTBA's concerns.*

- *Did the WTBA influence the rescinding of the NAHP? Yes, please see the response above.*

- *The original NAHP was rescinded in 2011. I would like to know if there are any specific examples/meaning specific tribes contacted, and what was the actual contact information used to do outreach to these specific tribes relating to these specific examples. From June 2009-July 2011 there were approximately 11 projects that submitted DT2405 forms. This was a new special provision and was never fully implemented. When the WisDOT TAA and WisDOT A started working for DOT in August 2010 one of our primary objectives was to fully implement the new provision.*

- *Which Tribes were contacted for the projects? The previous version of the hiring provision did not include a tribal contact tracking mechanism so there is no data available.*

- *Which Tribes did not have the correct contact information? In the fall of 2010, WisDOT TAA and WisDOT TA updated the tribal labor contact sheet based on direct contact with tribes. To the knowledge of the WisDOT TA, the contact sheet utilized in 2010 was correct. We did however update a few contacts based on our tribal outreach efforts in the fall of 2010. The original contact list was created in March 2009.*

- *Which Tribes did not respond after being contacted? We contacted TRIBES to update the contact sheet. All responded. If this question refers to which TRIBES did not respond to contractors during the 2009-2011 years, there is no data available because the previous version did not have a tribal contact tracking mechanism.*

- *Can you please include any documents that contain the explanation as to why the State had grounds to suspend the NAHP? Please see the meeting notes for TRANS-AC and the first Focus Group meetings for discussion and grounds for suspension. The official notice to TRIBES was issued on November 18, 2011. The WisDOT TAA and WisDOT TA reported at a 2011 GLITC meeting in addition, the suspension was announced during the annual Secretary's Consultation Meeting on September 19, 2011 – minutes also provided above.*

- *Please include a copy of the document from the State Secretary, stating the reason as to why this provision was suspended. Please see the materials above. No official notice was sent from the Secretary until the request to redraft the hiring provision was sent in August 2012. The TRIBE'S invitation/notice is also shown above. WisDOT OBOEC sent a notice, see above.*

- *If there are any documents regarding the industry that had an influence on this decision, and if it was based on WTBA, please include them. Yes, included above.*

- *If any documents pertain to who in the industry voiced their concerns to Madison about the NAHP were they not in favor of it because of the uncertainties involving the language of the NAHP?*

Yes. The WTBA Executive Director raised concerns at the TRANS-AC meeting, minutes are included above.

This concluded 2015 with this final request. It was not until the end of December that this information was received. During this time, it was important to find other representatives from WisDOT who also worked in the industry to ask these questions as well. There was a time when an allocated amount of time was set aside to meet with a WisDOT Representative and discuss the history of the NAHP and at this time all perspectives of the NAHP were discussed. This is to identify the different influences established and the impact on the NAHP from these groups. The reason for all of this is because there were several concerns with the application of the NAHP by the CI contractors on each project. The main issues were the lack of participation of the NAHP, lack of TSTW on the projects, CI contractors stating they are not hiring, the multiple classifications of nontribal skilled trades workers on the projects, lack of communication, and the collection of proper report data from the projects, along with cultural barriers on the projects.

For the DBE Reporters for 2015, there were 3 DBE Reporters Spring, Summer, Fall and Winter. This had been transpiring while these projects were currently active and ongoing, with an NAHP on a project located "on" or "partially on" tribal or reservation lands. These reports from these projects reflected many recommendations relevant to the NAHP and warranted requests by WisDOT, CI, and other entities involved with the concerns or issues related to their need to amend the NAHP since August 2015. This can be shown through the 2015 DBE Reporters, Regional Reports, and the MAR Reports.

2015 DBE Reporter

Spring

- *I-94 North-South Freeway Project (Milwaukee, Racine, and Kenosha Counties)*

Work Hours as of March 2015
The DBE Reporter spring quarterly reports there is no information available for this year of 2012

- *I-94 CTH Badger Interchange Project (Dane County)*

  Work Hours as of March 2015
  ****

- *US 41 Corridor Expansion Project (Brown and Winnebago Counties)*

  Work Hours as of March 2015
  ****

- *I-39/90 Expansion Project*

  Work Hours as of March 2015
  ****

- *Zoo Interchange*

  Work Hours as of March 2015
  ****

Summer

- *I-94 North-South Freeway Project (Milwaukee, Racine, and Kenosha Counties)*

  Work Hours as of June 2015
  ****

- *I-94 CTH Badger Interchange Project (Dane County)*

  Work Hours as of June 2015
  ****

- *US 41 Corridor Expansion Project (Brown and Winnebago Counties) NE Region*

  Work Hours as of June 2015
  Total Hours Worked 3,345,619
  Total Minority Hours Worked 208,230
  Total Female Hours Worked 76,048

- **WIS 441 (NE Region) as of June 2015**

  Total Hours Worked 151,214
  Total Minority Hours Worked 8,553
  Total Female Hours Worked 2,338

- **VERON Rd (SW Region) as of June 2015**

  Total Hours Worked 213,641
  Total Minority Hours Worked 13,707
  Total Female Hours Worked 7,001

- **I-39/90 Expansion Project**

  Work Hours as of as of June 2015
  Total Hours Worked 144,365
  Total Minority Hours Worked 9,654
  Total Female Hours Worked 4,389

- **Zoo Interchange**

  Work Hours as of as of June 2015
  Total Hours Worked 1,563,179
  Total Minority Hours Worked 273,455
  Total Female Hours Worked 52,695

Fall

- **I-94 North-South Freeway Project (Milwaukee, Racine, and Kenosha Counties)**

  Work Hours as of September 2015
  **

- **I-94 CTH Badger Interchange Project (Dane County)**

  Work Hours as of September 2015
  **

- **US 41 Corridor Expansion Project (Brown and Winnebago Counties) NE Region**

  Work Hours as of September 2015
  Total Hours Worked 3,534,801

Total Minority Hours Worked 222,437
Total Female Hours Worked 83,575

- **WIS 441 (NE Region)**

    Work Hours as of September 2015
    Total Hours Worked 231,911
    Total Minority Hours Worked 13,545
    Total Female Hours Worked 4,650

- **VERON Rd. (SW Region)**

    Work Hours as of September 2015
    Total Hours Worked 249,790
    Total Minority Hours Worked 16,393
    Total Female Hours Worked 8,658

- **I-39/90 Expansion Project**

    Work Hours as of September 2015
    Total Hours Worked 226,758
    Total Minority Hours Worked 14,869
    Total Female Hours Worked 6,915

- **Zoo Interchange**

    Work Hours as of March 2015
    Total Hours Worked 1,751,631.50
    Total Minority Hours Worked 305,620
    Total Female Hours Worked 59,151.60

Annual DBE Report as of September 30, 2015
Winter

- **I-94 North-South Freeway Project (Milwaukee, Racine, and Kenosha Counties)**

    Work Hours as of September 2015
    Total Hours Worked 3,238,343
    Total Minority Hours Worked 587,070
    Total Female Hours Worked 86,421

- **I-94 CTH Badger Interchange Project (Dane County)**

  Work Hours as of September 2015
  **

- **US 41 Corridor Expansion Project (Brown and Winnebago Counties) NE Region**

  Work Hours as of September 2015
  Total Hours Worked 3,189,134
  Total Minority Hours Worked 198,651
  Total Female Hours Worked 72,867

- **WIS 441 (NE Region)**

  Work Hours as of September 2015
  **

- **VERON Rd (SW Region)**

  Work Hours as of September 2015
  Total Hours Worked 138,716
  Total Minority Hours Worked 8,885
  Total Female Hours Worked 4,297

- **I-39/90 Expansion Project**

  Work Hours as of September 2015
  Total Hours Worked 117,592
  Total Minority Hours Worked 6,344
  Total Female Hours Worked 3,029

- **Zoo Interchange**

  Work Hours as of September 2015
  Total Hours Worked 1,185,891
  Total Minority Hours Worked 218,797
  Total Female Hours Worked 40,188

- **All Projects across Wisconsin Annually**

  Work Hours as of September 30, 2015
  Total Hours Worked 19,143,870
  Total Minority Hours Worked 2,061,325
  Total Female Hours Worked 507,925.60

All WisDOT projects across Wisconsin for 2015:
Total hours – 21,712,120.70

The DBE Reporter is used to represent the identification of the total number of hours worked, the total amount of hours available for "minorities," total female hours worked, and establishing an annual total along with the complete total of hours. This is then referenced when reviewing the regional reports established from the public records requests later on. This helps to identify the variances between things like the total hours worked and the minorities or females worked. If these numbers are accurate, then we move forward to begin to look for variances between the various reports. (*Please see Appendix B: Chapter 10.1 Chart WisDOT 2015 Regional Report*)

In analyzing the information in the DBE Reporters and the ALR for 2015, one important cat is to notice that women are counted twice: once as a "female" and once as a "minority." This is an important fact to know because this can throw off the reports or inflate the number. Looking at these two charts it is important to see the totals of workers and the hours are not matching up, there are almost double the numbers listed in the DBE reports versus the regional reports for Wisconsin. This now presents questions and prompts the need for another document to compare, and this led to the second public records request. This is the closest the TRIBES can identify this information as a baseline of qualitative information presented. This information which was presented is from all the regional reports from all construction projects across the state of Wisconsin. These regions are North Central, Northeast, Northwest, Southeast, and Southwest regions and encompass all of Wisconsin. This information is provided quarterly and presented by the WisDOT Regional TL. It is important to mention this information was all information reported to contractors by the method of self-reporting, this means the TSTW is the one who reports they are Native American. In 2015, in the regional report presented there was a total of 1.23% TSTW on all projects across Wisconsin and they attained about 1.40% of the hours available.

In 2014 the regional reports through 2015 shows a direct decline in the participation of TSTW as the number of workers on the projects went from 711 males or 1.29% and 59 females or .11% totaling 770 TSTW at 1.40% to all projects across Wisconsin. The hours consisted of 73,058.70 males or about 1.32%, and 8360.10 females or about 1.15%, totaling 81,418.80 hours worked or 1.47%. In 2015, TSTWs 660 or 1.14% males participated, and 54 or .09% females, totaling 714 TSTW at 1.23%. The total hours shown for TSTW participation in 2015 is 62,256.70 hours or 1.27% for males, and 6,086.90 hours for females or .12%, totaling 68,343.60 hours or 1.40% worked for the year across the state of Wisconsin.

This shows that from 2014 through 2015 there has been a decline. We first begin with the TSTW males, which shows a direct decline of 50 TSTW or .03% decline in participation and the hours for males. In the TSTW females show a decline of 4 TSTW or .02% and for males show a decline of 10,802 hours or .05% of TSTW participation of males, totaling and reflecting the total decline of over 13,074.20 hours or .07% for males and females on all projects across Wisconsin for TSTW.

If we look at these totals and compare them to the totals of the DBE Reporters, there is a discrepancy in the total hours available versus the Annual Regional Labor Reports. The DBE reporter shows the total amount of hours of all WisDOT projects for 2015 Total hours 21,712,120.10 and the Annual Regional Labor Reports show 4,897,733.10 leaving the amount of **16,814,387** hours unaccounted for all workers on Wisconsin Transportation projects for 2015.

Chapter 11

2016

In January 2016, the TLAC group scheduled a meeting with the following WisDOT representatives present: 1 representative from OBOEC, TA, TAA, Northwest Tribal Liaison (NWTL), Western Unit Labor Compliance Lead, Investigations Lead, DBE, FHWA, TLAC Coord., 2 from DWD, 3 from WTBA, and TLAC Consultants, and 11 tribal members from 6 TRIBES. This meeting began with the discussions of the Michigan TTAP programs of training available: DL Prep, Grade Staking, Heaving Equipment Operation and Safety, Heavy Forklift Operation and Safety, OSHA 10 Hour+, Survey Skills, Welding Techniques, Work Zone Safety and Work Zone Traffic Control "Flagger" Training. The discussion continued to talk about the updates as they related to the Statewide SNALDB where it was agreed for the database to be released on February 12, 2016, because the database has been developed for over two years. It has been said that the SNALDB would be completed because the DWD would not specify a definitive date of when the database would be completed. It was stated the WisDOT TA can retrieve data in several ways, and it was stated that WisDOT is working to have a consistent way to report this information, but one of the limitations of the CRCS is it can only track self-identification. The other issue was that the women were counted twice, once as a minority and once as a woman. They then followed up that the training would be available for this database from February 16 through 17. The WisDOT TA reports and updates the information compiled in a by-region full minority report. Then the discussion transitioned to the Statewide Native American Labor Database, as there was an inquiry about when the fully operational database would be released. The DWD stated it would tentatively be 2016, and the process for the MOU template for the TRIBES would then begin the discussion processes.

The next topic was the discussion of the Baseline Assessment and any related updates. The TLAC Consultant notes that Phase 1 has been distributed as 5 TRIBES have responded to the survey. The discussion of what was entailed in the phases was presented.

Phase one noted three main questions of the literature process which were:

- *Who (what agencies or organizations) is collecting the Native American labor workforce database regarding labor, highway construction, and transportation?*

- *What type of data is being collected and through what methods?*

- *What are the most frequently used data sets that are being collected for the Native American workforce regarding highway construction and transportation?*

Phase two focused on more the tribal level, "building Tribal capacity snapshots through an online survey to understand what types of data Tribes collect as well as the strengths, needs, and gaps that Tribes in Wisconsin face regarding strong participation in Wisconsin's highway construction and transportation industries." This was set to begin in January 2016, but before this survey was released it was recommended for this survey to be uniform for all TRIBES.

As we transitioned into the next topic, which is the WisDOT TA Reports and Updates, it was mentioned that the WisDOT TA was trying to establish a by-region full minority report. It was noted the multiple ways to obtain this information showing the variances of the information the WisDOT has already submitted. WisDOT's statement is they are working to have a consistent way to report Native American participation state-wide. The WisDOT Labor representative will then provide an overview of the data and an explanation for the variances between the headcount and the hours worked by TSTW. It was then brought forward about the multiple projects located "on," and "partially on" reservations as the NAHPs application can be enabled with the contractors simply stating they are not hiring or no follow-up. There were concerns about the pretrial coordination meetings being rushed and some other meetings being held, what was stressed at this meeting is the need for cultural training to be provided to Contractors' employees because there are concerns this training is not being disseminated to their employees when the owners or foremen are the only ones attending the training.

The next meeting scheduled was in March 2016 and wasn't a document showing who was in attendance for the meeting. The discussions began with the Michigan TTAP Training as it was stated these classes were free, but when the TTAP representative was contacted, it was stated the classes were $300 per person and $3000 for the classes. The size of the classroom was not clearly stated and is only limited to 10 attendees (if there are experienced operators, the class can be up to 12 to 13 attendees) with a minimum of 7 participants. The Michigan TTAP program does not provide certifications, and the only thing provided from the TTAP is provided for the completion of time certifications. It was also noted that all of the information provided about available training does not have any descriptions, and many of the trainings provided in the list were not available in this region. It was not known which of these trainings could be put together; training has not been utilized so there is no information available on any of them.

The DWD Native American Database has brought forward some issues:

- *Access to information —*

  - *All Tribes would have access to the TRIBES information. It was stated we needed to make sure that there was a limit to how much information was being released to any tribe. This would take a Legal Review along with a MOU for the TRIBES.*

- *The names of TRIBES needed to be amended.*

- *Tracking Descendants from Each Tribe:*

  - *There is no tracking mechanism in the database to track if someone is a descendant. The TRIBES made sure this was to be added to the enrollment dropdown.*

  - *Creation of one document for TRIBES to use for identifying Tribal and non-tribal employees when working on WisDOT and BOA projects on reservations or partially on tribal lands.*

  - *Look at the DT2405-1 form from the NAHP and revamp this document to use moving forward.*

There was another TLAC meeting in April with the following WisDOT representatives present: 1 representative OBOEC, TA, Labor Compliance (LC), Western Unit Labor Compliance Lead, Tribal Liaison NE, FHWA, TLAC Coordinator, Consultant, and TLAC 3 from NADBE and WTBA, 4 from DWD, 11 tribal members from 7 TRIBES. The meeting began with the TTAP classes and if any information had been received. It was stated the Michigan TTAP TRIBES have been redirected to the TTAP website, but this information was outdated, classes were not certified, and the cost was a concern when it was stated the classes would be free. The discussion also went towards the DWD SNALDB as it was having updates and these updates consisted of the confidentiality and data access by other entities was the primary concern. With the concerns brought forward, this DWD representative stated additional work would take 40 to 160 extra hours. DWD was to provide an estimate for the costs of the updates of the Database at the next meeting. Many of these classes on the list were not being offered.

The prices referenced were an issue because the cost is approximately $3000 per class. As previously noted in the TLAC meetings, the Training provided was stated to be free. One of the TRIBES' representatives said she believed that if there are over 20 participants, then the classes are free. It was also noted by another one of the TRIBES the certifications should detail what components have been completed so contractors know what has been trained. The TRIBES noted the importance of OSHA 30 as it is in high demand.

The meeting proceeded on to the TLAC Coordinator who had recently transitioned out of their position and a new TLAC Coordinator was appointed. This person who had been hired is also the same Tribe as the WisDOT TA. The WisDOT then transitioned into the DWD Statewide Native American Labor Database where it was noted the data collection has been implemented and the access for the TRIBES is still being worked on. There was an emphasis of the TRIBES regarding the confidentially and data access from other tribes and other entities as this is a primary concern. It was also noted in the database its original intent or purpose is to include the ability of TRIBES to track Tribal members and to increase the exposure of Native American workers to contractors. The DWD noted the additional security provided could take 40 to 160 additional hours.

The next bullet was to discuss the Baseline Assessment updates. In this was the WisDOT TA who stated the final report has not been received as comments are currently pending, and changes need to be made before it can be distributed. The consultant extinguished resources before completing the scope of the project. Nine of the 11 Tribes responded to the survey. A quantitative report is needed to determine gaps and needs.

In July 2016 the following WisDOT representatives were present: 1 representative from TA, TL, NWTL, NETL, NCTL, SWTL, Labor Compliance (LC), Western Unit Labor Compliance Lead, FHWA, DWD, TLAC Coordinator, and TLAC Consultant,

2 from WTBA, 9 tribal members from 8 TRIBES. This meeting began with a discussion about the TTAP OSHA 30 Training, which would cost more than $5,485 through the Northeast Technical College. With the DWD Statewide Native American database, there was an issue with the release of confidential tribal information. The TRIBES stated they would not release this information. This is the reason for the database team to focus on the accessibility and the MOU aspects of the database.

The Baseline Assessment had noted the completion of the original contract, as the report has been reviewed, and would've been released after edits from the TLAC consultant. The brochures for the recruitment and referrals warranted revisions, and it was suggested, when they are sent to the Construction contractors, to wait for the off-season of construction to obtain the best responses, or this will result in a low participation turnout.

As the WisDOT proceeded on to give the Statewide Tribal Liaison updates, it was stated there was a new interim TL position. The discussion then went on to the NAHP and the active projects throughout the state and two scheduled Pre-tribal Coordination meetings between the TRIBES and the construction industry. The discussion then transitioned to the NAHP language which states, "partially on or adjacent to" reservations of Indian lands. It was stated that the application of the NAHP needs endorsement from the TRIBES, Executive Office, and the WTBA. This is to be brought forward in the Great Lakes Inter-tribal Council (GLITC). Further discussion included the desire to maintain relationships with the surrounding counties and contractors as they have been noting the goal is to get people hired, there was a statement that stated that it is equally frustrating when contractors go through the Pre-tribal Coordination meeting and then there is none hired because the contractors just simply state they are not hiring.

This then preempted the discussion about how to bring contractors and workers together. It also identified how the contractors are made aware of the NAHP and how the contractors are made aware of the proximity of the reservations. This all led to the discussion about how the construction industry would be able to utilize the DWD Native American database to obtain the ready willing and able to work. The next topic transpired before the Partnership Agreement (PA) which was last signed in 2010/2011. The reason this was brought forward is because the PA is a living breathing document, and it warrants updating. It was recommended for the PA to be forwarded to one ITTF as the revisions for this document can lead up to or over a year to complete as it is not in the ITTF's Scope of work to analyze this. It was recommended by the WisDOT TA representative to bring this up at the Secretaries Consultation meeting in August 2016.

In October 2016 a meeting was scheduled with the following representatives from WisDOT present: 1 representative from TA, TAA TLAC Coord., OBOEC, LC, DWD, Local #139, and FHWA, 3 from WTBA, and 6 from tribal members of 4 TRIBES. This is only through the name lettering, which was present from the last meeting, there were no meeting minutes for the attendance. The discussion began with the training options available again, then proceeded to note the preference for classroom training over webinars as this was conferred with the WTBA who was also in agreement with the classroom training being ideal but cost prohibitive. Before the discussion of the MOU for the DWD Database, the TLAC Group convened on progress on the State Tribal Labor reports, Baseline Assessments, Training material, Funding available, Recruitment and referral Surveys, Cultural Awareness Training, and Annual Assessments. The work team then continued focusing on the accessibility estimates as well.

The update for the Baseline Assessment noted there have been no edits now as the contract is complete and a new RFP will be released. The updated Recruitment and Referral surveys will be shared by the WTBA with their contractors, but it was estimated there would be a low turnout due to being prime time construction season. The rest of the information from the meeting was the same as the previous meeting minutes from July 2016.

November was the last meeting for 2016 and had the following representatives present: 1 representative from TA, DWD, NCTL, NETL, SETL, SWTL, NWTL, BOTS, AICCW, BIA, FHWA, 2 WTBA, and 17 tribal members from 9 TRIBES. The meeting began with a brief introduction and history of the TLAC Group as there has been a large changeup in the TLAC Committee. It was discussed that there were no current updates for the DWD Database. The TLAC Coordinator mentioned the best practices tool kit was being established. There was a brief history of the document "The Partnership Agreement (PA)" which established the Inter-tribal Task Force. The discussion then expressed the need for the update of the current PA emphasizing the expansion of the subcommittee to introduce this to their tribal representatives. It was recommended to reach out to each of the TRIBE's leadership to get their input on the revisions.

For the DBE Reporters for 2016, there was 2 DBE Reporters, Spring Summer, and Winter. This had been transpiring while these projects were currently active and ongoing, with an NAHP on project located "on" or "partially on" tribal or reservation lands. These reports from these projects reflected many recommendations relevant to the NAHP and warranted requests by WisDOT, CI, and other entities involved with the concerns or issues related to their need to amend the NAHP since August 2015. This can be shown through the 2016 DBE Reporters, Regional Reports, and the MAR Reports.

2016 DBE Reporter

Spring

- *I-94 North-South Freeway Project (Milwaukee, Racine, and Kenosha Counties)*

  Work Hours as of March 2016

  The DBE Reporter spring quarterly reports there is no information available for this year of 2012

- *I-94 CTH Badger Interchange Project (Dane County)*

  Work Hours as of March 2016

  ****

- *US 41 Corridor Expansion Project (Brown and Winnebago Counties)*

  Work Hours as of March 2016

  ****

- *I-39/90 Expansion Project*

  Work Hours as of March 2016

  ****

- *Zoo Interchange*

  Work Hours as of March 2016

  ****

Summer

- *I-94 North-South Freeway Project (Milwaukee, Racine, and Kenosha Counties)*

  Work Hours as of June 2016

  ****

- *I-94 CTH Badger Interchange Project (Dane County)*

  Work Hours as of June 2016

  ****

- *US 41 Corridor Expansion Project (Brown and Winnebago Counties) NE Region*

  Work Hours as of June 2016

  ****

- *WIS 441 (NE Region)*

  Work Hours as of June 2016

  ****

- *VERON Rd (SW Region)*

  Work Hours as of June 2016

  ****

- *I-39/90 Expansion Project*

  Work Hours as of June 2016

  ****

- *Zoo Interchange*

  Work Hours as of June 2016

  ****

Fall

- *I-94 North-South Freeway Project (Milwaukee, Racine, and Kenosha Counties)*

  Work Hours as of September 2016

  ****

- *I-94 CTH Badger Interchange Project (Dane County)*

  Work Hours as of September 2016

  ****

- *US 41 Corridor Expansion Project (Brown and Winnebago Counties) NE Region*

  Work Hours as of September 2016

  ****

- *WIS 441 (NE Region)*

    Work Hours as of September 2016
    **

- *VERON Rd (SW Region)*

    Work Hours as of September 2016
    **

- *I-39/90 Expansion Project*

    Work Hours as of September 2016
    **

- *Zoo Interchange*

    Work Hours as of September 2016
    **

Winter
Annual DBE Report as of September 30, 2016

- *I-94 North-South Freeway Project (Milwaukee, Racine, and Kenosha Counties)*

    Work Hours as of September 30, 2016
    **

- *I-94 CTH Badger Interchange Project (Dane County)*

    Work Hours as of September 30, 2016
    **

- *US 41 Corridor Expansion Project (Brown and Winnebago Counties) NE Region*

    Work Hours as of September 30, 2016
    **

- *WIS 441 (NE Region) September 30, 2016*

    **

- *VERON Rd (SW Region) September 30, 2016*

    **

- *I-39/90 Expansion Project September 30, 2016*

  **

- *Zoo Interchange*

  Work Hours as of September 30, 2016

  **

- *All Projects across Wisconsin Annually*

  Work Hours as of September 30, 2016

  **

All WisDOT projects across Wisconsin for 2016:
Total hours – No information available to establish the total
amount of hours for 2016.

The DBE Reporter is used to represent the identification of the total number of hours worked, the total amounts of hours available for "minorities," total female hours worked, and establishing an annual total along with the complete total of hours. This is then referenced when reviewing the regional reports established from the public records requests later. This helps to identify the variances between things like the total hours worked and the minorities or females worked. If these numbers are inaccurate, then we move forward to begin to look for variances between the various reports. *(Please see Appendix B: Chapter 11.1 Chart WisDOT 2016 Regional Report)*

In analyzing these DBE Reporters, and after reviewing the reports, it is clear that this information was not provided in the quarterly DBE Reporters. This makes it difficult to take those numbers and compare the numbers against the ALR for 2016. As mentioned previously, one must notice that women are counted twice, once as a "female" and once as a "minority." This is an important fact to know as well because this can throw off the reports or inflate the numbers. Looking at these two charts it is important to see these totals of workers and the hours are not matching up there are almost double the numbers listed in the DBE reports versus the regional reports for Wisconsin. This now presents even more questions as to why this information was not included in the DBE Reporter for the whole year of 2016 and prompts the need for more documents to compare and led to the public records request for information. This is the closest TRIBES can identify the information as a baseline of qualitative information which is annually presented at the Wisconsin Tribal Transportation Conferences. This information reflects the regional reports from all construction projects across the state of Wisconsin and is provided quarterly and presented by the WisDOT Regional TL at TLAC meetings. The information reported to contractors is all by the method of self-reporting, as this means the TSTW is the one who reports they are Native American to the contractors they are working for. In 2016 in the regional report presented there was a total of 1.17% TSTW on all projects across Wisconsin and they attained about 1.24% of the hours available.

The previous year in 2015 the regional reports thought up to 2016 show a direct decline in the participation of TSTW as the number of workers on the projects went from 660 males or 1.23% and 54 females or .09% totaling 714 TSTW at 1.23% to all projects across Wisconsin. The hours consisted of 62,256.70 males or about 1.40% and 6086.90 females or about .12% totaling 68,343.60 hours worked or 1.40%. In 2016, TSTW's 531 or 1.08% male participation and 46 or .09% females totaling 577 TSTW at 1.17%. The total hours shown for TSTW participation in 2015 is 47071.00 hours or 1.13% for males and 4612.60 hours for females or .11% totaling 51683.6 hours or 1.24% worked for the year across the state of Wisconsin.

This shows that from 2015 through 2016 there has been a decline. We first begin with the TSTW males, which shows a direct decline of 129 TSTW or .15% decline in participation and the hours for males. In the TSTW females show a decline of 8 TSTW or .00% and males show a decline of 15,185.70 hours or .27% of TSTW participation of males, totaling and reflecting the total decline of over 16,660 hours or .16% for males and females on all projects across Wisconsin for TSTW.

If we look at these totals and can compare them to the totals of the DBE Reporters, this will present clear discrepancies between the total hours available versus the Annual Regional Labor Reports. The DBE reporter would show the total amounts of hours of all WisDOT projects for 2016 if the information was present, but since the information was not included in the DBE Reporter, we will put for Total hours 0.00 and the Annual Regional Labor Reports show 4,165,183.80 hours, as we are not able to conclude any unaccounted-for hours for workers on Wisconsin Transportation projects for 2016 without the DBE Reporters.

Chapter 12

2017

In January 2017 the following WisDOT representatives were present: 1 representative from OBOEC, TA, NWTL, NCTL, SETL, SWTL, Western Unit Labor Compliance Lead, DBE, FHWA, AICCW, TLAC Coord., from TLAC Consultants, 3 from WTBA, and TRANS, 4 from DWD, and 9 tribal members from 6 TRIBES. This meeting began with discussions about the MTTAP. OSHA training was brought forward once again, but this time it was to obtain estimates of how many want training and suggestions for locations. It then went into a presentation by the DWD. It was noted that a WTBA representative had inquired who the end user was for this project. It was also inquired if the WTBA Representative would have access to the potential employees as she utilizes the database for positions and research for possible job candidates. It was explained by the DWD representative these identification numbers are only available to a handful of security people within the DWD and iterated that this program or database cannot sort by ethnicity as this was excluded to avoid any litigations related to discrimination. The WTBA representative iterated this system isn't providing contractors with the ability to seek tribal members. This is a concern for the CI because contractors will not reach out to TRIBES for this information. The WisDOT TA spoke to the original intent of this database; to share data in hopes of supplying referrals to Tribal members for available positions for projects located within tribal communities. One of the TRIBES stated that all entities involved need to take a hard view at all of this because the original goal was to share and fulfill workforce needs between TRIBES. The MOU will be sent to the TRIBES to be signed by the Tribal Leadership. There was also discussion of the TRIBES' Sovereignty as it related to the MOU for the DWD database because it allows the gathering of information from people of dual citizenship, a political classification rather than a TRIBE member and United States citizen.

The TLAC discussions regarding the DWD Database were concerning because the database has become diluted, and the contractors are not able to utilize the database fully for data employer tagging of Tribal individuals. It was stated by the construction industry and TRIBES: "Why create a database when it can't be utilized because of the foundational function the database was created to do." It was brought forward by the TRIBES present at this meeting. There were 6 TRIBES, and they all agreed to create Tribal Database from within the TRIBES, thereby removing the DWD and WisDOT's authority on the database.

The night before the TLAC meeting, at approximately 4:56 pm on January 24, 2017, an email was submitted to the TLAC group TRIBES stating to the WisDOT TA: "One of the TRIBES will be taking the lead on delivering the annual report and the tool kit TLAC products and has indicated there may not be a need for a formal RFP. Will there be representatives from the TRIBES available should you have questions on their procurement process?" The WisDOT TA stated: "We have not executed a contact at this point, so we are still early in the process, but I wanted to be sure you had a few tools to keep the discussion moving forward tomorrow. The reason this email was sent the day before the TLAC meeting is because the TLAC Coordinator notified one of the TRIBES stating the WisDOT TA had called them inquiring why the meeting was taking place, then one of the TRIBES' leadership referenced their working relationships with the WisDOT TA, as they are there:

"Really good friends" and sent the closed door agenda to the WisDOT TA because they wouldn't let anything happen to the WisDOT TA given their relationships. The TLAC member was informed via a phone call the night before the scheduled TLAC meeting that the comprehensive data intended for the Closed-door session involving the TRIBES agenda had been shared with the WisDOT TA by a prominent TRIBES Leader. This act addressed numerous concerns raised during the meeting, but unfortunately undermined the meeting's intended impact and bypassed the established channels through which the TRIBES were meant to address these matters. This resulted in the upending of the closed-door meeting as the WisDOT TA or any other WisDOT representatives were not allowed in these meetings. The closed-door meetings were established because many times the tribes don't have enough time to meet in large groups before these meetings. The closed-door sessions were for the TRIBES to voice each other's concerns and proceed forward as a whole unified group addressing the issues of all the TRIBES in the TLAC meetings. The topics in the email presented by the WisDOT TA made it clear that she had obtained a copy of the TRIBES closed-door Agendas. This agenda was only sent to the tribal leadership.

The agenda consisted of the following topics:

- *The WisDOT representative stated, "Since I believe the tribes may be discussing the annual assessment and took kit projects, I am including the planning documents prepared for both projects."*

- *There was a tribal request to spend some time tomorrow drafting some language to be included in the RFP for the Annual Assessment during the tribal closed session of the TLAC meeting.*

- *While we are no longer developing an RFP according to Lac du Flambeau procurement procedures, we are still planning to finalize the scope of the report, timeline, and expectations. It is also imperative that the tribes indicate what they would like to see included in An Annual Native American Labor Assessment.*

- *There has been some discussion about revisiting the baseline assessment due to the quality, content, and incompleteness of the report.*

When the discussion went to the IGA, this became very tense because the IGA was being moved elsewhere without any consultation with any of the TRIBES. This information was being delegated to the Tribes from the WisDOT TA as the IGA was to switch hands, removing the TLAC Coordinator as well. What is interesting is when going into this meeting one of the TLAC members mentioned accountability because so many topics were not being completed which led to the TLAC members singling out another TLAC Member for not documenting or taking any notes. The TLAC member then stated there was no need to take notes as he was establishing an audio recording for the preservation of the meeting minutes for the betterment of the TLAC. It is important to note that over the next 3 to 4 years in these meetings, the meeting minutes were recorded as well as the Closed-door sessions and ITTF Meetings. They have been preserved to maintain the integrity and accountability of all entities with these documents. This is also the same meeting in which the TLAC member making accusatory statements also stated their TRIBE did not have the manpower or workforce to take on this IGA.

Later in the meeting, it was mentioned who the IGA would be turned over to as it was the same one who had mentioned they lacked the workforce or manpower to handle the IGA. One of the TRIBES stated that to be a sovereign TRIBE the TRIBES need to establish their database. The WisDOT TA noted the NAHP has been recently updated and adopted but has yet to be implemented. There was also a comment regarding the CRCS reporting of TSTW. The concern is that the numbers are inaccurate because they were labeled as 2 in the CRCS reports, which is 1-a minority, 2-labeled as a woman. It was mentioned that there is a need to travel onto projects to make sure they are accurate numbers being reported for these NAHP-specific projects. As the topic then led into the Annul

Assessment, there were concerns with this RFP process established by the WisDOT TA. It was noted that this was sent out to only 15 contractors across Wisconsin and only received 6 responses, and of those 2 of the replies were inconclusive, so there were only 4total reports. It was suggested by one of the TRIBES to generate a list of contractors who work on these projects each year for WisDOT. It was also recommended that the Wisconsin WTBA conference be on January 26, 2020, and why not go to the conference and hand out the survey? This was decided by the TRIBEs for WisDOT TA and TLAC Coord to get this done, but it was never completed.

The next concern was to address the RFP process because the WisDOT TA had scheduled a teleconference a few months prior and was trying to push the RFP through the current Tribe working on the IGA. The estimate for this to be done was $100,000, and it is worth noting that they only contacted one of the TRIBES to okay this to go through, but it was the position of the TRIBES that without proper discussion with the TLAC group they would not recommend anything. This is because the TLAC funds associated with it warranted all TRIBES to have an equal say in this process. This directly showed nothing had been completed with the brochure, there was no accountability, and was dismissed by the WisDOT. The final topic mentioned is the TRANS had stated in previous meetings they would be offering the OSHA 30-hour training, but this was messed up by miscommunication from departments of DOT, TRANS and DWD programs, who had all backed away from their previous statements of offering the OSHA 30. It was also mentioned that Big Step does not offer OSHA 30 for contractors as well.

The Base Lines Assessment was presented, and it was stated by the WisDOT TA it was going to settle on the assessment to move forward. The baseline assessment did not include transportation WisDOT projects general data, as it relates to the Native American Labor Data, because it is presented from across the state of Wisconsin. The SNALDB will not be used as previously as everyone is waiting on the final edits to the database. One of the TRIBEs states the biggest issues is getting in touch with TSTW and being ready and willing to travel to projects, drug tests, and driver's licenses.

The establishment of the survey for the CI, when the recommendation was brought forward, to push the surveys at the WTBA because this is the one place where all of the contractors are who are also the same ones doing the work and bidding on the projects each year. This was stated because the WisDOT TA had only sent the survey to the TRIBES, and there were only 16 surveys sent out and only 6 responses, 3 to 4 of them were usable data. The WisDOT TA had publicly notified that they are accepting a new position as prior to this the person was a Tribal Liaison.

The next meeting began with the amendments and revisions to the Partnership Agreement in February 2017. This was held in the Inter-tribal Task Force Meetings.

A few months later, in May 2017, TLAC reconvened as the following representatives were in attendance from WisDOT: 1 representative from OBOEC, TA, SWTL, SETL, NWTL, NCTL, NETL, FHWA, BIA, WTBA, AICCW, DTST/PPAA, AICCW, and CI, 4 from DWD and UMOS, 8 from WisDOT, 7 tribal members from 5 TRIBES. It was stated by the WisDOT TA that the IGA, which had been signed by one of the TRIBES, was now being transferred over to another TRIBE. Part of this process requires this to be finalized and submitted to the Governor's office but has yet to be signed. Once this has been completed the TRIBE will then be charged with the responsibility of completion of the baseline assessment, TRANS programs, and the original 8-recommendations continuing throughout 2017. This was done without the consultation or approval of the TLAC Committee. It was recommended, because TLAC funds are associated with the IGA, there should be a clearly defined process for when important decisions are involved in the

TLAC and not just with only one tribe. The IGA was then transferred at the discretion of WisDOT TA, directly excluding any input from the rest of the TLAC Group, thereby transferring $190,000 in funding for the NAHP, SNALDB, DWD, and training. There was a discussion regarding the database and the active TSTWs, as well as the verification processes for the TSTWs. Previously it has been stated that the TRIBES did not have to sign up to utilize the database. In a review of the TLAC group's history regarding the development of the statewide Native American database and at the last meeting where it was discussed this database had gotten diluted from its original intent. It was the recommendation of the TLAC group to go back to the beginning and develop their database, because there are two constraints and the TLAC Group and CI are not able to do what the database was originally intended for, which is to obtain ready willing and active TSTW for projects within the regions the work is taking place throughout Wisconsin. WisDOT TA stated at this current time there is no way for contractors to identify Native Americans within the DWD database. It was also stated the true intent of the database was to establish the reporting information and enhance the communications between the CI contractors.

At this time the WisDOT OBOEC and TA began to interject and state that the database program is not compulsory for the TRIBES and each tribe can decide if they wish to participate. The tones used by these two individuals reflected derogatory language and tones as these individuals became very upset when it was mentioned the TRIBES would like to go back to the drawing board excluding the DWD from the development of the database, because this is the decision of 9 TRIBES present at the January 2017 meeting, to begin working a TRIBES own database thereby excluding any affiliation of any other entities other than the TRIBES. The WisDOT representatives used aggressive, belittling, and condescending tones and language when this was brought forward and became confrontational.

The WisDOT TA then discussed the DWD Database and how it was utilized to provide targeted recruitment materials for one of the TRIBES to hold a workshop for upcoming projects. What was not discussed was this information here as it was utilized for a flooring and drywalling and not a Transportation project. This information was not the information requested as the original intent was to obtain this information for transportation-related sections. The information by the WisDOT TA was used to give the perception that the Database was working to help gather the information related to transportation-related projects with the intent of pushing TRIBES towards the utilization of the DWD database. The purpose of the original intent for the development of the Native American Labor database is to have control over this information, but if the TRIBES are not the controller of this information, then there is a concern with the release of the private information because TRIBES are defined as a sovereign nation and have the ability to self-govern. The Tribes do not have to release their statistical information unless requested, but if a database is created with another agency, they can establish information reports without consent. If the DWD is the Owner of the database and only issues a license to the TRIBES, they can access this information without the consent of the TRIBES. As the controller of the database, and all the Native American Labor information contained in the DWD Native American Labor Database, they can give information to the Wisconsin State and Department of Transportation, utilizing the Tribal information at their discretion. This was documented because the contractor who released their TSTW information to WisDOT TA was contracted to do this by the WisDOT Representative and submitted this information directly showing this information. In February 2020 this information had been gathered by the contractor and submitted.

The WisDOT OBOEC then asked about the next steps for the DWD database. DWD responded the communications needed to take place with Tribal leadership of a TRIBE to discuss the MOU. This TRIBE is the same TRIBE that is managing the Inter-Governmental Agreement, ITTF, and TLAC Program and the TLAC Coord. The WisDOT TA stated this TRIBE is looking to sign this MOU with the DWD and looking to do this on behalf of all the tribes with one MOU. This is the same database that was voted down at the January 2017 meeting.

There was an inquiry for clarification of the DWD database as it was asked how is the current database different from the database at the last meeting in January 2017? WisDOT TA explained there has been enhancement based on TLAC input, but the database is still not able to be used for the original intent of the TLAC group and Contractors which is accessing the database to recruit TSTWs. The WisDOT TA responded, *"At this time there is no way for contractors to identify TSTW in the DWD database, and the NAHP as Civil Rights Laws is preventing this use."* It was then stated that Citizenship is not a Civil Rights Law violation, and this issue will be forwarded to the DWD's attorneys because there is no concrete decision currently. This discussion concluded with the WisDOT TA noting the database is being used for targeted utilization – targeting a community for contractors providing limited accessibility at this time.

The NAHP and labor reports were the next discussion. WisDOT TA reported that is currently working on these reports, along with WisDOT DTSD, communicating with CI regarding the NAHP application on projects over the past three years in preparation for the audit in hopes of having information to present at the next meeting. It was brought forward at this time there has been discussion of revisiting the NAHP and WisDOT will be reaching out to contractors regarding the list of contractors requesting plans. One of the TRIBES requested a few changes to the NAHP relating to the time frames between TRIBES and contractors to submit information. It was noted this process should be equal and balanced for all entities. It was mentioned by the WisDOT TA these concerns needed to be elevated to the next level, which is to the Secretary of Transportation, as TLAC does not have the authority to move these changes forward.

The WisDOT OBOEC noted two issues with TERO and NAHP and the varying timelines, as the WisDOT TA is currently working on the form to adhere to consistency when contractors are communicating with TRIBES regarding projects and employment opportunities. The NAHP was drafted with Tribal leaders, and this would need to be brought forward to the Tribal leaders at the GLITC meeting. This concluded with the WisDOT bringing forward that one of the TRIBES has signed the contract to continue forward with the completion of the original 8-recommendations not yet completed.

The next day in May the Tribe who is being awarded the MOU and IGA's was contacted to confirm the statements made by WISDOT TA stating a MOU is being signed with the DWD, as this TRIBE is looking at doing this on behalf of all TRIBES with one MOU. In speaking with this TRIBES Leadership, the question was asked if he had signed a MOU encompassing all the TRIBES. This TRIBE's Leadership mentioned there was no MOU signed until after the attorney had had an opportunity to review it. The next day a phone call was made to the TRIBE who is being awarded the IGA stating this document has not been signed at this time and does not plan on signing anything until their TRIBE has had a chance to see and read that the IGA is reviewed with their attorneys. It was then explained these discrepancies are different from what has been mentioned at the TLAC meeting. The TRIBE stated in this phone conversation at approximately 4:13 pm the TRIBES leadership stated, *"Look I'm going to be frank with you,"* and said: *"I do not have time for this BU** SH**, and if anyone crosses my path, I will ruin their f***king careers!"* In an attempt to keep the conversation moving forward the mention of the comments made by one of the TRIBES regarding the discussion that transpired on January 23, 2017, asking if the database had become diluted as one of the TRIBES or CI was not able to fully utilize it. The TLAC group recommended that the database be created in-house and start by going back to the drawing board:

- *One of the TRIBES is looking to sign a MOU with the DWD; they are looking at it on behalf of all TRIBES with 1 MOU, WisDOT TA stated this is the same DWD Database which was voted down by the TRIBES.*

- *One of the TRIBES was put into a pilot project without any other TRIBES' consultation or knowledge after the database was voted down.*

- *IP is nothing more than a Statuary Outline, TERO quantifiable to exercise tribal sovereignty, changed within 30 days to hiring provision contracting TRIBES, hiring opportunities, and limitation for referrals on time. Revisiting the legal application to TERO and NAHP was discussed with Tribal Leaders to ask what they would all like to see happen.*

The next week this information was brought forward to the TRIBES Leadership mentioning the statement that was made. Nothing had ever resulted from this. It was also mentioned that at this time the new acting TLAC COORDINATOR is also a WisDOT OBOEC Representative.

In June 2017, a request for the list of all NAHP Projects in Wisconsin from 2009 until June 2017 was sent to the WisDOT TA who responded in 09, 2019, acknowledging the request to our Bureau of Project Development. An email was also sent requesting all projects for the NAHP from 2009 through 2017, keeping track of all the projects on which the NAHP has been implemented throughout Wisconsin. After speaking to the WisDOT Labor Development/EEO Compliance Specialist, I briefly asked if they possess the ability to gather information based on specific projects. They were able to locate this information within the CRCS program.

The WisDOT Labor Development/EEO Compliance Specialist was able to locate information after a specific project identification number was given through CRCS of how many people were on the projects as requested. It was then inquired if we have the ability to obtain this information for every project the NAHP was implemented on. The WisDOT Labor Development/ EEO Compliance Specialist stated there is a need to first consult with WisDOT TA to make sure the information could be released. The WisDOT Labor Development/EEO Compliance Specialist was walked through the process three different times to verify this information can be accurately gathered, and the information was gathered with success each time.

A list was compiled of projects based on what provisions are included in a contract. The WisDOT Representative then stated they were confused, as the WisDOT CRCS Specialists do not have control over which contracts contain certain provisions. Neither does the WisDOT TA. The WisDOT TA is not sure what report is referenced below. The WisDOT TA did speak to WisDOT CRCS Specialists, and they weren't sure either. Therefore, the WisDOT TA is requesting the bureau to provide a list of all projects that have contained the NAHP from its inception.

The WisDOT TA will work on establishing a report containing information reflecting projects that contain the provision and the results based on tribal reporting – including recommended best practices. *"We hope to share the results of this report at our next TLAC meeting. Perhaps this will assist with your analysis. Again, I will pass along your request and get back to you once I hear something."*

In July, another request had been sent because there was no response from the WisDOT TA. The second request was sent to obtain a list of all NAHP projects that have been implemented throughout the state of Wisconsin, including CRCS information for all those projects (Minority Reports).

Where this may sound redundant, this is what has been

submitted to the WisDOT to obtain the information needed in order to solve the current issues with the NAHP. Here is the list of items I would like to obtain: If you have any questions, please refer to the attachment which has been sent from Community Services Specialist (CSS) for WisDOT OBOEC in the past. This reflects a great deal of the information I would like to obtain from all projects the NAHP has been applied on or near the reservations within the state of Wisconsin from 2009 to 2017.

The information requested and I would like to obtain is a full list of all NAHP projects within the state of Wisconsin along with:

- *Total number of hours on the project broken down to each minority.*

- *Separate (if there is no one present please add a zero).*
  - *Men.*
  - *Women.*

- *Construction Trades:*
  - *Apprentice.*
  - *Journeyman.*
  - *Trainee.*

- *The total number of hours for each project.*

- *The quarterly information for these projects from each region.*

- *The total number of hours for NAHP projects each year includes:*
  - *Total number of quarterly hours for the projects based on regions.*
  - *Total hours available for the year.*
  - *Total number of Workers.*
  - *Construction group classifications.*

It was not until about a week after that a response from WisDOT was sent stating:

"WisDOT CSS has been compiling a list of projects that includes the previous NAHP and the new provision. They are currently out of the office today, but they will have the list submitted upon their return. WisDOT is evaluating 2013-16 projects and was hoping to send the complete report to you. This will be distributed at the consultation meeting next week. However, we do not have plans to evaluate the old provision. I did not understand your initial request to include CRCS data for the entire list. That is a bit more work than was assumed. This communication will be passed along to WisDOT CSS. This would require pulling individual data for each project, and unfortunately, the WisDOT TA does not have the staff to do this at this time, but discussions with WisDOT OBOEC and WisDOT CSS will take place to see if we can identify a possible timeline."

A rebuttal was sent the same day, stating:

This amount of work is relatively the same, but the only difference is that instead of the state quarterly information, this is more particular to the NAHP quarterly and annual information. It is the recommendation this is completed for all projects in which the NAHP has been implemented either on or near the reservations. Once the detailed list is available of all the projects to which the NAHP has been applied then it will be the request of the information from which WisDOT CSS already understands what data is needed. This is a request for only the NAHP information and not all the projects from across the state. The information is specific projects throughout the construction seasons from 2009 to 2017.

It is recommended to be able to review all the projects dating back to 2009 to accurately show a baseline or trend from which it is over 5 years. If there are only 3 years, it is only part of the information, and will be difficult to show the baseline or trend. This information has not been shown before as this is the purpose of the recommendation to show all the information to make sure the TRIBES, State, and WisDOT representatives all understand any trend that may be presented from the NAHP Data. Without access to this information, it is difficult for TRIBES to accurately analyze and address any concerns or implement the best resolutions to continue building the working relationship. Showing the old information may present what has worked in the past or what has not worked.

A few weeks later an email was sent in error from the WisDOT CSS to a TRIBE, because this was to be sent to the WisDOT TA and this is known because of the person identified in the communication stating that this was sent by accident to one of the TRBES. Soon after this, the WisDOT CSS vacated their position and was appointed the TLAC Coordinator. The communication states: "WisDOT TA,

WisDOT DTSD's thoughts on this request are that it be approved by TLAC.... Is that possible? This means that one of the TRIBES is requesting information that represents all tribes, not just their TRIBE. Is that a way of stalling this for a little bit to see if this is something all TLAC participants want to see? Or is this for personal/TRIBES use? In this case, this would need to be approved by all TRIBES that they agree to have this information provided to this TRIBE, does that make any sense? I mean I know it does not include any personal information, but if what was done before was by contacting the tribe whose project was located, wouldn't it be their data? Let me know if any of this makes sense.

The next time there was any other communication wasn't until August 2017.

The ITTF meeting which scheduled consecutively before the TLAC meeting. This meeting was established for the revisions of the Partnership Agreement. The reason this meeting is mentioned is that the NAHP project-specific information is requested along with the information reporting provided quarterly as these requirements are products of the TRIBES' government-to-government relationships between TRIBES, Contractors, and other entities. This information is submitted and given to the DOT. It was stated by the WisDOT TA in a derogatory and demeaning tone. It stated: *"Oh, this information is available, but there are only reports available, but the reports available would only be available the way they (WisDOT) would like to provide them. There is information and reports, but you only get the information the way we want to give it to TRIBES."* This was the fourth time this information has been requested.

The next meeting in August was the TLAC meeting and had 7 representatives of the TRIBES present. The main topic was the data request for the NAHP as this information reflects the average amount of the TSTW shown on projects is only from the results of all the WisDOT projects and not NAHP Project-specific. The difference is instead of including all projects across the state of Wisconsin, the NAHP projects specifically would only include projects located on or partially on TRIBES' reservations throughout Wisconsin. This equates to about 10% of all projects. The information presented was the average number of TSTW and reflects the information from all the WisDOT projects across the state of Wisconsin broken down quarterly and presented annually. NAHP concerns brought up were:

- *The tracking and reporting data for all our projects.*

- *The language of the provision has a lack of authority and accountability.*

- *To make this more formal in the closed-door session request voting from the TRIBES and created motions for action items.*

- *The discussion of the DWD Database and the IGA with one of the TRIBES, and how it would directly affect all TRIBES.*

- *The statements from DWD that one of the TRIBES would create one agreement that would blanket all the TRIBES. It was mentioned at the May 2017 TLAC meeting that TRIBES did not feel they had the authority to speak on behalf of all the other TRIBES. Each TRIBE should be allowed to speak on their own behalf as it is the responsibility of each to sign their agreements.*

- *WisDOT TA asked about the language of the dual citizenships as they are not minorities, and the CIS is not able to utilize the DWD database because this information is not available to look at for contractors when they are looking for Americans.*

- *It was official that the New TLAC Coordinator was working for the past six months as TLAC Coordinator and also as the WisDOT Community Services Specialist for OBOEC with the WisDOT under WisDOT TA. She is also the person who stalled the records request of information and is not the TLAC Coordinator and will be responsible for the completion of the surveys and reaching out to the contractors.*

- *NAHP on BOA and WisDOT projects. TSTW is not able to obtain positions after the Pre-Tribal Coordination Meeting.*
  - *Proper notifications to all the TRIBES located within the regions of the work being done.*
  - *Big Issues with the contractors attending the Pre-Tribal Coordination Meetings.*
  - *Language, Accountability in the NAHP.*
  - *Proper tracking information forms for Contractors for all NAHP projects.*
  - *The screening process for working on airport projects time.*
  - *Time allotted for Contractors and TRIBES' Communication needs to be fair, as this is an agreement.*

The discussion continued with the history of trying to obtain the requested data. The previous statements were brought which have all been documented stating the WisDOT TA originally stated there was no information in 2014-2015, and 2015-2016 when the same information was requested then stating, "there is little or no information available." In 2016-2017, during the third request for this information, the information is only available in the information shared for 2013 to 2017. When this last statement was made regarding the third request for this information, it was stated to the WisDOT TA in the TLAC Executive summary of the original 8-recommendations from 2012 stated in recommendation 4:

> ***Monitoring Reporting and Assessment.*** Where the WisDOT TA iterate the TRIBES their Tribal communities have some of the highest unemployment rates in the state. This fact has heightened concerns for tribal governments to strongly advocate for increased employment opportunities. Access to accurate and comprehensive information regarding Native American employment on WisDOT projects has also been raised as a big concern. Enhanced monitoring and reporting will yield the appropriate information needed to adequately assess Native American labor activities.
>
> ***Goal 1:*** Enhance the monitoring and reporting of Native American labor activities on WisDOT projects.
>
> - **Objective A:**[58] *Report regularly to the Great Lakes Inter-tribal Council (GLITC), WisDOT Inter-tribal Task Force (ITTF), tribal labor offices, governments, and industry on existing state and federal reports[59] regarding Native American[60] hiring and data gathered from the inter-tribal Native American employment database.*
>
> - **Objective B:**[61] *Conduct an annual assessment to identify trends, patterns, and challenges to improve Native American*

---

58. Committee Comment: Provide tribes an opportunity to pull reports at any time. Also, provide reporting to WTBA, unions and other construction industry stakeholders as well.

59. State and federal reports include Charts 15 and 16, 1392, Civil Rights Compliance system reporting, Trans, and Equal Employment Opportunity reviews.

60. Current state and federal reporting identify individuals based on self-identification as "Native American." The classification of tribal governments as minorities, versus sovereign governments with their own membership, has been of concern to the tribes. Tribes have requested the tracking of tribal membership and affiliation.

61. Committee Comment: Run report both in July and at the end of the construction season (coincides with 1392 reporting cycle). End of the year is the best time of year to run the report, when the season is complete.

> *employment outcomes, reporting, and overall effectiveness of the Native American labor initiative.*

- **Objective C:**[62] *Report regularly to stakeholders.*

This was when the fourth request was made when the WisDOT TA stated they have data the way WisDOT records information and not the way tribes record it. The reports are available only the way the WisDOT provides them. It was then stated the Legal representative was working for WisDOT. It was stated that it is hard to obtain funding if there is no accountability because the collective share was not listed, and the lack of information gathering was not addressed. One of the tribes emphasized it makes it difficult for the TRIBES to proceed forward and address other issues with the lack of information.

The Baseline assessment topic came up as there was further information needed, but it was first recommended this would be sent out to be bid on, then when it was inquired about the process WisDOT TA stated this was going to be in-house rather than sent out as an RFP by the TRIBE who had recently obtained the IGA. The Regional reports reflected the information presented was only part of the information and did not include the full information of the total amount of the hours available for the projects. It was also mentioned the hours need to be associated with the NAHP project specifically, and not just reported from all projects across Wisconsin. Having this done will present more accurate information regarding the NAHP projects and reflect the closest actual numbers of the TSTW on NAHP-specific projects.

This was the last meeting documented for 2017 and the information documented is the information for the TSTW, which has been compiled through rigorous work tracking

---

62. Committee Comment: Add Job Service (DWD) as a reporting entity because they maintain this information and to further help facilitate connecting people with jobs. https://wisconsindot.gov/Documents/doing-bus/civil-rights/tribalaffairs/tlac-exec-rec-final-com-approved-7-26-12.pdf

down the quarterly reports for 2017. There are some parts marked red only because there was no information available at the time. After speaking with the WisDOT Representative from NE Region, he was able to provide a total for the total amount. This total was subtracted from the totals attained from WisDOT and then calculated to show variances. These variances in the headcount were 17,879 total workers unaccounted for and over 208,218 hours not accounted for.(Please see Appendix B: Chapter 12.1 Chart WisDOT 2017 Regional Report)

In analyzing the information in the DBE Reporters for 2017, it is clear this information has been removed from the DBE Reporters and the ALR for 2017. Let's be reminded once again that women are counted twice: once as a "female" and once as a "minority." This is an important fact to know as well because this can inflate the report numbers. Looking at these two charts, it is important to see there is only one report to review the totals of tribal and non-tribal skilled trades workers and the hours are not able to be verified with these other resources. Without the numbers from the DBE reports, the Annual Regional Reports are the only source of information to go by on any of these reports for Wisconsin. This prompted the need for another document to compare, as this led to numerous public records requests. This is the closest the TRIBES can identify this information as a baseline of qualitative information presented. This information which was presented is from all the regional reports from all construction projects across the state of Wisconsin. These regions are North Central, Northeast, Northwest, Southeast, and Northwest regions encompassing all of Wisconsin. This information is provided quarterly and presented by the WisDOT Regional TL. It is important to mention this information was provided, but in the other two, the information was calculated by taking the total annual amount and subtracting the three quarters, leaving the result which was then input in the second quarter line for them minorities. This was given by the WisDOT Regional Liaison who was able to provide the total for 2017. All this information is information that is reported to contractors by the method of self-reporting, this means the TSTW is responsible for reporting themselves as Native Americans to the employer, because if the contractor requested this information, it is considered a violation of Civil Rights. In 2017, in the regional report presented there was a total of 2.70% TSTW on all projects across Wisconsin and they attained about 2.96% of the hours available.

This information has been gathered from quarterly and annual reports from TLAC and ITTF Meetings. This information reflects the non-tribal and TSTW on WisDOT Projects from as early as 2009 and going through 2017. This information will show the following information out of the tentative 32-week construction season for how many hours were available for TSTW and how many people also participated.

The below chart shows hours recorded for Tribal and Non-Skilled Trades Workers hours worked on all projects throughout Wisconsin, and in 2009 reflects the first record of self-identified TSTW on WisDOT projects across the state. Of the 7,096 total Skilled Trades workers on projects in Wisconsin, there were only 101 documented TSTWs who had chosen to self-identify themselves. The Skilled Trades Workers averaged about 155 hours per person, and this is equal to about $3\frac{1}{2}$ weeks on a tentative 32-week construction season on WisDOT projects across Wisconsin.

- **1.42%** *Tribal workers on projects.*

- **1.66%** *of the hours on the projects.*

2009	Tribal Total M & F		Non Tribal Total M & F		Total Workers
Regional Native American	Workers	101	Non Native Workers	6,995	7,096
Totals 2010	Hours	15,734	Non Native Hours	933,143.6	948,877.60

2010: Increase of **511 TSTW**, each averaged about **114 hours per person**, and this is equal to about two and a half weeks $(2^1/_2)$ of work on a tentative 32-week construction season on WisDOT projects across Wisconsin.

- **1.61% Increased (+.14 %)** *Tribal workers on projects.*

- **1.31% Increased (+.35%)** *in the hours on the projects.*

2010	Tribal Total M & F		Non Tribal Total M & F		Total Workers
Regional Native American Totals 2010	Workers	612	Non Native Workers	37,442	38,034
	Hours	69,834.6	Non Native Hours	5,269,534.4	5,339,369.00

2011: Increase of **241 TSTW** and increased TSTW hours of 26,000 worked. This averages out to each TSTW working about **112 hours per person** and this is equal to about $2^3/_4$ weeks of work on a tentative 32-week construction season on WisDOT projects across Wisconsin.

- **1.85% Increased (+.2%)** *Tribal workers on projects.*

- **1.97% Increased (+.66%)** *in the hours on the projects.*

2011	Tribal Total M & F		Non Tribal Total M & F		Total Workers
Regional Native American Totals 2010	Workers	853	Non Native Workers	45,166	46,019
	Hours	95,518.3	Non Native Hours	4,740,926.5	4,836,444.80

NAHP was rescinded

2012: Decrease of 31 TSTW and cut almost 9,900 hours. The TSTW averages about **104.2 hours per person** and this is equal to about $(2^1/_2)$ weeks of work on a tentative 32-week construction season on WisDOT projects across Wisconsin.

- **1.55%** *Decreased (-.30%) Tribal workers on projects.*

- **1.73%** *Decreased (-.24%) in the hours on the projects.*

2012	Tribal Total M & F		Non Tribal Total M & F		Total Workers
Regional Native American Totals 2010	Workers	822	Non Native Workers	52,085	52,907.00
	Hours	85,625	Non Native Hours	4,857,326.6	4,942,951.60

NAHP was rescinded

2013: Decrease of **11** TSTW with a decrease of hours to 922 hours. The TSTW averages about **104 hours per person** and this is equal to about a little more than $(2^1/_2)$ weeks of work on a tentative 32-week construction season on WisDOT projects across Wisconsin.

- **1.78%** *Increased (+.23) Tribal workers on projects.*

- **1.87%** *Increased (+.14%) in the hours on the projects.*

2013	Tribal Total M & F		Non Tribal Total M & F		Total Workers
Regional Native American Totals 2010	Workers	811	Non Native Workers	44,864	45,675
	Hours	84,702.80	Non Native Hours	4,435,311.20	4,520,014.00

These numbers are reflective Manpower? Of 100.13% which was recorded and sent from WisDOT

2014: Yields a decrease of **41** TSTW with a decrease of 3,284 hours. The TSTW averages about **105 hours per person** and this is equal to about a little more than $(2^1/_2)$ weeks of work on a tentative 32-week construction season on WisDOT projects across Wisconsin.

- **1.39%** *Decreased (-.39%) Tribal workers on projects.*

- **1.47%** *Decreased (-.40%) in the hours on the projects.*

2014	Tribal Total M & F		Non Tribal Total M & F		Total Workers
Regional Native American Totals 2010	Workers	770	Non Native Workers	3,476	4,213
	Hours	81,418.8	Non Native Hours	5,454,601	5,536,019.80

2015: Yield a decrease of **60** TSTW with a decrease of 13,075.2 hours. The TSTW averages about **101 hours per person** and this is equal to (21/2) weeks of work on a tentative 32-week construction season on WisDOT projects across Wisconsin.

- **1.23%** *Decreased (-.16%) Tribal workers on projects.*

- **1.40%** *Decreased (-.07%) in the hours on the projects.*

2015	Tribal Total M & F		Non Tribal Total M & F		Total Workers
Regional Native American Totals 2010	Workers	714	Non Native Workers	57,383	58,097
	Hours	68,343.6	Non Native Hours	4,829,329.5	4,897,733.1

2016: Yields a decrease of **107** Skilled Trades Workers with decreased hours of 17,987.2 hours. The TSTW averages about **83 hours per person** and this is equal to about (2) weeks of work on a tentative 32-week construction season on WisDOT projects across Wisconsin.

- **1.22%** *Decreased* (-.01%) *Tribal workers on projects.*

- **1.33%** *Decreased* (-.07%) *in the hours on the projects.*

2016	Tribal Total M & F		Non Tribal Total M & F		Total Workers
Regional Native American Totals 2010	Workers	607	Non Native Workers	49,072	49,679
	Hours	50,356.4	Non Native Hours	352,329.1	402,703.5

2017: Yields a decrease of **588** Skilled Trades Workers with decreased hours of 48,556 hours. The TSTW averages about **95 hours per person** and this is equal to a little more than (2) weeks of work on a tentative 32-week construction season on WisDOT projects across Wisconsin.

- **.89%** *Decreased* (-.33%) *Tribal workers on projects.*

- **.99%** *Decreased* (-34%) *in the hours on the projects.*

2017	Tribal Total M & F		Non Tribal Total M & F		Total Workers
Regional Native American Totals 2010	Workers	19	Non Native Workers	2,125	2,144
	Hours	1,800.40	Non Native Hours	180,558.6	182,359.00

The statistics reflect work done throughout the state of Wisconsin from 2009 until 2017. This has been through the first NAHP, and when it was rescinded and implemented in 2017, the NAHP dropped more than one full percent (1%), but then the season is only halfway through, and these percentages have a chance to come up. This is directly affecting all

TRIBES communities by letting contractors come on to the reservations, dictating who is hired when the only person who has authority to dictate who works on reservations is the Tribal Nations.

2009-2017 Annual Regional reports

norities	Caucasian	African	Hispanic	Asian	Native American	2 Races or more	Total Non-Native
rcentages of Workers	84.20%	4.62%	9.02%	0.56%	1.42%	0.17%	98.58%
rcentages of Hours	84.51%	4.43%	9.01%	0.30%	1.66%	0.09%	98.25%
Total from 2010 Regional Report for Wisconsin							
rcentages of Workers	87.07%	3.68%	7.16%	0.45%	1.61%	0.03%	98.39%
rcentages of Hours	84.59%	3.79%	9.82%	0.47%	1.31%	0.02%	98.68%
Total from 2011 Regional Report for Wisconsin							
rcentages of Workers	89.96%	2.67%	5.20%	0.40%	1.85%	0.04%	98.27%
rcentages of Hours	89.63%	2.43%	5.61%	0.34%	1.97%	0.02%	98.01%
Total from 2012 Regional Report for Wisconsin							
rcentages of Workers	90.61%	2.67%	4.83%	0.38%	1.55%	0.07%	98.56%
rcentages of Hours	90.14%	2.21%	5.44%	0.43%	1.73%	0.05%	98.22%
Total from 2013 Regional Report for Wisconsin							
rcentages of Workers	89.62%	3.06%	5.18%	0.38%	1.78%	0.14%	98.36%
rcentages of Hours	89.48%	2.35%	5.79%	0.41%	1.87%	0.11%	98.02%
Total from 2014 Regional Report for Wisconsin							
rcentages of Workers	88.99%	3.72%	5.34%	0.34%	1.39%	0.21%	98.61%
rcentages of Hours	87.70%	3.54%	6.69%	0.32%	1.47%	0.28%	98.25%
Total from 2015 Regional Report for Wisconsin							
rcentages of Workers	87.79%	3.94%	5.95%	0.46%	1.23%	0.63%	98.77%
rcentages of Hours	87.80%	3.30%	6.54%	0.36%	1.40%	0.60%	98.00%
Total from 2016 Regional Report for Wisconsin							
rcentages of Workers	87.17%	3.59%	6.50%	0.44%	1.22%	1.08%	98.78%
rcentages of Hours	90.74%	2.79%	4.64%	0.17%	1.33%	0.33%	98.34%
Total from 2017 Regional Report for Wisconsin							
rcentages of Workers	90.49%	3.31%	4.43%	0.19%	0.89%	0.70%	90.49%
rcentages of Hours	89.11%	4.25%	4.54%	0.26%	0.99%	0.85%	98.16%

The Original Intent of the Native American Hiring Provision:

Mission: Identify ways to monitor and track employment outcomes and areas for further effort and service, and *to help create opportunities and be a good-faith document for upcoming opportunities on or near the reservations.*

These numbers reflect the decline in opportunities for the eleven Federally Recognized Tribes of Wisconsin. It wasn't until a breakdown of the NAHP was done from the perspective of a contractor and what they need to do to get out of doing this provision I realized this:

- *The numbers are from all the Projects within the state of Wisconsin and not just the NAHP Projects.*

- *The Tribal Labor contacts have had to deal with many contractors' issues and many challenges. Here is a list of a few that have happened on some of the NAHP projects.*

- *The Challenges of Applying the NAHP:*

  - *Obtaining opportunities for TSTW on WisDOT projects.*

  - *FBI Background checks (Takes 7 to 10 business days) delay hiring. (BOA Projects)*

  - *The contractors see the statute language as optional and not definitive.*

  - *Subcontractors not showing up to the Pre-Tribal Coordination meetings.*

  - *Long-term Employment of TSTW.*

  - *Seasonal Workers or Short-Term opportunities.*

  - *Language states the contractor does not have to hire anyone.*

  - *Contractors who had previous issues are telling other contractors they don't have to do anything for the project.*

  - *Contractors are threatening to go straight up to Governor Walker and the Secretary saying they don't have to do this provision. This needs to be disseminated down to the Secretary of DOT to the contract and this needs to be adhered to by NAHP.*

  - *Stalling of data from the CRCS information when requested from TRIBES.*

Chapter 13

2018

The next meeting was 5 months later in January 2018 and the following WisDOT representatives were present: 1 representative from TA, SETL, NETL, NWTL, SWTL, NCTL, AICCW, TLAC Coordinator, TLAC Consultant, FHWA, State DOT technical expert for TRANS policy, DWD and ITTF, 2 from TRANS, 3 from WTBA, 12 Tribal members from 7 TRIBES. In this meeting, the discussions began with an allotted amount of $173,000 from the TRIBE with the IGA stating there is still this amount of funds available from the previous year. It was also mentioned the Baseline Assessment will be completed by May 2018. The WisDOT TA transitioned into the NAHP and the progress of the revisions which now included an online form, the amendments for the TRIBES and CI contractors to have equal times to submit their information for the Tribal Coordination meetings. They also mentioned that WisDOT can now monitor the contractor's competition and return of electronically submitted forms, with the ability to forward on an as needed basis. The discussion then continued to the addition of language for internships and apprenticeships to the NAHP mentioned, concluding on the delegation of authority of the NAHP and the binding authority moved to Labor Compliance Department as well as the implementation of the Labor Compliance Checklist.

The next topic was the DWD database as the TRIBE with the IGA is still in review of the MOU. This is the same MOU that was stated by the WisDOT TA that was being signed and just awaiting the signature of the Secretary of DOT. It is noted this TRIBE maintaining the IGA still has not signed this document almost a year later. The TLAC Coordinator delegated to the TRIBES that this TRIBE with the IGA would administer and pull the information to be sent to the TRIBES. This was the meeting minutes provided by the TLAC Coordinator and the WisDOT TA.

Here are some of the meeting minutes that were not included. These were recorded and transcribed. It is important to notice there is a lot of technical information missing, addressing key issues, and dealing with the funding. This is the purpose of a second set of meeting minutes, which were directly transcribed from the actual meeting minutes audio clip recorded:

The meeting began stating the purpose of this meeting was to establish a plan in the first quarterly meeting for 2018 with various areas like training, DWD Database, and outreach to the youth, looking at youth apprenticeships, NAHP, and many other resources to provide the stability needed to help the TRIBES in creating ways to enhance sustainably economic opportunities within all TRIBES communities across Wisconsin.

The TLAC Coordinator began to discuss the topic of TLAC Updates and reports, Baseline reports, Labor reports, Administrative, 2 Trans Scholarships for the WTBA Conference, and the available funding from 2017 of $173,000 moving forward into 2018. The WisDOT TA began discussing the 8-recommendations, dated the provision with the amendments to the NAHP, and looked at ways to help enhance opportunities through cooperative agreement with the TRIBE who obtained the IGA. There were recommendations of amendments to the NAHP presented from the last meeting minutes, along with the reviews from the WisDOT Bureau of Development from late August, as these recommendations were to make the process more efficient and to address any questions presented by CI contractors. Some questions asked were:

- *Prebid Documentation Process:*
  - *Contractors contact the Tribal Labor Representatives for each TRIBE when working on any NAHP projects, and document all communications to become eligible bidders, utilizing the online form and submitting to WisDOT TA notifying TRIBES who the eligible bidder is.*
  - *Contractors asking why they are contacting the Tribal Nations.*
  - *Reaching out to Tribal labor representatives, the TRIBES can notify contractors about:*
    - *Local Contractors*
    - *DBES*
    - *Borrow pits*
    - *Trucking*
    - *etc....*

The second portion of the discussion referenced the time constraints requirement amending the existing time constraints: "*A minimum of 3 business days would effectively be changed to a minimum of 5 business days for the Tribal labor representatives to respond with adequate information.*" The reason this was changed is because the Tribes should be afforded the same equal treatment with working in any agreement or provisions. If any contractor is afforded 5 business days, then the Tribes should be afforded the same. Previously, the TRIBES were only afforded 3 business days, and the contractors were afforded 5 business days.

- *"Recommendation" How to provide guidance for the contractors for setting up the Pre-Tribal Coordination Meetings process, setting Tribal Coordination meetings, a form online accessible for contractors recording and reporting processes same as an original form.*

- *Tribal Coordination Meeting. What are the rules and define the process? Some of the items touched on in this whole process are to help make this provision clearer and easier to understand expectations to forms, as much of this vagueness in the language has been eliminated and replaced after the accomplishment of a definitive, defined process now in black and white to help eliminate any misconceptions of the provision.*

This led to the question asking about the NAHP and its location of information, and what the format of these timelines were as it relates to the tracking information. The WisDOT TA responded there is no process for NAHP, the collection of the NAHP information, and stated that the Civil Rights and Compliance System (CRCS) is the way WisDOT has been tracking NAHP information and reporting this information in reports to TRIBES over the past few years. The CRCS blanketed TSTW numbers on projects but combined all the projects from across the state of Wisconsin.

The original intent of the NAHP is to help obtain information and statistics on how many TSTW are on NAHP Projects and not all projects from the state of Wisconsin. WisDOT TA stated: *"There was no process established for NAHP tracking information,"* and a TLAC Representative countered the WisDOT TA stating: *"This information which has been presented to the TRIBES is invalid and inaccurate as the numbers are fluffed, or inflated, but yet the WisDOT is reporting all of this information to all the TRIBES. The WisDOT TA stated the information was from NAHP, CRCS, and it has no verification process for this information."* It was explained these reports don't cover just the NAHP. The intent of the first NAHP provision was to request any information for all the projects the NAHP has been applied to. In the creation of the NAHP, its purpose was designed for NAHP project-specific, and the information reported to TRIBES over the past 3 to 4 years has not been NAHP-specific for the projects as the information is from the CRCS program reflecting these numbers which are not accurate, because it does not reflect the accurate amounts of non-tribal and TSTW on the NAHP-specific projects. The

WisDOT TA became upset and started speaking in a derogatory, aggressive, and counter-productive manner, repeatedly attempting to discredit, and demanding what was wanted.... It was explained to the WisDOT TA that what is being requested is the same forms required by the Federal Government (i.e., form 3121) as the TRIBES can restrict the federal government if not more strictly, and would like to obtain all the NAHP-specific projects to have the following:

Total number of hours on the project broken down to each minority,

- *Separate (if there is no one present please add a zero)*
  - *Men*
  - *Women*

- *Construction Trades*
  - *Apprentice*
  - *Journeyman*
  - *Trainee*

- *The total number of hours for each project.*
- *The quarterly information for these projects from each region.*
- *The total amount of hours for NAHP projects quarterly and annually for each year including:*
  - *Total number of quarterly hours for the projects based on regions*
  - *Total hours available for the year*
  - *Total number of Workers*
  - *Construction group classifications.*

The Tribal and non-Tribal, Tribal Skilled Trades Workers (TSTW) hours will be utilized to allocate hours for available projects. This allocation will follow the new 3121 federal requirement form, ensuring that the information is presented separately from the CRCS Report. In addition, an NAHP Report will be generated and presented during the TLAC quarterly meetings to provide the released information. The TLAC TA stated "fine!" and abruptly moved forward to the next section and concluded, moving forward this should be a monthly requirement for work on total hours available, but a CI contractor stated they were concerned with the requirement of releasing employee's names and positions available because stated they are not supposed to be releasing the information to TRIBES, and they will not be releasing the information to the TRIBES. This then concluded with a DWD statement that the DWD database is only self-reporting or self-identifying, so it is not accurate. Tribal IDS come into play because they are not able to record or verify the information.

The final part of the discussion was the audio clips and recording of the information. It was inquired as to why these audio clips were not preserved for accountability of the TLAC Group and all the entities involved. It was stated there will no longer be any audio clips of meeting minutes available. This was concluded with a statement this is concerning because it directly affects the accountability of the TLAC Group and the original 8-recommendations.

During February 2018, the Draft recruitment and referral survey was sent out to all TRIBES for a final review as the next step was to submit to the list of contractors. The purpose of the survey is to create an awareness and increased awareness of understanding the construction industry hiring practices and standards. Information to be gathered includes the application process, recruitment periods, recruitment methods, qualifications/skills needed for the job, lead time for hiring, availability of entry-level positions each year, and how the amount of those entry-level positions is determined.

TLAC Recruitment & Referral Survey

The purpose of this survey is to create awareness and increase understanding of construction industry hiring practices and standards. Information to be gathered includes: application process, recruitment periods recruitment methods, qualifications/skills needed for the job, lead time for hiring, availability of entry level positions each year, and how the amount of those entry level positions are determined.

Your Contact Information	
Your Business Name	
Date Completed *(for written surveys)*	
What type of construction work do you do:	
How many people do you employ full time:	_____ Less than 50 _____ 51 to 100 _____ 101 to 200 _____ 201 to 300 _____ 301 to 400 _____ 401 to 500 _____ 500 +
How many people do you employ seasonally:	_____ Less than 50 _____ 51 to 100 _____ 101 to 200 _____ 201 to 300 _____ 301 to 400 _____ 401 to 500 _____ 500 +
What areas of the state do you primarily work:	_____ NE _____ NC _____ NW _____ SE _____ SW _____ Entire State
What type of contractor are you?	_____ Prime _____ Sub-Contractor
Who is the primary person responsible for hiring:	_____ Owner _____ Manager _____ EEO Officer _____ HR Manager _____ Other – please describe
What is your application process:	_____ Written Application _____ Online _____ Apply In Person

TLAC Recruitment & Referral Survey

What are your recruitment methods:	_______ Newspaper Advertisements _______ Job Center website _______ Other Online – Please describe _______ Other – Please describe
Does your business accept referrals for possible employment? If yes, is there any specific or recommended time of year or date that these are accepted? Who should referrals be addressed to – please provide contact information.	_______ Yes/No Date _______________ Please provide contact information: _____________ ____ ____
Do you have a specific recruitment period? If yes, please explain the process. If no, please share why.	
What skills are you looking for in qualified applicants:	
What type of education and certifications are you looking for in qualified applicants:	
What else might you look for when hiring qualified applicants:	
What is your interview process, including timeline:	
Do you typically have a certain number of entry level positions available each hiring session? If no, please provide information on your reasoning.	_______ 0-10 _______ 10-20 _______ 20-30 _______ 30-40 _______ 40-50 Other _____________________
Do you offer new hires on-the-job training? What type of training do you offer?	
Do you offer advancement opportunities?	

TLAC Recruitment & Referral Survey

What type of advancement opportunities do you offer?	
What do you look for in an employee in order to advance them?	
When do you typically call back your seasonal employees?	
When do you start building teams/crews?	
Are you a Union Contractor?	
What Apprenticeship program(s) are you affiliated with?	
Are you a DWD Certified Apprenticeship Trainer?	
Could you provide a website link to your job openings?	Link here

Thank you for your participation.

You may also take this survey online at http://www.surveymonkey.com/s/TLACrecruitmentsurvey

If you have any questions, please contact
or via email at

After this review meeting, there was another meeting scheduled for the NAHP Amendments as the draft was prepared for April 2018.

Revisions Team 4-30-2018
WisDOT/Tribal Government Work Team
TLAC

Native American Hiring.

Pre-Bid
Before bid submittal, [prospective contractor shall] contact the (insert specific tribe who will serve as the labor contact) to provide information on hiring procedures and future employment opportunities, and gather information on the tribal work force and tribal resources (ex. NADBE, tribal businesses, products, potential worker, etc,.).

(Insert tribe) tribal labor office contact information: (insert specific contact information)
    Example: (tribal labor contact, name and title)
    (Address)
    Office:
    Cell:
    Email:

Maintain documentation of all efforts made to communicate with (insert specific tribe who will serve as contact). Pre-bid, complete DT---- and submit in conjunction with the Proposal Request Form [Insert Link to Form and reference email submission]. The Eligible Bidders list will not be updated until this form is received.

After Execution
The contractor shall contact the (insert specific tribe who will serve as contact) and discuss the following requirements.

The contractor will provide the (insert specific tribe who will serve as contact) with the following information regarding available employment opportunities for prime and subcontractors at a minimum 5 business days before the tribal coordination meeting:
    Job classification/trade
    Job qualifications and required skills
    Employment period
    Wage
    Copy of job application
    List of subcontractors, contact information (ex. Name, email, phone, etc.)
    List of available internships

After receiving employment opportunities, the (insert specific tribal labor contact) may provide employment referrals or recruitment sources throughout the life of the project to obtain qualified referrals.

Document all efforts made to communicate job opportunities and the results of hiring activities throughout the life of the contract. Utilize DT [insert form language] and submit to (Insert tribe) and (insert unit mailbox) on the 15th of every month for the previous month until all work complete date has been provided by the department per standard

Revisions Team 4-30-2018
WisDOT/Tribal Government Work Team
TLAC

specifications 105.11.2.1.4. Final report should be indicated on the form. Report shall include prime contractor and subcontractors data.

Tribal Coordination Meeting

Between execution of contract and the project preconstruction conference, the contractor and (insert tribe) will setup and coordinate a meeting, establish an agenda and date, and location. This meeting may also include potential interview or introduction with potential employees. Any cost incurred would be incidental to the overall projects cost. Contractor should notify and invite WisDOT Statewide Tribal Liaison, 4802 Sheboygan Ave, RM 451, P.O. Box 7965, Madison, WI 53707-7965, kelly.jackson@dot.wi.gov, 608-266-3761 and Regional Tribal Liaison (Insert Regional Liaison and contact information) and Regional Labor Compliance Specialist (insert Regional Labor Compliance specialist and contact information). Prime contractor and all subcontractors shall be present. Discuss available employment opportunities and other tribal areas of interest such as scope of work, Tribal regulations, borrow sites, waste sites, and available aggregate.

<u>USER GUIDANCE</u>

<u>Applicability:</u>

Project should be identified as candidates for the provision during the scoping to determine when this provision will be included in projects. Currently this provision would apply to projects located on or partially on lands held under the ownership and jurisdiction of the tribes.

<u>Suggested wording for advertising:</u>

This contract requires pre-bid contact with the Tribe whose lands the project is located on or partially on held under the ownership and jurisdiction of the tribes and additional documentation will be submitted [on form…] with the Proposal Request Form (available online). See special provisions and contact (insert project manager and contract information), for information on this requirement.

<u>Suggested policy considerations:</u>

Any time this provision is included within a contract the regional tribal liaison should be included. A pre-advertising meeting between the regional project manager, regional tribal liaison, statewide tribal liaison and the tribal labor contact should be arranged. WisDOT shall provide a timeline, basic scope of work and all relevant online links to project plans, bidding and advertising procedures and assist with outreach expectations, recommendations for tribal coordination meeting agenda and identify any other tribal project coordination needs or requirements. This is also an opportunity to discuss the DBE goals sets and outreach processes required as part of ASP 3, when federal funds are used. This meeting should include the following:
     Timeline [set standards]

<u>Suggested addition for Notes to Construction/Reporting:</u>

[Form TBD] Reporting will be provided to Labor Compliance Specialist, Tribes and Statewide Tribal Affairs. [Need to set up mailbox for report submission]

<u>Suggested information for PM (Project Manager) for pre-bid inquiries:</u>

This is a standard special provision. This is where we would likely reference where to find the supportive language regarding the provision. Purpose, background, etc. For further

3 of 4

information on the future of statewide hiring provision, contact Kelly Jackson, 608-266-3761

Documentation:
(Form DT TBD) will be submitted via email on the 15th of every month for the previous month. The mailbox is managed by statewide tribal affairs. If additional information is needed or requested contact Kelly Jackson, 608-266-3761. Labor Compliance Specialists may add additional information as requested to the monthly reports. Example: Total hours worked to date, etc.

Statewide Native American Labor Database:
At this time this resource is not available. Statewide Tribal Affairs is working with DWD to enlist a tribal component onto the Job Centers program. This will be included in the provision but is not available at this time.

4 of 4

The next meeting was scheduled for May 2018 and the following WisDOT representatives were present: 1 representative from TA, Western Labor Compliance, Environmental Specialist, Statewide TL, SETL, NETL, NCTL, NWTL, DBE, Labor Compliance Program Chief, Unit, DOA, Environmental Specialists, UMOS, and TLAC Coordinator, 2 from DWD, Consultant, WTB, and FHWA, 3 from DTSD, and Statewide Investigations and 12 tribal members from 5 TRIBES. This meeting brought forward the discussion of the review of the TLAC implementation plans for the 8-recommendations as five work teams have been developed to implement the recommendations. The information prepared in the WisDOT TA reports is reported from the CRCS information and is inaccurate as there is a difference between these numbers vs. the NAHP project-specific information. This meeting began with the review of the TLAC Implementation Plan (Original 8-recommendations) adopted back in 2012:

- *Recommendation 1 – Statewide Native American Labor Initiative.*

    - *The TLAC Coordinator position was developed.*

- *Recommendation 2 – Statewide Native American Labor Database Build capacity for Tribes.*

- *Recommendation 3 – Standardized Recruitment and Referral in the construction industry.*

- *Recommendation 4 – Monitoring, Reporting and Assessment:*

    - *How to monitor and report Native Americans TSTW.*

- *Recommendation 5 – Partnership Building and Communication.*

- *Recommendation 6 – Education Resources, Preparedness, and Career Development.*

- *Recommendation 7 – Construction Industry Incentives for Native American Hiring:*

    - *TLAC coordinator is working on an Awards Program.*

- *Recommendation 8 – NAHP for "on" or "partially on" tribal lands.*

- *Government-to-government relationships between the state and the Tribes.*

After the review of this information, the question was raised: "Why has the CRCS data been used in the past?" WisDOT TA responded that with the NAHP revisions, Tribes will have consistent data. Right now, TRIBES is gathering its own. It was then noted that the CRCS data shows gaps in Native American hiring, was told that newer data was not available, and that data varied widely. When this information was requested for the regional data from the CRCS and Tribal liaison reports. The information was brought forward and asked why the recording meeting minutes had changed moving forward. The TRIBE with the IGA stated they will no longer be offering this information. TLAC members mentioned the concerns of accountability as this is the same TRIBE as in a meeting in January 2017, their Leadership stated there needs to be accountability for the people in the TLAC Group to make sure the 8-recommendations are being completed, and now this same representative is stating there is no need for the accountability. Also in this same meeting, the TRIBE directly stated they lacked the staff and had much less manpower to work on an IGA. In the next meeting, they were given the IGA without any consultation between the TLAC Group members. This was dictated by the WisDOT TA as it is shown in the email communication which was sent the evening before the TLAC meeting. Once this was brought forward the Tribes Leadership from the TRIBE with the IGA became upset with the factual statements and began to use unprofessional language stating: "*I don't have time for this Sh#t!!*" The TLAC member this was directed at then stated to the TRIBES leadership: "We are all here to work collectively and there is no reason to be talking to me or anyone like this. We are here to work in a conducive manner and will not tolerate anyone talking to them in this manner. We need to work collectively in the best interests of all TRIBES. Later it was mentioned by one of the TRIBES' leadership, who was present, that the upset tribal leadership walked up to them after and stated the TLAC member needed to choose a side and abruptly left the meeting. A few days after the meeting, one of the TRIBE's called a meeting stating the Business Committee will address the comments made. This was never addressed, and a year went by thereby dissolving any accountability for the TLAC group. A final comment was made by the tribe leadership who has the IGA attempting to discredit the audio clips and stated there will be no more recorded meeting minutes. The audio clips were recorded and transcribed, these meeting minutes were then archived.

Once again, another Public Records Request had been submitted in mid-May 2018, making it the Fifth Public Records Request. After numerous requests since 2014, they still have not been completed. It was not until June 2018 that an actual cost was associated with receiving the information for the WisDOT information of the NAHP-specific projects. The letter was submitted by the Northeast Regional Office Records Coordinator. When the information was requested from the Bureau of Aeronautics (BOA), a letter from the Labor Compliance and DBE Program Manager stated that the BOA projects in the NAHP would require approximately 304 reports. There are 19 projects, 8 reports per year the project was active, approximately two years (average) for the duration of those projects, equals 304 reports. If each report takes ten minutes to generate, save and send electronically, then that is 3,040 minutes (or 50.6 hours) to fulfill the request.

During this year there was a Secretary's Consultation meeting, and, in this meeting, The Secretary of Transportation made a direct statement related to the NAHP tracking information as this information was inflated and skewed. The Secretary's direct statement was: *"This had better not be going on."* As the year went on, when the records request had been submitted, there were over 126 projects. It was not until further analysis had eluded both NAHP and NAHP projects. In review of all the information, it was clear to see that out of the 126 projects identified, they were only able to obtain information for 56 projects. This is interesting because this is when it was stated the information for the rest of the projects was no longer available through CRCS, due to being archived and therefore no data could be reported. The requesting of the BOA's open records from their coordinator to confirm my calculations for this request and pending a response: *"The Labor Compliance and DBE Program Manager will respond to you with an approximate calculation of cost once the adequate steps to calculate cost and fulfill your request have been completed."* The information from the BOA has never been obtained since the last communication from 2017. This is the response received from WisDOT TA:

> *"The data request included not only annual data but also required that the report be provided quarterly since 2009 by the project. This request was provided to BOA and OBOEC in July. Since the request required the extraction of at minimum 800 separate CRCS reports per year, and due to the time and resources needed to compile this report within both BOA and OBOEC, it was forwarded to our Open Records legal review process. As indicated, this request was denied. The Department is not required to create a new record that does not already exist, compile existing information in a new format, or obtain a record from another agency, Wis. Stat. 19.35 (1)(L). The Department is required to provide only documents in existence at the time of the request.*
>
> *While this request was denied by the Open Records team, this was brought up at the TLAC meeting in August. Since we did not have a record of an Inter-tribal request to utilize TLAC resources, recorded or documented, it was not considered at this time. We may not be able to pull the data by quarter or in the exact format requested but will discuss what data and what resources are needed to extract that data.*

The WisDOT TA is compiling a report on all the current NAHP projects (2013-2017) and shall provide an overview during the next TLAC meeting. We do not have plans to evaluate data from the provision that was suspended and is no longer active. The WisDOT TA does not see how evaluating a provision that no longer exists would lend to enhancing current policies and programs.

WisDOT TA attempted to clarify the reference highlighted within the Secretary's 8 Recommendations. Recommendation 4: Monitoring, Reporting, and Assessment section. This goal and the objectives have been implemented and are included in the TLAC's work plan. These reports have been provided quarterly to TLAC, ITTF, THPOs, and GLITC (as requested). TLAC conducted a Baseline Assessment in 2016 and is currently conducting a Baseline Annual Assessment for Native American Labor statewide. In addition, NAHP includes a requirement that tribes may request reports from Prime Contractors throughout the life of a project. This recommendation in no way, applies to this request.

The reason this was brought forward was because shortly after this an email was received related to the NAHP Open Records Request. This information was received from the WisDOT OBOEC/Now the acting TLAC Coordinator where there were over 126 projects. In these projects, none of them were specified which ones were NAHP-Specific projects, and it was not until analyzing this information an email was sent back to the WisDOT DTSD NE Records Coordinator.

WisDOT was sent a list of 104 projects, and, in return, we have received a total of 55 projects. Of those, there are projects from which the NAHP has been suspended; there are 40 projects on our list of information that are directly from the period of the suspension of the NAHP. This leaves a total number of 15 projects. Of these, only 4 of the projects have the relevant information needed.

Sometime in August, another Open Records Request was filed; again to the WisDOT TA. This request was for labor data on both the expired Native American Hiring Provision (2009-2012) and the new provision adopted in March 2013 (2013-2017), because the information received in the original was inaccurate and there were numerous concerns with the information received. This information from the record request only shows a total of 4 projects where, with the application of the NAHP, out of a total list of 104 projects we have only been able to obtain the information for only 4 projects leaving data for 53 projects unaccounted for.

This Public Record Request has only shown me 4 projects where we have been made aware of the NHAP out of a total list of 104 projects, leaving no data for 51projects.

Here are a few concerns:

- *The information requested was for NAHP Specific Projects, but if the NAHP was suspended then why is this information on the report?*

- *The communications sent July in 2018 at 8:03 am: "There were 104 projects on the list we provided Madison, however, 48 of those are no longer accessible through CRCS, therefore no data could be reported." Of those projects there are approximately 24 projects from 2010 along with those Projects there are 14 federally funded and 3 State managed projects that require the federal highways forms, the 1392 forms, where are those forms for these projects or who is the person of contact for the FHWA to receive these reports for all of the FHWA 1392 forms for all of the following 23 federally funded plus the additional 14 federally funded and 18 State managed plus the additional 3 projects? This would total 37 federally funded projects and 21 State managed projects.*

The Complete List of CIP Records Requests of projects from NAHP 2009-2019

Unique Contract ID	CNNTLPCN	County	Contract Description	Vendor Name	Awarded Amounts	Final Cost	Region	Highway	Voucher Status
20080212029	8160-13-71	Bayfield County	Washburn - Red Cliff Rd, Washburn / Bayfield St	ZENITH TECH., INC. - WAUKESHA	$382,627.16	$388,934.93	NW	Sth 13	SF
20091208024	1199-10-72	Douglas County	Solon Springs - Superior	ZENITH TECH., INC. - WAUKESHA	$947,034.18	$939,986.19	NW	Ush 53	SM
20091208025	1540-03-62	St Croix County	River Falls - Roberts	B. R. AMON & SONS, INC.	$2,935,770.90	$2,800,892.21	NW	Sth 65	SF
20091208026	1560-29-71	Sawyer County	Hayward - Drummond	LARSON CONSTRUCTION CO., INC.	$517,176.85	$534,302.26	NW	Ush 63	SF
20100112010	1530-00-78	Pierce County	Prescott - Ellsworth	MATTISON CONTRACTORS, INC.	$309,063.23	$329,035.10	NW	Ush 10	SF
20100112012	7505-00-70	Trempealeau County	Independence - Whitehall	ZENITH TECH., INC. - WAUKESHA	$186,527.49	$186,162.98	NW	Sth 121	SM
20100209014	7170-00-71	Buffalo County	Wabasha - Durand	MATTISON CONTRACTORS, INC.	$195,717.66	$231,480.06	NW	Sth 25	SF
20100209016	7520-03-71	Jackson County	Hixton, S State St	ZENITH TECH., INC. - WAUKESHA	$77,080.94	$101,564.32	NW	Sth 95	F
20100209017	8150-16-71	Bayfield County	Hayward - Brule	NORTHWOODS PAVING, A DIV. OF MATHY CONSTRUCTION CO.	$4,992,128.52	$4,881,284.61	NW	Sth 27	SM
20100309032	1020-00-78	St Croix	Hudson - Baldwin And Hudson - Menomonie Rd	MONARCH PAVING COMPANY	$7,339,185.85	$6,837,570.38	NW	I 94	F
20100309033	1637-07-73	Trempealeau County	Harmony St, City Osseo	A-1 EXCAVATING INC.	$1,229,089.76	$1,279,307.68	NW	Ush 53	F
20100309034	7560-01-71	Trempealeau County	Arcadia, Main St	A-1 EXCAVATING INC.	$1,092,420.87	$1,277,692.25	NW	Sth 95	F
20100309037	8640-00-70	Dunn County	Menomonie - Boyceville	B. R. AMON & SONS, INC.	$4,156,603.13	$3,894,429.18	NW	Sth 79	F
20100413028	8140-26-60	Sawyer County	Hayward - Brule	MONARCH PAVING COMPANY	$1,210,951.48	$1,141,421.30	NW	Sth 27	F
20100427031	8160-14-72	Bayfield County	Bayfield - Cornucopia	C & W TRUCKING COMPANY OF BAYFIELD	$1,928,384.61	$2,085,178.36	NWL	Sth 13	SF
20100427038	8170-08-61	Sawyer County	Ojibwa - Stone Lake	MONARCH PAVING COMPANY	$2,190,023.09	$2,092,406.55	NW	Sth 27	SM
20100511025	2340-00-72	Racine	Waterford - Racine	MANN BROS., INC.	$1,237,044.98	$1,331,702.18	SE	Sth 20	F
20100511052	1196-04-79	Barron County	New Auburn - Rice Lake	MONARCH PAVING COMPANY	$7,758,441.23	$7,565,931.03	NW	Ush 53	F
20100511053	1199-14-60	Washburn County	Sarona - Spooner	MONARCH PAVING COMPANY	$1,145,436.18	$1,199,294.25	NW	Sth 253	SF
20100511054	7080-05-72	Clark, Jackson County	Fairchild - Black River Falls	MATHY CONSTRUCTION COMPANY	$3,931,475.90	$4,036,041.11	NW	Ush 12	F
20100511055	7540-00-70	Jackson County	Merrillan - Black River Falls	RUZIC CONSTRUCTION CO., INC.	$383,190.88	$381,127.63	NW	Ush 12	SF
20100511059	8110-06-61	Dunn County	Connersville - Bloomer	MONARCH PAVING COMPANY	$2,029,783.57	$1,963,759.96	NW	Sth 64	F
20100608052	1021-00-64	St Croix, Jackson	Hudson - Menomonie And Osseo - Black River Falls	MATHY CONSTRUCTION COMPANY	$11,241,538.74	$10,989,643.96	NW	I 94	F
20100608056	1520-06-73	Clark County	Fairchild - Neillsville	AMERICAN ASPHALT OF WISCONSIN	$2,186,609.84	$2,257,516.38	NW	Ush 10	F
20100622006	9660-01-60	Menominee	Shawano - Langlade	NORTHEAST ASPHALT, INC	$2,344,449.99	$2,248,184.16	NC	Sth 55	SM
20100713011	9650-18-60	Menominee County	Neopit - Antigo	NORTHEAST ASPHALT, INC	$1,394,327.49	$1,316,268.35	NC	Sth 47	SM
20100713017	1022-00-78	Eau Claire County	Eau Claire - Osseo Rd	ZENITH TECH., INC. - WAUKESHA	$3,464,909.31	$3,865,021.25	NW	Ush 53	F
20100713018	1530-07-63	Buffalo, Trempealeau County	Durand - Osseo	THE KRAEMER COMPANY, LLC	$1,560,337.04	$1,474,660.77	NW	Ush 10	F
20100810017	1633-04-74	Trempealeau County	City Galesville, Main St	ZENITH TECH., INC. - WAUKESHA	$4,176,095.00	$4,533,429.20	NW	Ush 53	F
20100810018	7030-08-73	Clark County	Neillsville - Marshfield	MATTISON CONTRACTORS, INC.	$118,949.56	$130,658.78	NW	Ush 10	F
20100810022	9227-01-06	Nw Wide	Northwest Region Various Highways	AMERICAN PAVEMENT SOLUTIONS, INC.	$1,968,841.45	$1,879,215.56	NW	Var Hwy	F
20100914001	1674-00-76	Sauk	Lake Delton - Sauk City Rd	CHIPPEWA CONCRETE SERVICES, INC.	$6,839,628.93	$7,067,698.67	SW	Ush 12	F
20100928002	0385-15-70	Milwaukee County	Milwaukee Intermodal Station	C.D. SMITH CONSTRUCTION, INC.	$18,092,023.00	$0.00	SE	Non Hwy	
20101026011	8213-02-60	Rusk County	Thorp - Ingram	B. R. AMON & SONS, INC.	$2,476,932.55	$2,451,430.76	NW	Sth 73	F
20101109011	1020-07-77	St Croix County	Hudson - Menomonie	MONARCH PAVING COMPANY	$4,141,261.91	$4,029,544.31	NW	I 94	F
20101109012	1196-00-76	Washburn, Douglas County	Minong - Solon Springs And Spooner - Minong	MONARCH PAVING COMPANY	$2,054,362.80	$1,894,081.07	NW	Ush 53	SF
20101214013	1120-10-74	Winnebago County	Sth 26 - Breezewood Ln, Sth 44 - Witzel Ave	CENTURY FENCE COMPANY	$284,745.00	$274,435.45	NE	Ush 41	SM
20101214014	1120-10-81	Winnebago County	Sth 26 - Breezewood Ln, Sth 26 - Sth 21 Fencing	CENTURY FENCE COMPANY	$239,280.30	$227,956.46	NE	Ush 41	SM
20110111018	1022-08-76	Eau Claire County	Eau Claire - Osseo	MATHY CONSTRUCTION COMPANY	$2,154,052.67	$2,260,259.86	NW	I 94	F
20110111019	7120-01-63	Dunn County	Durand - Eau Claire Rd	MONARCH PAVING COMPANY	$3,770,535.63	$3,817,581.29	NW	Sth 85	SF
20110111020	7130-00-70	Trempealeau County	Centerville - Independence	ZENITH TECH., INC. - WAUKESHA	$320,332.69	$536,008.02	NW	Sth 93	F
20110111023	8080-08-73	St Croix County	Hudson - Somerset	MATTISON CONTRACTORS, INC.	$149,999.66	$154,593.41	NW	Sth 35	F
20110111025	8650-01-72	St Croix	Elmwood - Sth 64	LUNDA CONSTRUCTION COMPANY	$373,280.86	$390,812.50	NW	Sth 128	SF
20110308026	1133-04-88	Brown	De Pere - Suamico	RC EXCAVATING, INC.	$1,398,941.20	$1,378,063.03	NE	Ush 41	F
20110308030	9202-07-74	Brown County	De Pere - Suamico	VINTON CONSTRUCTION COMPANY	$3,292,874.94	$3,511,897.69	NE	Sth 29	F

Unique Contract ID	CNNTLPCN	County	Contract Description	Vendor Name	Awarded Amounts	Final Cost	Region	Highway	Voucher Status
20110308031	9202-08-74	Brown County	De Pere - Suamico	RC EXCAVATING, INC.	$125,026.53	$124,225.74	NE	Sth 29	F
20110308039	1050-01-63	Chippewa County	Chippewa Falls - Cadott	CPR, INC. (BROOKFIELD)	$1,451,852.27	$1,798,253.16	NW	Sth 29	F
20110308040	1050-01-64	Chippewa County	Chippewa Falls - Cadott	CPR, INC. (BROOKFIELD)	$1,848,080.06	$2,305,283.87	NW	Sth 29	F
20110308042	1570-00-71	Polk County	St Croix Falls - Turtle Lake	THE KRAEMER COMPANY, LLC	$6,423,091.46	$6,595,994.30	NW	Ush 8	SF
20110412014	1133-04-75	Brown County	De Pere - Suamico	VINTON CONSTRUCTION COMPANY	$451,154.10	$484,890.32	NE	Ush 41	F
20110412016	9202-07-72	Brown County	De Pere - Suamico, Cth J-Cth Ec South Frontage Rd	RELYCO, INC.	$3,613,190.84	$4,040,379.52	NE	Sth 29	SF
20110412025	1180-00-73	Ashland County	Ashland - Saxon	NORTHWOODS PAVING, A DIV. OF MATHY CONSTRUCTION CO.	$2,367,646.70	$2,766,559.44	NW	Ush 2	SF
20110412026	1550-02-71	Polk County	Clear Lake - Cumberland	MATTISON CONTRACTORS, INC.	$228,832.10	$217,826.10	NW	Ush 63	F
20110412035	7050-02-70	Clark County	City Neillsville, Hewett St	AMERICAN ASPHALT OF WISCONSIN	$1,853,245.42	$1,761,803.17	NW	Sth 73	SF
20110412040	1022-07-75	Dunn, St Croix County	Baldwin - Menomonie	MONARCH PAVING COMPANY	$4,396,489.94	$4,407,236.33	NW	I 94	F
20110510018	1130-35-71	Outagamie County	Oshkosh - Appleton	VINTON CONSTRUCTION COMPANY	$3,711,034.89	$4,187,288.76	NE	Ush 41	F
20110510021	1133-06-70	Brown	De Pere - Suamico	EDWARD KRAEMER & SONS, INC	$4,337,577.25	$4,535,511.11	NE	Off Sys, Ush 41	F
20110510022	1133-09-72	Brown	De Pere - Suamico, Glory Rd - Morris Ave, Glory Rd Bridge	ZENITH TECH., INC. - WAUKESHA	$2,356,283.96	$2,281,644.10	NE	Ush 41	SM
20110510024	3824-01-71	Fond Du Lac County	Wild Goose Prairie Trail And West Pioneer Rd	PHEIFER BROTHERS CONSTRUCTION CO., INC.	$1,848,192.40	$1,872,952.02	NEL	Cth Vv	F
20110510029	6230-13-60	Outagamie County	City Seymour	MCC, INC.	$103,679.64	$111,113.64	NE	Sth 54	F
20110510032	9202-08-85	Brown County	De Pere - Suamico	ZENITH TECH., INC. - WAUKESHA	$9,997,759.09	$10,570,848.17	NE	Sth 29	SM
20110510039	1023-00-76	Jackson County	Black River Falls - Tomah	MATHY CONSTRUCTION COMPANY	$5,520,075.00	$5,489,750.10	NW	I 94	F
20110510040	1198-00-71	Douglas County	Solon Springs - Superior	NORTHWOODS PAVING, A DIV. OF MATHY CONSTRUCTION CO.	$7,396,356.38	$8,153,982.01	NW	Ush 53	SF
20110614018	1009-39-36	Ne Wide	Signing & Marking And Local Rd Pavement Marking & Signing	CENTURY FENCE COMPANY	$570,536.00	$524,477.15	NE	Var Hwy, Loc St	SM
20110614019	1120-53-60	Outagamie County	W College Ave, City Appleton	LALONDE CONTRACTORS INCORPORATED	$1,065,373.66	$1,171,964.23	NE	Sth 125	SM
20110614021	1133-03-82	Brown County	De Pere - Suamico	HOFFMAN CONSTRUCTION COMPANY	$38,198,943.35	$38,261,598.94	NE	Ush 41, Non Hwy	F
20110614022	1133-06-77	Brown County	De Pere - Suamico	VINTON CONSTRUCTION COMPANY	$1,358,987.79	$1,357,088.25	NE	Ush 41	SF
20110614032	1180-50-60	Douglas	Wentworth - Brule	RJS & CJS, A JOINT VENTURE	$547,000.00	$747,486.05	NW	Ush 2	F
20110614033	1190-44-71	Douglas County	City Superior, Belknap St	CHIPPEWA CONCRETE SERVICES, INC.	$1,771,540.16	$1,922,683.06	NW	Ush 2	SM
20110614034	1196-00-74	Washburn County	Minong - Solon Springs	LUNDA CONSTRUCTION COMPANY	$289,316.56	$273,026.46	NW	Ush 53	F
20110614042	8060-02-60	Polk County	Somerset - St Croix Falls	MONARCH PAVING COMPANY	$997,286.15	$984,123.03	NW	Sth 35	F

Unique Contract ID	CNNTLPCN	County	Contract Description	Vendor Name	Awarded Amounts	Final Cost	Region	Highway	Voucher Status
2012			NO NATIVE HIRING PROVISION						
20130514045	9231-07-70	Vilas	Woodruff - Lac Du Flambeau	INTEGRITY GRADING AND EXCAVATING, INC.	$3,530,073.73	$4,015,189.23	NC	Sth 47	F
20130611011	1120-09-76	Winnebago County	Sth 26 - Breezewood Ln	INTEGRITY GRADING AND EXCAVATING, INC.	$10,665,185.63	$10,438,427.25	NE	Ush 41	SF
20140408016	2060-15-71	Milwaukee County	Howell Ave, City Oak Creek	PAYNE AND DOLAN, INC	$14,996,519.56	$17,763,472.40	SE	Sth 38	SM
20141111010	9202-10-71	Brown County	Shawano - Green Bay	NORTHEAST ASPHALT, INC	$5,644,817.73	$6,489,224.31	NE	Sth 29	SM
20150310022	1133-04-73	Brown County	De Pere - Suamico	ARBOR GREEN, INC.	$410,757.95	$239,339.72	NE	Ush 41	SM
20150512033	1009-32-33	Brown County	Oneida Wetland Mitigation Bank	RC EXCAVATING, INC.	$1,082,479.04	$1,054,996.78	NE	Non Highway	
20150714021	9286-04-71	Brown County	Village Hobart	NORTHEAST ASPHALT, INC	$93,561.90	$79,040.05	NEL	CTH J	SM
20150915009	6520-03-60	Outagamie County	Shiocton - N County Line	NORTHEAST ASPHALT, INC	$3,294,987.81	$3,396,198.53	NE	STH 187	SM
20160209017	1133-09-80	Brown County	De Pere - Suamico	HIGHWAY LANDSCAPERS, INC.	$208,811.01	$182,129.01	NE	STH 172	SM
20160412037	9155-14-70	Langlade County	Pickerel - Argonne	NORTHEAST ASPHALT, INC	$1,148,072.52	$1,155,860.65	NC	STH 55	F
20160510039	9155-13-60	LAnglade County	Pickerel - Argonne	NORTHEAST ASPHALT, INC	$926,459.13	$878,574.19	NC	STH 55	
20160510041	1000-08-88	NW Wide	NW Region Freight Mitigation	CHIPPEWA CONCRETE SERVICES, INC.	$837,192.66	$795,894.18	NW	Var Hwy	SM
20160510052	8780-00-70	Sawyer County	Moose Lake Rd - Pine Point Rd	MONARCH PAVING COMPANY	$825,291.43	$384,024.31	NWL	CTH S	
20161108015	9231-08-70	Iron County	Woodruff - Manitowish	AMERICAN ASPHALT OF WISCONSIN	$1,406,330.44	$0.00	NC	STH 47	
20170110012	6950-03-73		Dexterville - Port Edwards	EARTH, INC.	$2,624,672.68	$185,487.85	NC	STH 54 Wood County	SM
20170314030	1570-02-73		Village Turtle Lake	A-1 EXCAVATING INC.	$4,143,570.61	$50,143.22	NW	USH 008, Barron County	SM

Unique Contract ID	CNNTLPCN	County	Contract Description	Vendor Name	Awarded Amounts	Final Cost	Region	Highway	Voucher Status
20170509029	1058-25-70		SHAWANO - GREEN BAY STH 29 & STH 156 INTERSECTION	JAMES PETERSON SONS, INC.	$5,187,383.01	$0.00	NC	STH 029, SHAWANO COUNTY	
20110712009	1175-18-70	Iron County	Town Mercer And Mercer Downtown Enhance	MUSSON BROS., INC.	$5,652,418.08	$5,770,546.35	NC	Ush 51, Loc St	SM
20110712010	6064-02-72	Green Lake County	Columbus - Princeton	NORTHEAST ASPHALT, INC	$873,824.30	$1,074,048.33	NC	Sth 73	SM
20110712011	1022-00-87	Eau Claire, Trempealeau County	Eau Claire - Osseo	HAAS SONS, INC.	$1,214,732.65	$1,158,838.52	NW	I 94	SF
20110712013	7540-01-70	Jackson County	Fairchild - Black River Falls	MATHY CONSTRUCTION COMPANY	$3,175,903.06	$3,289,753.46	NW	Ush 12	F
20110712016	1133-03-72	Brown County	De Pere - Suamico	VINTON CONSTRUCTION COMPANY	$29,540,517.22	$29,577,982.94	NE	Ush 41	SM
20110809014	1133-04-78	Brown County	De Pere - Suamico	RC EXCAVATING, INC.	$376,861.25	$394,825.34	NE	Ush 41	F
20110809015	1440-28-60	Sheboygan	Fond Du Lac - Sheboygan	NORTHEAST ASPHALT, INC	$744,610.74	$703,274.81	NE	Sth 23	SF
20110809016	3822-01-71	Fond Du Lac	Cth T Bridge & Apps	RUZIC CONSTRUCTION CO., INC.	$236,967.71	$225,289.92	NEL	Cth T	SM
20110809017	4998-02-71	Manitowoc County	C Two Rivers, 17th St, East Twin River Bridge	LUNDA CONSTRUCTION COMPANY	$13,477,696.08	$13,733,069.86	NE	Local St	F
20110809018	9202-07-84	Brown County	De Pere - Suamico	ELMSTAR ELECTRIC CORPORATION	$515,918.00	$510,311.21	NE	Sth 29	SM
20110809022	1024-00-72	Eau Claire County	Menomonie - Eau Claire	MONARCH PAVING COMPANY	$415,285.97	$434,725.00	NW	I 94	F
20110809024	8560-13-71	Burnett County	Danbury - Minong	B. R. AMON & SONS, INC.	$4,876,627.54	$4,659,229.11	NW	Sth 77	F
20110809025	8865-00-70	Polk County	New Richmond - Wanderoos	MCCABE CONSTRUCTION, INC.	$1,172,735.80	$892,006.17	NW	Sth 65	F
20110913005	1227-07-71	Brown County	Milwaukee - Green Bay	VINTON CONSTRUCTION COMPANY	$1,318,162.73	$1,520,150.57	NE	I 43	SF
20110913007	1022-00-77	Eau Claire, Trempealeau County	Eau Claire - Osseo	ZIGNEGO COMPANY, INC.	$34,050,000.04	$35,854,553.63	NW	I 94	F
20111108008	1196-00-75	Douglas County	Minong - Solon Springs	HOFFMAN CONSTRUCTION COMPANY	$4,891,945.41	$5,000,132.74	NW	Ush 53	F
20110308041	REJECTED								
20111108007	REJECTED								

Once the proper information was obtained from the NAHP projects, another public records request was submitted. This is because the projects needed to be identified along with the TSTW on each of these projects, and this is where the below was established:

Project	County	Region	Vendor Name	Worker Type	Native American or Alaskan M	F	TOTAL	Total Available Hours (Male)	Total Available Hours (Female)	Total Available Hours	% Native American or Alaskan Hours
1130-35-71	Outagamie C	RCND10 Oshkosh - Appleton STH 125 & STH 96 INTERCHANGES	VINTON CONSTRUCTION COMPANY	Apprentice	0.0	0.0	0.0	689.5	0.0	689.5	0.0
				Journeyman	245.0	0.0	245.0	15,055.5	520.3	15,575.8	1.5
				Trainee	0.0	0.0	0.0	2.0	0.0	2.0	0.0
				Grand Total	245.0	0.0	245.0	15,727.0	520.3	16,247.3	1.5
1133-03-72	Brown	RECSTE De Pere - Suamico MORRIS AVENUE - MEMORIAL DRIVE	VINTON CONSTRUCTION COMPANY	Apprentice	0.0	0.0	0.0	7,907.3	0.0	7,907.3	0.0
				Journeyman	3,070.3	0.0	3,070.3	116,012.6	1,781.3	117,793.9	2.6
				Trainee	0.0	0.0	0.0	173.0	0.0	173.00	0.0
				Grand Total	3,070.3	0.0	3,070.3	124,092.6	1781.3	125,874.2	2.4
1133-03-82	Brown	RECSTE De Pere - Suamico MORRIS AVENUE - MEMORIAL DRIVE	HOFFMAN CONSTRUCTION COMPANY	Apprentice	0.0	0.0	0.0	7,289.1	0.0	7,289.10	0.0
				Journeyman	8,265.00	96.0	8,361.0	174,093.6	4,418.4	178,512.0	4.6
				Trainee	0.0	0.0	0.0	59.5	0.0	59.5	0.0
				Grand Total	8,265.0	96.0	8,361.0	181,442.2	4418.4	185,860.6	4.5
1133-04-73	Brown County	RECSTE De Pere - Suamico MORRIS AVE - MEMORIAL DRIVE	ARBOR GREEN, INC.	Apprentice	0.0	0.0	0.0	0.3	0.0	0.3	0.0
				Journeyman	0.0	0.0	0.0	1,755.0	26.0	1,781.0	0.0
				Trainee	0.0	0.0	0.0	0.0	0.0	0.0	0.0
				Grand Total	0.0	0.0	0.0	1,755.3	26.0	1,781.3	0.0
1133-04-75	Brown	RECSTE De Pere - Suamico MORRIS AVE - MEMORIAL DRIVE	VINTON CONSTRUCTION COMPANY	Apprentice	0.0	0.0	0.0	102.5	0.0	102.5	0.0
				Journeyman	57.8	0.0	57.8	2,388.5	166.3	2,552.8	2.2
				Trainee	1.5	0.0	1.5	1.5	0.0	1.5	100.0
				Grand Total	59.3	0.0	59.3	2,490.5	166.3	2,656.8	2.2
1133-04-78	Brown	RECSTE De Pere - Suamico ORANGE LANE - MEMORIAL DRIVE	RC EXCAVATING, INC.	Apprentice	0.0	0.0	0.0	0.0	0.0	0.0	0.0
				Journeyman	0.0	0.0	0.0	2,611.5	0.0	2,611.5	0.0
				Trainee	0.0	0.0	0.0	0.0	0.0	0.0	0.0
				Grand Total	0.0	0.0	0.0	2,611.5	0.0	2,611.5	0.0
1133-04-88	Brown	MISC De Pere - Suamico MORRIS AVE - MEMORIAL DRIVE	RC EXCAVATING, INC.	Apprentice	0.0	0.0	0.0	79.5	0.0	79.5	0.0
				Journeyman	557.3	0.0	557.3	7,203.6	0.0	7,203.6	7.7
				Trainee	0.0	0.0	0.0	0.0	0.0	0.0	0.0
				Grand Total	557.3	0.0	557.3	7,283.1	0.0	7,283.1	7.7
1133-06-70	Brown	RECSTE De Pere - Suamico ORANGE LN - GLORY RD	EDWARD KRAEMER & SONS, INC	Apprentice	8.0	0.0	8.0	996.0	0.0	996.0	0.8
				Journeyman	148.5	0.0	148.5	18,120.2	739.3	18,859.5	0.7
				Trainee	0.0	0.0	0.0	0.0	0.0	0.0	0.0
				Grand Total	156.5	0.0	156.5	19,116.2	739.3	19,855.5	0.7
1133-06-77	Brown	RECSTE De Pere - Suamico ORANGE LN - GLORY RD	VINTON CONSTRUCTION COMPANY	Apprentice	0.0	0.0	0.0	176.8	0.0	176.8	0.0
				Journeyman	56.5	0.0	56.5	6,595.5	178.8	6,774.3	0.7
				Trainee	9.0	0.0	9.0	13.5	0.0	13.5	66.6
				Grand Total	65.5	0.0	65.5	6,785.8	178.8	6,964.6	0.9
1133-09-72	Brown	RECSTE De Pere - Suamico, Glory Rd - Morris GLORY RD- MORRIS AVE	ZENITH TECH., INC. - WAUKESHA	Apprentice	47.0	0.0	47.0	495.8	0.0	495.8	9.4
				Journeyman	34.0	0.0	34.0	12,980.9	11.5	12,992.4	0.2
				Trainee	0.0	0.0	0.0	3.0	0.0	3.0	0.0
				Grand Total	81.0	0.0	81.0	13,479.7	11.5	13,491.2	0.6
1133-09-80	Brown	RECSTE De Pere - Suamico GLORY RD- MORRIS AVE	HIGHWAY LANDSCAPERS, INC.	Apprentice	0.0	0.0	0.0	0.0	0.0	0.0	0.0
				Journeyman	0.0	0.0	0.0	218.5	313.0	531.5	0.0
				Trainee	0.0	0.0	0.0	0.0	0.0	0.0	0.0
				Grand Total	0.0	0.0	0.0	218.5	313.0	531.5	0.0
1175-18-70	Iron County	RECST Town Mercer And Mercer Downtown BEACHWAY DRIVE - CTH J	MUSSON BROS., INC.	Apprentice	92	0.0	92.0	2,619.5	71.5	2,691.0	3.4
				Journeyman	572.8	0.0	572.8	27,561.3	1,051.7	28,613.0	2.
				Trainee	10.3	0.0	10.3	62.7	0.0	62.7	16.
				Grand Total	675.1	0.0	675.1	30,243.5	1123.2	31,366.7	
1190-44-71	Douglas	PVRPLA City Superior, Belknap St HILL AVENUE TO EAST 2ND STREET	CHIPPEWA CONCRETE SERVICES, INC.	Apprentice	0.0	0.0	0.0	541.7	18.3	560.0	
				Journeyman	307.6	0.0	307.6	7,087.6	87.8	7,175.4	4.
				Trainee	0.0	0.0	0.0	109.0	0.0	109.0	
				Grand Total	307.6	0.0	307.6	7,738.3	106.1	7,844.4	3.

Project	County	Location	Contractor	Trade	(1)	(2)	(3)	(4)	(5)	(6)	(7)
6-00-74	Washburn	BRRHB / Minong - Solon Springs / TOTAGATIC RIVER BRIDGE B-65-0028	LUNDA CONSTRUCTION COMPANY	Apprentice	0.0	0.0	0.0	143.5	0.0	143.5	0.00%
				Journeyman	11.8	0.0	11.8	972.7	34.5	1,007.2	1.17%
				Trainee	0.0	0.0	0.0	62.5	0.0	62.5	0.00%
				Grand Total	11.8	0.0	11.8	1,178.7	34.5	1,213.2	0.97%
6-00-75	Douglas	PVRPLA / Minong - Solon Springs / CTH T TO CTH Y (SB)	HOFFMAN CONSTRUCTION COMPANY	Apprentice	0.0	0.0	0.0	513.3	0.0	513.3	0.00%
				Journeyman	31.5	0.0	31.5	16,361.3	42.5	16,403.8	0.19%
				Trainee	0.0	0.0	0.0	0.0	0.0	0.0	0.00%
				Grand Total	31.5	0.0	31.5	16,874.6	42.5	16,917.1	0.19%
6-00-76	Washburn,	RDMTN / Minong - Solon Springs And Spooner - / BUS 53 (MINONG) TO CTH T (NB)	MONARCH PAVING COMPANY	Apprentice	0.0	0.0	0.0	0.0	96.8	96.8	0.00%
				Journeyman	263.1		263.1	3,801.3	370.8	4,172.1	6.31%
				Trainee	0.0	0.0	0.0	288.2	85.3	373.5	0.00%
				Grand Total	263.1	0.0	263.1	4,089.5	552.9	4,642.4	5.67%
8-00-71	Douglas	RECST / Solon Springs - Superior / CTH B INTERSECTION	NORTHWOODS PAVING, A DIV. OF MATHY CONSTRUCTION CO.	Apprentice	0.0	0.0	0.0	2,314.0	459.5	2,773.5	0.00%
				Journeyman	1,647.6	0.0	1,647.6	23,739.6	892.5	24,632.1	6.69%
				Trainee	0.0	0.0	0.0	266.3	74.5	340.8	0.00%
				Grand Total	1,647.6	0.0	1,647.6	26,319.9	1426.5	27,746.4	5.94%
9-14-60	Washburn	RSRF10 / Sarona - Spooner / USH 53 TO USH 63	MONARCH PAVING COMPANY	Apprentice	0.0	0.0	0.0	61.5	11.3	72.8	0.00%
				Journeyman	141.1	0.0	141.1	3,404.2	421.8	3,826.0	3.69%
				Trainee	0.0	0.0	0.0	110.3	0.0	110.3	0.00%
				Grand Total	141.1	0.0	141.1	3,576.0	433.1	4,009.1	3.52%
7-07-71	Brown	MISC / Milwaukee - Green Bay / MASON STREET RAMPS	VINTON CONSTRUCTION COMPANY	Apprentice	0.0	0.0	0.0	248.0	0.0	248	0.00%
				Journeyman	99.0	0.0	99.0	6,014.2	193.3	6,207.5	1.59%
				Trainee	0.0	0.0	0.0	6.0	0.0	6.0	0.00%
				Grand Total	99.0	0.0	99.0	6,268.2	193.3	6,461.5	1.53%
0-00-71	Polk County	PVRPLA / St Croix Falls - Turtle Lake / GLACIER DRIVE TO STH 35	THE KRAEMER COMPANY, LLC	Apprentice	0.0	22.5	22.5	1,262.0	94.5	1,356.5	1.66%
				Journeyman	1,004.3	0.0	1,004.3	22,099.5	1,044.5	23,144.0	4.34%
				Trainee	128.8	0.0	128.8	552.0	46.3	598.3	21.53%
				Grand Total	1,133.1	22.5	1,155.6	23,913.5	1185.3	25,098.8	4.60%
0-02-73	Barron	RECST / Village Turtle Lake / CTH K/NORWAY STREET	A-1 EXCAVATING INC.	Apprentice	0.0	0.0	0.0	3,937.3	0.0	3,937.3	0.00%
				Journeyman	63.1	0.0	63.1	12,638.0	239.4	12,877.4	0.49%
				Trainee	0.0	0.0	0.0	0.0	0.0	0.0	0.00%
				Grand Total	63.1	0.0	63.1	16,575.3	239.4	16,814.7	0.38%
4-00-76	Sauk	RECST / Lake Delton - Sauk City Rd / IH 90/94 - TERRYTOWN ROAD	CHIPPEWA CONCRETE SERVICES, INC.	Apprentice	0.0	0.0	0.0	1,515.5	0.0	1,515.5	0.00%
				Journeyman	0.0	0.0	0.0	17,660.4	526.8	18,187.2	0.00%
				Trainee	0.0	0.0	0.0	6.3	0.0	6.3	0.00%
				Grand Total	0.0	0.0	0.0	19,182.2	526.8	19,709.0	0.00%
60-15-71	Milwaukee	RCND20 / Howell Ave, City Oak Creek / OAKWOOD RD TO GRANGE AVE	PAYNE AND DOLAN, INC	Apprentice	1,291.5	0.0	1,291.5	8,309.3	10.0	8,319.3	15.52%
				Journeyman	1,300.8	18.0	1,318.8	87,516.7	997.0	88,513.7	1.49%
				Trainee	0.0	0.0	0.0	0.0	0.0	0.0	0.00%
				Grand Total	2,592.3	18.0	2,610.3	95,826.0	1007.0	96,833.0	2.70%
8-02-71	Manitowoc	BRRPL / C Two Rivers, 17th St, East Twin River / EAST TWIN RIVER BRIDGE	LUNDA CONSTRUCTION COMPANY	Apprentice	0.0	0.0	0.0	796.5	0.0	796.5	0.00%
				Journeyman	507.0	0.0	507.0	37,577.7	6.0	37,583.7	1.35%
				Trainee	0.0	0.0	0.0	0.0	0.0	0.0	0.00%
				Grand Total	507.0	0.0	507.0	38,374.2	6.0	38,380.2	1.32%
0-03-60	Outagamie	PSRS40 / Shiocton - N County Line / STH 54 - NCL	NORTHEAST ASPHALT, INC	Apprentice	0.0	0.0	0.0	694.5	0.0	694.5	0.00%
				Journeyman	29.8	0.0	29.8	9,053.5	734.3	9,787.8	0.30%
				Trainee	0.0	0.0	0.0	0.0	0.0	0.0	0.00%
				Grand Total	29.8	0.0	29.8	9,748.0	734.3	10,482.3	0.28%
0-03-73	Wood	RECST / Dexterville - Port Edwards / LONESOME ROAD TO SMITH LANE	EARTH, INC.	Apprentice	0.0	0.0	0.0	193.8	0.0	193.8	0.00%
				Journeyman	3.5	13.5	17.0	10,599.3	846.3	11,445.6	0.15%
				Trainee	0.0	0.0	0.0	71.5	0.0	71.5	0.00%
				Grand Total	3.5	13.5	17.0	10,864.6	846.3	11,710.9	0.15%
0-01-70	Jackson	RSRF30 / Fairchild - Black River Falls / N JCT OLD HWY 12 ROAD TO RUF	MATHY CONSTRUCTION COMPANY	Apprentice	0.0	0.0	0.0	331.8	0.0	331.8	0.00%
				Journeyman	263	110.3	373.3	11,156.2	949.7	12,107.9	3.08%
				Trainee	0.0	0.0	0.0	0.0	0.0	0.0	0.00%
				Grand Total	263.0	110.3	373.3	11,490.0	949.7	12,439.7	3.00%

Project	County	Project Description	Contractor	Class							
8560-13-71	Burnett	RCND20 / Danbury - Minong / STH 35 TO DEER LAKE ROAD	B. R. AMON & SONS, INC.	Apprentice	0.0	0.0	0.0	175.8	0.0	175.8	0.00
				Journeyman	585.8	170.5	756.3	14,772.5	1,095.00	15,887.5	4.77
				Trainee	0.0	0.0	0.0	0.0	0.0	0.0	0.00
				Grand Total	585.8	170.5	756.3	14,948.3	1,095.0	16,043.3	4.71
8650-01-72	St Croix	BRRHB / Elmwood - Sth 64 / UP RAILROAD BRIDGE B-55-0008	LUNDA CONSTRUCTION COMPANY	Apprentice	0.0	0.0	0.0	160.5	0.0	160.5	0.00
				Journeyman	0.0	0.0	0.0	1,916.8	134.0	2,050.8	0.00
				Trainee	0.0	0.0	0.0	10.0	0.0	10.0	0.00
				Grand Total	0.0	0.0	0.0	2,087.3	134.0	2,221.3	0.00
8780-00-70	Sawyer	PVRPLA / Moose Lake Rd - Pine Point Rd	MONARCH PAVING COMPANY	Apprentice	0.0	0.0	0.0	0.0	0.0	0.0	0.00
				Journeyman	25.0	5.3	30.3	3,632.8	330.2	3,963.0	0.76
				Trainee	0.0	0.0	0.0	0.0	0.0	0.0	0.00
				Grand Total	25.0	5.3	30.3	3,632.8	330.2	3,963.0	0.7
8865-00-70	Polk County	RECST / New Richmond - Wanderoos / CTH K INTERSECTION	MCCABE CONSTRUCTION, INC.	Apprentice	0.0	0.0	0.0	60.0	5.8	65.8	0.00
				Journeyman	112.8	0.0	112.8	2,008.5	84.0	2,092.5	5.3
				Trainee	16.0	0.0	16.0	44.8	0.0	44.8	35.71
				Grand Total	128.8	0.0	128.8	2,113.3	89.8	2,203.1	5.8
9155-13-60	LAnglade	PSRS40 / Pickerel - Argonne / CTH T TO NORTH COUNTY LINE	NORTHEAST ASPHALT, INC	Apprentice	0.0	0.0	0.0	122.8	0.0	122.8	0.00
				Journeyman	38.8	7.5	46.3	2,201.7	209.3	2,411.0	1.9
				Trainee	0.0	0.0	0.0	0.0	0.0	0.0	0.00
				Grand Total	38.8	7.5	46.3	2,324.5	209.3	2,533.8	1.8
9155-14-70	Langlade	RSRF10 / Pickerel - Argonne / SOUTH COUNTY LINE TO STH 64	NORTHEAST ASPHALT, INC	Apprentice	0.0	0.0	0.0	454.8	0.0	454.8	0.0
				Journeyman	283.5	5.5	289.0	3,563.8	148.0	3,711.8	7.7
				Trainee	0.0	0.0	0.0	0.0	0.0	0.0	0.00
				Grand Total	283.5	5.5	289.0	4,018.6	148.0	4,166.6	6.9
9202-07-72	Brown	RECSTE / De Pere - Suamico, Cth J-Cth Ec South / CTH J - CTH EB SOUTH FRONTAGE RD	RELYCO, INC.	Apprentice	0.0	0.0	0.0	705.0	103.0	808.0	0.00
				Journeyman	597.5	0.0	597.5	17,554.2	483.0	18,037.2	3.3
				Trainee	15.5	0.0	15.5	26.5	0.0	26.5	58.4
				Grand Total	613.0	0.0	613.0	18,285.7	586.0	18,871.7	3.2
9202-07-74	Brown	RECSTE / De Pere - Suamico / STH 29 RELOCATION USH 41 - CTH J	VINTON CONSTRUCTION COMPANY	Apprentice	0.0	0.0	0.0	539.5	0.0	539.5	0.00
				Journeyman	573.9	0.0	573.9	19,261.2	806.5	20,067.7	2.8
				Trainee	15.00	0.0	15.0	21.0	0.0	21.0	71.4
				Grand Total	588.9	0.0	588.9	19,821.7	806.5	20,628.2	2.8
9202-07-84	Brown	RECSTE / De Pere - Suamico / STH 29 RELOCATION USH 41 - CTH J	ELMSTAR ELECTRIC CORPORATION	Apprentice	0.0	0.0	0.0	734.0	0.0	734.0	0.0
				Journeyman	3.00	0.0	3.0	885.0	0.0	885.0	0.3
				Trainee	0.0	0.0	0.0	0.0	0.0	0.0	0.0
				Grand Total	3.0	0.0	3.0	1,619.0	0.0	1,619.0	0.1
9202-08-74	Brown	RECSTE / De Pere - Suamico / WIS 29 RELOCATION US 41-CTH J	RC EXCAVATING, INC.	Apprentice	0.0	0.0	0.0	16.8	0.0	16.8	0.0
				Journeyman	1.0	0.0	1.0	538.8	4.0	542.8	0.1
				Trainee	0.0	0.0	0.0	0.0	0.0	0.0	0.0
				Grand Total	1.0	0.0	1.0	555.6	4.0	559.6	0.1
9202-08-85	Brown	RECSTE / De Pere - Suamico / STH 29 RELOCATION US 41 CTH J	ZENITH TECH., INC. - WAUKESHA	Apprentice	222.5	0.0	222.5	2,029.5	48.5	2,078.0	10.7
				Journeyman	2,430.8	0.0	2,430.8	44,858.6	569.5	45,428.1	5.3
				Trainee	0.0	0.0	0.0	81.0	0.0	81.0	0.0
				Grand Total	2,653.3	0.0	2,653.3	46,969.1	618.0	47,587.1	5.5
9202-10-71	Brown	RSRF30 / Shawano - Green Bay / WCL-CTH J	NORTHEAST ASPHALT, INC	Apprentice	0.0	0.0	0.0	331.5	0.0	331.5	0.0
				Journeyman	109.3	0.0	109.3	13,504.0	116.8	13,620.8	0.8
				Trainee	0.0	0.0	0.0	0.0	0.0	0.0	0.0
				Grand Total	109.3	0.0	109.3	13,835.5	116.8	13,952.3	0.7
9231-07-70	Vilas	RCND10 / Woodruff - Lac Du Flambeau / WEST BOLTON LAKE LN - CTH D	INTEGRITY GRADING AND EXCAVATING, INC.	Apprentice	26.5	0.0	26.5	715.0	0.0	715.0	3.7
				Journeyman	3,402.7	165.0	3567.7	18,988.1	1,280.3	20,268.4	17.6
				Trainee	0.0	0.0	0.0	0.0	0.0	0.0	0.0
				Grand Total	3,429.2	165.0	3,594.2	19,703.1	1280.3	20,983.4	17.1
9231-08-70	Iron County	RSRF10 / Woodruff - Manitowish / LOWER SUGARBUSH LANE TO USH 51	AMERICAN ASPHALT OF WISCONSIN	Apprentice	45.0	0.0	45.0	805.5	0.0	805.5	5.5
				Journeyman	155.0	89.0	244.0	7,152.6	483.3	7,635.9	3.2
				Trainee	2.5	0.0	2.5	4.5	0.0	4.5	55.5
				Grand Total	202.5	89.0	291.5	7,962.6	483.3	8,445.9	3.4
9286-04-71	Brown	MISC / Village Hobart, CTH J / COUNTY LINE RD-HILLCREST DR	NORTHEAST ASPHALT, INC	Apprentice	0.0	0.0	0.0	5.5	0.0	5.5	0.0
				Journeyman	0.0	0.0	0.0	99.0	8.5	107.5	0.0
				Trainee	0.5	0.0	0.0	0.0	0.0	0.0	0.0
				Grand Total	0.0	0.0	0.0	104.5	8.5	113.0	0.0
Totals				TOTALS	31,818.1	1,533.6	33,351.7	1,138,055.9	34,447.4	1,172,507.3	2.3

Sometime in September 2018, an email was sent to one of the engineering firms who had been working on the mega projects, requesting a review of the WisDOT 2009-2012 Standard Specifications from the 441 Corridor Mega Projects. The purpose of the request is to obtain specific project IDs for the raze/removal/Clearing and Grubbing projects, verifying if the application of the NAHP was applied on these specific projects. These projects chosen were based on relevant information like the project locations, and if they were of a larger project like the 10-year mega project. After the communication was sent out a few days later, a response was received revealing these specific projects and stating: The engineering firm was not aware of the application of the NAHP in the Specials and provided the information of 4 project IDs used for the Razing and Removals on the 41 mega from 2009 to 2013.

- *9202-07-77*

- *9202-07-78*

- *9202-07-85*

- *9202-07-86*

This is important because these projects we also identified as projects located "on," "near," and "within a commutable distance" of a reservation. This is important because this information submitted has showed there were projects located within the criteria stated to implement the NAHP. It was not until after these projects were identified that the information was brought forward to the meeting, which was the purpose of showing directly the NAHP had not been implemented on these projects. The meeting scheduled was to address concerns resulting from this raised by multiple WisDOT representatives collectively working in extensive efforts, contacting, and scheduling numerous meetings to address the submission of multiple records requests and the concerns related to the analyzation of this information.

The following WisDOT Representatives were present: 1 representative from NETL, Labor Compliance Chief, DBE/Senior Labor Compliance Investigator, Labor Compliance Investigator, Labor Compliance Specialists, Labor Compliance Senior Records Coordinator, 2 from OBOEC, and tribal members of a TRIBE were all at WisDOT in the Northeast Regional Office who had discussed a number of concerns surrounding the records request of information submitted in May and August 2018. The next meeting was scheduled for October 2018. The meeting began with a discussion about the public records request and commenced when the WisDOT representatives had stated there was no information available from 48 projects, yet there is information for projects from as far back as 2004, which would include the timeframes mentioned. Previously it was mentioned that after 4 years this information was archived, but the request was submitted, and it reflected this was an inaccurate statement because there is information available longer than 4 years ago. The reason for this being brought to the surface is that some of these actual projects just happen to be located "on," "near," and "partially on" TRIBES' reservations. A perfect case of this is the information reviewed from the one mega project in Wisconsin. This project contains information relevant to the original general or public records requests dating back to 2015. This information was requested numerous times, but the WisDOT TA has said repeatedly: "There is little or no information," and "this information is not available." The Labor Compliance and DBE Program Manager then stated the reason this information was unavailable. It is because the WisDOT 41 Corridor Mega Projects were simply not picked for the NAHP to be applied to the projects. It was explained that this wasn't the reason the TRIBES had been denied the information, it was stated at recent meetings there was information available, but the TRIBES only get the information the way WISDOT wants to give the TRIBES this information. These statements were made by the WisDOT TA who had also specified the projects were from too long ago and had been archived, then shortly after the statement was amended to explain there is little or no information available. The Direct question was asked to the Labor Compliance and DBE Program Manager: "Why has the NAHP not been applied to these projects, as they meet the criteria of being located near and within the commutable distances of a TRIBE's reservation, because WisDOT does not have the authority to dictate which projects are selected for the application of the NAHP on any projects because the Provision should be applied to all projects which fall within the requirements stated above. This provision was established of the question asked to the WisDOT OGC, stating:

> *"Does the State of WisDOT have the legal authority to include and enforce TERO requirements as a WisDOT contractual requirement on any Federal-Aid Highway Program highway projects?" The WisDOT OGC responded with: "No, in brief, federal permission does not grant WisDOT legal authority to require such TERO[63] preferences on federally funded projects. There is no Wisconsin state statutory grant of authority to WisDOT to require TERO preferences. The rule of law in Wisconsin is that State agencies like WisDOT must find legal authority for a proposed action within the express or necessarily implied language of a statute. Any doubt is resolved in favor of the lack of legal authority."* [64]

The original intent of the NAHP was to promote economic opportunities with TRIBES with the goal aimed at working

---

63. Tribal Employment Rights Ordinances are not identical for all tribes. A TERO is a legislative act adopted by the governing body of a federally recognized tribe. In general, TEROs are a matter of tribal INTERNAL sovereignty. Tribes have authority to require private contractors to adhere to TERO ordinances on contracts with the tribe and as a condition of private contractor use of land over which a tribe has ample jurisdiction such as Indian trust land or restricted Indian land that is not subject to fee title alienation without the approval of the Federal Government.

64. Memo; February 27, 2012, page 1, WISDOT OGC response to WisDOT Secretary regarding TERO Preferences.

with TRIBES as equal partners focused on people economics and natural human environments to improve the quality of life for all people. This is done by the establishment of the Partnership Agreement, which was designed to acknowledge and support the government-to-government relationship and to support American Indian sovereignty. If any projects were located "on" or "partially on" the reservations, then the NAHP must be applied to these projects.

What is interesting is that in 1998, WisDOT had placed a Native American Hiring Preference on Federal Aid Projects located "on" or "near" Indian Lands. This required contractor(s) to make an aggressive, concentrated effort towards the employment of Native Americans. The reason for this is because it was stated by the WisDOT OGC that Wisconsin lacks the authority to implement TERO on projects and the common group was to establish the NAHP. To establish the EO#39, PA, NAHP MOU, MOA, IGA's, and any other agreements to enhance a positive government-to-government working relationship. Sometime in 2001, it was learned by the FHWA that TRIBES were not offered the opportunity to participate in Federal-aid highway programs offered through the state.

The Labor Compliance and DBE Program Manager representative spoke on the current mega projects across Wisconsin as one is currently still open and this information has not been archived, so this request of the NAHP TSTW labor information is still available because the provision predates one mega project as it has been around for so long. The question was once again asked: "Why has this provision been excluded from projects which are in accordance with the NAHP guidelines from 'on,' 'near,' 'partially on' and or 'within commutable distances' of a TRIBE's reservation? This project began in 2009 and was not completed until 2019, regardless of the numerous requests for this information and only told it is not available. The Labor Compliance and DBE Program Manager stated:

"We will be looking into this information as the project is still open and will send it over as soon as possible. Thanks for your insightful questions during the TLAC meeting. Next week when I return to the office, I will be setting up a meeting to discuss your reporting questions and needs. Are there any dates and times that work best for you between August 23 and August 31?"

Soon after this meeting, another meeting was scheduled in early October, but this meeting was not rescheduled until mid-November 2018. The following WisDOT representatives were present: 1 representative from TA, TLAC Coordinator, SETL, NETL, NETL Interim, NWTL, Statewide Tribal Liaison (SWTL), NCTL Investigations Lead (Statewide Investigations), SWI Labor Compliance Investigations (LCI), Eastern Unit Labor Compliance Lead (EULCU), Western Unit Labor Compliance Lead (WULCL), Labor Compliance Program Chief (LCPC), and invited 26 tribal members from 11 TRIBES, but only 2 TRIBES were present. This meeting scheduled by WisDOT is referenced to the recording and documentation processes used for the gathering of information for Tribal communities to learn the WisDOT reporting from our labor compliance team, as the agenda includes.

Agenda Items to be Discussed:

1) Introduction to WisDOT Reporting – Labor Compliance.

2) Types of Existing Labor Reports.

3) Review of Regional quarterly reports – labor data inclusive.

4) Open Discussion on Tribal Labor Data.

5) Review of DWD Labor Exchange data.

6) Annual Labor report for TLAC/Statewide.

With all the WisDOT representatives present and only one TRIBE at this meeting in reviewing this information it was stated numerous times there is no accurate way to track this information, but the real issue is "Accountability" because all of the information gathered and discussed was all through multiple requests sent to the WisDOT since 2015. This information is the same that the WisDOT TA has made clear there is little or no information for, or the information is available, but it is only available the way the WisDOT wants to give this information to the TRIBES. While this information has been requested there have been attempts to stall the release of it, or the submission of inaccurate documents. This can be shown through one of the requests that when it was previously stated this information is not available or it has been archived, then when the request was submitted and there were other projects which provided the information from the same period, which was stated to be "archived," all the information is available. It is apparent after this meeting, that it is the various WisDOT representatives who did not want any shape or form of accountability because the state has made so many attempts to discredit this information to be gathered and reported. The interesting fact is that this is the information presented from their projects, but they continue to misreport the information at quarterly and annual meetings and conferences to not just TRIBES, but Federal Agencies, State Agencies, and the public. This has continued to this day. Currently WisDOT still submits the information, which is inaccurate, thereby including the information from all projects across the state of Wisconsin and not just the NAHP-specific projects. The effect of the inaccurate information presented to not just the TRIBES, but to all agencies involved. It only helps to further eliminate the presence of TSTW on any WisDOT project directly showing the of honoring any agreements because this is the state and other agencies who neglect to supply the information as requested in the original 8-recommendations.

Shortly after these meetings, a few weeks later in October, the WisDOT DBE representative sent communications contained in an email reflecting the 41-project information, including the construction start and end dates of the mega project. This combination was received sometime towards the end of October, reflecting the information from projects located within the regions of the 41 Corridor Mega Project. Included in this was a list of all the projects on this mega project, showing the percentages of Tribal Skilled Trades workers on these projects and the percentages overall from Minorities, Native Americans, and others. This is a photo of the information requested of the active projects from one mega project, which started in 2009 and was not completed until 2020. In the top chart it shows the projects located in Winnebago County. In the second chart is all of the projects located within Brown County. Everything in both these charts shows they are all part of this one mega project.

Original Document sent from WisDOT DBE

Total Construction Contractor Employment Figures through August 31, 2018

Project Id	Description	Prime	Construction Contract Amount		Total Employees Head Count	Total Employees Work Hours	Women				Male Native Americans				Female Native Americans			
							Total Head Count	%	Total Work Hours	%	Total Head Count	%	Total Work Hours	%	Total Head Count	%	Total Work Hours	%
WINNEBAGO COUNTY																		
1120-09-71	Mainline US 45-Breezewood	Michels	$45,410,418	F	972	140,383.40	23	2.37%	3,462.80	2.47%	17	1.75%	3,272.50	2.33%	0	0.00%	0.00	0.00%
1120-09-72	Fencing 45 to CTH G	Century Fence	$441,219	F	15	1,272.50	0	0.00%	0.00	0.00%	1	6.67%	6.50	0.51%	0	0.00%	0.00	0.00%
1120-09-73	STH 114 Ramp Improvements	R & R Wash Materials	$383,651	F	82	2,447.50	4	4.88%	39.30	1.61%	0	0.00%	0.00	0.00%	0	0.00%	0.00	0.00%
1120-09-75	STH 76 Ramps	Michels	$3,153,472	F	272	12,231.50	13	4.78%	393.50	3.22%	9	3.31%	255.80	2.09%	0	0.00%	0.00	0.00%
1120-09-76	STH 26 - Breezewood Lane	Integrity Grading	$10,665,186	F	580	42,596.20	13	2.32%	708.80	1.66%	11	1.96%	809.50	1.90%	1	0.18%	88.50	0.21%
1120-09-79	Green Valley Rd & Dixie Rd	NEA	$969,655	F	108	1,579.30	9	8.33%	105.00	6.65%	3	2.78%	57.00	3.61%	0	0.00%	0.00	0.00%
1120-09-82	Wetland Mitigation Site	Mashuda Contractors	$1,200,000	F	41	5,807.50	7	17.07%	656.50	11.30%	0	0.00%	0.00	0.00%	0	0.00%	0.00	0.00%
1120-09-83	Breezewood Interchange	Michels	$27,456,950	F	837	121,723.80	27	3.23%	2,492.00	2.05%	14	1.67%	867.50	0.71%	0	0.00%	0.00	0.00%
1120-10-70	Salt Storage Facility-Oshkosh	Vinton	$1,324,093	F	128	3,927.10	5	3.91%	73.00	1.86%	2	1.56%	52.80	1.34%	0	0.00%	0.00	0.00%
1120-10-71	County K Overhead Overpass	Lunda	$2,226,889	F	173	10,849.70	0	0.00%	0.00	0.00%	1	0.58%	66.50	0.63%	0	0.00%	0.00	0.00%
1120-10-72	9th Avenue Interchange	Hoffman	$34,313,313	F	848	152,397.90	16	1.89%	2,246.30	1.47%	23	2.71%	5,721.50	3.75%	0	0.00%	0.00	0.00%
1120-10-74	Fencing WIS 44 to WIS 21	Century Fence	$284,745	F	4	698	0	0.00%	0.00	0.00%	1	25.00%	15.00	2.15%	0	0.00%	0.00	0.00%
1120-10-75	STH 44 Interchange Work	LaLonde Contractors	$314,678	F	59	1872.2	3	5.08%	116.00	6.20%	0	0.00%	0.00	0.00%	0	0.00%	0.00	0.00%
1120-10-76	STH 26 Crash Investigations	Vinton	$164,139	F	61	840.3	1	1.64%	13.50	1.61%	0	0.00%	0.00	0.00%	0	0.00%	0.00	0.00%
1120-10-78	WIS 26 - WIS 44 Mainline	Michels	$18,840,849	F	699	67,521.80	20	2.86%	1,942.80	2.88%	13	1.86%	1,495.80	2.22%	1	0.14%	193.00	0.29%
1120-10-81	Fencing WIS 26 - WIS 44	Century Fence	$239,280	F	4	700.00	0	0.00%	0.00	0.00%	1	25.00%	8.50	1.21%	0	0.00%	0.00	0.00%
1120-10-82	WIS 26 Intrchge Landscaping	Highway Landscapers	$192,415	F	25	872.50	7	28.00%	447.00	51.23%	0	0.00%	0.00	0.00%	0	0.00%	0.00	0.00%
1120-10-83	Lighting 9th Ave. Interchange	Outdoor Lighting Const.	$169,949	F	5	337.30	0	0.00%	0.00	0.00%	0	0.00%	0.00	0.00%	0	0.00%	0.00	0.00%
1120-10-84	STH 44 Median Work	Sommers Const.	$924,722	F	119	6,441.00	2	1.68%	268.30	4.17%	2	1.68%	47.00	0.73%	0	0.00%	0.00	0.00%
1120-10-85	Poberezny Road	NEA	$768,483	F	105	1,790.80	2	1.90%	44.50	2.48%	2	1.90%	22.50	1.26%	0	0.00%	0.00	0.00%
1120-11-71	Washburn St & Witzel Ave	LaLonde Contractors	$8,240,792	F	364	46,084.30	12	3.30%	1,351.80	2.93%	8	2.20%	613.00	1.33%	0	0.00%	0.00	0.00%
1120-11-72	Fountain Ave/Snell Rd (ARRA)	James Peterson	$3,900,000	F	342	17,683.60	12	3.51%	826.60	4.67%	7	2.05%	325.80	1.84%	0	0.00%	0.00	0.00%
1120-11-73	Fernau Ave, Snell Rd, & Stillman	Integrity Grading	$3,221,080	F	414	24,252.00	22	5.31%	675.30	2.78%	8	1.93%	252.80	1.04%	1	0.24%	18.00	0.07%
1120-11-74	Lake Butte Des Mortes (ARRA)	Hoffman	$15,295,973	F	742	83,973.50	32	4.31%	2,983.80	3.55%	14	1.89%	1,592.80	1.90%	0	0.00%	0.00	0.00%
1120-11-75	LBDM & 21 Interchange, WIM	Lunda	$54,180,900	F	795	194,509.70	14	1.76%	2,015.80	1.04%	17	2.14%	2,472.50	1.27%	1	0.13%	483.50	0.25%
1120-11-76	Fencing STH21-USH45	Century Fence	$149,104	F	6	602.50	0	0.00%	0.00	0.00%	1	16.67%	8.00	1.33%	0	0.00%	0.00	0.00%
1120-11-77	Razing/Removal	R & R Wash Materials	$522,853	F	24	2,033.50	1	4.17%	48.50	2.39%	0	0.00%	0.00	0.00%	0	0.00%	0.00	0.00%
1120-11-78	Razing/Removal	RLAM, Inc.	$277,291	F	22	598.80	1	4.55%	6.00	1.00%	2	9.09%	32.00	5.34%	0	0.00%	0.00	0.00%
1120-11-79	Razing/Removal	RLAM, Inc.	$96,038	F	28	782.50	1	3.57%	9.50	1.21%	1	3.57%	74.50	9.52%	0	0.00%	0.00	0.00%
1120-11-80	North Washburn Sidewalk	De Arteaga	$71,231	F	17	503.50	1	5.88%	8.00	1.59%	0	0.00%	0.00	0.00%	0	0.00%	0.00	0.00%
1120-11-81	Witzel Ave RAB & Street Lighting	Bodart Electric	$120,828	F	9	235.30	0	0.00%	0.00	0.00%	0	0.00%	0.00	0.00%	0	0.00%	0.00	0.00%
1120-11-83	USH 45 Interchange	Hoffman	$30,969,986	F	869	145,932.10	25	2.88%	5,265.30	3.61%	24	2.76%	5,204.50	3.57%	0	0.00%	0.00	0.00%
1120-11-88	USH 45 Interchange Landscaping	Highway Landscapers	$274,229	F	28	940.80	8	28.57%	286.00	30.40%	0	0.00%	0.00	0.00%	0	0.00%	0.00	0.00%
1120-11-89	LBDM Landscaping/Trail	Highway Landscapers	$1,451,590	F	87	5,086.60	7	8.05%	805.00	15.83%	1	1.15%	36.50	0.72%	0	0.00%	0.00	0.00%
6200-13-71	USH 45 & CTH T	Hoffman	$4,936,036	F	350	34,017.10	16	4.57%	1,369.50	4.03%	6	1.71%	549.00	1.61%	1	0.29%	55.50	0.16%
Winnebago County Subtotal			**$273,152,038**		**9,214**	**1,133,526.10**	**304**	**3.30%**	**28,660.40**	**2.53%**	**189**	**2.05%**	**23,861.80**	**2.11%**	**5**	**0.05%**	**838.50**	**0.07%**

Head count = # of employees on project, counted first time ss# entered on electronic payroll, counted once per project.

Female construction goal = 6.9% statewide

Minority Construction Goals: Winnebago County = .9%   Brown County = 1.3%   (based on 1970 census data)

Total Construction Contractor Employment Figures through August 31, 2018

CONNECTING WISCONSIN

Project Id	Description	Prime	Construction Contract Amount	NC-Asset Craft	Total Employees Head Count	Total Employees Work Hours	Women				Male Native Americans				Female Native Americans			
							Total Head Count	%	Total Work Hours	%	Total Head Count	%	Total Work Hours	%	Total Head Count	%	Total Work Hours	%
BROWN COUNTY																		
1133-03-70	Salt Storage Facility - Spirit Way	Peters Concrete	$1,052,748	F	115	3819.9	3	2.61%	4.00	0.10%	0	0.00%	0	0.00%	0	0.00%	0.00	0.00%
1133-03-71	US 41 and STH 29 Interchange	Hoffman	$96,912,405	F	1408	488,652.40	27	1.92%	8,633.80	1.77%	39	2.77%	20,588.00	4.21%	1	0.07%	141.50	0.03%
1133-03-72	Mason Street Interchange	Vinton	$29,540,517	F	697	125,978.40	20	2.87%	1,795.80	1.42%	14	2.01%	4,192.00	3.33%	0	0.00%	0.00	0.00%
1133-03-77	Oneida St Interchange, Mainline Glory to Mem	Lunda	$130,544,663	SC-PP	1310	538,878.40	59	4.50%	14,983.30	2.78%	21	1.60%	5,274.30	0.66%	0	0.00%	0.00	0.00%
1133-03-78	Lombardi Ave/CTH K Intchg	RC Excavators	$4,257,083	F	323	20,197.40	11	3.41%	825.50	4.09%	7	2.17%	286.30	1.42%	0	0.00%	0.00	0.00%
1133-03-79	Orange Ln to Larsen St	NEA	$7,158,398	F	309	21,847.10	7	2.27%	196.50	0.90%	3	0.97%	37.30	0.17%	0	0.00%	0.00	0.00%
1133-03-82	Early Structure/Early Fill; Beaver Dam	Hoffman	$38,198,943	F	842	185,860.60	24	2.85%	4,418.40	2.38%	37	4.39%	8,276.00	4.45%	1	0.12%	96.00	0.05%
1133-03-83	Steel Fabrication, Morris Ave-Memorial Drive	POM	$18,478,056	F	9	768.50	0	0.00%	0.00	0.00%	0	0.00%	0.00	0.00%	0	0.00%	0.00	0.00%
1133-03-88	Argonne Street Intersection	Vinton	$612,243	F	163	3,479.00	6	3.66%	117.50	3.38%	3	1.84%	46.80	1.40%	0	0.00%	0.00	0.00%
1133-04-73	STH 29 Landscaping	Arbor Green	$410,758	F	23	1,781.30	2	8.70%	26.00	1.46%	0	0.00%	0.00	0.00%	0	0.00%	0.00	0.00%
1133-04-75	Lambeau Street	Vinton	$451,154	F	166	2,673.80	7	4.17%	166.30	6.22%	4	2.38%	59.30	2.22%	0	0.00%	0.00	0.00%
1133-04-78	Clearing & Grubbing Phase 2	RC Excavators	$376,861	F	35	2,611.50	0	0.00%	0.00	0.00%	0	0.00%	0.00	0.00%	0	0.00%	0.00	0.00%
1133-04-80	Ninth Street Reconstruction	Vinton	$508,490	F	150	2,507.50	7	4.67%	75.00	2.96%	2	1.33%	9.30	0.37%	0	0.00%	0.00	0.00%
1133-04-88	Wick Drains	RC Excavators	$1,398,941	F	86	7,289.10	0	0.00%	0.00	0.00%	4	4.65%	557.30	7.65%	0	0.00%	0.00	0.00%
1133-06-70	Hemlock & Dutchman Crks Box Culverts	Ed Kraemer	$4,337,577	F	273	19,867.30	5	1.83%	739.30	3.72%	6	2.20%	156.50	0.79%	0	0.00%	0.00	0.00%
1133-06-71	Main Ave (CTH G) Intch; Orange-Glory Mainline	Michels Corp	$56,831,614	F	1158	260,493.40	35	3.02%	6,527.30	2.51%	17	1.47%	5,456.80	2.10%	1	0.09%	142.50	0.05%
1133-06-72	Scheuring Rd Interchange	Lunda	$14,703,942	F	582	74,057.40	13	2.23%	1,422.30	1.92%	20	3.44%	1,877.30	2.53%	0	0.00%	0.00	0.00%
1133-06-73	Depere-Suamico, Stormwater Detention Pond	Musson Bros	$1,028,388	F	97	7,387.00	4	4.12%	203.50	2.75%	10	10.31%	1,053.00	14.25%	0	0.00%	0.00	0.00%
1133-06-76	Shopko Detention Pond	Ed Gersek	$101,286	F	35	495.80	2	5.71%	13.50	2.72%	2	5.71%	12.50	2.52%	0	0.00%	0.00	0.00%
1133-06-77	Mid Valley Drive Realignment	Vinton	$1,358,986	F	273	6,971.30	9	3.30%	178.80	2.56%	6	2.20%	63.50	0.91%	0	0.00%	0.00	0.00%
1133-06-78	Lighting Scheuring Road	Elmstar Electric	$86,957	F	7	177.50	0	0.00%	0.00	0.00%	0	0.00%	0.00	0.00%	0	0.00%	0.00	0.00%
1133-06-83	Main Ave Lighting	Bodart Electric	$97,846	F	11	143.80	0	0.00%	0.00	0.00%	0	0.00%	0.00	0.00%	0	0.00%	0.00	0.00%
1133-06-85	Scheuring Rd TMP	Elmstar Electric	$95,529	F	25	673.50	1	4.00%	11.50	1.71%	1	4.00%	1.50	0.22%	0	0.00%	0.00	0.00%
1133-06-87	Fencing, Orange to Glory Rd	Century Fence	$191,353	F	8	566.50	0	0.00%	0.00	0.00%	0	0.00%	0.00	0.00%	0	0.00%	0.00	0.00%
1133-06-88	Grant Street Reconstruction	Vinton	$557,731	F	158	2,594.80	4	2.53%	45.50	1.75%	2	1.27%	47.50	1.83%	0	0.00%	0.00	0.00%
1133-09-72	Glory Rd Bridge	Zenith Tech	$2,356,284	F	166	13,501.70	2	1.20%	11.50	0.09%	2	1.20%	81.00	0.60%	0	0.00%	0.00	0.00%
1133-09-80	STH 172 Landscaping System Intchg	Highway Landscapers	$208,811	F	16	531.50	4	25.00%	313.00	58.89%	0	0.00%	0.00	0.00%	0	0.00%	0.00	0.00%
1133-10-71	Memorial Dr - Duck Crk NB I-43 Intchg	Hoffman	$31,104,303	F	516	108,421.00	17	3.29%	3,384.00	3.12%	8	1.55%	4,635.00	4.28%	0	0.00%	0.00	0.00%
1133-10-72	Lineville Road Interchange	Michels Corp	$29,414,291	F	790	108,095.00	32	4.05%	2,531.00	2.34%	12	1.52%	1,296.70	1.20%	1	0.13%	8.50	0.01%
1133-10-74	Lakeview Drive	Vinton	$3,324,127	F	281	16,322.30	9	3.20%	915.30	5.61%	9	3.20%	174.30	1.07%	1	0.36%	390.00	2.39%
1133-10-75	Velp Ave/USH 41 Intchg	Hoffman	$49,224,780	SC	756	167,471.60	25	3.31%	7,689.90	4.59%	13	1.72%	3,822.30	2.28%	0	0.00%	0.00	0.00%
1133-10-80	Beaver Dam BC, Island/Lone CDS, Velp Ave	Hoffman	$6,977,212	F	369	32,861.30	9	2.44%	732.30	2.23%	11	2.98%	1,401.30	4.26%	0	0.00%	0.00	0.00%
1133-10-84	N Segment Raze & Removal Ph 1	Ostrenga Excavating	$127,231	F	31	823.30	0	0.00%	0.00	0.00%	0	0.00%	0.00	0.00%	0	0.00%	0.00	0.00%
1133-11-74	IH 43 Early Structure/Early Fill	Lunda	$61,506,426	F	661	249,974.20	11	1.66%	3,816.00	1.53%	14	2.12%	3,985.50	1.59%	0	0.00%	0.00	0.00%
9202-07-72	CTH RK (S Frontage Rd) NW	Relyco, Inc.	$3,613,191	F	308	16,879.70	9	2.92%	586.00	3.10%	17	5.52%	613.00	3.25%	0	0.00%	0.00	0.00%
9202-07-73	CTH EB Ramps, Duck Crk Bridges	Hoffman	$18,357,167	F	725	78,949.90	20	2.76%	2,870.00	3.64%	23	3.17%	3,915.80	4.96%	1	0.14%	183.00	0.24%
9202-07-74	Shawano Ave/Taylor St	Vinton	$3,292,875	F	358	20,657.70	9	2.51%	806.50	3.90%	7	1.96%	588.90	2.85%	0	0.00%	0.00	0.00%
9202-07-77	Raze and Removal Phase 1	Ostrenga Excavating	$338,088	F	37	1,375.30	1	2.70%	9.30	0.68%	1	2.70%	47.80	3.48%	0	0.00%	0.00	0.00%
9202-07-78	Raze and Removal Phase 2	Peters Concrete	$125,298	F	56	1,301.80	2	3.57%	19.50	1.50%	0	0.00%	0.00	0.00%	0	0.00%	0.00	0.00%
9202-07-81	Clearing & Grubbing Phase 1	RC Excavators	$273,379	F	25	1,550.60	3	12.00%	13.30	0.86%	0	0.00%	0.00	0.00%	0	0.00%	0.00	0.00%
9202-07-84	Packerland/Dousman/Shawano Temp Signals	Elmstar Electric	$515,918	F	19	1,619.00	0	0.00%	0.00	0.00%	1	5.26%	3.00	0.19%	0	0.00%	0.00	0.00%
9202-07-85	Raze and Removal Phase 3	Stone Creek	$166,312	F	9	619.30	0	0.00%	0.00	0.00%	2	22.22%	135.80	21.93%	0	0.00%	0.00	0.00%
9202-07-86	Raze & Removal Phase 4	Peters Concrete	$48,825	F	21	120.30	0	0.00%	0.00	0.00%	0	0.00%	0.00	0.00%	0	0.00%	0.00	0.00%
9202-07-88	STH 29 Fencing; Shawano Ave Landscp & Bk	Hwy Landscapers	$659,273	F	62	1,866.80	5	8.06%	310.50	16.63%	0	0.00%	0.00	0.00%	0	0.00%	0.00	0.00%
9202-08-72	Dousman Street Obliteration	RC Excavators	$86,243	F	22	495.00	1	4.55%	5.80	1.17%	2	9.09%	88.30	17.64%	0	0.00%	0.00	0.00%
9202-08-73	Pamperin Pk Old Rd Obliteration; Shawano & E	Vinton	$214,677	F	104	1,093.50	2	1.92%	6.00	0.55%	1	0.96%	1.00	0.09%	0	0.00%	0.00	0.00%
9202-08-74	Obliterations	RC Excavators	$125,027	F	65	564.50	1	1.54%	4.00	0.71%	1	1.54%	1.00	0.18%	0	0.00%	0.00	0.00%
9202-08-77	Shawano Ave Landscaping & Trail	Vinton	$186,660	F	48	509.00	0	0.00%	0.00	0.00%	1	2.08%	1.80	0.35%	0	0.00%	0.00	0.00%
9202-08-78	Pamerin Park Trail	Peters Concrete	$201,660	F	43	1,047.50	1	2.33%	17.50	1.70%	0	0.00%	0.00	0.00%	0	0.00%	0.00	0.00%
9202-08-79	CTH EB/CNRR Grading & Culverts	Radtke Contractors	$510,652	F	77	2,254.80	0	0.00%	0.00	0.00%	1	1.30%	1.30	0.06%	0	0.00%	0.00	0.00%
9202-08-80	Elmhurst Ave Extension	Vinton	$1,734,371	F	262	7,654.30	8	3.05%	405.30	5.30%	3	1.15%	141.00	1.84%	0	0.00%	0.00	0.00%
9202-08-83	Freedom Mitigation Site	Relyco, Inc.	$448,258	F	34	1,146.80	2	5.88%	138.00	12.03%	0	0.00%	0.00	0.00%	0	0.00%	0.00	0.00%
9202-08-85	CTH RK, West & CTH J, J Underpass	Zenith Tech	$9,997,759	F	557	47,587.10	14	2.51%	618.00	1.30%	19	3.41%	2,653.30	5.58%	0	0.00%	0.00	0.00%
	Brown County Subtotal		$633,209,668		14,683	2,667,058.00	433	2.95%	65,576.80	2.46%	346	2.36%	71,588.30	2.68%	6	0.04%	971.80	0.04%

Head count = # of employees on project, counted first time ss# entered on electronic payroll, counted once per project.

Women construction goal = 6.9% statewide

Minority Construction Goals: Winnebago County = .9%   Brown County = 1.3% (based on 1970 census data)

Total Construction Contractor Employment Figures through August 31, 2018

CONNECTING WISCONSIN

10% Minority Aspirational Goal

	Construction Contract Amount	Total Employees Head Count	Total Employees Work Hours	Total Head Count	%	Total Work Hours	%	Total Head Count	%	Total Work Hours	%
				Women				Minorities and Native Americans			
Brown & Winnebago	$906,361,705	23,897	3,800,584	737	3.08%	94,237.20	2.48%	1,674	7.01%	241,194.90	6.35%

Head count = # of employees on project, counted first time ss# entered on electronic payroll, counted once per project.

Women construction goal = 6.9% statewide

Minority Construction Goals: Winnebago County = .9%   Brown County = 1.3% (based on 1970 census data)

he percentages of Native Americans were Male and Female and no Minorities were included except in the total

Total Construction Contractor Employment Figures through August 31, 2018

CONNECTING WISCONSIN

	Construction Contract Amount	Total Employees Head Count	Total Employees Work Hours	Total Head Count	%	Total Work Hours	%	Total Head Count	%	Total Work Hours	%	Total Head Count	%	Total Work Hours	%
				Women				Monority and Native Americans Male				Native AmericanFemale			
Brown & Winnebago	$906,361,705	23,897	3,800,584	737	3.08%	94,237.20	2.48%	1,674	7.01%	97,260.40	2.56%				
				Women				Native Americans Male				Native AmericansFemale			
Brown	$633,209,667.67	14,683	2,667,058	433	2.95%	65,576.80	2.46%	346	2.36%	71,588.30	2.68%	6	0.041%	971.8	0.036%
Winnebago	$273,152,038	9,214	1,133,526	304	3.30%	28,660.40	2.53%	189	2.05%	23,861.80	2.11%	5	0.054%	838.5	0.074%
Totals	$906,361,705	23,897	3,800,584	737	3.12%	94,237.20	2.49%	535	2.20%	95,450.10	2.39%	11	0.048%	1810.3	0.055%
Total M & F		24,634	3,894,821	Women NA added				11	0.048%	1810.3	0.055%				
				Total NA Male & Female				546	2.25%	97,260.40	1.22%				

Head count = # of employees on project, counted first time ss# entered on electronic payroll, counted once per project.

Women construction goal = 6.9% statewide

Minority Construction Goals: Winnebago County = .9%   Brown County = 1.3% (based on 1970 census data)

This is the formula used to get the average amount of workers in a tentative 32-week construction season for TSTW

BROWN COUNTY 72,560.10/352 =206.13/32=6.44 hours per week for the 352 TSTW in Brown County. This is only 1 year; we need to break it down for the past 10 years.

Equation: Total Tribal Hours/Total Tribal Headcount = 206.13 hours per person/32 Weeks Tentative construction season =6.44 hours per week. /10 years totaling .65 hours per week in a 32-week construction season for the 352 TSTW.

WINNEBAGO COUNTY 24,700.30/194=127.32/32=3.9 hours per week for the 194 TSTW in Winnebago County. This is only 1 year; we need to break it down for the past 10 years.

Equation: Total Tribal Hours/Total Tribal Headcount=127.32 hours per person/32 Weeks Tentative construction season= 3.9 hours per week/10 years totaling .39 hours per week in a 32-week construction season for the 194 TSTW.

The total percentage of Non-tribal vs. tribal hours on the 41-Corridor Mega Project located "On," "Near," and "within commutable Distance" of reservations from 2009 to 2018

Hours Worked

Current

Non Tribal Men & Women
3,894,822
Hours Worked
98.26%

Total Tribal
Men & Women
97,260.40
Hours Worked
1.74%

The thing to notice on the Brown and Winnebago information is it is combined. The participation of Native Americans and Minorities is also combined, thereby inflating the percentages up to 6.35%. This is where this information was overlooked in the original report, when this was submitted but an email was quickly submitted stating the concerns of the report created a few days later. At the time of the request for the information, the information specifically stated the Native American participation in these projects, but when it was submitted by the WisDOT Labor Compliance and DBE Program Manager, the information contained Native Americans and Minorities. The information requested was for the NAHP Project-Specific, including the total hours and the total hours of TSTW, but when this information was provided, an email was sent regarding these discrepancies and a request for some clarification because there was an allocated amount that had not been identified.

When looking at the employee labor headcounts from Brown County, the subtotal is 14,683 and the total number of Employee Headcounts allocated for the sheets provided is 1,867, which have been allocated for the sheet you have presented but there are 12,807 which have not been accounted for on this document. The 12,807 are documented as Caucasian and other minority workers. Analyzing the employee work hours from the Brown County subtotal is 2,667,058 and the total number of hours allocated, which is documented on this sheet, is a total of 319,674.10 leaving the amount of 2,347,383.90 which has not been allocated. These 2,347,383.90 hours are documented as Caucasian and other minority workers. Is there an explanation addressing the numbers which have not been accounted for on your spreadsheet with a large percentage of numbers having no justification? Are the women included along with the minorities and Native Americans, because there is no information on any non-minority women or Native Americans? What would these people be listed as, as this is a pretty large number? The women are included as minorities or Native Americans if they are both. Non-minorities are included in the totals. In closing the Senior Labor Compliance Investigator Labor Compliance Specialist WIS 441 Project WisDOT OBOEC, made a direct statement that the state was picking and choosing which projects they work on implementing the NAHP. This was brought up because it was asked if there was a total of over $906,361,705 for the projects and how much they were able to obtain, and it was at this point the WisDOT OBOEC representative stated the NAHP was not picked for these projects. It was then explained to the OBOEC Representative WisDOT does not have the authority to pick and choose which projects the NAHP shall be applied to as this NAHP was created to use the WisDOT was not implementing the Indian Preference or TERO. To allow WisDOT to proceed forward doing this has directly excluded the TRIBES from obtaining any portion of over $906,361,705 since 2009-2018, and not only that they have directly excluded Native American tribes from working on projects located on or near the Reservations. In the WisDOT Reporting that has transpired since 2009 until 2018, the Wisconsin Department of Transportation has been reporting these inaccurate numbers to the Construction Industry, Labor representatives, Unions, all Citizens and taxpayers, Federal Agencies, and TRIBES as WisDOT is reporting a 6.35%. The actual numbers from all these projects were 5.13% lower than reported for all of the entities mentioned above.

The Next TLAC meeting took place shortly after this. The following WisDOT representatives were present: 1 representative from TA, SETL, NETL, NWTL, SETL, SWTL, and Labor Compliance Program Chief, 3 Labor Compliance Specialists, and there are no meeting minutes of who attended this meeting, but there were emails sent to 21 tribal members of the TRIBES. This was the point where the meeting minutes were deleted, and this is also the point when the Closed-door sessions were also removed. The reason for this was requested. The TLAC Coordinator was dismissive and said the TRIBE with the IGA is not paying for the donuts and coffee or the space for that time. It was then asked if this was the decision of the whole TLAC Group or the decision of the Tribe who has the IGA. The TLAC Coordinator stated they were not going to get into this discussion right now.

The next topic for this meeting was the training for the TSTW, It was stated there was the OSHA 30-Hour General Industry training, which would be available. This was concerning because the WisDOT TL explained this training was adequate for the TSTW and there were no differences from the OSHA 30-Hour Construction. OSHA 30-Hour Construction teaches you a series of components that may potentially save your life on construction sites, and this is something that only those who have worked in the field would know. A show of hands was asked for how many have worked in the Construction/ Transportation industry. There were only 2 to 3 hands that were raised. The Construction Contractors were one of the hands and a TLAC Member was an OSHA 30 Construction card holder and has been in carpenter and Millwrighting. It was concerning that people who had never worked in the industry were trying to develop training when they never worked on a construction site, so they were completely unaware and oblivious to what takes place on these projects. When this was brought forward, this then put the TSTW at a high risk and now became liabilities because they did not receive adequate training and have the potential to injure themselves or someone around them.

After making this statement, the WisDOT TL stated there were few differences between the two OSHAs and that it would not affect the hiring of TSTW. This is when the CI contractor then spoke up and stated this was inaccurate and he was also concerned about the inadequate training. He then explained that the TLAC Member was accurate and agreed with the statement of the TSTW then becoming high risk, a liability on these projects and they would not hire them if adequate training wasn't provided. Below is a copy of the two OSHA 30-hour General industry and Construction trainings:

30-Hour General Industry

- Introduction to OSHA
- Managing Safety and Health
- Walking and Working Surfaces including Fall Protection
- Exit Routes, Emergency Action Plans, Fire Prevention Plans and Fire Protection
- Electrical
- Personal Protective Equipment
- Materials Handling
- Hazard Communication
- Hazardous Materials (Flammable and Combustible Liquids, Spray Finishing, Compressed Gasses, Dipping and Coating Operations)
- Permit Required Confined Spaces
- Lockout / Tagout
- Machine Guarding
- Welding, Cutting, and Brazing
- Introduction to Industrial Hygiene
- Bloodborne Pathogens
- Ergonomics
- Safety and Health Programs
- Fall Protection
- Powered Industrial Vehicles

30-Hour Construction

- Introduction to OSHA
- Managing Safety and Health
- Falls
- Electrocution
- "Struck-by " Hazards
- "Caught-In or Between" Hazards
- Personal Protective Equipment
- Health Hazards in Construction
- Stairways and Ladders
- Concrete & Masonry Construction
- Confined Space Entry
- Cranes, Derricks, Hoists
- Elevators & Conveyors
- Ergonomics
- Excavations
- Fire Prevention Plans & Fire Protection
- Materials Handling, Storage, Use & Disposal
- Motor Vehicles, Mechanized Equipment & Marine Operations
- Rollover Protective Structures & Overhead Protection
- Signs, Signals, and Barricades
- Powered Industrial Vehicles
- Safety and Health Programs
- Scaffolds
- Steel Erection
- Tools- Hand and Power
- Welding and Cutting

The next issue was the discussion of the baseline survey, which had not been completed as requested, which was to send this baseline survey out in mid-spring/summer. It was explained numerous times that there is a certain time of the year when it is best to release the surveys, because, without people from the industry able to voice their processes or concerns, it will be difficult to get any real quantifiable data. The WisDOT TA was told there is a small window right after the holidays, which is the best time to submit this survey to the contractors to do this. This was not considered and only resulted in more unquantifiable results.

The discussion of the Heavy Equipment training scheduled for the fall. Many of the people from the WisDOT do not even have experience in the field to understand the best times to hold training, 32-week tentative construction seasons, schedules of busy times/slow times, how to obtain a baseline assessment from the CI, to utilize the tools available within WisDOT, or to release a qualitative baseline assessment.

The original Baseline Assessment consisted of 16 contractors, and only 6 of them with useful information. Those contractors were the contractors who were contacted by one of the TLAC members directly, asking the contractors to fill out the assessment. The WisDOT TA tried to push this Baseline Assessment forward even after it was explained that is not even 1/32 of the CI, and there are over 76 Contractors who have worked in the industry in 2017. The first recommendation was for the WisDOT and TLAC Coordinator representatives to go to the Wisconsin Transportation Builders Association Conference to hand out surveys, thereby encompassing the whole CI. The Engineers, Contractors, Consultant firms, and Contractors who help establish the WisDOT Budgets for the industry are all present at these conferences. This was never followed up on in 2016 or even 2017, even when mentioned to do this in August, and everyone from the TLAC and WisDOT had agreed for this to be done. In 2016, TLAC members mentioned utilizing the list of contractors who were awarded the contracts for 2016 or 2017 as a second option. This would help establish a solid baseline of not only contractors but also establish a baseline of minimum requirements. It is now going into 2019 and these recommendations still have not been addressed. This information has the potential to help define the training needed based on the upcoming project's locations and the need for enhanced training if needed. If this was set for February-March, which is the best time for scheduling these trainings because the TSTW will be able to obtain a position in the spring when the season takes off, and work through the whole season. Because these recommendations were not acknowledged going on the third year, this only yielded 12 participants, all without a position after graduating their Heavy Equipment operating and no contractors lined up following the award of certifications with possible opportunities available, and the new students were without work for almost 6 months.

The next part of the discussion was the information given to a TLAC member. This information given was the 41-Corridor Mega Projects from 2009 through 2018 presented earlier. The State of Alaska and its people forever disclaim all right and title in or to any property belonging to the United States or subject to its disposition, and not granted or confirmed to the State or its political subdivisions, by or under the act admitting Alaska to the Union. The State and its people further disclaim all right or title in or to any property, including fishing rights, the right or title to which may be held by or for any Indian, Eskimo, or Aleut, or community thereof, as that right or title is defined in the act of admission. The State and its people agree that, unless otherwise provided by Congress, the property, as described in this section, shall remain subject to the absolute disposition of the United States. They further agree that no taxes will be imposed upon any such property, until otherwise provided by the Congress. This tax exemption shall not apply to property held by individuals in fee without restrictions on alienation. Let's not forget the direct statement by the former WisDOT OBOEC/current TLAC Coordinator and the WisDOT TA attempts to stall a TLAC representative from receiving this information. This information is only now being viewed for the first time by the TLAC Representatives. WisDOT TL spoke up stating there have been words put in the state's mouth and tried to discredit the information by stating this information has been previously litigated. It was explained the WisDOT Labor Compliance had just released the information in September. The CI asked how the TLAC Member knew this information was released previously. It wasn't then explained the history of when this information had been originally requested dating back to 2014 and the WisDOT TA has stated numerous times the information is not available, there is no information, there is limited information, there is information, but you only get the information the way the state will give the information. Another denied a public records request had been received, and it was refiled again for another request with the WisDOT Records Coordinator in August 2018, where it was stated, this would only cost between $256 and $320. When this information was received, this is the information that was brought forward but only more detailed from the WisDOT Labor Compliance.

Every time any questions are brought forward regarding data for the NAHP, they are swept under the rug, and it is stated, "What do we need to do to keep moving forward?" It is often pushed back by the WisDOT representatives and the WisDOT would begin to talk in a demeaning tone, becoming upset, and lashing out in hopes to discredit members of the TLAC and ITTF Meetings. This transpired in numerous meetings with the presence of many of the TRIBES, including Tribal Leadership, and their Labor representatives, Bureau of Indian Affairs, FHWA, WisDOT, and BOA employees and coworkers.

These issues still have not been addressed regarding what has transpired in the past. It is not just because of WisDOT, but it is some of the TRIBES that are equally responsible, because when these issues are brought to light, they are dismissed, and a direct statement is made: "What do we need to do to keep moving forward?" Rather than addressing the issues it was TRIBE'S leadership who made this statement, only to continue with sweeping this stuff under the rug versus dealing with the issues. It is quite evident if these issues are not acknowledged and addressed it is very difficult to move forward for the betterment of the TRIBES and their communities. All this information is based on the Legal Opinions commonly referred to by WisDOT from the WisDOT OGC stating that WisDOT and the State do not have the authority to enforce a provision they are not honoring and are only trying to elevate accountability of the WisDOT, with the blatant circumvention of the NAHP on projects for the past 10 years. This was created to help provide opportunities for TSTW workers to do the opposite. It is with the greatest importance to address all the issues associated with the NAHP, and it is once again my recommendation to push for the negotiation towards the Indian Preference and or TERO as it is the Eleven Federally Recognized Tribes' Inherent Rights as Sovereign Nations. This was created to help promote Self-Government and Economic Stability within the Tribal Communities.

In the State's arguments, the federal permission does not grant WisDOT legal authority to require such TERO Preferences on Federally funded projects. There is no Wisconsin state statutory grant of authority to WisDOT to require TERO preferences. The rule of law in Wisconsin is that State agencies like WisDOT must find legal authority for a proposed action within the express or necessarily implied language of a statute. Any doubt is resolved in favor of the lack of legal authority. Wisconsin has not proved the ability or law to do so within the boundaries of reservations. It is not the State of Wisconsin's right as the State of Wisconsin's Constitution was only adopted in 1848. Wisconsin does not possess the binding authority over the TRIBES to dictate what the Tribes can implement or not implement within the confines of their Indian lands. This information provided is first brought forward through the analysis of the Legal opinion from the WisDOT OGC you will read about in the next chapter.

Chapter 14

Analysis of WisDOT OGC
Legal Opinion

After a comprehensive analysis of the two responses presented, the most important facts selected two completely different interpretations, but were made on the same day and by the same person. One statement was transcribed as meeting minutes and did not have any backing or legal citations, while the second was a very detailed response that had citations, and referenced case litigations, and the federal code of law as well. Scrutinizing each response will help to show the negative impact on the TRIBES regarding the establishment of provisions as it impacts the economic opportunities for their communities. It is important to the function of IP or TERO to have these responses overturned because of the detrimental impact on the TRIBES communities. The decision of anyone other than the TRIBES to implement these IPs as long as they are grounded in their inherent sovereign status. This is the most rudimentary principle of Indian law and is reinforced by a host of Supreme Court decisions.

Consider this question in the context provided by WisDOT's first response, which was an oral response: Do the TRIBES have the ability to implement IP or TERO? His first response seems to indicate the following:

- *WisDOT does not have the statutory authority, and the federal government doesn't require the enforcement of hiring preference.*

- *(That does not mean that the Tribes cannot require it.)*

- *They (The Tribes) can require it on their reservations and lands in trust for the benefit of their members.*

- *If WisDOT has a contract that requires being on Tribal land, (WisDOT) cannot go on Tribal land without their permission and compliance.*

- *You (WisDOT) must comply in that instance, but it's not WisDOT that's requiring it, but the Tribe.*

- *This has been the Policy for the past 20 years.*

- *Transportation alliance in the treaties indicates that some state trunk highways on reservation/Tribal lands belong to the state for transportation purposes, and thus Tribes would not be able to apply hiring preference in those instances.*

From the meeting minutes at the TLAC meeting, WisDOT OGC made a direct statement that, "WisDOT lacks statutory authority, and the federal government doesn't require the enforcement of hiring preference.[65] This does not mean that the TRIBES cannot require it. They can require it on their reservations and lands in trust for the benefit of their members." This is correct as it is the responsibility of the TRIBES to enforce the IP and TERO, but WisDOT OGC fails to mention this is applicable on any project located on, near, or as defined within a commutable distance.[66] "*Roads 'near' an Indian reservation are defined as those within a reasonable commuting distance from the reservation.*"[67]

The WisDOT OGC proceeds to assert: "*If WisDOT has a contract that requires being on Tribal land, (WisDOT) cannot go on Tribal*

---

65. Memo; February 27, 2012, page 1, WISDOT OGC response to WisDOT Secretary regarding TERO Preferences.

66. The U.S. Equal Employment Opportunity Commission https://www.eeoc.gov/policy/docs/indian_preference.html

67. Indian Employment Preference on Federal-aid Projects https://www.fhwa.dot.gov/construction/cqit/indian.cfm

land without their permission and compliance. You (WisDOT) must comply in that instance, but it's not DOT, that's requiring it, but the TRIBES." The explanation makes it clear that WisDOT does not hold any authority or jurisdiction to work on projects located on or near because of the mentioned comment above. This would be forthcoming to review the process as stated by the FHWA: "Indian Reference in Employment on Federal-Aid Highway Projects on and near Indian Reservations."[68] As stated in its purpose which pronounces: "To consolidate all previous guidance for FHWA field officials, State Highway Agencies, and their sub-recipients and contractors regarding the allowance for IP in employment on projects on and *near* Indian reservations."[69] the final component presented in the last statement *"as this decision has been the process for over twenty (20) years,"* meaning nothing in this statement is not subject to change or, it does not mean that this process cannot be challenged or amended.

In conclusion, the final component of the statement that documented WisDOT's OGC said: "Transportation alliance in the treaties indicates that some state trunk highways on the reservation/Tribal lands belong to the state for transportation purposes, and thus TRIBES would not be able to apply hiring preference in those instances. Request for a copy of the 1854 treaty, which addresses transportation alliance." Further examination and an in-depth review of treaties revealed that it was the *Chippewa September 30, 1854;10 Stats.,1109; Ratified Jan. 10, 1855, Proclaimed Jan. 29, 1855.* The treaty proclaimed the only language related to the state trunk highways on the reservation/tribal lands stated: "All necessary roads, highways, and railroads, the lines of which may run through any of the

---

68. Indian Reference in Employment on Federal-Aid Highway Projects on and Near Indian Reservations https://www.fhwa.dot.gov/legsregs/directives/notices/n4720-7.cfm

69. Indian Reference in Employment on Federal-Aid Highway Projects on and Near Indian Reservation; Guidance, Section A https://www.fhwa.dot.gov/legsregs/directives/notices/n4720-7.cfm

reserved tracts, shall have the right of way through the same, compensation being made therefor as in other cases."[70] There is no direct statement that confers the ownership of lands to the state of Wisconsin or DOT. It is only through an act of Congress that can change the defining of boundaries.

In a more succinct assessment of the meeting minutes response, there was a lack or presence of citations or direct links that backed up any of the assertions made. It is important to ask the right questions. "Do the TRIBES have the ability to implement IP or TERO?" This question does not require any response from the WisDOT. The TRIBES maintain the sovereign rights to implement the IP or TERO as long as they are grounded in their inherent sovereign status. This is the most rudimentary principle of Indian law and is reinforced by a host of Supreme Court decisions, as stated earlier. WisDOT's positions seem in conflict with this principle as WisDOT has erroneously defined the scope of the projects as not falling within the boundaries that would invoke NAHP. The authority to define those parameters lies with the tribe and Congress, not with the state.

The legal opinion presented will necessitate a more in-depth analysis. The principal statement to take away from the first response is that "it is clear the WisDOT lacks the authority relevant to the application of IP and TERO as it is related to any jurisdictional rules or laws related to TRIBES. The TRIBES maintain the sovereign rights to implement the IP or TERO if they are grounded in its inherent sovereign status. This legitimate canon is the most rudimentary principle of Indian law and is reinforced by a host of Supreme Court decisions." This will be referred to as the "Meeting Minutes rebuttal," because it will be brought forward multiple times.

The opinion was prepared by WisDOT's OGC in advance and was intended to be distributed to the TLAC on Monday,

70. 1854 Treaty with the Chippewa; Article 3, https://files.dnr.state.mn.us/aboutdnr/laws_treaties/1854/treaty1854.pdf

February 27, 2012. The TLAC meeting was established some-time in the fall of 2011, with the directives to explore alternative methods to support and develop Native American labor opportunities on WisDOT and BOA Projects. TLAC is composed of representatives from the TRIBES, Unions, WisDOT Staff, and CI. The WisDOT OGC stated the responses supplemented the previous legal opinion which came to the same conclusion on August 04, 2008, but neglected to present any relevant information to support this statement. WisDOT has neglected to respond to the request for this information.

WisDOT OGC's legal opinion presented a response to the questions asked by the TRIBES. The first response was significantly different than the second response. The second question being asked states: "Does WisDOT have the legal authority to include and enforce TERO requirements as a WisDOT contractual requirement on any FHWA Program highway projects?" Asking a question, one must be careful with the context and wording of how the question is to be asked. The manner of how this question was being asked suggested there is more than one question being asked. This question presents multiple requests that require multiple responses. Here are the questions that were asked:

- *"Does WisDOT have the legal authority to include TERO requirements as a WisDOT contractual requirement on any Federal-Aid Highway Program projects?"*

- *"Does WisDOT have the legal authority to enforce TERO as a WisDOT contractual requirement on any Federal-Aid Highway Program projects?"*

The adequate response to the question would be, "Yes" because it is through coordination with Tribes and WisDOT as stated, in the process for the "Indian Preference in Employment on Federal-Aid Highway Projects on and near Indian Reservations; Classification code N 4720.7, March 15, 1993."[71] It clearly defines

---

71. Indian Reference in Employment on Federal-Aid Highway Projects on and Near

a process. Based on the pertinent information, The FHWA field offices were to encourage States to meet with Indian tribes and TERO to develop contract provisions for Federal-aid highway projects that would promote employment opportunities for Indians on reservations. Section C was amended in the background to include Section 140(d) of Title 23, U.S.C., and was amended by Section 1026 of the Intermodal Surface Transportation Efficiency Act of 1991 (ISTEA) to include that: "States may implement a preference for employment of Indians on projects carried out under this title *near* Indian reservations."[72]

The examination of the second part of the question asked by the TRIBES: "*Does WisDOT have the Legal authority to enforce TERO as a WisDOT contractual requirement on any Federal-Aid Highway Program projects?*" The rebuttal to this is: "The Indian employment preference applies to all Federal-aid projects on or near Indian reservations and within a commutable distance. A state may implement the preference on applicable Federal-aid contracts but is not required to do so."[73] However, it is not the responsibility of the WisDOT to enforce TERO. It is the state's responsibility to negotiate and work with the tribes as well when implementing the IP and TERO in any Federal-Aid Highway Program projects. In analyzing WisDOT's OGC legal opinion's articulating: "No. In brief, federal permission does not grant WisDOT legal authority to require such TERO preferences on federally funded projects. There is no Wisconsin state statute to grant authority to WisDOT to require TERO preferences. The rule of law in Wisconsin is that state agencies like WisDOT must find legal authority for a proposed action

Indian Reservation https://www.fhwa.dot.gov/legsregs/directives/notices/n4720-7.cfm

72. Indian Reference in Employment on Federal-Aid Highway Projects on and Near Indian Reservation, Background (B) (C) https://www.fhwa.dot.gov/legsregs/directives/notices/n4720-7.cfm

73. USDOT FHWA, Indian Employment Preference 23 U.S.C. §140(d) Date: September 20, 1994, https://www.fhwa.dot.gov/construction/contracts/940920.cfm

within the express or necessarily implied language of a statute. Any doubt is resolved in favor of the lack of legal authority."

This response has many components, so we must first begin by analyzing and decompressing this statement as there are multiple statements: the first statement presented in the brief stated: "NO," which explained that the tribes did not have the authority to implement TERO or Indian Preferences.

- *Federal permission does not grant WisDOT legal authority to require such TERO preferences on federally funded projects.*

- *There is no Wisconsin state statute granting authority to WisDOT to require TERO preferences.*

- *The rule of law in Wisconsin is that State agencies like WisDOT must find legal authority for a proposed action within the express or necessarily implied language of a statute.*

- *Any doubt is resolved in favor of the lack of legal authority.*

In addressing: "*Federal permission does not grant WisDOT legal authority to require such TERO preferences on federally funded projects,*" it is the responsibility of WisDOT and the TRIBES to negotiate regarding the applicability of the TERO laws to contracts. What has happened to the language about IP as well? This only discusses the TERO with no mention of IP. Where it has been stated, Wisconsin lacks a statute granting of authority of WisDOT to require TERO. This is an accurate statement because it is not the state of Wisconsin or WisDOT who has the authority,[74] it is the TRIBES.

To challenge the State of Wisconsin regarding the application of a statute can also be challenged through the state's process done by developing a theory of a case while including the applicable basis or (bases) for the challenge by addressing it through:

---

74. Memo; February 27, 2012, page 1, WisDOT OGC response to WisDOT Secretary regarding TERO Preferences.

Wisconsin's Administrative Procedure Act[75] *limits a rule challenge to only three grounds:*

1) violation of a constitutional provision,

2) failure to comply with statutory rulemaking procedures, and

3) exceeding the statutory authority of the agency.

The implementation of this rule of law, as a dynamic process, will also delineate the legal authority to provide action with the implied language of the statute. If it is found to be substantive grounds to invalidate an agency rule or a violation of a constitution provision as it is stated, the rule challenger must:

- *Prove unconstitutionality beyond a reasonable doubt. "It is not sufficient that the challenger shows that there is doubt as to the rule's constitutionality"*[76] *and*

- *"Convince the reviewing court that the agency's interpretation of the rule should be afforded little or no deference. Although a reviewing court is not bound by an agency's conclusions of law, courts often defer to the agency's interpretation of a rule."*[77]

Let's begin with: "23 U.S.C. 140(d) addresses Indian employment preferences in FHWA funded programs," as defined:

(d) Indian employment. – Consistent with section 703(i) of the Civil Rights Act of 1964 (42 U.S.C. 2000e-2(i)), **nothing in this section**

---

75. Challenging a State Agency Regulation; Wisconsin's Administrative Procedure Act, https://www.wisbar.org/NewsPublications/WisconsinLawyer/Pages/Article.aspx?Volume=90andIssue=10andArticleID=25970

76. Challenging a State Agency Regulation; Wisconsin's Administrative Procedure Act, Violation of a Constitutional Provision https://www.wisbar.org/NewsPublications/WisconsinLawyer/Pages/Article.aspx?Volume=90andIssue=10andArticleID=25970

77. Challenging a State Agency Regulation; Wisconsin's Administrative Procedure Act, Violation of a Constitutional Provision https://www.wisbar.org/NewsPublications/WisconsinLawyer/Pages/Article.aspx?Volume=90andIssue=10andArticleID=25970

> *shall preclude the preferential employment of Indians living on or near a reservation on projects and contracts on Indian reservation roads. States may implement a preference for the employment of Indians on projects carried out under this title near Indian reservations. The Secretary shall cooperate with Indian tribal governments and the States to implement this subsection [Emphasis added.]*

The WisDOT OGC presented an issue related to the context of qualitative citations, as the issue relates to questionable citations, and the use of such citation resources like "Wikipedia" is very concerning because of the source the citations come from. *"Then addressing a critical issue isn't right"* as stated by Judge Richard A. Posner, United States Court of Appeals for the Seventh Circuit in Chicago, directly asserts the questionability of the arguments made as it has been stated by the judge and a Tax lawyer by the name of Kenneth H. Ryesky, who also teaches at Queens College and Yeshiva University who has stated that: *"citation of an inherently unstable source such as Wikipedia can undermine the foundation not only of the judicial opinion in which Wikipedia is cited but of the future briefs and judicial opinions which in turn use that judicial opinion as authority."*[78] So, it is with great caution when drafting legal opinions, depositions, or contentions that one must refrain from the utilization of the citations of Wikipedia and referencing to anything related to Wikipedia. It is important to point out that the WisDOT OGC began the analysis where it is stated: (d) Indian employment. – Consistent with section 703(i) of the Civil Rights Act of 1964 (42 U.S.C. 2000e-2(i)), nothing in this section shall preclude the preferential employment of Indians living on or near a reservation.[79] This is a list of Indian Reservations and Off-Reservation Trust Land with descriptions.

---

78. Courts Turn to Wikipedia, but Selectively by Noam Cohenjan. 29, 2007 https://www.nytimes.com/2007/01/29/technology/29wikipedia.html

79. A list of Indian Reservations and Off-Reservation Trust Land with descriptions can be found at: http://en.wikipedia.org/wiki/List of Indian reservations in the United States

It is apparent, where it states the [Emphasis added] was not accurately depicted and should have read: [Emphasis added, bold refers to language added in 1991 amendment.][80] There were also important sections of the amendments that were not included but pertained to the projects which WisDOT also neglected to assert this information:

- *The legislative history is helpful. Title 23 U.S.C. § 140 was amended in 1987 by section 122 of the Surface Transportation Reauthorization and Uniform Relocation Assistance Act [STURRA]1. The purpose of the 1987 amendment (as set forth above, less the bold portion) was to confirm the antidiscrimination provisions of section 140 with Title VII of the 1964 Civil Rights Act on the issue of Indian preference in employment and contracting for certain Federal-aid highway projects.*

- *Before the 1987 amendment, the FHWA had interpreted 23 U.S.C. § 140 as precluding Indian employment preference on any Federal-aid project. This reasoning was based on an analysis of the competitive bidding and non-discrimination requirements of Title 23. The FHWA at that time determined that 23 U.S.C. § 140 precluded the application of section 703(i) of the Civil Rights Act of 1964 to other than Indian Reservation Road [IRR] projects funded under the IRR program under 23 U.S.C. § 204.[81]*

The assertion of WisDOT's analysis: "*WisDOT is required to assure FHWA that employment in connection with federally funded projects will be provided without regards to race, color, creed, national origin, or sex.*" In review of the EEOC Title VII Civil Rights Act of 1964[82] document which states: Any issue related to race, color, creed, national origin, or sex; it is important to also review:

---

80. Title 23 U.S.C. § 140(d) https://www.fhwa.dot.gov/construction/contracts/9409 20.cfm

81. Title 23 U.S.C. § 140(d) https://www.fhwa.dot.gov/construction/contracts/9409 20.cfm

82. EEOC Title VII Civil Rights Act of 1964 https://www.eeoc.gov/laws/statutes/ titlevii.cfm

Section 127 brings the anti-discrimination provisions of section 140 of Title 23,[83] United States Code, into conformity with Title VII of the 1964 Civil Rights Act, on the issue of Indian preference. Section 703(i) of Title VII makes Indian preference a permissible exception to the general prohibition against discrimination, thereby encoding a longstanding Federal policy towards Indians.[84]

Proceeding forward addresses the exceptions required, assurances that are allowed, are not mandated conditionally to utilize the federal funds, and that states may implement a preference for employment of Indians on projects carried out under this title near Indian reservations. This is only a partial response because in analyzing the last statement, WisDOT's OGC neglected to mention the following which should have been included: "On the reservation or within a commutable distance. As there was nothing to the effect of this. The FHWA field offices were to encourage States to meet with Indian tribes and TERO to develop contract provisions for Federal-aid highway projects which would promote employment opportunities for Indians on reservations."[85]

The reviewing of 23 CFR 635.117(d)[86] states it is permissible to implement procedures or requirements to extend preferential employment to Indians living on or near a reservation on eligible projects as defined in paragraph (e) of this section, it declines to mention the passage of commutable distance as well. The language avows it is permissible for state transportation department but there may be a question to the language as "shall," it is not obligatory for the state transportation for the implementation as stated: "Indian Preference

83. 23 U.S. Code § 140. Non-discrimination https://www.law.cornell.edu/uscode/text/23/140

84. 1991 Amendment, Indian Employment Preference on Federal-aid Projects https://www.fhwa.dot.gov/construction/cqit/indian.cfm

85. Indian Employment Preference on Federal-aid Projects https://www.fhwa.dot.gov/construction/cqit/indian.cfm

86. Labor and employment. 23 CFR 635.117(d).

shall be applied without regard to tribal affiliation" reveals that this word "shall" in 23 CFR 635.117(d) in its context is not a persuasive statement, because of the confusion with the language and its definition before 2013 when it had a different understanding. The language after 2013, as stated in this publishing in the Federal Aviation Administration (FAA), in the USDOT website is articulated. The Legal reference books like the Federal Rules of Civil Procedure no longer use the word "shall," even the Supreme Court has ruled that when the word "shall" appear in statutes, it means "may."[87] There was no emphasis added unless it was done by WisDOT's OGC. It is equally important to also look at 23 CFR 635.117(E)[88] as it also pertains to Labor, employment, and Indian Preference:

- *23 CFR 635.117(e) Projects eligible for Indian employment preference consideration are projects located on roads within or providing access to an Indian reservation or other Indian lands as defined under the term "Indian Reservation Roads" in 23 U.S.C. 101 and regulations issued there under.*

The WisDOT's statement regarding the citation to the Code of Federal Regulations (CFR), section *25CFR 170.912(a)* Tribal, State, and local governments "may" provide an Indian employment preference for Indians living on or near a reservation on projects and contracts that meet the definition of an Indian Reservation Road. (See 23 U.S.C. 101(a) (12) and 140(d), and 23 CFR 635.117(d).)" (*Emphasis added.*) The language in this statement is inaccurate as it should have been amended with the correct wording which is "Tribal Transportation Facility"[89]

---

87. What's the only word that means mandatory? Here's what law and policy say about "shall, will, may and must." https://www.faa.gov/about/initiatives/plain_language/articles/mandatory/

88. 23 CFR § 635.117 – Labor and employment. https://www.law.cornell.edu/cfr/text/23/635.117

89. Tribal transportation facility means a public highway, road, bridge, trail, transit system, or other approved facility that is located on or provides access to Tribal land and appears on the NTTFI described in 23 U.S.C. 202(1). https://www.law.

because this had a more expansive definition (See 23 U.S.C. 101(a) (12) and 140(d), and 23 CFR 635.117(d).):

- *23 U.S.C. 101(a)(12) refers to The term "Interstate System" means the Dwight D. Eisenhower National System of Interstate and Défense Highways described in section 103(c) and should have included 23 U.S.C. 101(a)(31) Tribal Transportation Facility.*[90]

- *23 U.S.C. 140(d), refers to Indian Employment. Consistent with section 703(i) of the Civil Rights Act of 1964 (42 U.S.C. 2000e-2(i)), nothing in this section "shall" preclude the preferential employment of Indians living on or near a reservation on projects and contracts on Indian reservation roads. States "may" implement a preference for the employment of Indians on projects carried out under this title near Indian reservations.*

WisDOT's OGC wholeheartedly failed to mention "on reservations or within a commutable distance". The Secretary "shall" cooperate with Indian tribal governments and the States to implement this subsection.[91]

In 1993, FHWA issued a notice entitled, "Indian Preference in Employment on Federal-aid Highway Projects on and Near Indian Reservations," and articulated the subsequent legal guidance has been consistent in the approach that the 23 U.S.C. 140(d) Indian employment preference is permissive, not mandatory. It is WisDOT's OGC who has conveyed repetitively stating: "Indian Preference is not mandatory the argument can be made that as long as these laws or ordinances are grounded to the tribe's inherent sovereign status and continue to be upheld with the Supreme Court decisions, as these powers originated from the principle that undeniable powers come

cornell.edu/cfr/text/25/170.912

90. Tribal transportation facility https://codes.findlaw.com/us/title-23-highways/23-usc-sect-101.html

91. Indian Employment https://www.fhwa.dot.gov/map21/docs/title23usc.pdf

from acts of Congress but are natural powers of a limited sovereign that have never been taken away as recognized in treaties and federal legislation.[92] So, when it is stated that "Indian employment Preference is permissive and not mandatory" it is concerning because what the WisDOT OGC is stating is that the WisDOT would have the power over Congress to control the application of the IP or TERO.

IP derived from historical relationships and "federal policy of according to some hiring preference to Indians in the Indian service dates at least as far back as 1834.[93] Since then, Congress repeatedly has enacted various preferences of the general type here at issue.[94] The purpose of these preferences, as variously expressed in the legislative history, has been to give Indians greater participation in their self-government as established to further the Government's trust obligation[95]

---

92. What is the legal basis for TERO?
http://www.councilfortribalemploymentrights.org/tero-faq/

93. Act of June 30, 1834, § 9, 4 Stat. 737, 25 U.S.C. § 45: "[I]n all cases of the appointments of interpreters or other persons employed for the benefit of the Indians, a preference shall be given to persons of Indian descent, if such can be found, who are properly qualified for the execution of the duties."

94. Act of May 17, 1882, § 6, 22 Stat. 88, and Act of July 4, 1884, § 6, 23 Stat. 97, 25 U.S.C. § 46 (employment of clerical, mechanical, and other help on reservations and about agencies); Act of Aug. 15, 1894, § 10, 28 Stat. 313, 25 U.S.C. § 44 (employment of herders, teamsters, and laborers, "and where practicable in all other employments" in the Indian service); Act of June 7, 1897, § 1, 30 Stat. 83, 25 U.S.C. § 274 (employment as matrons, farmers, and industrial teachers in Indian schools); Act of June 25, 1910, § 23, 36 Stat. 861, 25 U.S.C. § 47 (general preference as to Indian Labor and products of Indian industry). https://supreme.justia.com/cases/federal/us/417/535/#F7

95. Senator Wheeler, cosponsor of the 1934 Act, explained the need for a preference as follows: "We are setting up in the United States a civil service rule which prevents Indians from managing their own property. It is an entirely different service from anything else in the United States because these Indians own this property. It belongs to them. What the policy of this Government is and what it should be is to teach these Indians to manage their own business and control their own funds and to administer their own property, and the civil service has worked very poorly so far as the Indian Service is concerned...." Hearings on S. 2755 and S. 3645 before the Senate Committee on Indian Affairs, 73d Cong., 2d Sess., pt. 2, p. 256 (1934). https://supreme.justia.com/cases/federal/us/417/535

toward the Indian tribes;[96] and to reduce the negative effect of having non-Indians administer matters that affect Indian tribal life; as stated *in Morton v. Mancari, 417 U.S. 535 (1974).*[97]

Malabed v. North Slope Borough, 70 P.3d 416, 427-28 (Alaska 2003)

The Alaska Supreme Court held that such a "hiring preference violates the Alaska Constitution's guarantee of equal protection because the borough lacks a legitimate governmental interest to enact a hiring preference favoring one class of citizens at the expense of others and because the preference enacted is not closely tailored to meet its goals."[98] The ruling was made that North Slope Borough is not a tribe rather, but is a political subdivision of the State of Alaska which had enacted an ordinance granting employment preference to Native Americans even though they were not defined as a Native American. A Native American is defined as a person belonging to an Indian Tribe as defined: 25 U.S.C. Section 3703(10).[99] "Indian tribe" means any Indian tribe, band, nation, pueblo, or other organized group or community, including any Alaska Native village or regional corporation as defined in or established under the Alaska Native Claims Settlement

96. A letter, contained in the House Report to the 1934 Act, from President F. D. Roosevelt to Congressman Howard states: "We can and should, without further delay, extend to the Indian the fundamental rights of political liberty and local self-government and the opportunities of education and economic assistance that they require in order to attain a wholesome American life. This is but the obligation of honor of a powerful nation toward a people living among us and dependent upon our protection." H.R.Rep. No. 1804, 73d Cong., 2d Sess., 8 (1934). https://supreme.justia.com/cases/federal/us/417/535/#F10

97. 417 U. S. 554-555. Morton v. Mancari, 417 U.S. 535 (1974) https://supreme.justia. com/cases/federal/us/417/535/

98. 3-86 (quoting Malabed v. North Slope Borough, 70 P.3d 416, 427-28 (Alaska 2003)).

99. .25 U.S. Code § 3703. Definitions https://www.law.cornell.edu/uscode/text/25/3703

Act (43 U.S.C. 1601 et seq.), which is recognized as eligible for the special programs and services provided by the United States to Indians because of their status as Indians.[100]

The North Slope Borough consulted the Federal Equal Employment Opportunity Commission (EEOC) to determine if N.S. Borough qualifies for an exemption of federal equal employment opportunity laws, more specifically under section 703(i) of the Civil Rights Act of 1964 (the 703(i) exception), which excludes "hiring preferences" favoring Native Americans working on or near Indian reservations from the strictures of Title VII of the 1964 Civil Rights Act. While Mr. Malabed, Mr. Welch, and Mr. Emerson filed suit against North Slope Borough asserting they are non-native candidates and violating state and federal constructional guarantees of equal protection:

- *The Alaskan Human Rights Act,*

- *Federal Civil Rights Laws, and*

- *The borough's charter.*[101]

The district court ruled the Hiring preference violated the North Slopes Borough's charter and federal equal protection.

It is important to deduce the response related to the Alaskan Constitution, we must first identify the United States Constitution's, Indian Commerce and Treaty clauses as Congress possesses the plenary powers to regulate commerce "with the Indian tribes," once almost rendered superfluous by the Court decision[102] has now been resurrected and made largely the basis for

---

100. 25 U.S. Code § 3703. Definitions https://www.law.cornell.edu/uscode/text/25/3703

101. Malabed v. North Slope Borough, 42 F. Supp. 2d 927 (D. Alaska 1999) https://law.justia.com/cases/federal/district-courts/FSupp2/42/927/2501867/

102. United States v. Kagama, 118 U.S. 375 (1886). Rejecting the Commerce Clause as a basis for congressional enactment of a system of criminal laws for Indians living on reservations, the Court nevertheless sustained the act on the ground that the Federal Government had the obligation and thus the power to protect a weak and

informing judicial judgment concerning disputes concerning the justifications and agreements of Native Americans. The source of federal authority over Indian matters has been the subject of some perplexity, but it is now generally recognized that the power derives from federal responsibility for regulating commerce with Indian tribes and for treaty-making.[103]

Now understanding the context of language set forth here, we look at the United States' plenary power, and how this conveys to the Tribes. Looking further into the Alaska Constitution shows it lacks any language regarding provisions endorsing state action regarding Alaska Natives and grants no express powers from which implied powers could arise. The only provision of the Alaska Constitution addressing the state's relations with Alaska Natives is Article XII, Section 12,[104] which renounces any state authority similar to the federal government's protective powers. This relationship between the state of Alaska and Alaska Natives has been working in harmony following the original intent of the drafters of the constitution, thus offering Alaskan natives the same

dependent people. Cf. United States v. Holiday, 70 U.S. (3 Wall.) 407 (1866); United States v. Sandoval, 231 U.S. 28 (1913). This special fiduciary responsibility can also be created by statute. E.g., United States v. Mitchell, 463 U.S. 206 (1983). https://law.justia.com/constitution/us/article-1/44-commerce-with-indian-tribes.html

103. Morton v. Mancari, 417 U.S. 535, 551–553 (1974) https://law.justia.com/constitution /us/article-1/44-commerce-with-indian-tribes.html#fn-1285

104. The State of Alaska and its people forever disclaim all right and title in or to any property belonging to the United States or subject to its disposition, and not granted or confirmed to the State or its political subdivisions, by or under the act admitting Alaska to the Union. The State and its people further disclaim all right or title in or to any property, including fishing rights, the right or title to which may be held by or for any Indian, Eskimo, or Aleut, or community thereof, as that right or title is defined in the act of admission. The State and its people agree that, unless otherwise provided by Congress, the property, as described in this section, shall remain subject to the absolute disposition of the United States. They further agree that no taxes will be imposed upon any such property, until otherwise provided by the Congress. This tax exemption shall not apply to property held by individuals in fee without restrictions on alienation. https://ltgov.alaska.gov/information/alaskas-constitution/

rights and opportunities as all other Alaska citizens. Because of the dissent of languages between the constitutions, one must review Wisconsin's Constitution as well to see how they differentiate. The only excerpt located in the Wisconsin Constitution which addresses the TRIBES:[105]

> "Equality; inherent rights. Section 1. [As amended Nov. 1982 and April 1986] All people are born equally free and independent and have certain inherent rights; among these are life, liberty, and the pursuit of happiness; To have these rights, governments are instituted, deriving their just powers from the consent of the governed. [1979 J.R. 36, 1981 J.R. 29, vote Nov. 1982; 1983 J.R. 40, 1985 J.R. 21, vote April 1986]."

When a party claims an equal protection violation that does not involve a suspect class or fundamental interest, the court is presented with three questions:

1) Does the challenged statute create distinct classes of persons?

2) Is a class treated differently from others similarly situated? and

3) Is there a rational basis for different treatments?

As mentioned earlier at the beginning of this case, one important factor in the review of the North Slope Borough is they are not Federally Recognized Tribes.[106] "A federally recognized tribe is an American Indian or Alaska Native tribal entity that is recognized as having a government-to-government relationship with the United States, with the responsibilities, powers, limitations, and obligations attached to that designation, and is eligible for funding and services from the Bureau of Indian Affairs. Furthermore, federally recognized

---

105. Wisconsin Constitution Last amended in April 2015 Election. Published March 20,2019 https://docs.legis.wisconsin.gov/constitution/wi

106. What is a Federally recognized Tribe https://www.bia.gov/frequently-asked-questions

tribes are recognized as possessing certain inherent rights of self-government (i.e., tribal sovereignty) and are entitled to receive certain federal benefits, services, and protections because of their special relationship with the United States. At present, there are 573 federally recognized American Indian and Alaska Native tribes and villages, and North Slope Borough does not fit the criteria presented."[107]

The question that should be asked is: "How many tribes are located in Alaska now?"[108] There is only one, which is named Metlakatla Indian Community of the Annette Island Reserve in Southeastern Alaska.

The WisDOT OGC's legal opinion and statement recorded in the meeting minutes from the TLAC meeting in February 2012 is rather ironic, there has been no challenge or rebuttals to any of WisDOT OGC's responses in the past. These arguments redundantly brought forward by these legal opinions are ambiguous at best and do not have a solid footing, because the WisDOT OGC's statements reflect a more subjective point of view, and the legal opinion goes on to reflect only biased opinions. These can be previewed in the context of these responses.

In the review of a memo statement from Mr. Shawhan to the U.S. DOT sent on August 31, 1994. He had asked a few questions related to Indian Preference: *"To which projects does the Indian employment preference contained in 23 U.S.C. § 140(d) apply? Is the Indian employment preference permissive or mandatory?"* The response sent from the US DOT:

> The Indian employment preference applies to all Federal-aid projects on or near Indian reservations. It is discretionary. A State "may" implement the preference on applicable

---

107. What is a Federally recognized Tribe https://www.bia.gov/frequently-asked-questions

108. Are there any Federal Indian Reservations in Alaska https://www.bia.gov/frequently-asked-questions

Federal-aid contracts but is not required to do so. Title 23 U.S.C. § 140(d) provides:

Indian employment and contracting: Consistent with section 703(i) of the Civil Rights Act of 1964 (42 U.S.C. 2000e-2(i)),[109] nothing in this section shall preclude the preferential employment of Indians living on or near a reservation on projects and contracts on Indian reservation roads. States may implement a preference for the employment of Indians on projects carried out under this title near Indian reservations. The Secretary *"shall"* cooperate with Indian tribal governments and the States to implement this subsection. [Emphasis added, bold refers to language added in the 1991 amendment.][110]

The 1991 Amendment:[111] Title 23 U.S.C. § 140(d)[112] was further amended in 1991. Section 1026(c) of the Intermodal Surface Transportation Efficiency Act of 1991 [ISTEA], addressed the issue of Indian employment preference and added a new sentence to section 140{d):

- *States **"may"** implement a preference for the employment of Indians on projects carried out under this title near Indian reservations.*

- *For ISTEA section 1026(c), the legislative history indicates the following:*

- *Subsection (b) amends section 140(d) to authorize states to extend Indian employment preference programs to projects near reservations. Currently, such programs are limited to Indians living on or near reservations and to projects on IRR.*[113]

---

109. U.S. Equal Employment Opportunity Commission https://www.eeoc.gov/laws/statutes/titlevii.cfm

110. The 1991 Amendment https://www.fhwa.dot.gov/construction/contracts/940920.cfm

111. The 1991 Amendment https://www.fhwa.dot.gov/construction/contracts/940920.cfm

112. Sec.201.Federal lands and tribal transportation programs https://www.fhwa.dot.gov/map21/docs/title23usc.pdf

113. The 1991 Amendment https://www.fhwa.dot.gov/construction/contracts/940920.cfm

While the specific reference to reservations is contained in floor remarks made by Rep. Miller (D-CA) regarding section 126 of H.R. 2950 (the House version of the surface transportation reauthorization bill), the congressional intent of increased Indian employment is also expressed: "this bill extends Indian employment preferences so that more Indian Labor will be used when building on or near reservations."[114]

It is clear the ISTEA amendment made two separate changes concerning Indian employment preference. First, it permits an employment preference concerning all Indians, not just Indians living on or near a reservation. Second, the employment preference applies to all Federal-aid projects near reservations, not just Federal-aid IRR projects. The amendment also reiterates a state's authority to implement Indian employment preference provisions on federal aid projects near reservations. Although the 1987 STURRA amendment expressly permits a State to include Indian employment preference in its Federal-aid contracts, the 1991 ISTEA amendment clarifies the issue by the language, **"States may implement."** It is important to note that neither the STURRA nor ISTEA mandate that States utilize the preference in applicable contracts. A State may require the preference, but the State is not required to do so. The FHWA policy, however, has been to encourage the States to implement the Indian employment preference in applicable contracts.[115]

The TRIBES maintain the sovereign rights to implement the IP or TERO as long as they are grounded in their inherent sovereign status. This legitimate canon is the most rudimentary principle of Indian law and is reinforced by a host of Supreme Court decisions. It also mentions that Title VII of the 1964 Civil Rights Act in section 703(i) makes Indian

---

114. The 1991 Amendment https://www.fhwa.dot.gov/construction/contracts/9409 20.cfm

115. The 1991 Amendment https://www.fhwa.dot.gov/construction/contracts/9409 20.cfm

Preference a permissible exception to the general prohibition against discrimination, thereby encoding a longstanding Federal policy towards Indians.[116]

In many of these US-DOT, FHWA, USC, documents state the tribes, and the secretary shall work together, or the state may negotiate with the tribes, and this should be the foundation of the agreements for the IP and TERO to be allowed. If the State doesn't negotiate through the working type of process, then the TRIBES have inherent rights to exclude the WisDOT from contracting any work until an agreement has been negotiated as it is with the tribe's rights as stated: "The breadth of the power of Indian tribes to exclude non-Indians from territory reserved for the tribe was spelled out definitively by the Supreme Court in the case of Merrion v. Jicarilla Apache Tribe, 455 U.S. 130 (1982). The Court observed that an Indian tribe's power to exclude non-Indians from tribal lands is an inherent attribute of tribal sovereignty, essential to a tribe's exercise of self-government and territorial management."[117]

Understanding the power of the tribes and their reservations it is rather the inherited power of these tribes to exclude people in the same scope of authority and both as attributes directly infused to the tribe's sovereignty and it is the tribe's inherited right to exercise self-governance of their community within the boundaries of the Indian country. So, it is with the understanding that where it may be permissive federal statutes and regulations, and requires negotiations and possible MOA, MOU, PA, or EO may be the same tools needed as well, because it is clear the tribes also have the authority to not allow or exclude non-natives on the projects as well if they are located within the boundaries of Indian country.

The importance of understanding the language put in

---

116. Title VII of 1964 Civil Rights Act https://www.fhwa.dot.gov/construction/contracts/940920.cfm

117. Donovan v. Navajo Forest Products Indus., 692 F.2d 709 (10th Cir. 1982).

place has been set there as a moral obligation because of the different levels of sovereignty. It is often mentioned in TLAC and ITTF meetings that the relationship is much like a marriage, and it is imperative to negotiate and work together. This is not like a marriage but should only be interpreted as "Equals" and nothing more. Also important to understand is that tribes are not like a municipality township or incorporation and should not be treated like one. The tribe's sovereignty is in nature hard to define or explain but should always be looked at a minimum, to be equivalent to that of a state in its status. Things like IP Laws or TERO are all effective tools to enhance the working relationships because the state does not have civil authority over tribes regardless of the public law 280. Remember that tribes retain broad inherent civil jurisdiction over their tribal members with things like:

- *Qualifications for Tribal membership.*

- *Rules for tribal member lands.*

- *The prosecution of tribal members who are found in violation of the tribal laws or ordinances.*[118]

It is important to remember the purpose of these preferences, as variously expressed in the legislative history, has been to give Indians greater participation in their self-government. This has also helped to further the Government's trust obligation toward the TRIBES; and to reduce the negative effect of having non-Indians administer matters that affect Indian tribal life, over the lives and destinies of the TRIBES. The Court held that the preference was political, rather than racial.[119] [T]his preference does not constitute 'racial discrimination.' Indeed, it is not even a 'racial' preference. Rather, it is an employment

---

118. Limits on Tribal Jurisdiction https://www.wisbar.org/NewsPublications/Wisconsin Lawyer/Pages/Article.aspx?Volume=89andIssue=1andArticleID=24550

119. Morton v. Mancari, 417 U.S. 535 (1974) The purpose of these preferences https://supreme.justia.com/cases/federal/us/417/535/

criterion reasonably designed to further the cause of Indian self-government and to make the BIA more responsive to the needs of its constituent groups. It is directed to participation by the governed in the governing agency. The preference, as applied, is granted to Indians not as a discrete racial group, but, rather, as members of quasi-sovereign tribal entities whose lives and activities are governed by the BIA... Furthermore, the preference applies only to employment in the Indian service.[120] As long as the special treatment can be tied rationally to the obligations required of Congress toward the Indians, such legislative judgments will not be disturbed. Here, where the preference is reasonable and rationally designed to further Indian self-government, we cannot say that Congress' classification violates due process. [121]

The administrative agencies are finding the cases and any other relevant information related to IP and TERO as presented above where it is stated IP is permissive only reflects a personal illogical view by WisDOT's OGC, as we continue to move forward these responses reflect a biased position. These statements are an indistinct attempt at the utilization of persuasive language use as these testimonials lack a robust presence of adequate historical backing, case laws, and legal statutes. The inaccurate or subjective statements relating to IP, one must truly understand IP will require immersing yourself into tribal laws., To truly understand the preference one must understand this rationally is connected to the special treatment and obligations of Congress toward members of a political status and community of members of quasi-sovereign with dual citizenships. The TRIBES maintain the sovereign rights to implement the IP or TERO as long as they are grounded in its inherent sovereign status. This legitimate

---

120. Morton v. Mancari, 417 U.S. 535 (1974; preference does not constitute 'racial discrimination https://supreme.justia.com/cases/federal/us/417/535/

121. Morton v. Mancari, 417 U.S. 535 (1974) special treatment can be tied rationally to the fulfilment of Congress https://supreme.justia.com/cases/federal/us/417/535/

canon is the most rudimentary principle of Indian law and is reinforced by a host of Supreme Court decisions. As long as IP can be tied rationally to TRIBES as the right to self-govern, then the State lacks jurisdiction or authority to make any decisions regarding Indian preference.[122] Moving forward with issues like in the case discussing powers exercised between a State Board of Health and a Committee on Water Pollution, a question needed to be asked about the powers, are the levels of powers between a state and a municipality, state to state, or state to township?, under Ch. 144, Stats., and the delegation of powers has been by legislative bodies and the restrictions upon their exercise have been relaxed. However, for the rights of citizens under our constitution and laws, administrative agencies exercising legislative or judicial power, or both powers in combination, must be held to act within the limits prescribed by the statute creating them. They have no general legislative or general judicial powers. They have only those specifically granted or necessarily implied.[123]

The issue identified is relevant to the balance of powers or who holds the legislative powers between the State Board of Health and the Committee. The issue they have is from an incident related to Water Pollution as it relates to the jurisdiction and delegation of powers exercised by legislative bodies to the legislative delegation of judicial powers under the rights of the citizens. It is quite clear that they have inadequate familiarity with this subject of Indian Law and are quite unaware of the pundit structure of the tribal governments, the executive branches, constitutions, laws, and administrative agencies.

---

122. Morton v. Mancari, 417 U.S. 535 (1974) special treatment can be tied rationally to the fulfilment of Congress https://supreme.justia.com/cases/federal/us/417/535/

123. State Board of Health and the Committee on Water Pollution powers https://www.courtlistener.com/opinion/4234224/american-brass-co-v-state-board-of-health/

City of Appleton v. Transp. Comm'n of Wisconsin

The main component discussed is the ability of the city to exercise the township's permitting process because they believed they were excluded from having to do the process as the circuit court concluded. This case is not about what happened in this case, but rather about the context or language from what is brought forward, but it is related to statutes between the city (Appleton) and the Town as it relates to a permitting process to install sewer lines or utilities across city lines into the town. It relates directly to the cohesiveness of multiple entities or municipalities involved when proper communication is essential when crossing over into different municipalities. This again is another irrelevant statement because when dealing with one of the TRIBES it is the state who must negotiate with any one of the EFTROW, thereby disrupting any argument when addressing TRIBE's "Sovereignty and Self Determination Rights," located "on," "near," or "within a commutable distance" of Indian roadways, Indian country, Indian trust lands, fee lands, and reservations. As stated earlier it is in the interests of the state and the Tribes to negotiate as the civil and inherent jurisdiction belongs to the TRIBES, and further dismantling any question of this case and the use of its language by WisDOT's OGC.

With the efforts to interject his prejudiced opinion through implied assertions, neglecting to include any citations or backing, thereby only signaling these egregious statements by Mr. Thiel like: *"No Wisconsin statute authorizes WisDOT to implement the characteristics of a TERO, which include an Indian employment preference, exclusive or preferential use of Indian enterprises or services, or payment of TERO imposed taxes."* It is not the WISDOT who possesses the authority, but it is the TRIBES, as long as they maintain the Sovereign rights to implement the IP or TERO, as long as they are grounded in its inherent sovereign status. This legitimate canon is the most rudimentary principle of Indian law and is reinforced by a host of Supreme Court decisions and backed by the TRIBES who hold the authority as this transpires when working both "on," "near," or "within a commutable distance" of Indian roadways, Indian country, Indian trust lands, fee-lands, and reservations.[124]

Mitton v. Wisconsin Dept. of Transportation

The WisDOT OGC then tries to articulate the principles to establish the authorities while considering *"Permissive Federal Statutes"* as the Mitton's are in procession lands including a site of Indian Burial grounds within seven acres, which WisDOT attempts to condemn from the Mitton family as a portion of one acre is needed for the construction of HWY 29 rights-of-way. It was ruled that because DOT had not established land replacement, this argument failed. The courts concluded that WisDOT lacks an expansive condemnation authority to condemn it. The owner may commence an action in the circuit court of the county where the property is located. It was agreed in the 1994 case that the DOT had abused its authority in condemning $5^{1}/_{2}$ acres. The DOT does not have the authority to condemn these lands without being within reasonable grounds.

The WisDOT OGC references another set of federal statutes worth exploring IP/TERO related to DBE.[125] These arbitrary rebuttals are moot attempts at blurring the original inquiry as it pertains to IP or TERO. The DBE is established Tribal Firms or businesses and applicable to the Tribal Business but does

124. What is the legal basis for TERO? https://cter-tero.org/contact/

125. Disadvantaged business enterprises https://cms.dot.gov/sites/dot.gov/files/docs/mission/civil-rights/disadvantaged-business-enterprise/55851/official-questions-and-answers-disadvantaged-business-enterprise-program-regulation-49-cfr-26-4-25.pdf
Indian Tribes and Alaska Native Corporations https://cms.dot.gov/sites/dot.gov/files/docs/mission/civil-rights/disadvantaged-business-enterprise/55851/official-questions-and-answers-disadvantaged-business-enterprise-program-regulation-49-cfr-26-4-25.pdf

not apply to the questions that were asked as the DBE directly talks about the Ownership of Companies or Firms: How do recipients determine the eligibility of firms owned by an Indian Tribe or an Alaska Native Corporation? (Section 26.73 (h) (i)) (Posted 2/12/02) Any Indian Tribe may own a DBE firm as an entity. It is not necessary, in these cases, that disadvantaged individuals (i.e., natural persons) own the firm.[126] The DBE statutes would apply to tribally owned companies but hold no binding language relevant to the application of DBE for Tribal communities or their members. See footnote for a copy of the link to the DBE Application for TOB.[127] The Statute which is referred to at the end of Mr. Thiel's response concludes: *"This section does not apply if federal law does not require, as a condition of using federal funds, this state to establish goals for the participation of disadvantaged businesses or the employment of disadvantaged individuals in projects using federal funds."*[128]

The Federal DBE program, articulated by The WisDOT OGC prohibits targeting any individual minority group or gender groups that reflect misinterpretation or the deficiency to articulate, comprehend, or support the grounds of his argument. The essential component to always remember related to Indian Preference is that: preferences do not constitute "racial discrimination." Indeed, it is not even a "racial" preference. The preference/ordinance is reasonable and rationally designed to further Indian self-government and is not the position of the courts to say that Congress' classification violates due process. Indian preference is reasonably and directly related to a legitimate, nonracially based goal. This is the principal

---

126. Indian Tribes and Alaska Native Corporations Indian Tribes and Alaska Native Corporations https://cms.dot.gov/sites/dot.gov/files/docs/mission/civil-rights/disadvantaged-business-enterprise/55851/official-questions-and-answers-disadvantaged-business-enterprise-program-regulation-49-cfr-26-4-25.pdf

127. Link for DBE Application for Tribally owned Businesses; https://www.reginfo.gov/public/do/DownloadDocument?objectID=55126701

128. Statues reference DBE Program Wis. Stat. s. 84.072(8); https://docs.legis.wisconsin.gov/statutes/statutes/84/072/8

characteristic that generally is absent from proscribed forms of racial discrimination. Rather, it is an employment criterion reasonably designed to further the cause of Indian self-government and to make the BIA more responsive to the needs of its constituent groups. It is directed to participation by the governed in the governing agency. The preference is similar to the constitutional requirement that a United States Senator, when elected, be "an Inhabitant of that State for which he shall be chosen," Art. I, § 3, cl. 3, or that a member of a city council resides within the city governed by the council. As long as the special treatment can be tied rationally to the fulfillment of Congress's unique obligation toward the Indians, such legislative judgments will not be disturbed.[129] Native American Tribes and their members are classified as governmental and political entities and are not to be defined as racial groups. This principle is embedded in U.S. law from the very beginning and explicitly recognized by the Supreme Court in Morton v. Mancari in 1977.[130] Chief Justice John Marshall first articulated in American jurisprudence the existence of a unique legal relationship, established through treaties, between the federal government and Indian Tribes. "Their relationship to the United States resembles that of a ward to his guardian." Cherokee Nation v. Georgia, 30 U.S. 1 (1831). Marshall's formulation of the unique legal relationship between the Indian Nations and the U.S. government thus recognized the right of Tribes to govern themselves on their lands as "quasi-sovereign domestic dependent nations," as well as a federal "duty of protection" to safeguard tribal treaty rights.[131]

---

129. 417 U.S. 535 (1974) Morton, Secretary of the Interior, ET AL. v. Mancari ET AL. No. 73-362. Supreme Court of United States. https://scholar.google.com/scholar_case?case=4402198579492121596andhl=enandas_sdt=6,50

130. Tribes are governments, not racial classifications https://indianlaw.org/story/tribes-are-governments-not-racial-classifications

131. The Federal Government's Relationship to Tribes, Pre-Mancari http://indianlaw.org/sites/default/files/Morton%20v.%20Mancari%20Memo%20May%203%202018.pdf

This component is imperative to evoke where the discussion of "race, color, sex, or national origin," individual minority, and DBE Statuses are all presented as able to, as mentioned above, *"Sex, Race, Color, or National origin"* with the statement regarding the Preferences, because of the language in Section 703(i) of Title VII of the Civil Rights Act of 1964, as amended, 42 U.S.C. § 2000e-2(i) (1982),[132] provides an exception to Title VII's general non-discrimination principles allowing certain employers under certain circumstances to exercise an employment preference in favour of American Indians. That section provides[133] statements of excluding tribes from the Title VII clauses. Along with this, it is important to note that the DBE statuses technically do not apply if you read how this is articulated because Native Americans are not minorities or a racial class of people, they are defined as a political classification of both a United States citizen and a Tribal member of their tribe.

Milwaukee County Pavers Assoc. v. Fiedler

The DBE Tribal applications make it clear the DBE is for individuals who are potential or new owners of a business such as Corporations, Limited Liability Corporations (LLC), or Sole Proprietorships, but also of a race, color, sex, or national origin of which none are a tribe. Indian tribes are included because they are disadvantaged individuals, but the arguments are based on a racial group, "African Americans," in a predominately "African American city" where the DBE has received most of the work because the required percentages for DBE are all irrelevant. After all, tribes are not of individuals of a

132. 48 C.F.R. § 1452.204-71 (1987) (emphasis added). https://www.eeoc.gov/policy/docs/indian_preference.html

133. 48 C.F.R. § 1452.204-71 (1987) (emphasis added). https://www.eeoc.gov/policy/docs/indian_preference.html

particular race, color, sex, or national origin. "As long as the special treatment can be tied rationally to the fulfillment of Congress's unique obligation toward the Indians, such legislative judgments will not be disturbed."[134]

When these laws were first drafted, the attorneys drafted and reviewed these documents, and it is important to reflect on the processes for a moment. During this time, there was a lack of set standards or laws established for dealing with not just tribes but American Indians or Native American Indians and only tried to mold the laws around the Tribes to make sure they were adhering to the laws they were once excluded from. In analyzing the process of how the laws were established in the beginning, it seems there are two different standards applied. We must also analyze and interpret if the Vagueness Doctrines[135] can be applied to any of these laws or situations because it seems there is not enough information, or there by a lack of, and leaving the decisions open to biased decisions because of the way the laws are articulated, it is important to ask the questions if when there is no mention to the issues presented or a limited amount of information present to make unbiased decisions.[136] It is important to identify funding sources as these projects are from the federal government, which then are submitted to the states and sent to the tribes. Whereas if it was directly sent to the TRIBES and not disseminated down to the TRIBES by the state it is safe to say the TRIBES would have more leverage for the implementation of the IP Laws and TERO Ordinances. The next chapter will begin to discuss all the influences from the various entities and the impact

---

134. What is Indian Preference? http://www.councilfortribalemploymentrights.org/tero-faq/

135. Vagueness Doctrines By requiring fair notice of what is punishable and what is not, vagueness doctrine also helps prevent arbitrary enforcement of the laws. https://www.law.cornell.edu/wex/vagueness_doctrine

136. Skilling v. Unites States (No. 08-1394) 554 F. 3d 529, https://www.law.cornell.edu/supct/html/08-1394.ZS.html

they all have on a Tribe's Sovereignty and right to self-government. The entities mentioned are from TRIBES themselves or other TRIBES, FHWA, WisDOT, WTBA, and CI Contractors.

Chapter 15

Identifying the Influences Surrounding These Agreements

The WisDOT and other CI have had a direct role with the establishment, call for amendments, and the suspension of the NAHP. This can be shown through the actions mentioning entities' comments in focus groups, TRANS-AC, and TLAC meeting minutes. As these entities continue working diligently together to further diminish and remove the authority of TRIBES on any projects located "on," "near," or "within a commutable distance" of Indian roadways, Indian country, Indian trust lands, fee lands, and reservations. These influences not only undermine the true intent of the NAHP but challenge the authority of the TRIBES within the confines of their reservations. The TRIBES need to comprehend these processes for the protection of the TRIBES *"nationhood status and retain inherent powers of self-government,"*[137]

These TRIBES were excluded from much of the establishment, call for amendments, and the suspension of the NAHP process in 2011. This was done through the established focus group meetings by the WisDOT, and other agencies thereby directly impacting the TRIBES communities, circumventing IP and TERO process on any projects located on or near Indian Country, and only helping to further the TRIBES continued highest unemployment rates for roads and highways projects

---

137. inherent powers of self-government, https://www.bia.gov/frequently-asked-questions

with the NAHP applied to them. This industry was composed of WisDOT, FHWA, DWD, CI, Union Laborers, NAMC-WI, AICTA, AACC, TRANS-AC, WTBA, TA, SETL, NETL, NWTL, SWTL, NCTL, AICCW, TLAC Coordinator, TLAC Consultant, State DOT technical expert for TRANS policy, ITTF, TRANS, local municipalities, and counties all having some type of direct influence or relation to the projects located on or near or within a commutable distance of Indian Roadways, Indian Country, Trust lands and Reservations. The NAHP at the direction of WisDOT and the WTBA held two focus group meetings, on September 08, 2011, and September 13, 2011. Both of these first two focus group meetings lacked the participation of the TRIBES on a provision directly impacting their economic opportunities located on projects located on or near IRR, Indian Country, Trust lands, and Reservations. The WisDOT TL or TA representatives continue even today to reiterate to the TRIBES they have the highest unemployment rates while WisDOT has established these same focus group meetings which led to the suspension of the NAHP which WisDOT had helped to establish and implement. The consequences of the discontinuation of the NAHP reduced participation of the TRIBES from 2011 until sometime in 2013, directly impacting any economic opportunities for the TRIBES eliminating economic opportunities for over two years for any TSTW. This should be taken into note as well that even before the establishment of the NAHP this even further impacted the TERO and IP, so it is important we look back to the participation rates before NAHP to see the true detrimental effects or influences this has had on the TRIBES.

Chapter 16

Influences of FHWA Surrounding the TERO/IP or the NAHP

It has been revealed numerous times the status of various subjects throughout this book, but it is important to scrutinize, construe, and empathize with the documents created as far back as March 1993. The subject of IP in Employment on Federal Aid Highway projects on and near Indian reservations as the purpose of this was to establish guidance from the FHWA, State highway agencies, and their sub-recipients and contractors regarding the allowance for IP in employment on projects on and near Indian reservations.

Section 122 of the Surface Transportation[138] and Uniform Relocation Assistance Act of October 1987, a Memorandum was established by the FHWA Administrator to Regional Administrators, stating the FHWA field offices were to encourage states to meet with the Indian Tribes and TERO Offices to establish contract provisions for Federal Highway projects which would promote opportunities for Indians *"on"* reservations.

It is also important to notice that section 140 of Title U.S.C.[139] had been amended by section 1026 of the Intermodal

---

138. Section 122, Indian employment and contracting, Surface Transportation and Uniform Relocation Assistance Act (STURAA) of 1987, amended 23 U.S.C. § 140 (1982 and Supp. III) by adding subsection (d). This subsection now provides: https://www.fhwa.dot.gov/construction/contracts/870508.cfm

139. 23 U.S. Code § 140. Nondiscrimination (d) Indian Employment. https://www.law.cornell.edu/uscode/text/23/140

Surface Transportation Efficiency Act of 1991 (ISTEA)[140] which included: "States 'May' implement a preference for employment of Indians on projects carried out under this title *'near'* Indian reservations." What was also added in 1987 was subsection (d) which states to allow IP in employment on Federal and Federal-aid Indian Reservation Roads (IRR).

When looking at the language, one must scrutinize the information to identify the facts presented, which are:

- *STURRA Act of 1987 states in section 140 of Title 23, United States Code (U.S.C.) (d)* **to allow Indian preference in employment on Federal and Federal-aid Indian Reservation Roads (IRR).**

- *Section 122 of the STURRA of 1987 in October released a Memorandum from FHWA that began to encourage States to meet with Indian tribes and Tribal Employment Rights Offices (TERO)* **to develop contract provisions for Federal-aid highway projects which would promote employment opportunities for Indians on reservations.**

- *Section 140(d) of Title 23, U.S.C., was amended by Section 1026 ISTEA Act of 1991, which states:* **"States may implement a preference for employment of Indians on projects carried out under this title "near" Indian reservations."**

The State is encouraged to meet with Indian Tribes and TERO or IP to develop contract provisions for Federal Aid Highway projects which would promote opportunities for Indians on reservations. This is clear the state lacks the authority to deny the applicability of TERO for projects located on reservations. What else is clear is the States may also implement a preference for the employment of Indians on projects carried out under this title **"near"** *Indian reservations.*

---

149. Section 1026 of the Intermodal Surface Transportation Efficiency Act of 1991 (ISTEA) https://books.google.com/books?id=z7tXdWZ0j7wCandpg=PA331andlpg=PA331and dq=section+1026+of+the+Intermodal+Surface+Transportation+Efficiency+Act+of+1991+ (ISTEA)andsource=blandots=6Mq3oSwxxUandsig=ACfU3U2oYK7N-9X5_MVeP-LTC-9XZg l5vgandhl=enandsa=Xandved=2ahUKEwiBh4zHw4vnAhXRW8OKHTOUB1AQ6AEwCXoE CAsQAQ#v=onepageandq=section%201026%20of%20the%20Intermodal%20Surface%20 Transportation%20Efficiency%20Act%20of%201991%20(ISTEA)andf=false

This means the State is encouraged to communicate with Tribes as it relates to the Federal Aid Highway projects to implement the developed Contract provisions for Indians **"on"** reservations. It also identifies that for any project located **"near"** Indian reservations, the State **"may"** implement a preference for Indians near reservations referring to a possible negotiation of percentages of participation of Native Americans on the projects.

For Clarification of section 140(D) of Title 23, U.S.C. the term for Indian Reservation Roads (IRR) was also articulated which stated: "Eligible projects for Indian preference consideration are those projects which are on IRRs (*i.e., roads within or providing access to an Indian reservation or other Indian lands as defined under the term "Indian reservation roads" in Section 101 of Title 23, U.S.C., and regulations issued pursuant thereto*), or are not on IRRs, but are near the boundaries of reservations and other Indian lands. BIA maps showing Indian land areas can be obtained from the BIA area offices listed in the attachment, roads "near" an Indian reservation are those within a reasonable commuting distance from the reservation. IP is to be applied without regard to Tribal Affiliations or places of enrollment all with the established goals of developing IP in the project development, State and tribal, representatives negotiate to determine the Indian employment goals for the contractor's workforce while also considering the availability of skilled and unskilled Indian Workers, the type of work to be performed, contractors' employment requirements, about projects "near" reservations. Once the Indian employment goals have been established, these goals can only be changed by the state, only after consultation with the Indian Tribal government representative, TERO/Tribal Employment and Contracting Rights Office (TECRO), IP representatives, and the contractor, only after the consideration of the good faith effort of the contractor together with the ability of the Tribal Government, TERO/TERCO/IP to refer workers in numbers and time for the contractor to meet the goal and perform the work.

After the Indian Employment goal has been inserted into the contract, the State will follow normal contract compliance, or contract administration oversight procedures to effect compliance. The State may elect to invite TERO/ TECRO/IP representatives to assist with monitoring efforts of any part of the compliance process. When the state reviews the contractor's employment practices, if goals are not reached after consideration of good faith efforts, they will take appropriate enforcement actions or file sanctions for failure to meet the goals. These sanctions should be predetermined in advance and inserted as a part of the contract to facilitate enforcement. The final part to address is the TRIBES TERO Tax, which has been established and applied to contracts for projects performed *"on"* reservations but has no tax authority off reservations. TRIBES has an agreed rate for services rendered, recruitment (i.e., employment referral, and related supportive services as these proceeds are used by tribes to develop and maintain skills banks, help fund job referral, counseling, liaison, and other related services and activities related to the employment and training of Indians). The FHWA's longstanding policy is to participate in state and local taxes and does not discriminate against or otherwise single out federal aid highway construction contractors for special or different tax treatments. If the TERO tax rate on highway construction contracts is the same as on contracts on the reservation, such costs are eligible for federal aid reimbursement.

This is the FHWA's influence as they have stated they are there to provide information, advice, and assistance to the State, Tribal Governments, and TERO/IP representatives, all of which is trying to achieve the intent of ISTEA and to assist in meeting these requirements as the intended audience is the State, local Governments, Tribal and TERO/IP contractors. It is clear to see the FHWA and their attempts to be a resource in relaying the clarification of these laws or federal codes of law. It is also clear to see the process, which had been established back in 1987-1991, is not being followed the correct way it should be done as it relates to IP or TERO. This is clearly shown in many of the first meetings, consultations documented through the meeting minutes resulting in the dismissal of the TERO and IP and the implementation of the NAHP, it is presented through the documents like the legal opinions for WisDOT OGC from 2008 and 2012 stating WisDOT does not have the authority to implement TERO or IP thus implementing the NAHP to remove the authority from the Tribes. While examining the legal opinion of the WisDOT OGC, this presents a view that is subjective and not objective because the articulation of the information lacks the premise of the gathering of the information not being from both sides. The only positions presented are justifications of why the WisDOT does not have to apply these ordinances or references, but only partial truths have been presented in legal opinions to the tribes. Now we will take a look at the WisDOT and other influences surrounding the TERO, IP, and the NAHP.

It is also important to note the fact the misinformation presented to the other entities directly conflicts with the actual documents in the illustration of the context of information is not the same as it has been presented by the FHWA to the WisDOT. This is detrimental because this information is then relayed to Wisconsin's CI, State and local Municipalities, Tribal representatives, and the public. The information that has been wrongly given or stated by the FHWA directly shows the influence the FHWA has on all entities, so it is with the greatest caution to make sure the most accurate information is presented and relayed exactly how it is presented.

Chapter 17

Influences of WisDOT Surrounding the TERO/IP or the NAHP

In taking a look at the WisDOT, it is important to understand that some of the information has been documented as early as 2001, which shows the working relationships or partnerships between WisDOT as they place an NAHP in Federal Aid Projects on or near Indian lands. There is little information from back then when the FHWA Wisconsin Division embarked on a mission to visit each Tribe to begin to initiate the government-to-government relationships. This took place in August 2001 as each tribe was offered the opportunity for one-on-one meetings where the FHWA had learned the TRIBES have not been offered the opportunity to participate in Federal Aid Highway programs offered throughout the state of Wisconsin.

FHWA stepped up working diligently to ensure that TRIBES are not only offered the opportunity to participate but are taking an active role with the State to ensure this happens. Early progress includes the TRIBES being offered the opportunity for the first time to participate in WisDOT's Transportation Enhancements Program. From the participation of the FHWA, it was brought forward that many of the WisDOT State personnel were unaware that TRIBES were eligible to participate in WisDOT programs. WisDOT began to embark on education processes to ensure their staff is aware of this, able to assist TRIBES, and begin developing statewide policy within TRIBES.

This led to the development of EO#39 which recognized the sovereignty of the TRIBES and the unique government-to-government relationship that exists between the State and the TRIBES, which was signed February 27, 2004. This was called the State Tribal Consultation initiative which had been established to establish consideration to demonstrate the need for the state and TRIBES to begin coordinating and streamlining more closely while delivering services to improve the provision of governmental services and economic development to both tribal communities and citizens of the state to eliminate wasteful spending of taxpayer money.

The EO#39 states:

"Whereas, the State of Wisconsin, a sovereign state within the United States, recognizes the unique status of Indian Tribes and their right to existence, self-government, and self-determination; as JIM DOYLE, Governor of the State of Wisconsin, by the authority vested in me by the Constitution and the laws of this State, do hereby:

1. Direct cabinet agencies to recognize the unique legal relationship between the State of Wisconsin and Indian Tribes, respect fundamental principles that establish and maintain this relationship, and accord Tribal governments the same respect accorded other governments.

2. Direct cabinet agencies to recognize the unique government-to-government relationship between the State of Wisconsin and Indian Tribes when formulating and implementing policies or programs that directly affect Indian Tribes and their members, and whenever feasible and appropriate, consult the governments of the affected Tribe or Tribes regarding state action or proposed action that is anticipated to directly affect an Indian Tribe or its members.

3. In instances where the State of Wisconsin assumes control over formerly federal programs that directly affect Indian Tribes or their members, direct cabinet agencies, when feasible and appropriate, to consider Tribal needs and endeavor to ensure that Tribal interests are taken into account by the cabinet agency administering the formerly federal program; and

4. Direct cabinet agencies to work cooperatively to accomplish the goals of this order.

5. General Provisions.

a. Nothing in this order shall require cabinet agencies to violate or ignore any laws, rules, directives, or other legal requirements or obligations imposed by state or federal law.

b. Nothing in this order shall require cabinet agencies to violate or ignore any agreements or compacts between one or more Indian Tribes and the State of Wisconsin or one or more of its agencies.

c. If any provision in this order conflicts with any laws, rules, agreements, or other legal requirements or obligations imposed by state or federal law, the state or federal law shall control.

d. Nothing in this order prohibits or limits any cabinet agency from asserting or pursuing any action or right or taking any position under state or federal law or any existing agreement concerning the interests of the State of Wisconsin or any of its state agencies.

e. Nothing in this order creates any right, benefit, or trust responsibility, substantive or procedural, enforceable at law by a party against the State of Wisconsin, its agencies, or any person.[141]

---

141. Executive Order # 39 http://witribes.wi.gov/docview.asp?docid=23379andlocid=57

In analyzing this important document, it is important to notice that it directly states: "*The State of Wisconsin, a sovereign state within the United States, recognizes the unique status of Indian Tribes and their right to existence, self-government, and self-determination,*" This is important later on when clarifying the premise of the IP and TERO and TRIBES right to self-determination and self-government. It is also important to take a look at the General Provisions presented as well and understand the language presented because it contradicts many of the statements made earlier, and information presented by WisDOT the OGC TA, and the DBE later on.

We next take a look at the establishment of the 2005 PA as the intent this document seeks to embark on the journey involved in building and sustaining a true government-to-government relationship between the TRIBES, FHWA, and WisDOT, with the goal of such a relationship aimed at moving beyond the agency mindset of simply consulting with Indian nations as a legal requirement, but instead, working with Indian nations as equal partners focused on people, economics, natural, and human environments to improve the quality of life for all people. It is equally important to remember this agreement as it states, "*the parties place value in working as '*__equal partners__*,' and are guided by __moral, ethical and professional principles__.*" This is important because some of the documents and participants brought forward along with their statements and actions show this partnership agreement is not, and has not, been adhered to. This can be shown with the application of the IP or TERO. This can be directly shown in the Legal opinions presented by WisDOT OGC where the legal opinion is one-sided to dismiss IP and TERO. It can also be shown through the development of the NAHP established by the WisDOT to let their contractors work on projects located on or near Indian Lands or the TRIBES' reservations. This influence was also from the representative of FHWA which had misspoken in an email where it was stated by FHWA

Division Office Mr. William Starks the federal laws provide authority to use a TERO clause in Federal Aid Contracts but does not mandate it. He also stated the State DOT has the discretion to implement its own program promoting employment among the less advantaged populations consistent with state laws and with their efforts such as TRANS in Wisconsin. The FHWA representative had misspoken when he should have made a clear statement as it relates to the STURRA act of 1987 stated in section 140 of Title 23, United States Code (U.S.C.) (d)[142] *"allow Indian preference in employment "on" Federal and Federal-aid Indian Reservation Roads (IRR);"* as well as the Section 122 of the STURRA of 1987, *"released the memo from the FHWA to the State stating they are encouraged to meet with the tribes and TERO to development of contract provisions for Federal-aid highway projects which would promote employment opportunities for Indians "on" reservations,"* and finally Section 140(d) of Title 23, U.S.C., as amended by Section 1026 ISTEA Act of 1991 which states: *"States 'may' implement a preference for employment of Indians on projects carried out under this title 'near' Indian reservations."* Mr. Stark's statement directly impedes these sections and is quite a vague statement in that it does not state anything near or on reservations or IRR lands.

This is concerning because when the FHWA makes an inaccurate statement to the WisDOT OGC this causes the spread of misinformation and eventually causes one group to establish and misinform other groups causing great confusion. The purpose of this email was to schedule a meeting between the FHWA and the WisDOT OGC and at this time there were none of the TRIBES representatives present. In the 2005 PA, it is stated: *"The parties place value in working as 'equal partners,' and are guided by moral, ethical and professional principles."* If there was a statement of equability where everyone is to be treated as

---

142. Indian Preference in Employment on Federal-Aid Highway Projects on and Near Indian Reservations 4720.7 March 15, 1993. https://www.fhwa.dot.gov/legs regs/directives/notices/n4720-7.cfm

equals, then from the beginning processes the question needs to be asked why were the TRIBES representatives not at the table even as early as 2008?

A few days later, on May 16, 2008, an email was produced from WisDOT OGC, with the subject header stating: "*No WisDOT Authority to Mandate or Require or Participate in TERO.*" The WisDOT OGC states TERO provisions of federal law are permissive in an earlier March 15, 1993 FHWA Notice 4720.7, it fails to mention as permissive but it does state that the FHWA encourages the States to meet with Indian TRIBES and TERO/IPO to develop contract provisions for Federal-Aid highway projects promoting employment opportunities for Indians "**on**" reservations, and relays the information presented above the three sections once again along with the memorandum.[143] When asked if the Indian Employment Preference is permissive or mandatory the FHWA responded with: "The IP applies to all Federal-Aid projects contained in 23 U.S.C. § 140(d) and is discretionary." This was not the statement made as it was stated that the TERO provisions are permissive. A state may implement the preference on applicable Federal-aid contracts but is not required to.

Discretionary powers do not impose an obligation on a decision-maker to exercise them or to exercise them in a particular manner, and permissive is allowed but not obligatory; optional. This is different from Title U.S.C. § 140(d) where it is states: "*States may implement a preference for employment of Indians on projects carried out under this title 'near' Indian Reservations.*" It is important to be sure to relay the accurate information because the FHWA's statement once again was inaccurate, but in the background, it was clear that it is discretionary on only projects located "**near**" the Indian reservations, but then it does go on to say that the secretary shall cooperate with Indian

---

143. Subject Indian Preference On Federal Aid highway projects on and near Indian Reservations, Code N 4720.7 Date: March 15, 1993, https://www.fhwa.dot.gov/legs regs/directives/notices/n4720-7.cfm

Tribal Governments and states to implement this subsection.

In the 1991 Amendment, it was stated, in the ISTEA section 1026(c) subsection (b) amends section 140(d),[144] to authorize states to extend Indian employment preference programs to projects near reservations. Currently, such programs are limited to Indians living on or near reservations and to projects on IRR and continues to say: "This bill extends Indian employment preferences so that more Indian labor will be used when building on or near reservations."

Section703(i) of Title VII of the Civil Rights Act 1994 as amended 42 U.S.C. §2000e-2(i) 1982[145] provides an exception of non-discrimination principles to exercise employment preferences in favor of American Indians as it states in the statutory language that an employer seeking to avail itself of IP exception must meet the 3 following conditions:[146]

The employer must be located on or near an Indian reservation.

- *The employer's preference for Indians must be publicly announced; and*

- *The individual to whom preferential treatment is accorded best be an Indian living on or near a reservation.*

It was also stated by the WisDOT, authority conferred by the Wisconsin state statutes must find authority in the four corners of the statute book; if there is any doubt, the authority does not exist. It is clear to also exemplify the Tribes do not apply to the four corners of the Wisconsin state book of

---

144. INFORMATION: Indian Employment Preference 23 U.S.C. §140(d) Date: September 20, 1994, From: Director, Office of Engineering Refer To: HNG-22 https://www.fhwa.dot.gov/construction/contracts/940920.cfm

145. Section 703(i) of Title VII of the Civil Rights act of 1994 as amended 42 U.S.C. §2000e-2(i) 1982. https://uscode.house.gov/view.xhtml?path=/prelim@title42/chapter 21andedition=prelim

146. May 16, 1988, Code N915.027 https://www.fhwa.dot.gov/construction/contracts/940920.pdf

statutes because Wisconsin has stated, in EO#39: "*The State of Wisconsin, a sovereign state within the United States, recognizes the unique status of Indian Tribes and their right to existence, self-govern-ment, and self-determination,*" and if the State of Wisconsin truly recognizes the unique status of the Indian TRIBES and their right to existence, self-government, and self-determination, they would understand that the foundation of the right to self-determination and self-government is at the foundation, which is the sovereign right to implement IP or TERO. The reason this is being shown is to show the influence the state and FHWA have enforced over the Tribes and the applicability of the TERO and IP.

These two case laws presented:

- *City of Appleton Transportation Commissioner, 116 Wis. 2d 352, 342 N.W.2d 68 (Ct. App. 1983)*[147]

- *American Brass v. Wisconsin State Board of Health, 245 Wis. 440, 15 N.W.2d 27 (1944).*[148]

These arguments lack relevance on the subject for WisDOT to state the requirements of TERO provisions in its contracts to enter into TERO agreements or expend money for Express TERO purposes. These arguments are the same as mentioned earlier in the February 2012 Legal Option released by WisDOT OGC stating WisDOT is within the authority for the applica-tion of the DBE programs. This argument is not pertinent to the application of TERO or IP because DBE is only relevant to minority-owned businesses and the state of Wisconsin to state it prohibits using specific separate goals for individual minority or gender groups and not the Tribes because they are

---

147. City of Appleton transportation Commissioner, 116 Wis. 2d 352, 342 N.W.2d 68 (Ct. App. 1983) https://law.justia.com/cases/wisconsin/court-of-appeals/1983/83-358-6.html

148. American Brass v. Wisconsin State Board of Health, 245 Wis. 440, 15 N.W.2d 27 (1944) https://www.courtlistener.com/opinion/4234224/-american-brass-co-v-state-board-of-health/

considered a political classification, that of dual "citizenship," and TRIBES is not defined as a race or a minority because of this political classification. It is clear to see the direct influence in the early stages and application of the NAHP.

The meeting minutes presented reflect many of the first meetings were scheduled and representatives were invited by the WisDOT TA in many of the first meetings leading to the suppression of IP or TERO and the implementation of the NAHP. This can be seen throughout 2011 during the series of WisDOT TRANS-AC and focus group meetings which led to the suspension of the NAHP and its intent, because when the invites were sent out there was only one tribe who was present, and this is why it was noted that "**a**" tribal representative was present. There should have been documented emails sent to all of the TRIBES, as this was an important decision that directly impacted them. Without direct consultation from all of the TRIBES, this has had a detrimental effect on their communities, and this is where it can be attributed that the NAHP was suspended already in July 2011.

This meeting consisted of all of the entities associated with the NAHP except the one TRIBE who had participated in this meeting. It was WisDOT TA and OGC iterating that Wisconsin does not have the statutory authority to implement TERO without even communicating with the TRIBES, as it was stated by the FHWA to begin the consultation process towards the implementation of TERO or IP on projects located **"on"** or **"partially on"** reservations, and this is also where the FHWA Representative states: *"Congress said there will be no discrimination because of race, religion, sex, etc. Congress also said states may implement Native American hiring preferences if they would like to. Federal law authorizes but does not mandate it. FHWA policies encourage states to implement what they can that is consistent with their state laws."* The misinformation was also reiterated by the WisDOT TA as well as the OGC and this is also relayed to the WTBA and throughout the CI, but it is important to see the direct influences of the information and the importance of making sure the accurate factual information is being relayed rather than an interpretation, because in the language it states this is discretionary **"near"** reservations, and in section 122 of the STURRA of 1987, *"released the memo from the FHWA to the State encouraging them to meet with the Tribes and TERO to development of contract provisions for Federal-aid highway projects which would promote employment opportunities for Indians 'on' reservations."* So it is with the utmost importance to relay the correct information, or it may have a detrimental effect on the very same people these documents have been created to help.

Without the proper participants, it is difficult to state everyone is being treated as equals as stated in the PA and the EO#39. With the inaccurate information being relayed from the FHWA to WisDOT, it is easy to see how the objective statements being relayed by the WisDOT TA, OGC, DBE, OBOC, AICCW, MANC, WTBA, and CI and Union Representatives all have sighted their direct influence at the influence of the FHWA statement: which established the creation of a provision which holds no binding authority to hold the contractors accountable for the non-compliance or direct violations of the provision, because it contains loopholes for the CI to do work located on or partially on reservations, Indian lands or IRR where the NAHP has stated that CI **"may"** utilize TSTW on projects located on or partially on the reservations IRR or Tribal lands. In November, the WisDOT OBOC and TA notified the TRIBES of the suspension of the NAHP. It was also the WisDOT who scheduled the meetings and invited all the following parties, bringing everyone to the table, but looking at most of 2011, and up until November 2011, there was only 1 tribal representative at these meetings; like the TRANS-AC meetings, 2 Focus Group meetings then there was a clear list of tribal representatives or an established WisDOT Tribal Task Force, so the question needs to be asked why weren't the TRIBES invited to the meetings until after all this was done and the provision was suspended, which directly violates the PA in a statement: "*Whereas, the State of Wisconsin, recognizes the unique status of Indian Tribes and their right to existence, self-government, and self-determination*" and then states in the EO#39 with the statement of: "*the parties place value in working as '**equal partners**,' and are **guided by moral, ethical** and **professional principles**.*" Where is the level of equality between the partners lacking to invite TRIBES to these meetings if guided by "moral, ethical, and professional principles?" The TRIBES did not have a seat at the table to voice their concerns and to rebut any of the concerns from any of the other parties, when this is clearly shown the influences were not in the best interests of the TRIBES, their communities, or their members.

WisDOT later amended the provision to remove the Native American Tracking form DT2405 which was established by WisDOT's forms technician. This was done at the request of the WTBA. The language of the original provision asserts the application of the provision was to be applied on all projects located "on," "near," and "within commutable distances," but through the direct influences of all of the entities who were involved in the TRANS-AC, and the two focus group meetings where there was no participation from any of the TRIBES. The language wasn't amended, but the provision was suspended without discussion between the Tribes, and it was later changed to "on" or "partially on" reservations, IRR, or Indian lands. The original language of the NAHP had stemmed from the WisDOT OGC because of his statements that the TRIBES lacked the authority to implement TERO preferences. This can be shown back in May 2008 when it was stated: No WisDOT Authority mandate was required to participate in TERO Ordinances. There are no other legal opinions presented that show the direct development of the NAHP other than by WisDOT and its employees, because it was WisDOT's creation to establish this provision so the Construction Industry, Unions, WTBA, DWD AICC would be able to work within the boundaries of reservations, IRR, and Indian lands. The objective legal opinion created by the WisDOT OGC was then presented to the TRIBES.

Analyzing the facts presented by the various WisDOT agencies, the clear influence was confoundingly presented when the question asked: *"Does the State of Wisconsin Department of Transportation ('WisDOT') have the legal authority to include and enforce Tribal Employment Rights Ordinance ('TERO') requirements as a WisDOT contractual requirement on any Federal-Aid Highway Program highway projects?"* WisDOT/OGC explicates in his answer stating: *"No. In brief, federal permission does not grant WisDOT legal authority to require such TERO preferences on federally funded projects. There is no Wisconsin state statutory grant of authority to WisDOT to require TERO preferences. The rule of law in Wisconsin is that State agencies like WisDOT must find legal authority for a proposed action within the express or necessarily implied language of a statute. Any doubt is resolved in favor of the lack of legal authority."*

This was presented in the Correspondence Memorandum presented to the WisDOT Secretary of the Department of Transportation on February 24, 2012, which the OGC official had stated was consistent with the previous legal opinion, which came to the same conclusion on August 04, 2008. This memo, along with all of the documented meeting minutes, shows who is asking the questions and making requests. The TLAC Group is composed of the group of Tribal Members or Individuals which are composed of the majority of entities who have a direct impact on the rescindments of the Indian Preference, TERO, but also the implementation and the suspension of the NAHP as it was composed of the TRIBES, Industry representatives, Unions, WisDOT Staff, and representatives from DWD, OBOEC, Civil Rights Compliance, DBE, Tribal Affairs, TRANS-AC, DTSD, NAMC, AACC, and AICC. These groups are the same ones who have been pushing control of the application of the NAHP as there has only been limited Tribal participation at the beginning of the development process of the NAHP, and the established foundation of influences due to the lack of participation, which has directly impacted all tribes.

Through further analysis, this letter, which was submitted by WisDOT's OGC, and was set to be distributed to all TRIBES on February 27, 2012, at the TLAC meeting in various locations because of meeting minutes for the same dates, regarding the requests made to the WisDOT, there was no line of communication or any further dialog following these requests being fulfilled. The information requested was listed as a recommendation/action to WisDOT DTSD Management and was presented back in 2012. The original requests were as follows:

- *Request for the total hours and total contract dollar amounts for each project cited in the Native American Hiring Provision data.*

- *Request to provide more education to the committee on the EO#39 and the WisDOT PA.*

- *Request for a copy of the 1854 treaty which addresses the transportation alliance.*

- *Recommendation to take the PA to the Tribal Task Force to revise and strengthen the document.*

- *Request for information on the amount of federal dollars allocated to WisDOT projects.*

- *Recommendation to elect a Tribal government representative on TRANS-AC.*

- *Charter a separate task force to work directly with TRIBES and internal WisDOT staff to explore a policy that addresses projects that are "on" or "partially on" tribal lands.*

- *Request for historical data that led up to the suspension of the NAHP.*

- *TRIBES wants to point out that if contractors are hiring minorities, they still meet their goal, but that does not do anything for Tribal members, especially when work is on tribal lands.*

The meeting minutes contained a request for the reports from the TRIBES regarding the US41 Mega Project and Trans Program. The TRIBES mentioned the use of the federal dollars in relation to the sovereign status of the TRIBES and their relationship with the federal government. The TLAC Members clarified Tribal members are not racial minorities, they are members of a sovereign nation, and they should not be referred to as minorities if the contractors are hiring minorities, they still need to meet their goals. It was emphasized this does nothing for the tribal members, especially when work is on tribal lands. The request from the TLAC Group is to see specific numbers of Tribal Members participating in these projects because there is a concern that we don't have solutions to obtain these specific numbers.

When the WisDOT/OGC presented WisDOT's Legal Opinion regarding TERO, it was different from the previous statements given three days earlier. The influence of the WisDOT OGC legal opinions reflected the objectivity of the OGC and WisDOT, but in this meeting the statement was similar, this is from the TLAC meeting minutes in Lac du Flambeau which stated:

> *"WisDOT does not have the statutory authority, and the federal government doesn't require the enforcement of hiring preference.* **That does not mean that the Tribes cannot require it. They can require it on their reservations and lands in trust for the benefit of their members.** *If DOT has a contract that requires being on Tribal land, they cannot go on Tribal land without their permission and compliance.* **You must comply in that instance, but it's not DOT, that's requiring it, but the Tribe."**

These statements changed from WisDOT's legal opinion in a matter of three days. They later presented an analysis with enough change because the legal opinion and the analysis presented were one-sided it only benefited the entities associated with the WisDOT construction industry, except the people whom the intent of the provision had been established for, but this collection of meeting minutes had stated something that the TRIBES are within authority of requiring TERO ordinances or Indian Preference laws within the boundaries of their reservations, IRR, or Indian Lands. It also stated they must apply to contracts, and if WisDOT has a contract, no one is allowed, without permission and compliance of the Tribes.

This only helped establish a foundation for future requests because the meeting minutes for any future meetings lacked any dialog or information being followed through, beginning from 2015 through 2018. The TRIBES inquired for the information to WisDOT TA numerous times, and this was documented in meeting minutes as early as 2012 and continued through 2018. At the time of the requests, there had been a series of events that transpired. The first request was listed on February 27, 2012, and again on March 06, 2013, where it was stated by WisDOT TA that WisDOT currently tracks tribal affiliation, and so there is no way of reporting the number of tribal members working on NAHP project-specific projects. When this information had been requested to obtain the NAHP labor reports information, TLAC representatives were told there was little or no information available; meanwhile, the NAHP was suspended and not applied to projects until it was shown on June 30, 2014, where the Standardized Special Provisions log of revisions (STSP). This is interesting because there was mention that the NAHP was being applied to all projects across the state of Wisconsin by WTBA's representative.

It wasn't until February 17, 2014, that the NAHP was re-adopted. This was not at the discretion of the TRIBES, but the whole process had been WisDOT delegated to the TRIBES. They were told the conditions that needed to transpire before the NAHP could be adopted. Contained in the new provision, was more language that stated this needed to be filled out by eligible bidders. If this DT1633 form was not completed and documented, showing valid good faith communications of the upcoming project, then contractors would not be eligible for bidding on the project.

The next section amended in the language of the NAHP was where it states the contractors receive three business days. The amendment was to make sure both the TRIBES and the contractors had equal time. If the contractors have 5 business days to send the information before the pre-tribal coordination meetings, then the TRIBES shall be afforded the same opportunity to respond. The next section amended was the applicability of the NAHP, changed from "on" or "near" reservations, IRR, and Indian lands, to "on" or "partially on" reservations, IRR, and Indian lands, thereby further constraining the TRIBES from implementing their provision established by the WisDOT, the DT2405 form, the WisDOT Native American tracking form created by a WisDOT forms technician, their process had been removed from the NAHP process back in 2011. A recommendation was made to put the Native American tracking form back into the process for the contractors to submit to the TRIBES. There was also no language that the contractors must implement the hiring of TSTW on NAHP projects located on or partially on Indian lands, reservations, and IRR. The language states that contractors "may" utilize TSTW on these projects.

It is all-important to note the WisDOT agencies like the TA, DWD, DBE, CRCS, OBOEC, and TRANS-AC, directly implemented their influences on these Ordinances, NAHP, which can be seen from 2009 through until the current review of the meeting minutes, or even the audio clips contained in many of the actual meeting minutes. This information was first requested back in 2014 and numerous times until 2018. When this information was requested, there was always some excuse, or delay in time between communications, and after requesting this information it often took anywhere from 6 to 12 months to obtain a small amount of the information, if any at all. This can be best noted by the fact that the WisDOT employee from OBOEC, who was also working as the TLAC coordinator, sent an email in error stating that perhaps this was a way of stalling the requestor from receiving the requested NAHP labor reports. This presented an accidental email that was sent to one of the TRIBES and directed to the WisDOT TA giving the perception of attempts to stall the TLAC group from receiving any information and presenting a potential of questionable ethics, because this was sent in error to the requestor of the labor reports, but it was directed to the WisDOT TA from the acting TLAC coordinator. This transpired in 2017.

When this was brought forward there were attempts to dismiss these concerns, or there were stalling tactics when the information was requested, and we were told there was little or no information. Then it wasn't until a meeting in 2018 that the WisDOT DBE made a direct statement about this information, which had originally been requested back in 2015, that this information is still available because this project is not closed yet. It was at this time the WisDOT DBE representative stated that this project was not chosen for the application of the NAHP. It was then explained to the WisDOT DBE representative, "how interesting, because it was not the decision of the WisDOT to delegate when this NAHP was applicable as this was to be implemented on all projects located on, or partially on reservations, or IRR." When this information was documented from CRCS it was information that was not available, there is little information available, then information has now been archived, and an email was received showing WisDOT OBOEC representative (current TLAC coordinator) directly attempting the stalling of the release of the information requested to present to the TRIBES. In 2017 a direct statement from WisDOT TA had stated this information is available from WisDOT, but it is only available in the way WisDOT TA wants to give the TRIBES this information, because they only get what WisDOT wants the tribes to have.

Let's not forget the concerns with the potential bidding process for the IGA also with the Federal Procurement process, which is stated in the section Ethical Conduct and Conflicts of Interest, Standards for Employees:

The Regulations contain provisions applicable to all government employees, regardless of assignment. Among these topics treated (which relate to procurement) are:

1. Private business or employment that creates an accrual or apparent conflict between their private interest and those of the government.

2. The use of "inside" information gained through a government position or the use of such position to further a private interest or gain.

3. Dealings with present and former personnel involving a violation of statute of government policy.

4. Membership in associations.

5. Conduct prejudicial to the government.

6. Bribery and grift.
7. Gratuities.

8. Use of Government Facilities, property, and manpower.

This is brought forward because the IGA established and released by the WisDOT TA on March 23, 2013, was for two different items:

1. WisDOT Statewide Native American Labor Initiative for $190,000 of available funds.

2. WisDOT Inter-tribal Task Force Administration with $250,000 of Available Funds.

The important dates to watch for were:

1. Letter of Interest Deadline: Thursday, February 20, 2014.

2. Proposal Deadline: Friday, February 28, 2014.

It was not until May 13, 2014, when a Memorandum of Agreement (MOA) was signed between the WisDOT and one of the TRIBES which is an IGA. This is important because the WisDOT TA representative is also a Tribal member of one of the TRIBES but is also the same tribe that was awarded the Pilot IGA. The WisDOT TA also was the same person who drafted and released the Pilot IGA out for bid. This presents a potential violation of the Federal Procurement process because it is a direct conflict of interest for WisDOT TA to award their tribe the IGAs. The total RPF for IGA totaled over $440,000 in funds. It was stated this was an annual agreement, then it became an annual three-year agreement. As part of the Federal Procurement Process, this is the same part mentioned in the WTBA as well for establishing the RFP and potential conflicts of interest.

At one of the TLAC meetings in Thursday April of 2017, the tribes received an email the night before the meeting, Wednesday of the April 2017 4:56 pm, from the WisDOT OBOEC TL representative that stated:

"One of the TRIBES will be taking the lead on delivering the annual report and the tool kit TLAC products and has indicated there may not be a need for a formal RFP. I believe there will be representatives from one of the TRIBE's available should you have questions on their procurement process."

This IGA was transferred from one tribe and given to another without any consultation from the whole TLAC Group as these are TLAC funds associated. It was stated there should have been a discussion, or a drafted RFP process again. When this process was asked about, it was stated by the WisDOT

OBOEC (and TA representative) that the funds were going to end the discussion because they were not changing it. If the TRIBES are recognized as a government and this is a government-to-government relationship, then we as the TRIBES need to be consulted as a government when there are any changes to the MOU, MOA, or any other agreements. Proper consultation was not given when one of the TRIBES' MOA was terminated and turned over to another one of the TRIBES without any consultation of the TLAC group*f*

This is quite concerning, because at the last TLAC meeting in January one of the TRIBEs expressed they did not even have the manpower or resources to create a list of their TSTW, but they wanted to take over the grant and the IGA. This was documented in audio clips and transcribed to meeting minutes as well. The question to ask is why was this all done without the consent of the TLAC Group and pushed through by the hand of the WisDOT TA, and the acting TLAC Coordinator. Was this only to circumvent the RFP process or procurement process? The TRIBES' one requirement is to have a procurement process established for the Competitive Bidding Process. At the TLAC meeting it was stated by WisDOT TA, one of the TRIBES interested in obtaining the IGA does not have to RFP, because they were going to sole source the process. It was explained to WisDOT TA that even if a penny associated with TLAC funds is federal dollars attached, then it is not able to be sole-sourced and needs to follow the federal procurement process. The DWD established the database, which was estimated to cost $61,515.99. After the database was completed in 2017, the WisDOT DWD mentioned the CI, or the TRIBES would not be able to utilize the DWD database for what it was originally intended for. In this TLAC meeting in January 2017, the TLAC group stated they would like to go back to the beginning because the DWD database does not perform any of the functions the TRIBES and CI requested it to do. At the next TLAC meeting in May 2017, the DWD had begun to present the DWD database, but it was stated in the January 2017 TLAC meeting that the TLAC group voted to go back to the beginning and create their database tribally owned because the DWD created a database which does not do what had been requested. When it was mentioned that this was already decided against, WISDOT OBOEC and WisDOT TA both became upset and yelled at one of the TRIBES' TLAC members and kept pushing the database regardless of what anyone had said.

During the creation of the baseline assessment, this plan was poorly established and lacked the proper follow-through by the TLAC coordinator and the WisDOT TA correctly, because there wasn't a control when this was sent out the first time, it was only sent to 15 contractors, and only yielded 6 responses. It was recommended to go to the WisDOT page for the construction to obtain a list of contractors to whom the baseline assessment should be sent. This was mentioned at the January 2017 TLAC meeting and documented in the meeting minutes, but the WisDOT TA acting TLAC coordinator, and Wis DOT OBOEC representative vigorously attempted numerous times to push the Baseline Assessment through. It is not possible to proceed forward when someone is trying to force the funding to be applied from the TLAC group when the group has not decided on it or had an opportunity to speak on this subject. This baseline assessment cost $18,400 and had no information that was adequate or presentable because there was no control or any quantifiable information.

This final statement received from WisDOT TA, along with the objective legal opinions presented by the WisDOT OGC makes it quite apparent the influences WisDOT has, they are standing behind people making biased statements like: "*WisDOT does not have the statutory authority, and the federal government doesn't require the enforcement of hiring preference.*" When a question should have been asked: "At *what point does the Tribes of Wisconsin interject their authority to implement their TERO Ordinances/Indian*

Preference Laws on all projects located 'on' or 'partially on' Reservations, Indian Lands, or IRR?"

When does the WisDOT contact the TRIBES notifying them of upcoming projects located "on," "near," or within "commutable distances" of the reservations? This is the point where the WisDOT and TRIBES begin working together relating to their government-to-government working relationships as stated in the EO, PA, MOU, MOA, and IGA. This is because the WisDOT and TRIBES have equal seats at the table, instead of trying to keep pushing the past under the rug. Once this is acknowledged then everyone can move together in a positive direction to work together.

Chapter 18

Influences of the WTBA Surrounding the TERO/IP or the NAHP

We shall now look at the Wisconsin Transportation Builders Association (WTBA) beginnings, linked to several contractor-related groups that were organized in 1902. They worked to promote highway building in Wisconsin at a time when the automobile was increasingly becoming an important and popular means of transportation. In 1939, after the consolidation of a number of these organizations, WTBA emerged as the primary trade association representing the interests of the highway construction industry. A year later, in 1940, WTBA moved from Milwaukee to Madison, Wisconsin's capital, to be closer to legislative decision-makers. The Association expanded its activities from solely road-building activities to working on issues such as highway industry safety and balancing environmental protection with mobility for travelers and products. Today, WTBA has more than 280 member companies, including contractors, consultants, and a broad range of other firms that supply diverse products and services to the transportation construction community.

- *State Government Relations: WTBA continuously monitors and proactively supports state legislation that advances investment in transportation construction and shapes an acceptable regulatory environment. The Association is extremely active at each stage of the Biennial Budget process, where most of these decisions are made.*

- *Federal Government Relations: WTBA actively monitors and communicates its positions on key federal transportation legislation to Wisconsin's Congressional delegation. WTBA members are extremely active in ARTBA (American Road and Transportation Builders Association) and TRIP (The Road Information Program) and have held numerous leadership positions. The Association sponsors a member "Fly-In" each year to maintain a continuous dialog with the delegation and its staff. WTBA also organizes member communications directly with the delegation, at critical points in the federal legislative process.*

- *Contracting and Engineering Services: WTBA provides extensive, up-to-date information on all transportation construction projects to be let with federal or state funding statewide. The Association also provides accurate, timely information on bids received and awarded.*

- *Safety Services: WTBA contracts with a transportation safety construction consultant to Staff a WTBA Safety Committee that works closely with OSHA to improve member safety performance, provide timely information on changing safety regulations, and respond to member questions. The Association is also active in federal and state safety regulatory processes.*

To analyze the influences of the WTBA on not just TERO/IP, but also the NAHP. On December 2, 2011, the question was asked if WTBA has any influences on the NAHP, it was the WisDOT TA who stated that WTBA does have a direct influence as there is a document from September 08, 2011, which had resulted from the Trans-AC meeting which took place on July 27, 2011. This document addressed only the concerns of the WisDOT agencies like the DBE, DTSD, TA, and OBOC. There were also groups like the NAMC, AACC, FHWA, Construction industry, Unions, and the WTBA. The Document concluded the following concerns from the WTBA as it related to the WisDOT NAHP:

Training and Outreach

- *Not involved with the language development process and vetting of the provision.*

- *Would like more education and outreach regarding NAHP implementation?*

Applicability

- *The provision is being included in contracts all across the state (as a result of the "on" or "near" boundaries), whereas they were under the impression that it would only apply to contracts that are "on" or "partially on" the reservation.*

Provision Language

- *Would like to know what the "spirit" of the provision means?*

- *Who decides?*

- *What are the criteria?*

- *Concerned with this provision statement – "if the tribe requests, the contractor shall meet with the Tribal Contact person to discuss Native American employment issues" – because of the additional burden, negative perception, and legal issues it lays on contractors.*

- *Concern with the statement that "engineer may withhold monies due the contractor if the contractor fails to submit this form."*

Tracking and Monitoring

- *The submission of the DT2405 tracking form is due 30 days after the work is substantially complete, which they feel is too subjective and conveys a negative message. Contractors are fearful of discrimination lawsuits if they do not hire recommended Native Americans that they believe are unqualified or hire from the union bench.*

General Concerns

- *Overall, WTBA cautioned that NAHP is communicating the wrong message to contractors and is receiving several questions from their members. NAMC representative Brian Mitchell also asked about the inclusion of subcontractors in the provision language and would like clarification as to whether or not the provision also applies to them.*

- *There is not a lot of hiring going on at this time, concerns were raised concerning perceptions that contractors are just not hiring Native Americans, and with the potential conflicts with the impacts of contractors' union obligations.*

There was also one more concern from the National Association of Minority Contractors (NAMC) which states:

"Does the provision apply to subcontractors?"

After analyzing the concerns brought forward by the WTBA and how they impact the NAHP, but also impact the implementation of the Indian Preference or TERO. The reason many of these concerns and questions had been asked is because the entities were already looking at ways to circumvent the NAHP, IP, or TERO processes. Once it was found there was too much authority in the NAHP, then it was the WTBA who sighted their influence on this NAHP, which led to the removal of the DT2405 Native American tracking form, the language change from "shall" to "may" is concerning to Native Americans on projects, lead to no language of accountability or enforcement within the NAHP because it leads from being definitive to subjective language.

In one of the many meetings speaking with the numerous WisDOT representatives associated with the establishment of the NAHP, it was mentioned how the structure of the WTBA established the budgets for the WisDOT, which reflects how the WTBA influences the WisDOT budgets each year as the WTBA was charged with establishing the budgets for the past 5 years. One of the WisDOT representatives voiced their concerns as it relates to the influences surrounding the NAHP. It is not just the WisDOT agencies that pose their influences on the NAHP, but it also comes from the CI, DBE, Construction Unions, and the WTBA. One other important fact is to remember that for any PA the DOI and FHWA would have to go through an approval process before these can be agreed upon.

WisDOT is charged with establishing a budget for transportation each year. It is also WisDOT that then bestows the WTBA to establish a budget for an allocated amount of work to be done within the state. For WisDOT, for the past 5 years and even possibly prior, when WisDOT does this, then it is the WTBA's board of directors, which is composed of 17 members of 11who are the owners of the construction companies, and these are a small portion of the companies who obtain a certain percentage of work from which they are also charged with establishing the same budgets. These budgets created by the WTBA are then submitted to the WisDOT and released for bid as a part of the federal procurement process. The board of directors are also the owners of the same construction companies who have bid on these projects, and the same contractors who have awarded these projects. This has been going on tentatively since 2014 when the questions had been asked at the first interview with the WisDOT representatives, well, also the same companies who helped establish the budgets. In 2019 I became aware of the list of the board of directors as it was pulled directly from the WTBA information at the time there was a compiled list for the public, but over the years this list has become more private on the website: https://wtba.org/about/

The website helps give the history of the WTBA, but it was not until using more search engines like Google, Chrome, and Safari, and researching Facebook accounts that I was able to get a more in-depth understanding of each person and the roles they played in their positions within the WTBA. It was not until I went to the Wisconsin Tribal Transportation Conference that I was able to obtain this information about who was the vice president and such, along with all of the key players in the WTBA. Attending these annual meetings throughout the state as a Trades Worker for training, but also as a Tribal member is how I began to obtain all of the information. This information is no longer available to the public. It took a great deal of time to research each person and the roles they play in the WTBA. There is also a state website called: https://lobbying.wi.gov This website calls out all of the information and who they lobby for as well.

The WTBA used to have an orange book with all of the key players, representatives, and contractors in the book. Since then this book has dissolved.

- ***Pat Goss, Executive Director,*** *Executive Director Wisconsin Asphalt Pavement Association (WAPA) deputy secretary of the Wisconsin Department of Transportation. I was the executive vice president of the Wisconsin Asphalt Pavement Association, which wasn't a political group, but it had that same membership-based quality. Before that, I served as the deputy secretary of the WisDOT, and before that I worked with the Metro Milwaukee Association of Commerce, which is the largest commerce group in the state. I also worked as the president of the Wisconsin Sports Development Corporation and before that, was the deputy secretary of the Department of Tourism. From 1992 to 1995, former member of Gov. Tommy Thompson's policy staff, and a large part of that was dealing with transportation issues.[149]*

- **Kevin Traas, Director of Policy and Finance** *Director of Transportation Policy and Finance of WTBA. Also ARTBA affiliation Glenn S. Grohman from Glenbeulah, Wisconsin is a Republican member of the U.S. House of Representatives from Wisconsin's 6th congressional district (R-Campbellsport). Traas says, "Federal funding accounts for 25 percent of Wisconsin's total transportation budget and about 55 percent of the highway construction budget.[150]*

---

149. https://lobbying.wi.gov/Who/PrincipalInformation/2019REG/_PrintProfile Principal/7980?print=True

150. https://lobbying.wi.gov/Who/LobbyistInformation/2019REG/Information/8747

- **Matt Grove, Director of Construction** Director of Engineering Policy/Highway Construction Industry Liaison to Government Agencies, for all operations related to the Highway Construction Industry in the State of Wisconsin. Duties include, but are not limited to: the Development and negotiation of WisDOT specifications and contract administration policy, Director of the WTBA Safety Committee, Industry representation on numerous technical and oversight committees, membership training, labor development, and minority contracting collaboration, dispute resolution, and mediation, union labor negotiations (Director of Wisconsin Transportation Employers' Council) and the mediation of state and federal labor compliance issues and union grievances.

- **Sean Stephenson, Director of Government and Member Relations** Sean Stephenson has worked in local, state, and federal politics for nearly a decade. Most recently, Sean served as Chief of Staff for Senator Joe Leibham. In that capacity, Sean served as a budget staffer on the Joint Finance Committee and helped usher through Senator Leibham's legislative priorities. Sean began working for Senator Leibham in the 6th Congressional District Republican primary in 2007 as a legislative aide.[151]

    Stephenson has also served as chief of staff for A Republican, Mayor Jim Schmitt of Green Bay, and as an aide to Congressman Mark Green serving as the U.S. Representative for Tennessee's 7th congressional district. Since 2019 Sean has also played a significant role in presidential, gubernatorial, state, and local campaigns. Sean grew up in Schofield, Wisconsin, and is a graduate of the University of Wisconsin-Green Bay.

- **Pam Fugina, Office, and Financial Manager** was listed for this year.

- **Patricia Hackett, Administrative Assistant** Current Assistant to Republication politician who was a state legislator and the 42nd Governor of Wisconsin from 1987 to 2000. Tommy G Thompson,

---

151. https://lobbying.wi.gov/Who/LobbyistInformation/2019REG/Information/8693

Hackett Consulting Previous: Thompson for Senate Campaign, Office of Governor Tommy G. Thompson-State of Wisconsin Consultant, Wisconsin Transportation Builders Association Hackett Consulting.

- **Michelle Klubertanz, Administrative Assistant** *I manage the Family Medicine department at the Fish Hatchery clinic.*

Board of Directors

WTBA is governed by a 17-member Board of Directors representing all sectors of the construction industry. Here is the link for the list of the Companies owned by WTBA Board of Directors Representatives and they were awarded these projects for January 2019, https://wisconsindot.gov/pages/doing-bus/contractors/hcci/bid-let.aspx

Below, I have compiled summaries of all of the chart information provided to show how much has been allocated by the WTBA. *(For the charts, please see Appendix C: Influences Discussed in Chapter 18)*

Influences of the WTBA surrounding the TERO/IP or the NAHP
(January to November 2019)

WisDOT APPARENT BID RESULTS FOR THE LETTING OF
January 15, 2019
*Total $137,809,890.42 attempting to bid on projects by the Construction Companies directly associated with the WTBA. On just **January 15, 2019**, the WTBA Board received the amount of **$47,602,329.79** Awarded Projects by WisDOT.*

WisDOT APPARENT BID RESULTS FOR THE LETTING OF
February 12, 2019
*Total $41,209,385.48 attempting to bid on projects by the Construction Companies directly associated with the WTBA. On just **February 12, 2019**, the WTBA Board received the amount of **$13,907,041.19** Awarded Projects by WisDOT.*

WisDOT APPARENT BID RESULTS FOR THE LETTING OF
March 12, 2019

*Total $136,865,534.48 attempting to bid on projects by the Construction Companies directly associated with the WTBA. On just **March 12, 2019**, the WTBA Board received the amount of **$43,375,426.07** Awarded Projects by WisDOT.*

WisDOT APPARENT BID RESULTS FOR THE LETTING OF
April 09, 2019

*Total $80,384,185.17 attempting to bid on projects by the Construction Companies directly associated with the WTBA. On just **April 09, 2019**, the WTBA Board received the amount of **$34,663,346.23** Awarded Projects by WisDOT.*

WisDOT APPARENT BID RESULTS FOR THE LETTING OF
May 12, 2019

*Total **$56,381,127.05** attempting to bid on projects by the Construction Companies directly associated with the WTBA. On just **May 12, 2019**, the WTBA Board received the amount of **$33,633,639.75** Awarded Projects by WisDOT.*

WisDOT APPARENT BID RESULTS FOR THE LETTING OF
June 11, 2019

*Total **$26,552,594.84** attempting to bid on projects by the Construction Companies directly associated with the WTBA. On just **June 11, 2019**, the WTBA Board received the amount of **$9,024,781.73** Awarded Projects by WisDOT.*

WisDOT APPARENT BID RESULTS FOR THE LETTING OF
July 09, 2019

*Total $367,670,063.71 attempting to bid on projects by the Construction Companies directly associated with the WTBA. On just **July 09, 2019**, the WTBA Board received the amount of **$16,007,745.67** Awarded Projects by WisDOT.*

WisDOT APPARENT BID RESULTS FOR THE LETTING OF
August 13, 2019

Total **$110,020,091.33** attempting to bid on projects by the Construction Companies directly associated with the WTBA. On just **August 13, 2019**, the WTBA Board of Directors received the amount of **$42,528,877.43** Awarded Projects by WisDOT.

WisDOT APPARENT BID RESULTS FOR THE LETTING OF
September 10, 2019

Total **$24,873,411.99** attempting to bid on projects by the Construction Companies directly associated with the WTBA. On just **September 10, 2019**, the WTBA Board of Directors received the amount of **$12,680,706.04** Awarded Projects by WisDOT.

WisDOT APPARENT BID RESULTS FOR THE LETTING OF
November 12, 2019

Total **$102,997,209.75** attempting to bid on projects by the Construction Companies directly associated with the WTBA. On just **November 12, 2019**, the WTBA Board of Directors received the amount of **$43,799,512.99** Awarded Projects by WisDOT.

2019 Total reports

Awarded	Percentage awarded to WTBA	Bid On but not awarded
$341,785,772.94	42%	$806,639,772.48
$1,084,763,494.22	Total projects left for 2019	
$297,223,406.89	Total Board of Directors of WTBA Companies awarded Projects	
27%	**Percentages that go to WTBA Companies and BOD**	

The totals for the year of **2019: $1,084,763,494.22** attempting to bid on projects by the Construction Companies directly associated with the WTBA. In 2019, the WTBA Board of Directors received the amount of **$297,223,406.89** Awarded

Projects by WisDOT. The following is the link taken directly from the WisDOT website for the 2019 Bid Letting: https://wisconsindot.gov/Pages/doing-bus/contractors/hcci/bid-let-2019.aspx

The owners of the following companies are also on the board of directors for the WTBA and have either attempted to bid on projects or were awarded these projects for 2019: American Asphalt of Wisconsin, Edgerton Contractors, Inc., Integrity Grading and Excavating Inc., James Peterson Sons Inc., Lunda Construction Company, Mega Rentals Inc., Musson Brothers Inc., Northeast Asphalt Inc., Payne and Dolan, Inc. Rock Road Companies Inc. Zenith Tech. Inc., Zignego Company Inc.

The awarded results for 2019

Awarded to the Board of directors for WTBA Construction Companies	Total Percentage of Projects Awarded 2019 to WTBA	Bid on but not awarded to the Board of Directors for WTBA Construction Companies
$1,567,112,750.10	39%	$4,138,920,964.08

In 2019, the awarded amount of state projects from the WisDOT is **$1,567,112,750.10** out of $4,138,920,964.08, which equates to about **39%** of the projects for the year. The significance of this is when you look at who is charged with establishing the projects, the WisDOT, have the WTBA establish the estimated budgets, and this team is also the same team, the WTBA, which is comprised of 17 board members and complete staff are also the owners of the construction companies bidding on these same projects they have been establishing these same budgets for.

In the bid letting for 2018, the Wisconsin Trade Builders Association (WTBA) is governed by a 17-member Board of Directors representing all sectors of the construction industry. The Board meets semi-monthly. WTBA was established in 1947.

Transportation Construction Support and Services State Government Relations WTBA continuously monitors and proactively supports state legislation that advances investment in transportation construction and shapes an acceptable regulatory environment. The Association is extremely active at each stage of the Biennial Budget process, where most of these decisions are made.

Federal Government Relations WTBA actively monitors and communicates its positions on key federal transportation legislation to Wisconsin's Congressional delegation. WTBA members are extremely active in ARTBA (American Road and Transportation Builders Association) and TRIP (The Road Information Program) and have held numerous leadership positions. The Association sponsors a member "Fly-In" each year to maintain a continuous dialog with the delegation and its staff. WTBA also organizes member communications directly with the delegation at critical points in the federal legislative process.

Contracting and Engineering Services WTBA provides extensive, up-to-date information on all transportation construction projects to be let with federal or state funding statewide. The Association also provides accurate, timely information on bids received and awarded.

Safety Services WTBA contracts with a transportation safety construction consultant to Staff a WTBA Safety Committee that works closely with OSHA to improve member safety performance, provide timely information on changing safety regulations, and respond to member questions. The association is also active in federal and state safety regulatory processes.

Here is a list of all the Wisconsin contractor companies associated with the WTBA: **James and Son, Kraemer,**

Lunda, Iverson Construction, Wisconsin Asphalt, Highway Landscapers, Integrity Grading and Excavating, Musson Brothers Inc., Michaels Corp., Peterson James Sons Inc., Payne and Dolan Inc., Rock Road Companies, Trierweiler Construction, Mega Rentals, Zenith Tech. Inc., Zignego Company Inc, Parisi Construction Co. Inc. *(For the charts, please see Appendix C: Chapter 18 Influences of the WTBA surrounding the TERO/IP or the NAHP (January to December 2018)*

WisDOT APPARENT BID RESULTS FOR THE LETTING OF
January 09, 2018

*Total **$118,152,127.99** attempting to bid on projects by the Construction Companies directly associated with the WTBA. On just January 09, 2018, the WTBA Board of Directors received the amount of **$5,280,382.81** Awarded Projects by WisDOT.*

WisDOT APPARENT BID RESULTS FOR THE LETTING OF
February 13, 2018

*Total **$121,083,239.17** attempting to bid on projects by the Construction Companies directly associated with the WTBA. On just February 13, 2018, the WTBA Board of Directors received the amount of **$33,052,478.54** Awarded Projects by WisDOT.*

WisDOT APPARENT BID RESULTS FOR THE LETTING OF
March 13, 2018

*Total **$158,094,067.15** attempting to bid on projects by the Construction Companies directly associated with the WTBA. On March 13, 2018, the WTBA Board of Directors received the amount of **$65,896,279.78** Awarded Projects by WisDOT.*

WisDOT APPARENT BID RESULTS FOR THE LETTING OF
April 10, 2018

*Total **$54,519,107.68** attempting to bid on projects by the Construction Companies directly associated with the WTBA. On just April 10, 2018, the WTBA Board of Directors received the amount of **$16,176,711.89** Awarded Projects by WisDOT.*

WisDOT APPARENT BID RESULTS FOR THE LETTING OF
May 08, 2018

Total $139,463,984.76 attempting to bid on projects by the Construction Companies directly associated with the WTBA. On just May 10, 2018, the WTBA Board of Directors received the amount of $54,991,509.65 Awarded Projects by WisDOT.

WisDOT APPARENT BID RESULTS FOR THE LETTING OF
May 22, 2018

Total $331,597,600.84 attempting to bid on projects by the Construction Companies directly associated with the WTBA. On just May 22, 2018, the WTBA Board of Directors received the amount of $248,898,946.81 Awarded Projects by WisDOT.

WisDOT APPARENT BID RESULTS FOR THE LETTING OF
June 12, 2018

Total $162,985,514.43 attempting to bid on projects by the Construction Companies directly associated with the WTBA. On just June 12, 2018, the WTBA Board of Directors received the amount of $69,655,609.71 Awarded Projects by WisDOT.

WisDOT APPARENT BID RESULTS FOR THE LETTING OF
July 10, 2018

Total $144,424,427.86 attempting to bid on projects by the Construction Companies directly associated with the WTBA. On just July 10, 2018, the WTBA Board of Directors received the amount of $70,039,639.59 Awarded Projects by WisDOT.

WisDOT APPARENT BID RESULTS FOR THE LETTING OF
July 24, 2018

Total $209,960,876.71 attempting to bid on projects by the Construction Companies directly associated with the WTBA. On just July 24, 2018, the WTBA Board of Directors received the amount of $0.00 Awarded Projects by WisDOT.

WisDOT APPARENT BID RESULTS FOR THE LETTING OF
August 14, 2018
Total $55,507,474.24 attempting to bid on projects by the Construction Companies directly associated with the WTBA. On just August 14, 2018, the WTBA Board of Directors received the amount of $17,603,648.51 Awarded Projects by WisDOT

WisDOT APPARENT BID RESULTS FOR THE LETTING OF
September 11, 2018
Total $57,441,258.17 attempting to bid on 2018 projects by the Construction Companies directly associated with the WTBA. On just September 11, 2018, the WTBA Board of Directors received the amount of $32,555,486.03 Awarded Projects by WisDOT

WisDOT APPARENT BID RESULTS FOR THE LETTING OF
November 13, 2018
Total $251,812,476.69 attempting to bid on projects by the Construction Companies directly associated with the WTBA. On just November 13, 2018, the WTBA Board of Directors received the amount of $90,007,436.58 Awarded Projects by WisDOT.

WisDOT APPARENT BID RESULTS FOR THE LETTING OF
December 11, 2018
Total $1,159,546,641.15 attempting to bid on projects by the Construction Companies directly associated with the WTBA. On just December 11, 2018, the WTBA Board of Directors received the amount of $708,599,325.50 Awarded Projects by WisDOT to the Wisconsin Transportation Builders Association (WTBA averaged 61% for December 2018).

In the Annual report for **2018**, the total amount left for projects was **$1,908,270,687.43**, and of that amount for funded projects, the Construction Companies directly associated with the WTBA in 2018, the WTBA Board of Directors received the amount of **$717,320,615.50** in funds Awarded for Projects by WisDOT. This is about 38% of the projects the WTBA Board of Directors was awarded for the year 2018. The owners of the following companies are also on the board of directors for the WTBA and have either attempted to bid on projects or were awarded these projects: Asphalt of Wisconsin, Edgerton Contractors, Inc, Integrity Grading and Excavating Inc., James Peterson Sons Inc., Lunda Construction, Michels Corporation, Mega-Rentals Inc., Rock Road Companies Inc., Musson Brothers Inc., Payne and Dolan Inc., Zenith Tech. Inc., Zignego Company Inc.

All of the bid letting information has been presented for any of the WisDOT projects awarded can be located in the following links from the 2018 WisDOT projects awarded located on the WisDOT website:

- **Link:** https://wisconsindot.gov/Pages/doing-bus/con-tractors/hcci/bid-let/2018/20181211.aspx

- **Link:** https://wisconsindot.gov/Pages/doing-bus/con-tractors/hcci/bid-let-2017.aspx

In the bid letting for 2017, the Wisconsin Trade Builders Association (WTBA) is governed by a 17-member Board of Directors representing all sectors of the construction industry. The Board meets semi-monthly. WTBA was established in 1947. *(For the charts, please see Appendix C: Chapter 18 Influences of the WTBA surrounding the TERO/IP or the NAHP (January to November 2017)*

WisDOT APPARENT BID RESULTS FOR THE LETTING OF
January 10, 2017

Total $77,587,099.18 attempting to bid on projects by the Construction Companies directly associated with the WTBA. On just January 10, 2017, the WTBA Board of Directors received the amount of $4,314,856.38 Awarded Projects by WisDOT.

WisDOT APPARENT BID RESULTS FOR THE LETTING OF
February 14, 2017

Total $22,149,075.18 attempting to bid on projects by the Construction

Companies directly associated with the WTBA. On just February 12, 2017, the WTBA Board of Directors received the amount of **$1,544,489.64** Awarded Projects by WisDOT

WisDOT APPARENT BID RESULTS FOR THE LETTING OF
March 14, 2017

Total **$247,955,431.61** attempting to bid on projects by the Construction Companies directly associated with the WTBA. On just March 14, 2017, the WTBA Board of Directors received the amount of **$25,380,350.46** Awarded Projects by WisDOT.

WisDOT APPARENT BID RESULTS FOR THE LETTING OF
April 11, 2017

Total **$171,101,027.90** attempting to bid on projects by the Construction Companies directly associated with the WTBA. On just April 11, 2017, the WTBA Board of Directors received the amount of **$44,911,181.57** Awarded Projects by WisDOT.

WisDOT APPARENT BID RESULTS FOR THE LETTING OF
May 09, 2017

Total **$143,352,550.27** attempting to bid on projects by the Construction Companies directly associated with the WTBA. On just May 09, 2017, the WTBA Board of Directors received the amount of **$59,040,749.13** Awarded Projects by WisDOT.

WisDOT APPARENT BID RESULTS FOR THE LETTING OF
June 13, 2017

Total **$210,181,089.59** attempting to bid on projects by the Construction Companies directly associated with the WTBA. On just June 13, 2017, the WTBA Board of Directors received the amount of **$46,311,300.93** Awarded Projects by WisDOT.

WisDOT APPARENT BID RESULTS FOR THE LETTING OF
July 11, 2017

Total **$219,733,097.70** attempting to bid on projects by the Construction

Companies directly associated with the WTBA. On just July 11, 2017, the WTBA Board of Directors received the amount of **$86,467,160.07** Awarded Projects by WisDOT.

WisDOT APPARENT BID RESULTS FOR THE LETTING OF
August 08, 2017

Total $289,814,094.74 attempting to bid on projects by the Construction Companies directly associated with the WTBA. On just August 08, 2017, the WTBA Board of Directors received the amount of **$113,113,523.95** Awarded Projects by WisDOT

WisDOT APPARENT BID RESULTS FOR THE LETTING OF
September 12, 2017

Total $155,498,211.40 attempting to bid on projects by the Construction Companies directly associated with the WTBA. On just September 12, 2017, the WTBA Board of Directors received the amount of **$34,980,016.20** Awarded Projects by WisDOT

WisDOT APPARENT BID RESULTS FOR THE LETTING OF
November 14, 2017

Total $241,867,552.87 attempting to bid on projects by the Construction Companies directly associated with the WTBA. On just November 14, 2017, the WTBA Board of Directors received the amount of **$84,002,070.66** Awarded Projects by WisDOT.

WisDOT APPARENT BID RESULTS FOR THE LETTING OF
December 12, 2017

Total $283,814,853.89 attempting to bid on projects by the Construction Companies directly associated with the WTBA. On just December 12, 2017, the WTBA Board of Directors received the amount of **$55,046,256.74** Awarded Projects by WisDOT to the Wisconsin Transportation Builders Association (WTBA averaged 37% for December 2017).

Total Projects Let for 2017

$2,063,054,084.33	Total projects Let for 2017	
$555,111,955.73	Board of Directors of WTBA awarded for 2017	
27%	Percentages going WTBA Companies and BOD	
Awarded to the Board of Directors for WTBA Construction Companies	Total Percentage of projects awarded to the WTBA in 2017	Bid On but not awarded to the Board of Directors WTBA Construction Companies
$494,799,897.11	22%	**$1,343,203,604.72**

The link has been included in the WTBA Directory and Buyers Guide from 2015 to 2020.

The Wisconsin Transportation Builders Association (WTBA), according to their website https://www.wtba.org/ "has more than 280 member companies, including contractors, consultants, and a broad range of other firms that supply diverse products and services to the transportation construction community."

In general, WTBA's beginnings are linked to several contractor-related groups that were organized in 1902. They worked to promote highway building in Wisconsin at a time when the automobile was increasingly becoming an important and popular means of transportation. In 1939, after the consolidation of a number of these organizations, WTBA emerged as the primary trade association representing the interests of the highway construction industry. A year later, in 1940, WTBA moved from Milwaukee to Madison, Wisconsin's capital, to be closer to legislative decision-makers. The Association expanded its activities from solely road-building activities to working on issues such as highway industry safety and balancing environmental protection with mobility for travelers and products. Today the WTBA has more than 280 members composed of construction-related companies, including contractors, consultants, and a broad range of other firms that supply many diverse construction-related products and services to the transportation construction community. It is considered to represent the non-DBE highway construction firms operating in Wisconsin; however, it is noted that while WTBA is comprised mainly of non-minority-owned contractors, it does have DBE firms as members and a DBE firm on its Board of Directors, in addition to other member firms that are owned by women and minority individuals, but which are not DBE certified.

Above is the list of Projects let from 2017 through 2019 directly presented to the WisDOT Representatives statement that the WTBA is charged with the task of establishing the budget for the WisDOT each year. With Statements like this and the understanding of the federal procurement process, it had become aware that there is a possible direct violation of the federal procurement process in which the people who are establishing the State estimates for budgets each year are also the board of directors for the WTBA, who are the owners of these large corporate construction companies who are awarded an average of about **38%** of the projects they are bidding on. The amount bid on in 2018 is over 146 projects of those projects there was 56 projects awarded. So when you look at this perspective it is easy to see the monumental influence established by the WTBA to the WisDOT. The influence of the WTBA has had a direct impact on all the projects located on or partially on Indian Lands, reservations, or IRR. If the WTBA chooses not to help establish the budgets, then it will be the WisDOT who is charged with the implementation of the effects of all the projects, and the amount of money the construction companies are then held accountable for.

So, it is in the best interests of the WTBA to have the suppression of the IP and the TERO Ordinances, thereby establishing a provision with the WisDOT influenced by the WTBA and making sure this document was not binding to any construction contractors, thus leaving no accountability. This was then implemented in 2008 up until 2011, when the construction industry began to look at the process and things, they did not like about it, and drafted a document through the Focus Group Meetings and submitted it to the WisDOT, causing the NAHP to be suspended sometime in August or September 2011 and not reimplemented until 2013; but with a lot less accountability for contractors if they violated the NAHP.

It was also stated that WisDOT representatives all directly and indirectly associated with the establishment of the NAHP mentioned the structure of how the WTBA influences the WisDOT. It was stated by numerous WisDOT representatives that WTBA is charged with establishing the budgets for the WisDOT annually. It is clear there is some type of relationship established because this is also the same reason why the NAHP was suspended, because of the construction industry, WisDOT, WTBA, TRANS-AC, and DWD.

It was not until this clear relationship presented itself, sometime in 2015, the Partnering Initiative was established, which consisted of the following partnership: DOT, WTBA, and American Engineering Companies of Wisconsin ACEC WI, as this was established to improve working relationships as it related to the delivery of Wisconsin transportation projects. In this partnership, the main goals were to:

- *Focus on the delivery of the transportation program to achieve common goals.*

- *The initiative includes the goal of providing a "new way of doing business" in Wisconsin.*

- *Implementing as many of these proposals as possible and will track progress through this website.*

- *Evaluate what and when plan information is available to contractors before advertising coordinating with the industry to identify items contributing to blended prices and evaluate if new bid items should be created to reduce risk.*

- *Develop a process for designers to contact contractors for input in the design phase.*

- *Review existing region processes for plan review and assess/implement best practices for statewide use.*

Below is a list of entity descriptions for each of the areas associated with this Partnering Initiative:

- ***The Wisconsin Chapter of the National Association of Minority Contractors (NAMC-WI).*** *According to their website (https:// namcwi.org/), NAMC "is a nonprofit trade association that was established in 1969 to address the needs and concerns of minority contractors. While membership is open to people of all races and ethnic backgrounds, the organization's mandate, 'Building Bridges – Crossing Barriers,' focuses on construction industry concerns common to African Americans, Asian Americans, Hispanic Americans, and Native Americans." Their latest membership roster lists 63 firms and 10 corporate sponsors.*

- ***The American Indian Construction and Trades Association (AICTA).*** *According to the American Indian Chamber of Commerce of Wisconsin (AICCA) website (http://www.aiccw.org/aicta. php), the Chamber "created the American Indian Construction and Trades Association (AICTA), responding to the need for American Indians in the construction industry to have access to much-needed information about federal, state, and local government policies. AICTA also lobbies on behalf of American Indians in Wisconsin to give their voice on issues that affect the industry."*

- ***The African American Chamber of Commerce of Greater Milwaukee (AACC).*** *According to their website (http://aaccmke.org/Home_ Page.html), AACC "invites people of all races, ethnic backgrounds and both genders as members. Our mission is to develop programs that strengthen and grow businesses owned by African Americans."*

- ***Transportation Advisory Committee (TRANS-AC).*** *TRANS-AC is a permanent and critical standing committee that meets year-round focusing on the state construction contracts of WisDOT's* *federal-aid highway DBE program. The diverse committee is structured to have representation by prime contractor associations, minority contractor associations, minority chambers of commerce, minority and woman-owned DBE firms, small non-DBE firms, and two prime contractors from different areas of the state, along with WisDOT contracting and DBE staff.*

The majority of TRANS-AC time is spent on drafting, proposing, and reviewing program changes, including proposed and final US DOT rules revisions; monitoring the processing and granting of good faith waivers; tracking goal achievements; drafting contractor guidance; developing educational objectives and efforts; and addressing other issues and concerns presented by DBE firms, the construction industry, and other stakeholders. The full committee meets every other month; subject-area subcommittees meet to address specific issues. Members are rotated every 2 years to expand effective stakeholder engagement. The current members of TRANS-AC are:

- *Wisconsin Transportation Builders Association (WTBA).*

- *Wisconsin Chapter of the National Association of Minority Contractors (NAMC-WI).*

- *American Indian Construction and Trades Association (AICTA).*

- *Lunda Construction.*

- *Zignego Construction.*

- *Arrow-Crete Construction.*

- *WisDOT leadership and program representatives: Administrator from the Chief Engineers Office, Chief from Project Development Section.*

- *WisDOT DBE program representatives, including the DBE Program Manager, DBE Engineer, and DBE Good Faith Waiver Analyst.*

- *WisDOT representatives from Aeronautics and Transit.*

- *FHWA Wisconsin Division Civil Rights Program Manager.*

- *Transportation Advisory Committee – Consultants (TRANS-CAC). TRANS-CAC is a permanent standing committee that meets year-round and whose focus is on the state-solicited and awarded consultant contracts portion of the WisDOT federal-aid highway DBE program, including regular state highway consultant contracts, work orders under "master" (delivery order), management consultant contracts, mega project consultant contracts, and local consultant contracts. The primary work area for consultant contractors is design and construction engineering (project leader and inspection services) which accounts for many of our overall annual needs from consultant firms.*

  TRANS-CAC has an alternating meeting schedule; a full committee meeting alternates with a DBE-only teleconference. DBE consulting firm meeting the next month, and then the third month, the pattern is repeated.

  WisDOT evolved into using this meeting schedule after determining that both DBE and non-DBE consulting firms were significantly freer and open with their comments in a more controlled environment. This schedule has substantially greater and more productive discussions of industry issues and concerns.

  Like TRANS-AC, WisDOT continuously reviews and revises TRANS-CAC membership to promote effective stakeholder engagement. The following groups and interests are currently represented through membership in TRANS-CAC:

  - *American Council of Engineering Companies of Wisconsin (ACEC).*

  - *Wisconsin Chapter of the National Association of Minority Contractors (NAMC-WI).*

  - *Wisconsin Women's Business Initiative Corporation (WWBIC).*

  - *FHWA Wisconsin Division Civil Rights Program Manager.*

The opinions from the Trans-AC and Trans-CAC meetings are archived within the WisDOT, a records request would need to be filed to receive this this document, which directly correlates with the WTBA and their responses to the TRIBES.

These responses are slated by all the entities that directly influenced the ability of non-Tribal members to work within the boundaries of the reservation, adding even further to the high unemployment rates of the TRIBES. With the biased perspective of WisDOT's OGC's Legal opinion and other influences, which was only one-sided, the WisDOT now had the ability to work on Indian reservations land and IRRs because of this slated legal opinion, but also what needs to be mentioned is the potential of alleged influences from one last entity as well.

Chapter 19

Influences of Eleven Federally Recognized Tribes of Wisconsin (TRIBES) Surrounding the TERO/IP or the NAHP

In conferring the influences surrounding the implementation of NAHP, IP, and TERO the mention of influences does not only affect these documents but also has a potential influence on these other documents which may be affected, which are: NAHP, TERO, IP, EO, MOU, MOA, and PA. These documents are often implemented by representatives of the TRIBES. The challenge in the comprehension of the perplexing TRIBES is to first understand the prerequisites for becoming a leader of TRIBES. For these positions of Tribal leadership, or any other elected officials for TRIBES, there are no clear prerequisites or formal requirements, such as education, tacit knowledge, experience, or understanding of Tribal Laws and Judicial systems or Government structures. So, it is with great concern for establishing a baseline of prerequisites to become Tribal leaders, because any of the documents mentioned can be simply influenced by a political official who has no knowledge of history or the detrimental effects of these documents to be implemented. Because these positions require no formal education or even any experience on how to run businesses or understand the governments, these people are the people who are running multibillion-dollar businesses and are influenced by and plagued by nepotism and conflicts of interest, questionable integrity, or lack of ethics.

Often statements like this were made through conversations between TRIBES growing up in Indian Country: "*It is not what you know but who you know or the name in your families which define the people in these positions.*" The unfortunate reality is not just the perceptions, but presents a clear need to obtain requirements like education, infield or hands-on experience working in government for TRIBES, and could only benefit from such classes as Tribal Governments, Federal Contracting or Compacting, Principles of Federal Indian Law, Tribal Criminal Law, Procedure, and Ethics, or even to understand your own government structure, the rate branches of government how each branch functions and how to develop laws and establish laws for the members of your TRIBES.

In the past it has been apparent that some people in these positions lack any of this education, and this can lead to things like nepotism, conflicts of interests, or even incidents of quid pro quo, which is defined as: "*a favor or advantage granted or expected in return for something.*" A good example of this is for one entity to release information on the condition that this information is detrimental to the entities, and it is released to the other entity before the scheduled time when everyone is to meet and go over the information in a closed-door session. When this information was disclosed, which was only for the TRIBES, but it was given the WisDOT TL. This document contained a list of questions and concerns addressing issues. When this information was released, a Tribal Leader took the information which was delegated for only tribal leadership to view and gave it to the WisDOT TL. This then circumvents the whole discussion process needed between the TRIBES leadership and other tribal representatives first. Then after this, the tribes and their representatives are all able to proceed forward together. After this is done, the tribal leadership and tribal representatives then present their concerns to the WisDOT TL collectively as the TLAC Group. When this process was circumvented, it was also stated by WisDOT TL stating: "*Tribal leader would always let the WisDOT TA representative know what is going on, because the Tribe's leader and the WisDOT TA are really good friends.*"

This statement presents a whole other level of perception of unethical or dubious behavior, and questionable integrity all directly impeding on the past, present, or future working relationships between TRIBES and State officials and any other agencies affiliated with any of these Agreements. This emerged because of the release of confidential information intended to only be presented to the TRIBES, prior to the TRIBES-only meeting scheduled to take place before this in a closed-door session. This presented the perceptions of unethical practices that were directly intended to circumvent the procurement processes related to the IGA and the funding associated, as the individual who was the WisDOT TA is also the same Tribe, and they awarded their tribe the IGA. When they were not able to complete this process accordingly, the WisDOT TL representative then moved this IGA and funds over to another tribe without the consultation of any members of the TLAC Group. The other Tribe that had received these funds from the IGA had stated in the previous meetings that they did not have the manpower or resources to take on the IGA, and then when it was commented on, this Tribal Leadership made a comment directly to the person who had inquired on this concern that if anyone crosses his path, he will ruin their career.

The reason for this comment was five months later it was stated by the WisDOT TL that this other tribe had signed the IGA and would be accepting the funding. This Tribe would also be operating as the TLAC Coordinator. The individual who became the new TLAC Coordinator was working as a WisDOT Employee at the WisDOT OBOEC. For months, this person was also sitting in on the closed-door sessions and reporting this information back to the WisDOT TA. This is a direct violation of ethics and presents a questionable level of integrity. When this was done, there were no opportunities presented for discussion between the Tribes and the IGA about the TLAC funds just being given to another Tribe without any consultation between the Tribes. The IGA was transferred to the other tribe by the WisDOT TA representative in the late afternoon of the day before the TLAC meeting. When asked, the WisDOT declined to move the IGA or even take another look at it because the statement from the WisDOT TA stated that it was going to the specific Tribe and this was not going to change the decision of the WisDOT representative, end of story. This information was all new to the tribes, while a public request for the NAHP TSTW project-specific labor reports was made to the WisDOT TL and it was disseminated to the TLAC Coordinator. A few weeks later, an email was received, this was sent in error from the acting interim TLAC Coordinator as it stated:

> *"My thoughts on this request is that it be approved by TLAC.... Is that possible? I mean he is requesting information that represents all tribes, not just Oneida. Is that a way of stalling this for a little bit to see if this is something all TLAC participants want to see? Or is this for personal/Oneida use? In that case, I would think it would need to be approved by all tribes that they agree to have this information provided to the requestor, does that make any sense? I mean I know it does not include any personal information but if what was done before was by contacting the tribe whose project was located, wouldn't it be their data? Let me know if any of what I said makes sense."*

This email directly exposes the Interim TLAC Coordinator and WisDOT's representative's attempts to stall the release of any information, while also working as the Community Services Specialist for WisDOT OBOEC this email was sent in error when it was directed to the WisDOT TA representative with the direct statements to stall the records request of the TSTW reports from the NAHP specific projects.

As this all took place and the IGA and the funding moved over to the other Tribe, over the next year things progressed to worsen. Some of the items had been mentioned in a TLAC meeting, but one of the TRIBES representatives inquired about why there is a need for the documentation of meeting minutes, and it was stated these meeting minutes were no longer going to be documented and, in fact, there will be no more closed-door sessions; this was brought forward by the one of the TRIBE's representatives and the TLAC Coordinator. It was then stated the audio clips would not be archived, and the TLAC Coordinator voiced her concerns about recording the meetings. Then the TLAC Coordinator stated: "*The discussion on the meeting minutes is over, end of discussion.*" A statement was made that it is not the decision of the TLAC Coordinator, or any one TRIBE, because this is a group, and no one has any more authority than any another TRIBE. We are all here to work together collectively and it is rather concerning that there are no more meeting minutes because this is a public meeting. The purpose for the preservation of the meeting minutes for accountability was stated by the TRIBE who stated in a meeting last year: "*We need to have progress and accountability for the people in this group.*" One of the TRIBES' representatives became upset and said they did not have time for this S#$T, became upset and stormed out of the meeting, but before leaving the meeting stated to another TRIBE's representative that the individual who asked these questions had to pick a side; and then stormed out of the meeting.

Soon after this meeting concluded, the discussion about the incident related that the TRIBES' representatives were present, but when the representative was talked to in this manner nothing was done and the person asking the questions was talked to. This tribal representative had become upset and left the meeting for a short time. He became upset because he was caught in his statements and became frustrated, and when he began to lose his composure, he took a moment to conduct himself.

This continued for about six months later at another TLAC meeting. In this meeting, in November 2018, it was stated by the TLAC Coordinator that there would be no more meeting minutes, and now it was stated there aren't closed-door sessions for the TRIBES to discuss the current issues. The TLAC Coordinator was asked: *"What is the justification for the removal of the closed-door meetings?"* The TLAC Coordinator stated there is no reason they should have to pay for closed-door sessions. It was explained that this should have been covered throughout the IGA Funding and this should have been the decision of the TLAC Group as the TLAC Coordinator does not have the authority to delegate anything to any TRIBES without the approval of the TLAC Group first.

In this meeting, there was a conversation regarding the training for TSTW. Topics discussed where the timing of the training was important as they didn't want to have training in the middle of the working season, and to not have the training in the fall because if they completed the training then the TSTW would not be able to find employment because it was the end of the season. Another concern was to make sure adequate training was available because, in the OSHA 30 Training, there are two different classes: One for Construction and the other for General Industry. One of the concerns was that, in OSHA 30, there are two different kinds of training, and to be sure the right training is provided because this is important. If a person is not given the right training, then for working on a construction project, people can lose their lives on these projects because the correct information was not given to them. A contractor from the industry also mentioned that this is important because of the seriousness of working in the construction industry, that if they don't have the correct training, they will not be hired.

The TLAC Coordinator had stated this shouldn't matter and that they would be okay. It was at that point it was asked how many people in the meeting have worked in the construction industry. Only one or two raised their hands and it was explained this is concerning that we have people who have never worked in the industry, because the people with no experience are delegating how training and processes are implemented without any consideration to the industry, as the people who raised their hands had stated. An example of this was the training which was given. This training was provided on June 18 to 20, 2019, and it was not adequate. One of the committee also stated that he was concerned because TSTW wasn't receiving the adequate training needed to be working in the Construction Industry:

1. They become a Risk Factor to themselves and anyone around them in the construction projects.

2. They will not have the adequate Certification needed to obtain the positions relevant to construction.

3. Wasting TLAC funding and not to mention now you're wasting the time of the Tribal Skilled Trades Workers.

Adequate training is the training for OSHA #510 – Occupational **Safety and Health Standards for the Construction Industry**. Below is a link to the OSHA Construction vs. General Industry doc, which directly shows the differences in the classes. It is concerning when the level of risk is elevated and could have been prevented but has the potential to directly affect our community. It is rather concerning that WisDOT continued to offer this training, even though it was explained that this was incorrect training and had the potential of seriously elevating the risk level and injury or even death because people will now not have the adequate training needed. This was stated to Both WisDOT representatives from Tribal Affairs, one of the Regional Tribal representatives and the TLAC Coordinator.

Below is a link to the PDF, which shows the direct differences between the two trainings offered:

- *OSHA 30-Hour Outreach Course for Construction Industry, 30-Hour Construction Industry Required Course Topics Mandatory (15 hours) Electives (12 hours).*

- *OSHA 30-Hour Outreach Course for General Industry, 30-Hour General Industry Required.*

This link presented displays the discrepancies between the training provided and the training required for the Transportation Industry, and this is located on the OSHA website with the United States Department of Laborers. Here is the link: https://www.osha.gov/laws-regs/regulations/standardnumber/1926

The TSTW who obtained this certification may not be able to obtain a position on any construction-related projects, because this is not the correct certification as these are directly related to Industrial or Manufacturing related projects. This is concerning because they will not become aware of these hazards on the projects and become a higher risk factor to not just themselves but also other workers on the project.

In Closing

The many influences directly or indirectly affect, not just the NAHP, PA, and MOU, but also to the safety of those working in the industry. It is chilling that the training for all new TSTW looking to get into the industry across the state of Wisconsin is being defined by a group of individuals who have had no experience in the industry and never worked in the field in the CI, but yet they are delegating what training should be applied. This comes at a cost to all entities involved:

1) The costs of high liability to the contractors because the tribal skilled trades worker was told they have the training to be on these fast-paced projects but are not adequately trained.

2) The TSTW are affected because they do not have adequate training to prevent them or their coworkers from injury or even loss of life on the projects.

3) Wasting Tribal funding to get the adequate training for TSTW.

4) Wasting or misappropriating taxpayer money on inadequate training; and

5) Wasting all of the above-mentioned time as well as resources.

Therefore, it is my recommendation to take a good look at the people who are in these positions and follow up with an assessment of how to resolve all the concerns. It is difficult because not it is clear to see where the levels of influence come from on all sides, but it has been brought to light that some of these others are not yet known.

It is also important to look at all the conflicts of interest presented, including some other possible conflicts of interest such as the Stroebel, Brooks Bill to Swap Federal Money, and curtail regulations which were established on November 18, 2015. This was established to help by Representative Brooks (R-Saukville) as he proposed:

> *Representative Rob Brooks (R-Saukville) and I have proposed legislation that would "swap" a portion of federal funds within local transportation programs with already existing state transportation dollars, thereby removing costly and unnecessary federal regulations and red tape from local highway projects.*

Another clear example of the influences is the State Buyout of Federal Funds for Local Transportation Programs, which was established in 2010 as the purpose for this was for:

> *Eliminating federal funds from local road programs and replacing them with state funds would reduce the magnitude of oversight and allow projects to be designed and constructed at a faster pace and a lower cost to taxpayers. By streamlining the use of federal funds and providing counties with more efficient options to do business, local transportation providers will have the opportunity to do more with*

less. The state could more appropriately use federal funds on its larger, more complex projects. Local projects would still be required to comply with the state facilities development process, specifications, and other state laws and regulations such as the Wisconsin Environmental Protection Act.

If these two acts are utilized with projects located near or projects within a commutable distance of Reservations, it is concerning to see how this could be perceived. Many people are unaware of this information, but the further I have dug into the information the more it has come out from when the previous governor was in office.

These acts directly show the circumvention of not just the federal processes but could even lead to the disruption of employment opportunities for TRIBES, and with these influences presented, it can only add fuel to the fire, because when looking at the context of all of the information presented in just the influences, the memorandums, working relationships, PA, and Hiring Provisions, along with TERO and IP. This detrimental effect from any of the influences has the opportunity to continue to further devastate Tribes, pushing the unemployment rates to all-time highs when provisions, laws, or ordinances are not implemented only continuing to further enhance the already high employment rates and making it difficult to fortify positive good faith working relationships without honoring these documents.

When everyone comes to the table, we all must have an equal seat to begin the healing process and acknowledge what has been done in the past to solidify a positive future for all working together in a good way, because it is not effective to just continue to push these items under the rug for the next person to clean up, when they need to be addressed now. Establishing the proposal of the document to ensure that the TRIBE's right to self-govern, and that it is acknowledged that contractors will be working within the boundaries of federally recognized tribes, will help the agreement or even negotiation process for all projects located near and within commutable distances, and enhance, not just the working relationships, but also the cohesiveness to all work together in a communal manner.

The reason for this being brought forward, is because it was not until research of the public website for the Wisconsin Department of Transportation and the Public Website of the WTBA, presented these influences. Statements made by the WisDOT Representatives through the past 5 years were brought forward because, when establishing estimates for annual budgets, this can be compiled by the WTBA or construction industry and, as part of Federal government's guidance on Administrative Requirements, this process has been streamlined by The Office of Management and Budget (OMB) for Federal Awards. This is important because of the federal Procurement Standards in the following sections:

- *§200.317 Procurements by States: When procuring property and services under the federal award, a state must follow the same policies and procedures it uses for procurements from its non-federal funds. The state will comply with Sec. 200.322 Procurement of recovered materials and ensure that every purchase order or other contract includes any clauses required by section 200.326 Contract provisions. All other non-federal entities, including sub-recipients of a state, will follow Sec. 200.318 General procurement standards through 200.326 Contract provisions.*

- *§200.318 General Procurement Standards:*

  (a) *The non-Federal entity must use its own documented procurement procedures which reflect applicable State, local, and tribal laws, and regulations, provided that the procurements conform to applicable Federal law and the standards identified in this part.*

  (a) *Non-Federal entities must maintain oversight to ensure that contractors perform following the terms, conditions, and specifications of their contracts or purchase orders.*

(a) *The non-Federal entity must maintain written standards of conduct covering conflicts of interest and governing the actions of its employees engaged in the selection, award, and administration of contracts.*

    (1) *No employee, officer, or agent may participate in the selection, award, or administration of a contract supported by a federal award if he or she has a real or apparent conflict of interest. Such a conflict of interest would arise when the employee, officer, or agent, any member of his or her immediate family, his or her partner, or an organization that employs or is about to employ any of the parties indicated herein, has a financial or other interest in or a tangible personal benefit from a firm considered for a contract. The officers, employees, and agents of the non-Federal entity may neither solicit nor accept gratuities, favors, or anything of monetary value from contractors or parties to subcontracts. However, non-Federal entities may set standards for situations in which the financial interest is not substantial, or the gift is an unsolicited item of nominal value. The standards of conduct must provide for disciplinary actions to be applied for violations of such standards by officers, employees, or agents of the non-Federal entity.*

    (2) *If the non-Federal entity has a parent, affiliate, or subsidiary organization that is not a state, local government, or Indian tribe, the non-Federal entity must also maintain written standards of conduct covering organizational conflicts of interest. Organizational conflicts of interest mean that because of relationships with a parent company, affiliate, or subsidiary organization, the non-Federal entity is unable or appears to be unable to be impartial in conducting a procurement action involving a related organization.*

(d) *The non-Federal entity's procedures must avoid the acquisition of unnecessary or duplicative items. Consideration should be given to consolidating or breaking out procurements to obtain a more economical purchase. Where appropriate, an analysis will be made of lease versus purchase alternatives, and any other appropriate analysis to determine the most economical approach.*

(a) *To foster greater economy and efficiency, and by efforts to promote cost-effective use of shared services across the Federal Government, the non-Federal entity is encouraged to enter into state and local intergovernmental agreements or inter- entity agreements where appropriate for procurement or use of common or shared goods and services.*

(a) *The Non-Federal entity is encouraged to use Federal excess and surplus property instead of purchasing new equipment and property whenever such use is feasible and reduces project costs.*

(a) *The Non-Federal entity is encouraged to use value engineering clauses in contracts for construction projects of sufficient size to offer reasonable opportunities for cost reductions. Value engineering is a systematic and creative analysis of each contract item or task to ensure that its essential function is provided at an overall lower cost.*

(a) *The Non-Federal entity must award contracts only to responsible contractors possessing the ability to perform successfully under the terms and conditions of a proposed procurement. Consideration will be given to such matters as contractor integrity, compliance with public policy, record of past performance, and financial and technical resources. See also § 200.213 Suspension and debarment.*

(a) *The Non-Federal entity must maintain records sufficient to detail the history of procurement. These records will include, but are not necessarily limited to, the following: rationale for the method of procurement, selection of contract type, contractor selection or rejection, and the basis for the contract price.*

(1)   The non-Federal entity may use a time and materials type contract only after a determination that no other contract is suitable and if the contract includes a ceiling price that the contractor exceeds at its own risk. Time and materials type contract means a contract whose cost to a non-Federal entity is the sum of:

(i) The actual cost of materials; and

(ii) Direct labor hours are charged at fixed hourly rates that reflect wages, general and administrative expenses, and profit.

(2)   Since this formula generates an open-ended contract price, a time-and-materials contract provides no positive profit incentive to the contractor for cost control or labor efficiency. Therefore, each contract must set a ceiling price that the contractor exceeds at its own risk. Further, the non-Federal entity awarding such a contract must assert a high degree of oversight to obtain reasonable assurance that the contractor is using efficient methods and effective cost controls.

(j)   The Non-Federal entity alone must be responsible, under good administrative practice and sound business judgment, for the settlement of all contractual and administrative issues arising out of procurements. These issues include but are not limited to, source evaluation, protests, disputes, and claims. These standards do not relieve the non-Federal entity of any contractual responsibilities under its contracts. The Federal awarding agency will not substitute its judgment for that of the non-Federal entity unless the matter is primarily a federal concern. Violations of law will be referred to the local, state, or Federal authority having proper jurisdiction.[152]

---

152. [78 FR 78608, Dec. 26, 2013, as amended at 79 FR 75885, Dec. 19, 2014; 80 FR 43309, July 22, 2015] https://www.law.cornell.edu/cfr/text/2/200.318

- ***§200.319 Competition:***

(a) *All procurement transactions must be conducted in a manner that provides full and open competition consistent with the standards of this section. To ensure objective contractor performance and eliminate an unfair competitive advantage, contractors that develop or draft specifications, requirements statements of work, and invitations for bids or requests for proposals must be excluded from competing for such procurements. Some of the situations considered to be restrictive of competition include but are not limited to:*

    (1) *Placing unreasonable requirements on firms for them to qualify to do business.*

    (2) *Requiring unnecessary experience and excessive bonding.*

    (3) *Noncompetitive pricing practices between firms or between affiliated companies.*

    (4) *Noncompetitive contracts to consultants that are on retainer contracts.*

    (5) *Organizational conflicts of interests.*

    (6) *Specifying only a "Brand Name" product instead of allowing "an equal" product to be offered and describing the performance or other relevant requirements of the procurement; and*

    (7) *Any arbitrary action in the procurement process.*

(b) *The non-federal entity must conduct procurements in a manner that prohibits the use of statutorily or administratively imposed state or local geographical preferences in the evaluation of bids or proposals except in those cases where applicable Federal Statutes expressly mandate or encourage geographic preference. Nothing in this section preempts state licensing laws. When contracting for architectural and engineering (A/E) Services, geographic location may be a selection for criterion provided its application leaves an appropriate number of qualified firms, given the nature and size of the project, to compete for the contract.*

(a) *The Non-Federal entity must have written procedures for procurement transactions. These procedures must ensure that all solicitations:*

(1) *Incorporate a clear and accurate description of the technical requirements for the material, product, or service to be procured. Such description must not, in competitive procurements, contain features that unduly restrict competition. The description may include a statement of the qualitative nature of the material, product, or service to be procured and, when necessary, must set forth those minimum essential characteristics and standards to which it must conform if it is to satisfy its intended use. Detailed product specifications should be avoided if possible. When it is impractical or uneconomical to make a clear and accurate description of the technical requirements, a "brand name or equivalent" description may be used to define the performance or other salient requirements of procurement. The specific features of the named brand that must be met by offers must be clearly stated; and*

(2) *Identify all requirements that the offerors must fulfill and all other factors to be used in evaluating bids or proposals.*

(d) *The Non-Federal entity must ensure that all prequalified lists of persons, firms, or products that are used in acquiring goods and services are current and include enough qualified sources to ensure maximum open and free competition. Also, the non-Federal entity must not preclude potential bidders from qualifying during the solicitation period.*[153]

---

153. The Office of Management and Budget's https://www.grants.gov/learn-grants/grant-policies/omb-uniform-guidance-2014.html (OMB) Guidance https://www.govinfo.gov/content/pkg/CFR-2014-title2-vol1/pdf/CFR-2014-title2-vol1-sec200-319.pdf

Chapter 20

Collective Solution Moving Forward

In conclusion, this is based on the presence of factual information and meeting minutes which, over Ten Years of the history of the NAHP and the TLAC, were all removed from the website in March 2019. This is where the same information contained in this dissertation came from because copies of all this information had been preserved to maintain the integrity of this NAHP/TLAC process. It was also to help provide accountability for these individuals and their actions resulting in the justification to nullify the current NAHP. The repudiation of the decisions made by WisDOT OGC thereby "recognizing the TRIBES' right of self-determination for Indian tribal governments while restoring these obligations to work with Indian tribal governments in a government-to-government relationship." Doing this would be an extensive restoration process thereby obligating the responsibility of WISDOT and other agencies to negotiate and commit to working with Indian tribal governments in these unique relationships, respecting tribal sovereignty and self-determination.

Doing this would then result in the preservation or restoration of the inherent rights of the TRIBES as sovereign nations, and all who reside within the state of Wisconsin. These agreements, compacts, bylaws, and constitutions continue to further elevate self-governance, regardless of the surrounding influences. We are all here to help promote and enhance economic opportunities on projects located on or near the reservation, thereby honoring and promoting Tribal Sovereignty and the inherent rights as domestic dependent nations composed of tribal members with dual citizenships and a political classification as stated for it to ever be resolved that a document should be established similar to this when working with any governmental agencies and any of the TRIBES across the nation.

With the appearance of the unswerving and ancillary influences, whether it is from the TRIBES, Federal Agencies, State Agencies, or Construction industries Contractors or Unions, it is important to note they all present a uniqueness of influence imposed, but it is clear the only influence which should be predominant is the influence from the TRIBES, because this directly relates to the work being done within the boundaries of their reservations. Regardless of the situations and influences. The TRIBES are the only entities with the final say when it comes to any agencies or construction contractors stepping within the boundaries of their reservation or obtaining any work from any other agencies, as this is the same process when they are contracted by TRIBES on these projects. This warranted the establishment and development of this document has been created thereby formally acknowledging the TRIBES and making a level of accountability:

Tribal Sovereignty and Self-Determination Form

The creation of a document that must be established for all federally recognized tribes when dealing with other agencies involving an MOU or MOA, PA, EO, or any other official documents moving forward, will thereby require acknowledging and respecting: Federal, State, Townships, Municipalities, Corporations, etc.

"Tribal Sovereignty and Self Determination Rights."

For Tribal Self-Government and Sovereignty, Tribal Rights, and Tribal responsibilities policies that affect Indian tribal governments in a unique and significant way, all Federally recognized tribes should begin their language in any agreement as follows:

Whereas: This document is to be incorporated for all Federally Recognized Tribes whereas any of the following may apply which may be located "on," "near," or "within a commutable distance" of Indian roadways, Indian country, Indian trust lands, fee lands, and reservations.

- *Indian preference law is one of the founding principles of the inherent rights as a sovereign nation and the tribe's rights to self-govern. IP has been established as a unique legal right that tribal members have that entitles them to first consideration for all employment, training, contracting, subcontracting, and business opportunities that exist on and in some cases near reservations.[154] The first appearance in Federal regulations was in 1834. Since then, most new laws and regulations related to tribes and Indian people include preference provisions. There are no federal laws that prohibit IP, additionally, court rulings have held that Indian preference is a political preference and not a racial preference, and as such does not violate the dictates of federal employment law.*

- *Indian Preference and TERO are enacted through the Tribe's authority to enforce an Indian/Native employment preference law grounded in its inherent sovereign status. This legal doctrine is the most basic principle of Indian law and is supported by a host of Supreme Court decisions. Inherent sovereign powers derive from the principle that certain powers do not necessarily come from delegated powers granted by express acts of Congress but are inherent powers of a limited sovereign that have never been taken away. Tribes have a basic relationship with the federal government as sovereign powers. This is recognized in both treaties and federal statutes. The sovereignty of tribes has been limited from time to time by treaties and federal legislation; however, what has not been expressly limited remains within tribal sovereignty.[155]*

---

154. Most Frequently Asked Questions about TERO; What is Indian Preference? http://www.councilfortribalemploymentrights.org/tero-faq/,

155. What is the legal basis for TERO? http://www.councilfortribalemploymentrights.

- ***Self-Determination:*** *"Indigenous Peoples have the right to self-determination. By virtue of that right, they freely determine their political status and freely pursue their economic, social, and cultural development," according to Article 3 of the U.N. Declaration of the Rights of Indigenous People. "Indigenous peoples, in exercising their right to self-determination, have the right to autonomy or self-government in matters relating to their internal and local affairs, as well as ways and means for financing their autonomous functions," according to Article 4 of the U.N. Declaration on the Rights of Indigenous People. "The most protected and sacred right of all peoples is the right to govern their affairs and make decisions without being coerced by other governments. This is an inherent right of peoples and for the Navajo people it has existed since time immemorial. However, Navajo law states that the Navajo Nation must still obtain it. The 'ultimate goal of the Navajo Nation is self-determination.'10 N.N.C. § 124 (A) (2002). The Commission recommends that the Navajo government, instead, recognize that the Navajo people's right to self-determination has been absolute since time immemorial and is not an aspiration as stated in Title 10 of the Navajo Nation Code. Moreover, Navajo written law must recognize the Navajo people's right to self-determination comes from the Holy People."*

- ***Tribal Employment Rights Ordinance*** *(TERO) stands for Tribal Employment Rights Ordinance or Office. TERO Ordinances require that all employers who are engaged in operating a business on reservations give preference to qualified Indians in all aspects of employment, contracting, and other business activities. TERO Offices were established and empowered to monitor and enforce the requirements of the tribal employment rights ordinance.[156] The primary purpose of the TERO program is to enforce tribally enacted Indian Preference law to ensure that Indian/Alaska Native people*

org/tero-faq/

156. What is TERO: What is the purpose of the TERO program? http://www.council fortribalemploymentrights.org/tero-faq/;

gain their rightful share of employment, training, contracting, sub-contracting, and business opportunities on and near reservations and native villages.

This should be concluded along with signatures from the representatives and certified by a witness as it would state agency has the "responsibility" and is "committed," to working with the Indian Tribal Governments in this unique relationship, "respecting tribal sovereignty and self-determination" if found in any violation to working in good faith may impose a series of civil penalties, suspension, or removal of any non-Indian representatives or agencies from the ability to do work located "on," "near," or "within a commutable distance" of (*This can be negotiated between the tribes and governmental agencies*) miles of Indian roadways, Indian country, Indian trust lands, fee lands and reservations.

Definitions

(Commonly Used Terms)

- **BIA:** *Bureau of Indian Affairs (U.S. Department of the Interior).*

- **BIA/FHWA Memorandum of Agreement:** *An agreement between the BIA and the FHWA that contains mutually agreeable roles and responsibilities for the administration of the IRR (Indian Reservation Road) and Highway Bridge Replacement and Rehabilitation programs.*

- **Consultation and Coordination with Indian Tribal Governments:** *This is the title of Executive Order 13084, signed by the President on May 14, 1998, that requires federal agencies to respect tribal self-government and sovereignty, tribal rights, and tribal responsibilities whenever they formulate policies that affect Indian tribal governments in a unique and significant way.*

- **Cooperative Agreement:** *An agreement between the BIA and other agency(s) used to reimburse that agency for goods or services provided to the BIA.*

- **Disadvantaged Business Enterprise (DBE):** *A business owned and operated by one or more socially and economically disadvantaged individuals. Socially and economically disadvantaged individuals include African Americans, Hispanic Americans, Native Americans, Asian Pacific Americans or Asian Indian Americans and any other minorities or individuals found to be disadvantaged by the Small Business Administration under Section 8(a) of the Small Business Act.*

- **Eleven Federally Recognized Tribes of Wisconsin (TRIBES)** *composed of the eleven separate tribes all with individual constitutions, by laws and establish individual governments, but all located within the state* *of Wisconsin. The tribes included are: Bad River Band of Lake Superior Chippewa Indians, Forest County Potawatomi Community, Ho-Chunk Nation, Lac Courte Oreilles Band of Lake Superior Chippewa Indians, Lac Du Flambeau Band of Lake Superior Chippewa Indians, Menominee Indian Nation of Wisconsin, Oneida Nation of Wisconsin, Red Cliff Band of Lake Superior Chippewa Indians, Sokaogon Chippewa Community, St. Croix Band of Chippewa Indians, Stockbridge-Munsee Band of Mohican Indians.*

— **FAA – Federal Aviation Administration:** *See U.S. DOT.*

— **FHWA – Federal Highway Administration:** *See U.S. DOT.*

— **Government-to-Government Relationship:** *Relationship that exists between federally recognized tribes and the federal government. Implicit in the relationship is recognition of tribal sovereignty as individual nations within the U.S., and the U.S. government's obligation to protect tribal lands. The relationship between tribal and state governments should also be characterized as government- to-government.*

— **Indian Country:** *As defined by federal law, Indian country includes all land within the limits of any Indian reservation under the jurisdiction of the U.S. government, notwithstanding the issuance of any patent, and including rights-of-way running through the reservation. In addition, Indian country also includes all dependent Indian communities as well as all Indian allotments to which Indian titles have not been extinguished. [The term "Indian country" has become the controlling term of art for jurisdictional issues in Indian law. Even though 18 U.S.C. § 1151 et seq. deals primarily with crimes and criminal procedures, the U.S. Supreme Court has held that the definition given by § 1151 also applies to state civil jurisdiction. The principle that section 1151 defines Indian country for both civil and criminal jurisdiction purposes is firmly established. The Court has also held that a tribe may exercise civil authority over Indian country as defined by 18 U.S.C. § 1151.45. In addition, the Supreme Court has held that land held in trust by the United States for a tribe is Indian country subject to tribal control whether or not that land has reservation status.]*

- **Indian Lands:** *Lands held in trust by the United States for individual Indians or tribes, or land titled to individual Indians or tribes subject to federal restrictions against alienation or encumbrance.*

- **Indian preference Law** *(IP) is one of the founding principles of the Inherent rights as a sovereign nation and the tribe's rights to self-governs. IP has been established as a unique legal right that tribal members have that entitles them to first consideration to all employment, training, contracting, and subcontracting and business opportunities that exist on and in some cases near reservations.[157] The first appeared in Federal regulations in 1834. Since then, most new laws and regulations related to tribes and Indian people include preference provisions. There are no federal laws which prohibit IP, additionally, court rulings have held that Indian preference is a political preference and not a racial preference, and as such do not violate the dictates of federal employment law*

- **Indian Preference and TERO** *are enacted through the Tribe's authority to enforce an Indian/Native employment preference law and is grounded in its inherent sovereign status. This legal doctrine is the most basic principle of Indian law and is supported by a host of Supreme Court decisions. Inherent sovereign powers derive from the principle that certain powers do not necessarily come from delegated powers granted by express acts of Congress but are inherent powers of a limited sovereign that have never been taken away. Tribes have a basic relationship with the federal government as sovereign powers. This is recognized in both treaties and federal statutes. The sovereignty of tribes has been limited from time to time by treaties and federal legislation; however, what has not been expressly limited remains within tribal sovereignty.[158]*

- **Indian Reservation Roads** *(IRR): Public roads located within or that provide access to an Indian reservation or Indian trust land or restricted Indian land that is not subject to fee title alienation without the approval of the federal government, or Indian and Alaska Native villages, group, or*

---

157. Most Frequently Asked Questions about TERO: What is Indian Preference? http://www.councilfortribalemploymentrights.org/tero-faq/

158. What is the legal basis for TERO? http://www.councilfortribalemploymentrights.org/tero-faq/

communities in which Indians and Alaskan Natives reside, whom the Secretary of the Interior has determined are eligible for services generally available to Indians under Federal laws specifically applicable to Indians. Roads on the BIA Road System are also IRR roads.

– **IRR Inventory**: *An inventory of roads that meet the following criteria: a) public roads strictly within reservation boundaries; b) public roads that provide access to lands, groups, villages, and communities in which the majority of residences are Indian; c) public roads that serve Indian lands not within reservation boundaries; and d) public roads that serve recognized Indian groups, villages, and isolated communities not located within a reservation.*

– **IRR Program Road/Bridge Inventory**: *An inventory of BIA owned IRR and bridges.*

– **IRR Program Stewardship Plan**: *The plan that details the roles and responsibilities of the BIA, FHWA and ITGs in the administration and operation of the IRR Program.*

– **Intergovernmental Agreement (IGA)**: *An agreement between two or more governments for accomplishing common goals, providing a service, or solving a mutual problem.*

– **Memorandum of Agreement (MOA)**: *A document describing in detail the specific responsibilities of, and actions to be taken by, each of the parties so that their goals may be accomplished. A MOA may also indicate the goals of the parties, to help explain their actions and responsibilities.*

– **Memorandum of Understanding (MOU)**: *A document that describes very broad concepts of mutual understanding, goals and plans shared by the parties.*

– **Native American**: *A member of any of the indigenous cultural groups of the western hemisphere, including American Indians, Alaska Natives, Native Hawaiians, and other indigenous peoples.*

– **Native American Hiring Provision (NAHP)** *established in 2009 by the Wisconsin Department of Transportation with the purpose to outline the requirements and procedures necessary to: "Encourages and promote* *the hiring of Native Americans on transportation construction projects that are located 'on' or 'near' reservations." The provision is applied to both state and federal projects. This was a direct result of the established Partnership Agreement set in place from the Eleven Federally Recognized Tribes of Wisconsin (TRIBES) and WisDOT. This all resulted out of the State Tribal Consultation which was the signing of the Executive Order #39 on February 27, 2004, as this was the beginning of the unique government-to-government relationship between the state and tribal governments requiring the strengthening of the working relationship between two governments.*[159] *The main purpose of the NAHP supports the government-to-government relationship between the state and the tribes and enhances Native American labor employment opportunities on state and federal transportation projects that are located on, or partially on, tribal or reservation lands.*[160] *This is because Tribes often have the highest unemployment rates on their reservations.*

— **Native Americans:** *This term broadly describes the people considered indigenous to North America who lived here prior to European colonization. The term includes "American Indians," "Indians," "Alaska Natives," "Eskimos," "Aleuts," and "Native Hawaiians."*

— ***Partnership Agreement (PA):*** *The Partnership Agreement is a document first created in 2005 because of Executive Order 39, "Relating to an Affirmation of the Government-to-Government Relationship Between the State of Wisconsin and Indian Tribal Governments Located Within the State of Wisconsin." Its purpose is to continue to create and define the processes by which the Wisconsin Department of Transportation (WisDOT) and the Wisconsin Division-Federal Highway Administration (FHWA) will work in collaboration with the eleven federally recognized tribes (tribes) of Wisconsin. This agreement is designed to acknowledge and support the government-to-government relationship and support American Indian sovereignty among State and Federal Agencies and the eleven tribes. This mutually beneficial relationship continues to grow.*

159. February 27, 2004, Executive Order #39; http://witribes.wi.gov/section.asp?linkid=283andlocid=57

160. Native American Hiring Provision: https://www.wisdottlac.org/

- *Public Law 280 (PL280) is a federal statute enacted by Congress in 1953. It enabled states to assume criminal, as well as civil, jurisdiction in matters involving Indians as litigants on reservation land. Previous to the enactment of Public Law 280, these matters were dealt with in either tribal and/or federal court. Essentially, Public Law 280 was an attempt by the federal government to reduce its role in Indian affairs. Six states which were obligated to assume jurisdiction from the outset of the law: Alaska, California, Minnesota, Nebraska, Oregon, and **Wisconsin**. States that have assumed at least some jurisdiction since the enactment of Public Law 280 include: Nevada, South Dakota, Washington, Florida, Idaho, Montana, North Dakota, Arizona, Iowa, and Utah.[161]*

- *Reservation: Lands reserved by a tribe during treaty negotiations with the federal government for tribal use. Indian reservations are held in trust for the tribe by the federal government.*

- *Self-Determination: "Indigenous Peoples have the right to self-determination. By virtue of that right, they freely determine their political status and freely pursue their economic, social, and cultural development," according to Article 3 of the U.N. Declaration of the Rights of Indigenous People. "Indigenous peoples, in exercising their right to self-determination, have the right to autonomy or self- government in matters relating to their internal and local affairs, as well as ways and means for financing their autonomous functions," according to Article 4 of the U.N. Declaration on the Rights of Indigenous People. "The most protected and sacred right of all peoples is the right to govern their affairs, make decisions without being coerced by other governments. This is an inherent right of peoples and for the Navajo people it has existed since time immemorial. However, in Navajo law it states that the Navajo Nation must still obtain it. The 'ultimate goal of the Navajo Nation is self-determination.'10 N.N.C. § 124 (A) (2002). The Commission recommends that the Navajo government, instead, recognize that Navajo people's right to self-determination has been absolute since time immemorial and is not an aspiration as stated in Title 10 of the Navajo Nation Code. Moreover,*

---

161. Frequently Asked Questions of Public Law 280 https://www.humanities.uci.edu/IDP/nativeam/pl280.html

Navajo written law must recognize the Navajo people's right to self-determination comes from the Holy People."

— **Self-Government:** *Is defined as the self-control, self-command government of a country by its people especially after having been a colony.*

— **Sovereignty:** *The status, dominion, rule, or power of a sovereign. Tribes have the power to make and enforce laws for their tribe and reservation, and to establish courts and other forums for the resolution of disputes.*

— **Tribal Employment Rights Ordinance** *(TERO) stands for Tribal Employment Rights Ordinance or Office. TERO Ordinances require that all employers who are engaged in operating a business on reservations give preference to qualified Indians in all aspects of employment, contracting and other business activities. TERO Offices were established and empowered to monitor and enforce the requirements of the tribal employment rights ordinance.[162] The primary purpose of the TERO program is to enforce tribally enacted Indian Preference law to ensure that Indian/Alaska Native people gain their rightful share to employment, training, contracting, subcontracting, and business opportunities on and near reservations and native villages.*

— **U.S. DOT – United States Department of Transportation:** *The federal cabinet-level agency with responsibility for highways, mass transit, railroads, aviation, and ports; headed by the secretary of transportation. The U.S. DOT includes the Federal Highway Administration, the Federal Transit Administration, Federal Aviation Administration and Federal Railroad Administration, among others. There are also state DOTs (known as WisDOT in Wisconsin).*

— **WisDOT – Wisconsin Department of Transportation:** *The state cabinet-level agency with responsibility for highways, mass transit, aviation, railroad development and ports, headed by the secretary of transportation.*

---

162. What is TERO; What is the purpose of the TERO program? http://www.council fortribalemploymentrights.org/tero-faq/

Appendix A

Original Timeline TLAC NAHP ITTF Meeting Minutes Highlight Notes

- *October 31, 2002 – The FHWA releases a report that the WisDOT placed an NAHP on Federal Aid Projects on or near Indian lands. This special provision also required that the contractors at all tiers shall make aggressive, concentrated efforts to employ Native Americans on these projects.[163] The WisDOT and FHWA partnered to work with Native American Businesses and individuals working on a government-to-government basis with the TRIBES.*

- *February 27, 2004 – The EO#39 was issued and signed, recognizing the sovereignty of the TRIBES of Wisconsin while also recognizing the government-to-government relationship between the state and tribal governments, requiring strengthening of the working relationship between the two governments. The State-Tribal Consultation Initiative was established, which was aimed towards increasing relations between state agencies and tribal governments to streamline and improve the services our governments provide to both tribal and non-tribal members.[164]*

- *May 24, 2005 – The PA was established between the TRIBES, Wisconsin Division Federal Highway Administration (FHWA), and WisDOT, which was created as a result of the EO#39 as this related to the affirmation of the government-to-government relationships established between the state of TRIBES. This was designed*

---

163. Outreach to Native Americans – Federal Highway Administration www.fhwa.dot.gov/tribal/state/oct31_03.htm

164. Wisconsin State Tribal Relations Initiative http://wiTRIBES.wi.gov/section_print.asp?linkid=283andlocid=57

to acknowledge and support the government-to-government relationship between TRIBES and State and Federal Agencies and to
support American Indian sovereignty.

- **June 28, 2005** – A policy was established regarding the consultation with WisDOT and TRIBES. This relationship is outlined in the
Constitution of the United States, treaties, statutes, laws, and court
decisions. The Wisconsin EO#39, issued in February 2004, affirms
the government-to-government relationship between the State
of Wisconsin and TRIBES. These relationships involve respectful
and cooperative communication and dealings that are designed to
achieve a consensus, to the extent possible, before a decision is made
or an action is taken, and to implement programs collaboratively.
The Wisconsin Department of Administration (DOA) is committed to such relationships with the TRIBES. The State will employ
its best efforts to achieve positive outcomes from its consultation
and collaboration. This policy intends to improve the planning and
delivery of state services to Tribal governments, Tribal communities, and Tribal members by developing principles and a process for
consultation on these service policies in Wisconsin. It is for this purpose that this policy has been developed.

- **May 08, 2008** – Meeting scheduled for WisDOT Office of General
Council (OGC) and FHWA Representative to meet on May 22, 2008.

- **May 16, 2008** – The WisDOT OGC stated their position is that:
"There is no WisDOT authority to mandate or require or participate in TERO." What is TERO? It stands for Tribal Employment
Rights Ordinances, which require all employers who are engaged
in operating a business on reservations to give preference to qualified Indians in all aspects of employment as this was established
to ensure Native Americans gain their rightful share to employment, training, contracting, subcontracting, and business opportunities on and near reservations and native villages.[165] The TERO
was enacted to address the high unemployment rates and eliminate

---

165. What is TERO https://cter-tero.org/tero-faq/#1

discrimination, which exists on reservations.

TERO is the TRIBEs' authority to enact and enforce an Indian/ Native Employment Preference law as it is grounded in its inherent sovereign status, which has been the most basic principle of Indian Law. This has been supported and recognized in treaties and federal statutes and supported by a host of Supreme Court decisions.[166]

Indian Preference Law is the unique legal right that tribal members have which entitles them to first consideration for all employment, training, contracting, subcontracting, and business opportunities that exist on and near reservations. Both TERO and IP have been in federal regulations since 1841.[167]

After this statement from the WisDOT OGC in May 2008: "There is no WisDOT authority to mandate or require to participate in TERO." In June 2008, a formal request was submitted to the WisDOT OGC for request for a formal legal opinion regarding TERO.

- *August 2008 – The WisDOT OGC offers a response stating: "WisDOT does not have the authority to enforce TERO." (A public records request for this information has been sent to the State of Wisconsin DOT 09112019.)*

- *March 2009 – The WisDOT Civil Rights and Labor Offices (CRLO) met with tribal representatives to begin to work on new specification language, including the point of contact for the TRIBES, their areas of interest, and the establishment of a data tracking form. At the Transportation Advisory Committee (TRANS-AC) meeting, the NAHP was discussed in a presentation regarding WisDOT TA developing draft special provision – NAHP utilizing Minnesota model. The WisDOT TA, in coordination with the TRIBES, drafts Wisconsin language, establishes the tribal contact list, identifies areas of interest and the tracking form. Provision is presented at the TRANS- AC meeting for review.*

---

166. What does TERO do https://cter-tero.org/tero-faq/#1

167. What is Indian Preference https://cter-tero.org/tero-faq/#1

- *May 2009 – The NAHP was approved by members of WisDOT, The Division of Transportation System Development (DTSD)[168] Administration, to proceed with NAHP.*

- *July 2009 – The establishment of the first DT-2405 Native American Tracking form, which was created by one of WisDOT's representatives on July 22, 2009.[169]*

- *August 2010 – New WisDOT TA staff is charged with fully implementing the new provision. This process included slight revisions to the form and the provision language to enhance its application in WisDOT contracts.*

- *June 2011 – Revisions to the Bureau of Project Development.*

- *July 27, 2011 –TRANS-AC This meeting consisted of 11 WisDOT Officials, 2 WTBA Representatives, 3 National Association of Minority Contractors (NAMC), African American Chamber of Commerce (AACC) with no participation from any of the TRIBES. In the meeting minutes, some of the information mentioned information from May 2008 concerns TERO in Wisconsin as the communication continued between the Governor and the TRIBES. It was also discussed the DT-2405 Native American Tracking form is used to track and evaluate Native American labor development activities across the state. This form is to be completed and sent to WisDOT TA staff. It was also mentioned by the WisDOT TA that: "WisDOT does not have statutory authority to implement TERO. This is also the direct statement made by WisDOT OGC when this determination of WisDOT's inability to implement TERO, the agency looked at alternative plans for expanding Native American labor development. The NAHP was a direct result of this. This provision was designed to encourage and promote hiring Native Americans employment on transportation projects on or near Indian reservations (on or near means within commutable*

---

168. WisDOT DTSD https://cter-tero.org/tero-faq/#1

169. See the PDF DT2405Wanda Little07222009 on Page: https://wisconsindot.gov/Documents/formdocs/dt2405.docx

distance). An important fact to note is this provision is not mandatory for all projects across the state of Wisconsin and only for projects specifically located within the requirements mentioned above. The TRIBES each have Labor Representatives, which all contractors are required to contact before bidding if the project is practically on or near Indian reservations. WisDOT's OGC is working on a written opinion that will be available for public distribution. There is also an Indian Employment Credit (see document for details)." The concerns presented by various entities were expressed by:

- *WTBA stated the NAHP language is subjective and would like to work on the language in the provision and talk about the best ways to implement it.*

- *WTBA – Contractors do not want to be considered non-cooperative because there are a lot of zeros on the tracking forms.*

- *WisDOT – The Division of Transportation System Development (DTSD)[170]*

- *WisDOT – A Focus Group is needed to further discuss NAHP. The group will consist of had been identified with key representatives from the CI, CU WisDOT officials, and TRIBES.*

- *August 11, 2011 – The meeting was called to review the original Native American Hiring Provision Employment statistics.*

- *August 16, 2011 – Focus Group Invitations to all tribal leaders to consider nominations from TRIBES to serve on a focus group to examine the provision. The invitation included: Nominations submitted by Tribal Leadership by the WisDOT Office of Business Opportunity and Equity Compliance (OBOEC) Director, Lac Du Flambeau (LDF), Ho-Chunk Nation (HCN) and Lac Courte Oreilles Band of Lake Superior Chippewa (LCO), Red Cliff Band of Lake Superior Chippewa (RC), Forest County Potawatomi (FCP), Sokaogon Chippewa Community Mole Lake Band of Lake Superior Chippewa (SCC), Menominee Indian Tribe of Wisconsin (MITW),*

---

170. WisDOT DTSD https://wisconsindot.gov/Pages/about-wisdot/who-we-are/dtsd/default.aspx

Stockbridge-Munsee Band of Mohican Indians (SMBM), Bad River Band of Lake Superior Chippewa (BRB), Oneida Nation of Wisconsin (ONW), and St. Croix Chippewa Indians of Wisconsin (SCCIW).

The WisDOT has been charged with revisiting the WisDOT's NAHP, a provision that encourages Native American labor opportunities on WisDOT projects located on or near reservations. The department will be hosting a focus group meeting, which will consist of various stakeholders, including TRIBES, to:

1. Review and propose provision language that communicates clear instructions to contractors.

2. Clarify tracking and enforcement components of the provision.

3. Develop an education and outreach plan to inform contractors and other industry representatives of the application and implementation of the provision.

September 2011 – Focus group meetings:

- *September 8, 2011 – In Madison, the Focus Group Meeting consisted of representatives who were present: 6-WisDOT, 1-FHWA, 2-WTBA, 1-Union, 1-AICCW, and 1-Tribal Representative. There were only 3 of the 11 TRIBES who were invited to this meeting to discuss the concerns regarding the NAHP. Many of the questions asked were:*

  - *Can WisDOT enforce NAHP on tribal lands? What is the recourse?*

  - *Can the state enter into individual agreements with each tribe that addresses NAHP?*

  - *What does "desired skill set" mean (on the tracking form)? A contractor can make the skill set as difficult as they want it to be.*

  - *Union currently has about 200 Native Americans on their rosters; can contractors request Native Americans specifically?*

  - *Does the union agreement become exempt when the work is on the reservation?*

- *Can Indian Reservation Roads (IRR) definitions be used to assist with defining "nearby"?*

- *Agency or WisDOT OGC's opinion that WisDOT does not have the authority to enforce TERO also implies that the TRIBES don't have the authority either.*

- *How do we go forward with the provision in its current form?*

- ***September 13, 2011*** *– The second focus group meeting convened in Madison, WI. Present were the following representatives: 7-WisDOT, 2-WTBA, 2-Union, 1-AICCW, 1-FHWA, and 1-Tribe. There were only 3 TRIBES who were Invited: HC, LDF, and LCO, which resulted in the following recommendations:*

  - *Come up with something that is more consistent and efficient, and less of a workload on contractors.*

  - *Willing to work with TRIBES during the off-season to do some education and tracking.*

  - *Have requirements for doing work on tribal land to be "flagged" as a special provision for projects that are located on or partially on the reservation.*

  - *See NAHP suspended until a plan is created and implemented.*

- ***September 19, 2011*** *– MITW WisDOT Tribal Consultation Meeting One of the TRIBES requested to be involved in the development of the NAHP to help look at legal issues regarding the application of tribal laws on hiring preference, especially state versus tribal laws.*

  - *Look at legal issues regarding the application of tribal laws on hiring preference, especially state versus tribal laws.*

- ***October 26, 2011*** *– An email was sent to one of the TRIBE'S Leadership relating to specific issues surrounding the construction on the US 41 Corridor located: "On" and "Near" the confines of their Reservation. One concern presented that is relevant to one of the initiatives completed was an NAHP for Indian Workers when they're on or near the reservation. Since the construction had moved up to their area:*

1. A Construction Company had hired one TSTW for three weeks, then laid him off.

2. Another company hired one of our trucking companies to haul all the junk from the Round-a-About and then no longer utilized his services.

3. Another Construction Trades company hired three TSTW for about a month and then laid them off.

What was observed by the current Tribal Labor Representative is the WisDOT NAHP doesn't have anything to enforce it if the Tribe doesn't contact WisDOT supporting this provision and the Indian Subcommittee. Please keep in mind we are not asking them to hire a hundred of our men or even 50, or 20, maybe not even 10.

- *November 18, 2011, provision suspended – WisDOT OBOEC sent email invitations to the TRIBES: This notice also includes the suspension of the NAHP. The official notice to TRIBES was issued on November 18, 2011. WisDOT TA also reported at a 2011 Great Lakes Inter-tribal Committee (GLITC) Meeting in addition, the suspension was announced during the annual Secretary's Consultation Meeting on September 19, 2011 (minutes also provided above). As a result, WisDOT convened two focus group meetings with various stakeholders, which included a tribal representative, WisDOT staff, CI, and union representatives. The two major outcomes of these focus group meetings were to:*

1. Suspend the current NAHP from future lets until revisions can be made; and

2. Establish the WisDOT TLAC.

- *December 8th, 2011 – The first TLAC meeting, there were 50 tribal members invited. Present at the meeting were the following representatives. 8-WisDOT, 5-WTBA, 1-AICC, 2-DWD, 1-FHWA, 0-Unions, and 20-tribal members of 9 of the 11 TRIBES. The committee developed strategies to enhance Native American Labor opportunities on state and federal projects. A PowerPoint was established to walk through the history of NAHP and TERO. A set of* eight recommendations were developed by TLAC over the first year. The final recommendations document was approved by committee resolution on July 26, 2012, and endorsed and supported by the WisDOT Secretary on September 17, 2012. The next steps of this effort were to establish five work teams to develop implementation plans that allocate the needed tasks, responsibilities, resources, budget, and timeline to carry the recommendations forward. The work teams met at least three times from September through November 2012. (This is also the conduit that was used to finalize the TLAC work plan and encourage the authorization of a $190,000 allocation of state aid to implement the plan). This was all concluded with a PowerPoint of the history of the NAHP.

- **January 6, 2012** – *WisDOT Official sent notice to tribal leaders to participate in subcommittees and next TLAC meeting: TLAC creates three subcommittees and begins developing recommendations to address the NAHP.*

- **January 31, 2012** – *The TLAC Connection Subcommittee Meeting was for the sake of establishing the proper outreach to contractors and included 3 to 5 to help assist with the effort for introductions, networking, and training. This was also the point of helping the contractor identify the individuals within each tribe as well. Discussion and dialog were referenced to the statement of: "On" or "Near" reservations.*

- **February 24, 2012** – *WisDOT OGC Legal Opinion was distributed to the Secretary of WisDOT reflecting statements made by WisDOT OGC: "It supplements my previous legal opinion that came to the same conclusion dated August 4, 2008." This is regarding the questions asked: "Does the State of WisDOT have the legal authority to include and enforce TERO requirements as a WisDOT contractual requirement on any Federal-Aid Highway Program highway projects?" WisDOT OGC's response to this was: "No". "In brief, federal permission does not grant WisDOT legal authority to require such TERO preferences on federally funded projects. There is no Wisconsin state statutory grant of authority to WisDOT to require*

TERO preferences. *The rule of law in Wisconsin is that State agencies like WisDOT must find legal authority for a proposed action within the express or necessarily implied language of a statute. Any doubt is resolved in favor of the lack of legal authority, which was followed up by a 5-page analysis."*

- **February 27, 2012** – *The TLAC meeting reflects that there was another TLAC meeting scheduled for the same day with the following recommendations and Action Items:*

  - *Request for the total hours and total contract dollar amounts for each project cited in the NAHP data.*

  - *Recommendation to provide more education to the committee on the EO#39 and the WisDOT PA.*

  - *Request for a copy of the 1854 treaty that addresses the transportation alliance.*

  - *Recommendation to take the PA to the Inter-tribal Task Force (ITTF) to revise and strengthen the document.*

  - *Request for the agency to look at set-asides, for example, those under the Dept. of Defense (DOD).*

  - *Request for information on the amount of federal dollars allocated to WisDOT projects.*

  - *Recommendation to elect a Tribal government representative on TRANS-AC.*

  - *Charter a separate task force to work directly with TRIBES and internal WisDOT staff to explore a policy that addresses projects that are "on" or "partially on" Tribal lands.*

  - *WisDOT OGC TERO Opinion –*

    WisDOT does not have statutory authority, and the federal government doesn't require the enforcement of hiring prefer-ence. **That does not mean that the TRIBES cannot require it. They can require it on their reservations and lands in trust for the benefit of their members.**

If DOT has a contract that requires being on Tribal land, it cannot go on Tribal land without their permission and compliance. You must comply in that instance, but it's not WisDOT that's requiring it, but the Tribe. *This has been the same decision for the past 20 years. Transportation alliance in the treaties indicates that some state trunk highways on reservation/Tribal lands belong to the state for transportation purposes, and thus TRIBES would not be able to apply hiring preference in those instances.* **Request for a copy of the 1854 treaty that addresses the transportation alliance.**

- **March 20, 2012** *– The TLAC Capacity Subcommittee Meeting was scheduled to demonstrate the Civil Rights and Compliance Systems (CRCS), and it was also used to help identify a standardized qualification system for referrals based on the skill sets and standards of the industry.*

- **April 09, 2012** *– At the TLAC meeting, it was identified that WisDOT TA would then release a solicitation for representation on the task force to redraft a policy for projects located on or partially on tribal lands. Requests for more education on the PA and 39 EO#39.*

- **May 17, 2012** *– The TLAC Joint Subcommittee Session was established for establishing the pre-requirements for Tribal Skilled Trades Workers (TSTW) to work on these projects with the NAHP being applied to those located on or near the reservations. There was also a review of the NAHP Labor Database and what would be reported.*

  If TLAC were to host a focus group with Native American employees with experience working in the construction industry, what information do you think would be beneficial to gather?

  - *Examples of the pathways to initial entry into the industry.*

  - *Examples of barriers to entry.*

  - *Include Native American Disadvantaged Business Enterprises (NADBE) perspective as an employer.*

- *Barriers to maintaining a job (e.g., family, finances, etc.).*

- *Cultural sensitivity/both ways for awareness.*

- *What are their areas of expertise?*

- *What are the needs of the industry?*

- *What training is needed to get the jobs?*

- *Benefits of working in the construction industry.*

- *Resources that are available to assist with the barriers that applicants may have.*

- *Just ask them about their lives.*

- *Potential earnings in these trades (see the white wage sheet that is included in every contract).*

- *June 26, 2012 – A TLAC meeting was set in place for the review of the committee's set of recommendations to enhance Native American labor opportunities on state and federal projects.*

  - **Recommendation #1** – *Centralize a Statewide Native American Labor Initiative*

  - **Recommendation #2** – *Statewide Native American Labor Data Management*

  - **Recommendation #3** – *Standardized Recruitment and Referral Process*

  - **Recommendation #4** – *Monitoring, Reporting and Assessment*

  - **Recommendation #5** – *Partnership Building and Enhanced Communications*

  - **Recommendation #6** – *Educational Resources, Preparedness, and Career Development.*

  - **Recommendation #7** – *Investigate Construction Industry Incentives for Hiring Native American Trans Graduates.*

- **Recommendation #8** – *NAHP for on or partially on Tribal/ Reservation Lands.*

- **August 31, 2012** – *A letter was sent from the Secretary of WisDOT inviting Tribal Leadership to participate in the third focus group meeting in the redrafting of the NAHP. This was sent to TRIBES Leadership.*

- **September 27, 2012** – *The redrafting session took place in Madison with the following representatives present: 2-WisDOT, 1-FHWA, and 6 tribal members from 4 of the TRIBES. In this meeting, WisDOT expressed to the TRIBES the priorities for revising the provision. The TRIBES, in turn, also expressed their concerns about the TSTW, training, and job opportunities available. It was stated these recommendations and efforts focused solely on those projects that are "On," "Near," or "Partially On" Tribal Lands while also examining any of the State's provisions, Memorandums of Understanding (MOU), or Memorandum of Agreements (MOA). Another meeting had been scheduled for October 17, 2012, in Madison. No agenda or meeting minutes were located from the meeting scheduled.*

- **February 11, 2013** – *The TLAC NAHP Redrafting session had the following representatives present: 4-WisDOT, 1-FHWA, and 9 tribal members from 6 of the TRIBES. In this meeting, the following was discussed:*

  - *Effects from the suspension of the original NAHP.*

  - *Develop recommendations to enhance labor and connect TRIBES with the key construction industry stakeholders that do the actual hiring on projects.*

  - *The NAHP was recommended to serve as a separate government-to-government relationship between the agency and TRIBES.*

  - *All meetings for projects are located on/partially on tribal lands; recruitment process; capacity and skills development; limitations on preference requirements on WisDOT contracts;*

apply to both federal and state aid contracts; this provision applies to on/partially on tribal lands.

- *February 25, 2013 – The TLAC preparation for the meeting was scheduled for a discussion of the proper procedures to enhance the Native American labor opportunities for projects located on or partially on tribal lands. The DWD endorsed the State-wide labor database to explore other partnerships or data sharing and funding opportunities. There was a process of reviewing the TLAC's Draft implementation plans, including the topics of the establishment of development of a partnership with the DWD for a database for the TRIBES. It was recommended for the database to be maintained by WisDOT, but there were concerns that the cost would have been significantly larger. ONW did not support the placement in an inter-tribal organization, as the concerns seemed to be surrounded by confidentiality.*

    - *The next topic was regarding the training and preparedness to help create a strategy to increase construction contractor and tribal participation, thus creating successful employment and future opportunities. In the NAHP draft there were two key components identified:*

        ○ *First, a contractual special provision shall be completed as it is under development.*

        ○ *The need for an MOA indicating the WisDOT policy needs and tribal commitments to ensure these efforts are successful.*

- *March 06, 2013 – The NAHP Redrafting session was scheduled at the U.S. 41 Brown County field office as the purpose of this meeting was to provide an overview of the NAHP and TLAC work done to date. Some of the discussions that have taken place are to reference the language of: "on," "near," or "partially on" tribal lands. It was also expressed by the TRIBES the concern with the exclusion of projects that are adjacent to or had the potential to impact tribal communities (access, etc.). It was recommended that the applicability of the provision explore options for inclusion in contracts* in those counties that contain tribal lands or sustain a significant Native American population.

With the previous statement as it relates to the Civil Rights exception language provided, Tribal preference is not a violation of the Civil Rights Act for actions and companies owned and operated on Indian lands. During this time there were recommendations for the purpose of gathering information into a statewide database, but WisDOT stated they do not track tribal affiliation as there is no way for WisDOT to report the information of TSTW, and the new language presented would include in the provision which would consider those eligible for employment opportunities as these TSTW are referred by the TRIBES.

- **March 07, 2013** – The TLAC meeting had the following representatives present: 7-WisDOT, 1-BIA, 2-WDOA, 1-DWD, 1-WTBA, 1-Operating Engineer (OE), 5 of 11 TRIBES where present and 3-CI. The purpose of this was to explain the implementation plan composed of the Native American Labor Initiative, which is composed of 4 components:

  - Data management with a statewide database.

  - Training and preparedness.

  - Incentives to connect industry to tribal workforce.

  - Recruitment and referral for tribal capacity.

  To help develop scopes of work, secure available funding, finalize the scopes of work, advertise, select, and award the contracts, all of which derive from the 8-recommendations.

- **March 22, 2013** – In the NAHP Redrafting session, a representative motioned to approve the NAHP, which was then seconded by another one of the TRIBES as the discussion included the distribution of the final draft to the TRIBES. A statement was made to reinvest for the application of the provision to areas located outside the boundaries of tribal lands was to be brought forward at the next meeting. It was at this time an Inter-governmental Agreement

Opportunities (IGA) for tribal governments and tribal colleges, which was released 03/22/2013 but was also due and must be postmarked on February 20, 2014, as this would establish available funds for the following areas:

- *WisDOT Statewide Native American Labor Initiative (NALI) consisted of $190,000 in funds available established in 2011, and whoever was awarded this was charged with developing strategies to enhance Native American Labor Opportunities on State and Federal projects. This included coordination and development of standardized recruitment and referral processes, monitoring and reporting labor data, and developing/ delivering training programs, which will all be analyzed and distributed at outreach meetings.*

- *WisDOT ITTF administration funds $250,000 available for the group to guide WisDOT on programs, policies, and projects that affect tribal communities through the implementation of the annual work plan, which was appropriated in 2014 to include the coordination of the ITTF meetings, creating and implementing the ITTF annual work plan including: joint safety initiatives, economic development programs, labor and business development, cultural resource programs, training, technical assistance which benefits the Tribal Transportation systems and WisDOT's government-to-government relations.*

Important deadlines were noted in a letter of interest deadline, which was 02/20/2014, and the proposal deadline, which was 02/28/2014, as all this information was to be submitted to the member of the same tribe who was also working as the WisDOT TA to review this information. It is stated for a conflict of interest to be present, there needs to be only a perception of a conflict of interest.

February 2014 – TRIBES NAHP Pilot Project HWY 47 2nd

- *February 14, 2014 – This was the adoption of the NAHP. This was the day revisions were accepted by the WisDOT and Tribal Governments.*

- *February 17, 2014 – The TLAC meeting was scheduled to go through the TLAC implementation overview PowerPoint which was reviewed. During this time there was a discussion of the Statewide Native American Labor Database (SNALDB), the NAHP, and Trans Update. WisDOT TA was to meet with various agencies all at the table: WDOA, DWD, BIA, Local 139OE, WTBA, WisDOT, TRIBES, FHWA, CRCS, etc.*

  When the NAHP was revised and approved, the DT2405 tracking form was no longer available for reporting this information while revising the title of the Preconstruction Meeting–Tribal Coordination meeting. It was also stated that this provision would be applied to projects adjacent to the tribal lands, but there was no mention of projects located within the boundaries of the reservations.

- *May 13, 2014 – LDF signed a MOA with the WisDOT with the following main purposes:*

  - *Implement the TLAC SNALDB while creating a Centralized statewide NALI to enhance Native American Labor Opportunities on state and federal projects.*

  - *Go through the development of the SNALDB infrastructure to establish labor assessment reports, thereby establishing recommendations based on the findings.*

  - *This is done with the purpose of monitoring and reporting Native American activities on WisDOT projects, increasing awareness, and understanding between TRIBES and contractors to ensure equitable opportunities for Native Americans can engage in these training opportunities.*

  - *Create pre-training expectations and qualifications to work in the construction industry.*

  - *Looking at Incentives and possibilities of the utilization of Native American labor, reporting, and accountability.*

The agreement went into effect May 01, 2014, but was not officially signed until May 13, 2014, by the TRIBES Leaderships and the State Secretary of WisDOT.

- *June 30, 2014 – it shows in the Standardized Special Provision (STSP) log of revisions, as the STSP# 107-200 shows the NAHP is a New STSP.*

- *October 24, 2014 – WisDOT/ Transportation Administrative Manual, Directive DIV 102 Title VI/Nondiscrimination Complaint Intake Procedure from the WisDOT OBOEC. The purpose of this is as a recipient of federal funds through the US DOT, WisDOT has been delegated the responsibility for investigating external complaints of discrimination by the FHWA, Federal Aviation Administration (FAA), Federal Motor Carrier Safety Administration (FMCSA), Federal Railroad Administration (FRA), Federal Transit Administration (FTA), and the National Highway Traffic Safety Administration (NHTSA). This is because WisDOT receives federal funding for many of its programs, and so Title VI applies to all WisDOT services. Any person who believes that, in the course of business with a WisDOT program or service, he or she or any specific class of persons or business entity has been subject to discrimination or retaliation prohibited by any of the federal or state Civil Rights statutes or common law principles, based upon race, color, national origin, sex, age or disability may file a complaint.*

- *October 30, 2014 – TLAC meeting where the representatives available were: 2-DWD, 6-WisDOT, 2-WTBA, 1-FHWA, and 5-tribal members from 4 of the 11 TRIBES. The topic of discussion was the introduction of the IGA with the TRIBES, which encompasses the 8-recommendations and the funding associated with the NAHP (See January 26, 2012, for 8-recommendations)[171]. There was a note at the end of this meeting that stated: NOTE: An inquiry to find out whether or not the committee should have by-laws to govern the committee in terms of appointments for representation and decision-making.*

---

171. https://wisconsindot.gov/Documents/doing-bus/civil-rights/tribalaffairs/tlac-exec-rec-final-com-approved-7-26-12.pdf

- **Early January 2015** – *Established a work team meeting for the NAHP database management in the TLAC and ITTF meetings where the database is one of the original 8-recommendations, some of which have established a series of topics presented, discussed, and identified for the establishment of the database.*

- **January 15, 2015** – *The TLAC implementation plan is the plan establishing the SNALDB along with the other items on the agendas of the TLAC Group. This list consists of the original 8-recommendations. The information identified is to be collected in the database to determine how this information is to be used in its primary functions like pre-screening applicants, collection of workforce information from each of the tribal labor offices, recruiting efforts, and tracking and monitoring mechanisms.*

- **January 28, 2015** – *The TLAC meeting's agenda was comprised of the SNALDB, the review of the regional business and labor reports, and the DWD business requirements needed for collaboration. It was brought forward on the 41-corridor mega project a small portion of the NAHP was applied to HWY 29, while the past 41-corridor mega projects did not have the NAHP on them and for some upcoming Safe Routes to School projects as well. There was a presentation of the database from the DWD to identify 3 specific areas:*

  - *Tribal Identification.*

  - *Skills Matching system.*

  - *Reporting and the frequency of reporting.*

- **April 30, 2015** – *The TLAC meeting agenda covered many past items like the Trans programs, the database notes, and the DWD replies to the questions asked in the previous meetings from January 2015 in Madison. The following representatives were present: 6-WisDOT, 2-DWD, 1-FHWA, 3-WTBA, and 4-TRIBES.*

  The discussion began with the following:

  - *Inquiry regarding whether WisDOT maintains copies of all TRIBES TERO/IP? Known TERO programs noted during the meeting include:*

- ° *Several TRIBES have submitted their information or are currently in progress with their IP and TERO programs.*

- *ACTION ITEM: Request that WisDOT obtain copies of all known TERO's Bureau of Indian Affairs (BIA) approved ordinances for the next meeting. To explore MOU and what action items would need to take place to make it happen and present at the next meeting. For the DWD to develop a timeline for specific functionalities and estimates for the July meeting. There was discussion regarding the training or Trans information from Native American members who have obtained the Trans certification.*

- *There was an update from the DWD database to construct the system as there were questions which were asked which stated:*

  - ° *When an individual identifies as a Native American, they can also identify as a specific tribal member. What level of access would the TRIBES like to have if given "administrative" or staff level access to the information exchange system? Would TLAC be interested in providing metadata to trigger that the utilization of this system by contractors is for DOT projects? DWD will develop a timeline for specific functionalities and estimates for the July meeting.*

In the review of TLAC's 1-year summary, it was presented that the two-year agreement was coming soon because it was TLAC's responsibility to carry out the remaining deliverables of the IGA. Next presented were the labor reports, which, as the provision is not applied to the Bureau of Aeronautics (BOA) projects as well as located within the boundaries of one of the TRIBES. There was a mention of the 4-projects that took place within one TRIBE'S reservation, including BIA, BOA, FHWA, and WisDOT past and upcoming projects. Mentioned was the Scheduling of a Tribal Coordination project meeting for one of the TRIBES. The follow-up ACTION ITEM is to request and provide an overview of the services offered by the Michigan Tribal Technical Assistance Program (MTTAP), including the training provided.

- *August 06, 2015 – The TLAC meeting agenda items for this meeting were to obtain copies of the TERO and IPs, and to obtain an overview of the services and training provided by MTTAP. There was also a discussion of the Native American Labor Database, where the DWD Budget and timeline were reviewed while also beginning the development of the MOU and the MOA. TLAC updates have consisted of the recruitment and referral survey, pre-training materials, Native American Focus Group, Cultural Awareness for Non-Native American Community, and the establishment of the Baseline Assessment. The next section was about the review of the Regional Business and Labor Reports from the state of Wisconsin and not Specific Projects.*

- *October 08, 2015 – The TLAC meeting had the following representatives present: 9-WisDOT, 2-DWD, 1-FHWA, 0-WTBA,1-Local 139OE, 1-Northeast Asphalt (NEA), 1-LDF Construction, 12-tribal members from 6 of the 11-TRIBES. This meeting led off with the following action items:*

  - *Contact MTTAP for Training opportunities.*

  - *MOU for the DWD Database.*

  Recruitment and Referral Survey was also discussed to be handed out to contractors in December or at the WTBA Conference. The baseline assessment was introduced, and regional reports from business and labor were presented. SNALDB was presented, and it was estimated that it would cost $45,900 to create a database.

- *December 10, 2015 – A need to understand the WTBA to identify the history and forming of this group. This was listed on the WTBA website when the research was done on December 10, 2015. The reason for the investigation of the WTBA was that the evidence had been brought forward in a series of Focus Group Meetings, which directly influenced the suspension of the NAHP, but also for the removal of the application of the TERO and IP Laws within the boundaries of the 11 TRIBES. A list of the board of directors for the WTBA is shown to reflect the fact that many of the board of* directors are comprised of owners of CI Companies. They are also the same contractors who are awarded the projects located within Wisconsin.

- *December 18, 2015* – *An email was sent to the WisDOT TL requesting several questions to be answered because there was documentation provided at the TLAC meetings leading to the history of the NAHP. This information had a list of all the documents surrounding the foundation of the TLAC Group and the NAHP. Some of the questions asked were:*

    - *Were the TRIBES conveying the reason for the NAHP being rescinded due to invalid contact information for TRIBES Labor Representatives or TRIBES' contact in general when contractors were trying to contact them and let them know there was work available on a project?*

    - *Was it the WisDOT's perspective that because concerns from the industry were voiced, the NAHP be rescinded or needed a complete overhaul on inclusivity?*

    - *Did the WTBA influence the rescinding of the NAHP?*

    - *The Original NAHP was rescinded in 2011. I would like to know if there are any case studies on the following:*

        - *Please provide all specific examples/meaning specific TRIBES contacted, and what was the actual contact information used to do outreach to these specific TRIBES relating to these specific examples.*

        - *Which TRIBES were contacted for the projects?*

        - *Which TRIBES did not have the correct contact information?*

        - *Which TRIBES did not respond after being contacted?*

    - *The NAHP was suspended in November 2011, and the following was requested:*

        - *I would like the Document and any other documents stating why this was suspended.*

- ◦ *Any documents that contain the explanation as to why the State had grounds to suspend the NAHP.*

- ◦ *A copy of the document from the Secretary of WisDOT stating the reason why this provision was suspended.*

- ◦ *Any documents regarding the industry that had an influence on this decision and if it was based on WTBA.*

- ◦ *Any documents that pertain to who in the industry voiced their concerns to Madison about the NAHP, as they were not in favor of it because of the uncertainties involving the language of the NAHP.*

- **2015 NAHP** – *WisDOT projects were located within the boundaries of a TRIBE'S reservation. The project scopes of work varied from:*

  - *Bureau of Aeronautics work.*

  - *Safe Route to School Project.*

  - *Wetland Mitigation.*

  - *2 WisDOT Highway Projects.*

  There were several concerns with the application of the NAHP by the CI on each project. The main issues were the lack of participation of the NAHP, lack of TSTW on the projects, CI stating they are not hiring, the multiple classifications of non-tribal skilled trades workers on the projects, lack of communication, and the collection of proper report data from the projects, along with cultural barriers on the projects.

- **January 27, 2016** – *TLAC meeting in Madison had the following representatives present: 7-WisDOT, 1-FHWA, 2-DWD, 1-WTBA, 2-CI, and 10-tribal members from 5 TRIBES. In this meeting, the discussion was relevant to the MTTAP and the classes available. A large list was brought forward, but it was stated these are not certifications in the construction industry, but the certifications are certifications of completion. The discussion continued to talk about the updates as they related to the Statewide SNALDB, where* it was agreed for the database to be released on February 12, 2016, because the database has been developed for over two years. It has been told that the SNALDB would be completed because the DWD would not specify a definitive date of when the database would be completed. They then followed up by saying that the training would be available for this database from February 16th through 17th. The WisDOT TA reports and updates as the information has been compiled a by-region, full minority report. It was stated the WisDOT TA can retrieve data in several ways, and it was stated that WisDOT is working to have a consistent way to report this information, but one of the limitations of the CRCS is it can only track self-identification. The other issue was that women were counted twice, one as a minority and one as a woman.

- **March 31, 2016** – The TLAC meeting scheduled the discussions that took place about the MTTAP and the classes they have available. MTTAP stated that the training was free, but when called, the representative from MTTAP stated that the classes cost $300 per person and $3000 for the class. The class size was not clarified. The certifications from classes are not certified and only presented upon completion. Of the classes listed, there were no current descriptions of the many remaining that could be put together but have not been utilized. The discussion of the DWD Database continued here, and it was discussed regarding the issues presented:

  - Access of Information.

  - Tracking of Descendants from each tribe.

  - BIA Rulings from 25CFR Part 169 "Right of ways."

  - Review of the MOU for each of the TRIBES.

- **April 28, 2016** – TLAC meeting. The following representatives were present: 5-WisDOT, 1-FHWA, 4-DWD, 2-Trans, 2-DBE, 2-CI, and 9-tribal members from 6 of the TRIBES. The items discussed were the MTTAP classes, as when directed to the TTAP website, this information was outdated, classes were not certified, and the prices were a concern when it was stated the classes were free. The discussion also went towards the DWD SNALDB as it had updates, which *consisted of confidentiality and data access by other entities, which was the primary concern. With the concerns brought forward, this DWD representative stated additional work would take 40-160 extra hours. DWD was to provide an estimate for the costs of the updates of the database at the next meeting.*

- *July 12, 2016 – The TLAC meeting had the following representatives present: 8-WisDOT, 1-FHWA, 1-WTBA, 1-DWD, and 8-tribal members of 11 TRIBES. The discussion was that an OSHA 30 Class through the Local Technical College would cost $5500. It was recommended to centrally house this training so all TRIBES could benefit from these opportunities. The discussion went on to the SNALDB changes, the estimate, and the updated timeline. Also recommended was the need for job fairs after the training. The NAHP and the reports noted there were 6 active projects and 2 pending between the TRIBES and the contractors. The topic of the language was held regarding "partially on" or "adjacent to." It was also recommended to extend or expand the application of the NAHP, but it was stated that an endorsement from the Executive office, the WTBA, and the TRIBES would be needed. It was recommended that the PA be updated as it is a living document. The FHWA Official retired. The second request for a list of the WisDOT and BOA Projects was requested at the public meeting. This was to be presented to the TLAC Group.*

- *October 18, 2016 – The TLAC meeting had the no representatives present to discuss progress on the State Tribal Labor reports, Baseline Assessments, Training material, Funding available, Recruitment and Referral Surveys, Cultural Awareness Training, and Annual Assessments. This was done by other entities.*

- *January 24, 2017 – An email was sent to the TLAC group the night before the TLAC meeting stating there were no meeting minutes as it related to the grant funding, which was being removed from one TRIBE and moved to another TRIBE. This was done without any consultation from the other TRIBES, and it was sent as an FYI Email from the WisDOT TA at 5:27 pm. This was done* because there were notes set for the TRIBES closed-door sessions, which had a baseline of information and questions, and this was one of the concerns that needed to be addressed. This was also followed up with a phone call from the TLAC Coordinator stating that the WisDOT TA got a copy of the meeting minutes and concerns regarding the NAHP. It was then stated by the WisDOT TA that their "Really good friend" would let them know if this was going on because of their relationship with one of the TRIBE'S leaders. The concerns were with the RFP Process, and the WisDOT TA stated there was no draft RFP process and the concerns with the lack of proper consultation. One of the TRIBES stated it was sovereign, and all TRIBES need to create their database.

- **January 25, 2017** – The TLAC meeting had the following representatives present: 10-WisDOT, 5-DWD/Trans 1-WTBA, 1-AICCW, 2-CI, and 12-tribal members from 6 TRIBES. The meeting discussions consisted of the MTTAP, and OSHA training was brought forward once again, but this time it was to obtain estimates of how many wanted it and suggestions for locations. Presented were the DWD updates for the SNALDB, and a concern was whether contractors would have access to the DWD SNALDB to post positions while also looking for potential candidates. It was stated there is no ability to focus on Native Americans being specifically selected for NAHP projects, which is not a function of the SNALDB. With the concerns of the privacy of this information, this is difficult for the database to be fully utilized by both the TRIBES and the CI with the issues of Civil rights.

  The Base Lines Assessment was presented, and the WisDOT TA stated it would settle on the assessment to move forward. The baseline assessment did not include transportation. WisDOT projects general data as it relates to the Native American Labor Data as it is presented from across the state of Wisconsin. The SNALDB will not be used as previously, as everyone is waiting on the final edits of the database. One of the TRIBE'S states the biggest issue is getting in touch with TSTW and being ready and willing to travel to projects, drug tests, and driver's licenses.

The establishment of the survey for the CI, when the recommendation was brought forward, to push the surveys at the WTBA because this is the one place where all the contractors are at who are also the same ones who are doing the work and bidding on the projects each year. This was stated because the WisDOT TA had only sent the survey to the TRIBES, and there were only 16 surveys sent out and only 6 responses, 3 to 4 of them were usable data.

The WisDOT TA had publicly notified that they are accepting a new position.

- **February 15, 2017** – The ITTF meeting agent began with an overview of the original PA, which was the beginning of the revisions of the PA.

- **May 03, 2017** – The TLAC meeting had the following representatives present: 8-WisDOT, 4-DWD, 4-UMOS, 1-AICCW, and 1-CI. It was stated by the WisDOT TA that the IGA, which had been signed by one of the TRIBES, was now being transferred over to another of the TRIBES, and they will continue to work on the baseline assessment. This was done without any consultation of the TRIBES as it was recommended by one of the TLAC Group because of the TLAC funds associated that there should be some sort of process where the group makes the decision and not just one tribe. This IGA was for the transition of the $190,000 in funding for the NAHP, SNALDB, DWD, and training. There was a discussion of the SNALDB regarding the active individuals and the verification process, and it was stated that the TRIBES did not have to sign up. This discussion was stated at the TLAC meeting on January 23, 2017, in which the discussion brought forward that the TRIBES had stated they wanted to go back to the drawing board and that this database could not do the functions it was designed to do as requested by the TRIBES and the CI and Labor Unions. WisDOT TA stated that, at this current time, there is no way for contractors to identify Native Americans within the DWD database.

The WisDOT TA stated there were only NAHP Labor Reports for the past 3 years because the WisDOT won't go back any further because they had stated that there was little or no information, and to go back to 2009 would take a large number of resources and time to obtain the information. A comment was made by WisDOT TA stating at the time (2009–2013) that the NAHP was a different provision, and that information was not available because there was no tracking information at this time. The NAHP was suspended, and the information has been archived. The NAHP was recommended for amendments because it does not reflect an equal standard amount of time for contractors to submit information, as the TRIBES had to respond within three business days.

It was brought forward that the TLAC Workplan, WisDOT TA, stated that one of the TRIBES had signed the contract to move forward with completing the unfinished items. On May 07, 2017, a phone call was made to one of the TRIBES inquiring if the agreement had been signed because it had been stated at the TLAC meeting earlier that the IGA had already been signed and that this would be for all TRIBES. One of the TRIBES had stated this document had not been signed at this time and did not plan on signing anything until their TRIBE had had a chance to see and read the IGA review with their attorneys. It was then explained these discrepancies were different from what had been mentioned at the TLAC meeting. The TRIBE stated in this phone conversation, at approximately 4:13 pm they were going to be frank with me and stated: "I did not have time for this BU** SH**, and if anyone crosses my path, I will ruin their f***king careers." In an attempt to keep the conversation moving forward, the mention of the comments made by one of the TRIBES regarding the discussion that transpired on January 23, 2017, regarding the database has become diluted as one of the TRIBES, or CI was not able to fully utilize the database. The TLAC group recommended that the database be created in-house and start by going back to the drawing board.

- One of the TRIBE'S MOUs is looking to sign a MOU with the DWD; they are looking at it on behalf of all TRIBES with 1 MOU. WisDOT TA stated this is the same DWD Database, which was voted down by the TRIBES.

- *One of the TRIBES was put into a pilot project without consultation with or knowledge of any other TRIBES after the database was voted down.*

- *IP is nothing more than a Statutory Outline, TERO quantifiable to exercise tribal sovereignty, changed within 30 days to hiring provision contracting TRIBES, hiring opportunities, and limitation for referrals on time. Revisit the legal application to TERO and NAHP was Discussed with Tribal Leaders to ask what they would all like to see happen.*

The next week this information was brought forward to the TRIBES Leadership, and the mentioned statement was made, and it was brought forward, and nothing had ever resulted from this.

It was also mentioned that at this time, the WISDOT OBOEC Representative would also be working as the interim TLAC Coordinator.

- *June 01, 2017 – A request for the list of all NAHP Projects in Wisconsin from 2009 until June 2017 was sent to the WisDOT TA, who responded on June 09, 2019, stating: "I have sent your request to our Bureau of Project Development. They can compile a list of projects based on what provisions are included in a contract. I am a bit confused; WisDOT CRCS Specialists cannot pull data based on which contracts contain certain provisions. Neither does the WisDOT TA. The WisDOT TA is not sure what report is being referenced below. The WisDOT TA did speak to WisDOT CRCS Specialists, and they weren't sure either. Therefore, the WisDOT TA is asking the bureau to provide a list of all projects that have contained the NAHP from its inception.*

  WisDOT TA is working on a report that will contain information from the past few years for projects that contain the provision and the results based on tribal reporting – including recommended best practices. We hope to share the results of this report at our next TLAC meeting. Perhaps this will assist with your analysis.

  Again, I will pass along your request and get back to you once I hear something."

- *July 6 to 11, 2017* – Another request for information to obtain the information from 2009 to 2017. Specifically, the NAHP required information that was project-specific to help identify the trends, but this was stalled from receiving information by one of the TRIBES' new acting TLAC Coordinators. The TLAC Coordinator was also working for WisDOT OBOEC at the same time, which directly presented a clear conflict of interest.

- *August 09, 2017* – The ITTF meeting in Rothschild discussed the PA revisions and other topics related to the relationships of the TRIBES, local municipalities, state, and federal agencies, and WisDOT are trying to foster better working relationships, addressing things like:

  ○ Cultural Sensitivity.

  ○ Training.

  ○ How to help become more efficient and better resolutions.

  ○ Expediting processes if working combatively on a project together.

  ○ Applicability of the TERO or IP.

  - Asked about Specific Projects and information reporting is provided quarterly, and the requirement is an individual Tribal government-to-government relationship with the individual TRIBES and contractors. Information is submitted at the end and given to the WisDOT and WisDOT TA stating this information is available, but the only reports available would only be available how the state currently provides them (the Process). The WisDOT TA also stated they have data presented the way WisDOT records information and not the way TRIBES records it. The reports are available only the way the WisDOT provides them. It was explained to everyone in the meeting that the reason for this information is it is gathered for accountability for the projects and data to be collected to help other partners and TRIBES gather or apply for grants.

- *It was stated by the WisDOT Consultant charged with drafting the revisions of the PA that it is hard to obtain funding if there is no accountability because the collective share wasn't listed, and the lack of information gathering was not addressed.*

- *There must be a value of outputs and inputs because it makes it difficult for all TRIBES to proceed forward and address other issues with the lack of information.*

- *What are the evaluation markers we are looking at (Annual Reports)?:*

  - *Measurable performance standards.*

  - *Completed.*

  - *Program based.*

  - *Projects.*

  - *Standards.*

  - *Accomplishments form.*

- *Are these goals being accomplished?*

- *What are the issues we have encountered, and how did we address them?*

- *When was it completed?*

All this information should then be evaluated for all the programs on an annual basis and needed changes as the training changes based on the regions of work for TSTWs.

The PA information or draft is not presentable for the TRIBES leadership to start the buy-in process from all agencies.

- ***August 10, 2017*** *– In the TLAC meeting, the following representatives were present: 7 members of the TRIBES. The information presented was the average number of TSTW reflects the information from all the WisDOT projects across the state of Wisconsin broken down quarterly and presented annually. NAHP concerns brought up were:*

- ○ *The tracking and reporting data for all of our projects.*

- ○ *The language of the provision has a lack of authority and accountability.*

- ○ *To make this more formal in the closed-door session requesting voting from the TRIBES and creating motions for action items.*

- ○ *The discussion of the DWD Database and the IGA with one of the TRIBES and how it would directly affect all TRIBES. The statement made by DWD is that one of the TRIBES would create one agreement that would blanket all the TRIBES. A TLAC member had mentioned that at the May 03, 2017, TLAC meeting, this statement was made and was followed up with form of the TRIBES did not feel they had the authority to speak on behalf of all the other TRIBES, as they should each have the responsibility to sign their agreements.*

- ○ *WisDOT TA asked about the language of the dual citizenships as they are not minorities, and the CI is not able to utilize the DWD database because this information is not available to look at for contractors when they are looking for Native American-specific data.*

- • *It was official that the New TLAC Coordinator was working for the past six months as TLAC Coordinator and as the WisDOT Community Services Specialist for OBOEC with the WisDOT under WisDOT TA. She is also the person who stalled the records request of information and will be responsible for the completion of the surveys and reaching out to the contractors.*

- • *NAHP on BOA and WisDOT projects. TSTW is not able to obtain positions after the Pre-Tribal Coordination Meeting.*

- ○ *Proper notifications to all the TRIBES located within the regions of the work being done.*

- ° *Big Issues with the contractors attending the Pre-Tribal Coordination Meetings.*

- ° *Language, Accountability in the NAHP.*

- ° *Proper tracking information forms for Contractors for all NAHP projects.*

- ° *The screening process for working in airports.*

- ° *The time allotted for Contractors and TRIBES Communications needs to be fair as this is an agreement.*

Regional Reports – *The information presented was only part of the information and did not include the full information on the total amount of hours available for the projects. It was also mentioned the hours need to be associated with project-specific and not just sent for all state projects. If this is done, this will reflect the information more accurately on NAHP and show the actual numbers or the closest numbers of TSTW on the Specific NAHP projects.*

- **January 24, 2018** – *The TLAC meeting was in Madison and the following representatives were present: 6- WisDOT, 0-FHWA, 1-WTBA, 1-DWD, 2-Trans, 1-AICCW, 2-Walbec Group, and 14-tribal members of 6 of the TRIBES.*

  - *It was stated by WisDOT TA there was an amount of $173,000 in the TLAC funds available for 2018.*

  - *WisDOT TA said the Baseline assessment would be finished by May 31, 2018.*

  - *The NAHP – Progress of the revisions to the NAHP which includes:*

    - ° *Online form.*

    - ° *The timeframe changed from three business days to five business days.*

    - ° *The Guidance of the Tribal Coordination meeting process was amended.*

WisDOT TA noted that they could monitor both forms electronically, and the forms can be forwarded as needed.

- *Discussion to add the internships and apprenticeships.*

- *A delegation of authority moving the NAHP from Labor Compliance Specialists and adding it to the Labor Compliance Checklist.*

- *One of the TRIBES is still reviewing the MOU for the DWD Database.*

- *There is no process for NAHP, the collection of the NAHP information, and stated: CRCS is the way WisDOT has been tracking NAHP information and reporting this information in reports to the TRIBES over the past few years.*

- *The CRCS numbers of blanketed projects numbers of TSTW on projects but combining all of the projects from across the state of Wisconsin.*

- *The original intent of the NAHP is to help obtain information and statistics on how many TSTW are on NAHP projects and not all the projects from the state. WisDOT TA stated in the NAHP tracking information that no process was established, and it was responded to her by stating that this information is invalid as the numbers are fluffed, but the WisDOT is reporting all of this information to all the Tribal Leadership.*

- *WisDOT TA stated the NAHP information was from CRCS, and there is no verification process for this information. The reports don't cover just the NAHP; the intent of the NAHP the first provision was to request any information for all the projects the NAHP has been applied to.*

- *In the creation of the NAHP, its purpose was designed for NAHP-specific projects. All the information reported to tribal nations over the past 3-4 years has not been NAHP-specific for the projects and is not the information* from the CRCS, as these numbers are not accurate because it does not reflect the accurate amounts of TSTW on the NAHP-specific Projects. It was then asked repeatedly by WisDOT TA, in a non-professional tone, what was wanted, and this was explained that the TRIBES would like to request the same form required by the Federal Government, which is form 3121, as the TRIBES can be as strict as the federal government, if not more strict, and we would like to obtain NAHP projects having the following:

- Total hours for each project are broken down indi-vidually as stated on the Federal form.

- Total headcount on each project broken down.

- Description of job positions.

- List of all wages on projects.

- **February 21, 2018** – This meeting was scheduled to review the TLAC recruitment and referral survey.

  - A copy of the updated survey was also handed out for amend-ments and review.

- **April 30, 2018** – A meeting in Madison at the WisDOT office was scheduled to make revisions for the NAHP.

- **May 01, 2018** – The TLAC meeting was scheduled, as the follow-ing representatives were present: 1-WisDOT, 1-FHWA, 1-DWD, 1-WTBA, 1-UMOS, and 8-tribal members from 5 of the TRIBES. This meeting brought forward the discussion of the TLAC imple-mentation plan 8-recommendations, as five work teams have been developed to implement the recommendations. The information prepared in the WisDOT TA reports is reported from the CRCS information and is inaccurate as there is a difference between num-bers vs. the NAHP-specific projects.

  - The baseline assessment report commented on the recommen-dation suggesting a shared database for labor.

- *June 19, 2019* – *A formal public Records Request was sent to the WisDOT Records Coordinator, and it was stated on June 21, 2018, that the fee associated with this records request is $256.00. This was determined based on 16 hours of search time at a cost of $16/hour. Payable to: WisDOT DTSD.*

- *August 01, 2018* – *An email was sent from the WisDOT TA regarding the Public Record Requests stating: This request was for labor data on both the expired Native American Hiring Provision (2009-2012) and the new provision adopted in March 2013 (2013-2017). The data request included not only annual data but also required that the report be provided quarterly since 2009 by the project. This request was provided to BOA and OBOEC in July. Since the request required the extraction of a minimum 800 separate CRCS reports per year, and due to the time and resources needed to compile this report within both BOA and OBOEC, it was forwarded to our Open Records legal review process. As Travis indicated, it was denied. The Department is not required to create a new record that does not already exist, compile existing information in a new format, or obtain a record from another agency, Wis. Stat. 19.35 (1) (L). The Department is required to provide only documents in existence at the time of the request.*

- *August 14, 2018* – *TLAC meeting. The meeting minutes used were the same meeting minutes from May 01, 2018, as these are even presented in the November meeting minutes notes.*

- *September 04, 2018* – *It was brought forward that WisDOT TA was not aware of any process regarding the establishment of the RFPS process. However, through further research, it was listed in the TLAC meeting minutes that they were the ones who had established the IGA.*

- *November 27, 2018* – *TLAC meeting. There was lots of discussion as it related to the training for TSTW, and it was concerning that the incorrect training was being provided for OSHA 30. It was Commercial and not the Construction OSHA. This helps show the following meetings that have taken place, whether they were related to the NAHP or any of the other recommendations over the past 10 years. It was also reflected in the time period.*

Appendix B

Chronological Order of Events, Meetings, Conferences, Communications, Emails and Annual reports, ETC...

- *1993 03-1993 IP Employment on FAHP On and near Indian Reservation*

- *2000 Page 54 Definition for Sovereignty*

- *2001 ****** no information****

- *2002*

    - *10-2002 – FHWA releases report that WisDOT "places NAHP in federal aid projects on or near Indian lands."*

- *2003 ****** no information****

- *2004*

    - *02-2004 Wisconsin State Tribal Relations Initiative*

    - *02-2004 Jim Doyle Executive Doyle drafted & signed Executive order #39*

- *2005*

    - *05-2005 Partnership Agreement TRIBES, Wisconsin Division of FHWA and WisDOT*

    - *06-2005 Jim Doyle DOA Consultation with Indian Tribes*

- *2006 ****** no information****

- *2007 ****** no information****

- 2008

  - *05-2008 FHWA to meet with WisDOT OGC 05082008*

  - *05-2008 WisDOT OGC Legal opinion "No WisDOT authority to mandate require or participate in TERO."*

  - *05-2008 WisDOT OGC Jim Thiel states No WisDOT Authority to Mandate or Require Participating in TERO*

  - *06-2008 Formal request for legal opinion submitted to OGC towards alternative job opportunities for tribes*

  - *08-2008 OGC offers a response that WisDOT does not have the authority to enforce TERO*

  - *08-2008 OGC *Is WisDOT Participation in a TERO Program Required by the FHWA? "TERO"*

- 2009

  - *2009-2015 Project from US 41 Corridor Mega Project*

  - *2009-2015 Delivery Schedule Winnebago and Brown County Construction Projects*

  - *03-2009 Presentation is given at TRANS-AC about NAHP. See December 08, 2011, PowerPoint*

  - *03-2009 The WisDOT CRLO and TA drafts special provision – NAHP in coordination with TRIBES, establishes the tribal contact list, identifies areas of interest and the tracking form. Provision is presented at the TRANS-AC meeting*

  - *05-2009 US 41 Labor Development Committee*

  - *05-2009 The NAHP was Approved by WisDOT Systems Development DTSD Denied information requests*

  - *07-2009 WisDOT created the Wisconsin Native American Tracking Form DT2405*

  - *09-2009 The Indian Preference Coordinator stated they are not receiving any updates on TSTW working or not working*

- 2010
  - *2010 Spring DBE Reporter*
  - *2010 Fall DBE Reporter*
  - *10-2010 Partnership Agreement Revisions*
  - *2010 Winter DBE Reporter*
  - *Annual 2010 Minority Reports Quarterly*
  - *Annual 2010 WisDOT Minority Analysis Report*

- 2011
  - *07-2011 Transportation Advisory Committee TRANS-AC*
  - *08-2011 Native American Employment WTBA/WisDOT*
  - *08-2011 WisDOT OBOEC Invites TRIBES to revisit the WisDOT NAHP*
  - *09-2011 WTBA/NAMC NAHP Concerns*
  - *09-2011 Madison NAHP Focus Group Meeting*
  - *09-2011 Madison NAHP Focus Group Meeting*
  - *09-2011 Menominee Nation WisDOT Annual Secretary Consultations meeting*
  - *10-2011 Communication to Tribal Leadership regarding issues surrounding construction on the US41 Corridor*
  - *11-2011 WisDOT OBOEC Invite all TRIBES regarding the suspension of the NAHP September 2011*
  - *12-2011 Oneida TLAC first official meeting*
  - *12-2011 TLAC NAHP PowerPoint*
  - *Annual 2011 Minority Reports Quarterly*
  - *Annual 2011 NAHP Report*

- 2012
  - *01-2012 Invite from WisDOT TAA. Invite to TRIBES to attend meeting*

- 01-2012 LCO TLAC Meeting
- 02-2012 WisDOT OGC Correspondence sent to Sec. of Trans. Legal Opinion to TRIBES
- 02-2012 TLAC Potawatomi Legal Opinion from WisDOT OGC
- 02-2012 LDF TLAC Meeting Legal Opinion from WisDOT OGC distributed to TLAC Meeting
- 03-2012 TLAC Meeting Demonstration of the CRCS system
- 04-2012 Potawatomi TLAC Meeting Minutes
- 05-2012 TLAC Joint Subcommittee Session Information for tracking in Database
- 07-2012 Oneida TLAC Meeting
- 07-2012 Executive Summary Committee Recommendations (8-recommendations)
- 07-2012 DBE Summer Report
- 08-2012 WisDOT email inviting Tribal Leadership first team meeting scheduled for Madison, WI
- 09-2012 NAHP Redraft Session in Madison, WI
- 10-2012 DBE Fall Reports
- Annual 2012 Minority Reports Quarterly
- Annual 2012 WisDOT Minority Analysis Report

- 2013

  - 02112013 NAHP Redrafting Session. NAHP recommended to serve as a separate government-to-government relationship between the agency and tribes
  - 02-2013 TLAC Preparation Meeting
  - 03-2013 NAHP Redrafting Session
  - 03-2013 Oneida TLAC Meeting
  - 03-2013 LDF NAHP Redrafting session

- 03-2013 NAHP Adopted

- 03-2013 Intergovernmental Agreement

- 03-2013 TLAC Final Implementation Plan 8-recommendations

- 03-2013 DBE Spring Reporter

- 07-2013 DBE Summer Reporter

- 10-2013 DBE Winter Reporter

- Annual 2013 Minority Reports Quarterly

- Annual 2013 WisDOT Minority Analysis Report

- 2014

  - 02-2014 Adopted NAHP

  - 05-2014 WisDOT LDF Memorandum of Understanding

  - 06-2014 Standardize Special Provisions 107-200 NAHP Implemented

  - No 07-304 March 08, 2010, State of California V. Edmund G Brown; Pages 12-15

  - 10-2014 Title VI/Nondiscrimination Complaint Intake Procedure

  - 02-2005 CA DOT decision to revoke its policy to include TERO on and near reservations from NIJC

- 2015

  - 01-2015 Work team notes NAHP Database Management TLAC/ITTF

  - 01-2015 TLAC Implementation Plan

  - 01-2015 Madison TLAC Meeting Minutes

  - 03-2015 Spring DBE Reporter

  - 04-2015 Rothschild TLAC Meeting Minutes

  - 07-2015 DBE Summer Reporter

- 08-2015 Menominee TLAC Meeting
- 10-2015 LDF TLAC Meeting Minutes
- 10-2015 Fall DBE Reporter
- 12-2015 History of WTBA
- 12-2015 NAHP response from WisDOT Tribal Affairs
- 12-2015 Winter DBE Reporter
- 2015 5 Projects WisDOT
- Annual 2015 Minority Reports Quarterly

- 2016
  - 01-2016 Madison TLAC Meeting
  - 03-2016 Mole Lake TLAC Meeting
  - 04-2016 Oneida TLAC Meeting
  - 07-2016 Stockbridge TLAC Meeting
  - 10-2016 Stevens Point TLAC Meeting
  - 11-2016 WisDOT ITTF, TLAC, THPO Meeting
  - Annual 2016 Minority Reports Quarterly
  - Annual 2016 DBE Reporters

- 2017
  - 01-2017 TLAC Agenda Madison, WI
  - 02-2017 Partnership Agreement Revisions Committee
  - 05-2017 Mole Lake TLAC Meeting
  - 07-2017 Email WisDOT DTSD to WisDOT TA Stalling of Record Request
  - 08-2017 Rothschild ITTF/Partnership Agreement Revisions
  - 08-2017 Rothschild TLAC Meeting
  - Annual 2017 Quarterly Region Reports
  - DBE Spring 2017

- 2018
  - 01-2018 Madison TLAC Meeting Minutes
  - 02-2018 TLAC Recruitment and Referral Survey Draft
  - 04-2018 Revisions for the NAHP Meeting
  - 05-2018 TLAC Meeting Oneida
  - 06-2018 Public Records Request to the WisDOT DTSD
  - 08-2018 TLAC Meeting Redcliff
  - 08-2018 NAHP Open Records Requests WisDOT DTSD
  - 10-2018 Tribally Owned Consultant Firm Communications
  - 10-2018 Oneida Open Records Meeting WisDOT NE Regional office
  - 10-2018 DBE Labor Compliance Specialists WIS 441 Project OBOEC
  - 11-2018 Inter-tribal Data Meeting
  - 11-2018 Communications with WisDOT Labor Compliance Specialists regarding 441 Project OBOEC
  - 11-2018 TLAC Meeting LDF
  - 12-2018 TLAC NAHP Solicitations Draft

Anything which has transpired since 2019 is unknown; other than between February and March 2019 when the location of all Tribal Labor Advisory Committee Meeting Minutes from 2008 to 2019 were all either deleted or removed and have not been reestablished since the updating of the new website: https://www.wisdottlac.org/

Chapter 3.1 Regional Report

Information received from the CRCS System from Labor Compliance

Total from 2009 Regional Report for Wisconsin

Minorties	Caucasian		African American		Hispanic		Asian		Native American		2 Races or more		Total Non Native		Total
Gender	Male	Female	Male	Female	Male	Female	Male	Female	Male	Female	Male	Female	Male	Female	Workers
Workers															
Q1	182	0	5	0	12	0	1	0	0	0	2	0	6,752	231	7,084
Q2	2,090	75	124	12	210	2	16	2	40	1	5	1			
Q3	213	10	6	0	6	0	1	0	3	0	0	0			
Q4	3,284	121	167	14	405	5	19	1	54	3	4	0			
2009 Q TOTAL	5,769	206	302	14	633	7	37	3	97	4	11	1			
Percentages of Workers	81.44%	2.91%	4.26%	0.20%	8.94%	0.10%	0.52%	0.04%	1.37%	0.06%	0.16%	0.01%	98.57%		
Percentages of Workers	84.35%		4.46%		9.03%		0.56%		1.43%		0.17%				
Hours Worked	Male	Female	Male	Female	Male	Female	Male	Female	Male	Female	Male	Female	Male	Female	Hours
Q1	9,988.00	0.00	84.00	0.00	166.00	0	7.30	0	0.00	0.00	245.50	0.00	902,633.70	30,509.90	948,877.60
Q2	143,447.30	3,724.30	6,213.50	428.30	12,214.70	71.3	528.50	5	3,500.30	17.00	280.00	101.00			
Q3	388,185.10	12,372.70	21,590.70	2,273.80	44,869.10	604	1,459.50	207.8	7,276.40	750.00	124.80	81.80			
Q4	235,100.90	9,089.80	10,067.70	1,350.50	27,422.50	166.3	638.60	33.3	3,956.50	233.80	0.00	0.00			
2009 Hours Total	776,721.30	25,186.80	37,955.90	4,052.60	84,672.30	841.60	2,633.90	246.10	14,733.20	1,000.80	650.30	182.80			
Percentages of Hours	81.86%	2.65%	4.00%	0.43%	8.92%	0.09%	0.28%	0.03%	1.55%	0.11%	0.07%	0.02%	98.25%		
Percentages of Hours	84.51%		4.43%		9.01%		0.30%		1.66%		0.09%		100.00%		

Chapter 4.1 2010 Regional Report

Information received from the CRCS System from Labor Compliance

Total from 2010 Regional Reportfor Wisconsin														
Minorties	Caucasian		African American		Hispanic		Asian		Native American		2 Races or more		Total Non Native		Total
Gender	Male	Female	Male	Female	Male	Female	Male	Female	Male	Female	Male	Female	Male	Female	Workers
Workers															
Q1	14,321	394	622	32	1141	17	63	7	265	15	5	0	36,451	971	38,034
Q2	799	19	23	1	37	0	4	0	10	0	0	0			
Q3	9,919	285	449	24	826	14	53	3	183	11	4	0			
Q4	7,170	208	294	11	679	11	41	2	119	9	1	0			
2009 Q TOTAL	32,209	906	1,388	11	2,683	42	161	12	577	35	10	0			
Percents of Workers	84.68%	2.38%	3.65%	0.03%	7.05%	0.11%	0.42%	0.03%	1.52%	0.09%	0.03%	0.00%			
Percents of Workers	87.07%		3.68%		7.16%		0.45%		1.61%		0.03%		98.39%		
Hours Worked	Male	Female	Male	Female	Male	Female	Male	Female	Male	Female	Male	Female	Male	Female	Hours
Q1	2,317,668.90	59,522.80	101,011.40	4,934.60	268,400.40	4397.8	10,936.90	1799.8	33,745.90	2,465.80	346.60	0.00	5,131,807.70	137,726.70	5,339,369.00
Q2	485,536.30	13,513.40	20,999.90	1,112.30	52,596.50	1084.8	950.60	169.3	7,427.90	585.50	102.80	81.80			
Q3	1,028,829.50	28,929.90	44,770.30	2,129.60	113,833.80	2342	5,239.10	1135.8	16,837.50	902.10	175.80	0.00			
Q4	568,495.60	14,161.20	26,429.90	1,085.30	80,911.90	831.5	4,397.90	494.8	6,936.60	933.30	173.60	0.00			
2009 Hours Total	4,400,530.30	116,127.30	193,211.50	9,261.80	515,742.60	8,656.10	21,524.50	3,599.70	64,947.90	4,886.70	798.80	81.80			
Percents of Hours	82.42%	2.17%	3.62%	0.17%	9.66%	0.16%	0.40%	0.07%	1.22%	0.09%	0.01%	0.00%	98.68%		
Percents of Hours	84.59%		3.79%		9.82%		0.47%		1.31%		0.02%		100.00%		

Chapter 5.1 2011 Regional Report

Information received from the CRCS System from Labor Compliance

Total from 2011 Regional Reportfor Wisconsin																
Minorties	Caucasian		African American		Hispanic		Asian		Native American		2 Races or more		Total Non Native		Total
Gender	Male	Female	Male	Female	Male	Female	Male	Female	Male	Female	Male	Female	Male	Female	Workers
Workers															
Q1	1,661	27	78	9	142	1	3	13	22	3	0	0	43,856	1,263	45,972
Q2	11,734	342	309	14	672	10	44	2	231	16	5	1			
Q3	15,411	470	442	24	861	7	59	4	308	24	6	1			
Q4	11,338	357	333	18	694	7	59	2	231	18	5	1			
2009 Q TOTAL	40,144	1,196	1,162	18	2,369	25	165	21	792	61	16	3			
Percentages of Workers	87.32%	2.60%	2.53%	0.04%	5.15%	0.05%	0.36%	0.05%	1.72%	0.13%	0.03%	0.01%	98.14%		
Percentages of Workers	89.92%		2.57%		5.21%		0.40%		1.86%		0.04%				
Hours Worked	Male	Female	Male	Female	Male	Female	Male	Female	Male	Female	Male	Female	Male	Female	Hours
Q1	169,122.20	1,682.80	5,852.10	386.00	14,264.30	136.5	338.50	0	1,758.80	45.00	20.80	0.00	4,616,666.70	124,259.80	4,836,444.80
Q2	1,198,204.20	30,900.30	29,552.60	1,192.00	77,362.80	618.6	3,231.80	237.8	24,159.30	2,167.90	141.40	88.50			
Q3	1,878,670.80	55,726.90	48,407.20	3,078.30	108,475.70	1135.2	7,758.70	403.3	42,456.60	3,639.80	298.30	7.50			
Q4	974,300.70	26,243.30	27,344.80	1,917.10	68,943.90	403.1	4,183.40	94.3	19,505.60	1,785.30	192.50	8.30			
2009 Hours Total	4,220,297.90	114,553.30	111,156.70	6,573.40	269,046.70	2,293.40	15,512.40	735.40	87,880.30	7,638.00	653.00	104.30			
Percentages of Hours	87.26%	2.37%	2.30%	0.14%	5.56%	0.05%	0.32%	0.02%	1.82%	0.16%	0.01%	0.00%	98.01%		
Percentages of Hours	89.63%		2.43%		5.61%		0.34%		1.97%		0.02%		100.00%		

Chapter 6.1 Chart 2012 Regional Report

Information received from the CRCS System from Labor Compliance

Minorties	Caucasian		African American		Hispanic		Asian		Native American		2 Races or more		Total Non Native		Total
Gender	Male	Female	Male	Female	Male	Female	Male	Female	Male	Female	Male	Female	Male	Female	Workers
Workers															
Q1	3,251	57	100	3	194	1	10	1	39	4	1	0	50,608	1,425	52,855
Q2	13,946	455	391	20	814	11	61	1	235	32	8	3			
Q3	17,538	542	482	29	902	13	65	3	303	27	13	0			
Q4	11,785	305	366	19	614	9	59	2	166	16	8	3			
2009 Q TOTAL	46,520	1,359	1,339	19	2,524	34	195	7	743	79	30	6			
Percentages of Workers	88.01%	2.57%	2.53%	0.04%	4.78%	0.06%	0.37%	0.01%	1.41%	0.15%	0.06%	0.01%			
Percentages of Workers	90.59%		2.57%		4.84%		0.38%		1.56%		0.07%		98.44%		
Hours Worked	Male	Female	Male	Female	Male	Female	Male	Female	Male	Female	Male	Female	Male	Female	Hours
Q1	253,107.40	2,945.90	5,051.10	502.00	16,845.60	8	952.90	257.5	2,943.30	251.50	8.00	0.00	4,734,974.40	122,352.20	4,942,951.60
Q2	1,440,283.30	37,344.10	32,633.00	1,381.00	83,679.00	404.5	6,032.00	461.5	23,183.50	2,883.20	473.60	38.00			
Q3	1,747,481.10	49,789.50	42,638.60	2,029.10	106,645.80	1066.8	7,742.00	593.6	34,208.50	4,549.60	1,261.70	109.00			
Q4	901,915.10	22,775.80	23,654.50	1,277.10	59,462.70	752.5	4,679.60	516.3	15,889.30	1,716.10	427.40	100.00			
2009 Hours Total	4,342,786.90	112,855.30	103,977.20	5,189.20	266,633.10	2,231.80	19,406.50	1,828.90	76,224.60	9,400.40	2,170.70	247.00			
Percentages of Hours	87.86%	2.28%	2.10%	0.10%	5.39%	0.05%	0.39%	0.04%	1.54%	0.19%	0.04%	0.00%	98.22%		
Percentages of Hours	90.14%		2.21%		5.44%		0.43%		1.73%		0.05%		100.00%		

Chapter 7.1 Chart 2013 Regional Report

Information recieved from the CRCS System from Labor Compliance

Total from 2013 Regional Reportfor Wisconsin

Minorties	Caucasian		African American		Hispanic		Asian		Native American		2 Races or more		Total Non Native		Total
Gender	Male	Female	Male	Female	Male	Female	Male	Female	Male	Female	Male	Female	Male	Female	Workers
Workers															
Q1	2,803	41	91	0	194	3	8	1	33	1	3	0	46,313	1,289	48,413
Q2	13,058	375	397	26	686	12	49	4	237	17	18	2			
Q3	16,182	505	494	39	866	11	55	7	300	27	17	2			
Q4	10,412	302	338	13	584	8	46	2	178	18	12	1			
2009 Q TOTAL	42,455	1,223	1,320	13	2,330	34	158	14	748	63	50	5			
Percentages of Workers	87.69%	2.53%	2.73%	0.03%	4.81%	0.07%	0.33%	0.03%	1.55%	0.13%	0.10%	0.01%			
Percentages of Workers	90.22%		2.75%		4.88%		0.36%		1.68%		0.11%		98.32%		
Hours Worked	Male	Female	Male	Female	Male	Female	Male	Female	Male	Female	Male	Female	Male	Female	Hours
Q1	202,349.40	2,382.30	5,245.00	0.00	13,201.30	206.8	448.70	77	2,247.20	18.50	134.80	0.00	4,304,192.20	131,119.00	4,520,014.00
Q2	1,204,104.20	35,479.10	32,633.90	2,229.70	85,587.00	1049.4	4,890.20	1022.3	21,323.50	1,384.10	1,845.10	34.50			
Q3	1,712,185.60	58,836.10	42,003.80	3,181.10	104,924.10	1559.3	7,625.80	919.3	36,066.50	4,179.50	1,867.50	38.80			
Q4	806,382.20	22,568.50	20,027.90	710.70	54,377.20	614.5	3,428.00	127.8	17,805.40	1,678.10	930.50	81.80			
2009 Hours Total	3,925,021.40	119,266.00	99,910.60	6,121.50	258,089.60	3,430.00	16,392.70	2,146.40	77,442.60	7,260.20	4,777.90	155.10			
Percentages of Hours	86.84%	2.64%	2.21%	0.14%	5.71%	0.08%	0.36%	0.05%	1.71%	0.16%	0.11%	0.00%			
Percentages of Hours	89.48%		2.35%		5.79%		0.41%		1.87%		0.11%		100.00%		98.02%

Chapter 8.1 Chart 2014 Regional Report

Information received from the CRCS System from Labor Compliance

Minorties	Caucasian		African American		Hispanic		Asian		Native American		2 Races or more		Total Non Native		Total
Gender	Male	Female	Male	Female	Male	Female	Male	Female	Male	Female	Male	Female	Male	Female	Workers
Workers															
Q1	3,027	52	157	5	211	3	8	1	33	0	12	0	52,801	1,624	55,195
Q2	14,525	449	566	30	880	19	55	5	217	17	20	0			
Q3	18,144	603	718	36	1014	21	62	5	264	25	39	3			
Q4	11,966	417	526	20	786	17	46	6	197	17	39	3			
2009 Q TOTAL	47,662	1,521	1,967	20	2,891	60	171	17	711	59	110	6			
Percentages of Workers	86.35%	2.76%	3.56%	0.04%	5.24%	0.11%	0.31%	0.03%	1.29%	0.11%	0.20%	0.01%	98.60%		
Percentages of Workers	89.11%		3.60%		5.35%		0.34%		1.40%		0.21%				
Hours Worked	Male	Female	Male	Female	Male	Female	Male	Female	Male	Female	Male	Female	Male	Female	Hours
Q1	285,751.60	3,534.80	11,453.10	1,124.50	26,489.80	252.3	597.20	397.5	2,643.40	0.00	1,274.50	0.00	5,296,978.40	157,622.60	5,536,019.80
Q2	1,426,545.80	38,316.50	47,619.60	2,761.20	98,944.70	1410.4	4,472.50	863.5	20,842.10	2,205.90	4,320.50	0.00			
Q3	1,988,450.20	63,056.10	76,390.70	5,125.70	143,955.70	3506.1	6,323.90	1053.1	35,392.80	4,560.30	4,806.40	43.50			
Q4	1,017,880.80	31,478.80	49,191.70	2,416.60	94,129.90	1601.2	3,573.40	637.3	14,180.40	1,593.90	4,806.40	43.50			
2009 Hours Total	4,718,628.40	136,386.20	184,655.10	11,428.00	363,520.10	6,770.00	14,967.00	2,951.40	73,058.70	8,360.10	15,207.80	87.00			
Percentages of Hours	85.24%	2.46%	3.34%	0.21%	6.57%	0.12%	0.27%	0.05%	1.32%	0.15%	0.27%	0.00%	98.25%		
Percentages of Hours	87.70%		3.54%		6.69%		0.32%		1.47%		0.28%		100.00%		

Total from 2014 Regional Reportfor Wisconsin

Chapter 9.1 Chart 2009-2014 Regional Report

2009-2014 Annual Information received from the CRCS System from Labor Compliance

Total from 2009-2014 Regional Report for Wisconsin

TOTALS	Caucasian		African American		Hispanic		Asian		Native American		2 Races or more		Total Non Native	Total Workers
2009 Q TOTAL	5,769.00	206.00	302.00	14.00	633.00	7.00	37.00	3.00	97.00	4.00	11.00	1.00	6,983.00	
Percentages of Workers	81.44%	2.91%	4.26%	0.20%	8.94%	0.10%	0.52%	0.04%	1.37%	0.06%	0.16%	0.02%	98.57%	14,067.00
Percentages of Workers	84.35%		4.46%		9.03%		0.56%		1.43%		0.17%		100.00%	
2009 Hours Total	776,721.30	25,186.80	37,955.90	4,052.60	84,672.30	841.60	2,633.90	246.10	14,733.20	1,000.80	650.30	182.80	933,144	Hours
Percentages of Hours	82%	3%	4%	0%	9%	0%	0%	0%	2%	0.11%	0%	0%	98.25%	1,882,021.20
Percentages of Hours	84.51%		4.43%		9.01%		0.30%		1.66%		0.09%		100.00%	
2010 Q TOTAL	32,209.00	906.00	1,388.00	11.00	2,683.00	42.00	161.00	12.00	577.00	35.00	10.00	-	37,422.00	Total Workers
Percents of Workers	84.68%	2.38%	3.65%	0.03%	7.05%	0.11%	0.42%	0.03%	1.52%	0.09%	0.03%	0.00%	98.39%	96,015.00
Percents of Workers	87.07%		3.68%		7.16%		0.45%		1.61%		0.03%		100.00%	
2010 Hours Total	4,400,530.30	116,127.30	193,211.50	9,261.80	515,742.60	8,656.10	21,524.50	3,599.70	64,947.90	4,886.70	798.80	81.80	5,269,534	Hours
Percents of Hours	82.42%	2.17%	3.62%	0.17%	9.66%	0.16%	0.40%	0.07%	1.22%	0.09%	0.01%	0.00%	98.68%	96,015.00
Percents of Hours	84.59%		3.79%		9.82%		0.47%		1.32%		0.02%		100.00%	
2011 Q TOTAL	40,244.00	1,196.00	1,162.00	18.00	2,369.00	25.00	165.00	21.00	792.00	61.00	16.00	3.00	45,119	Total Workers
Percentages of Workers	87.32%	2.60%	2.53%	0.04%	5.15%	0.05%	0.36%	0.05%	1.72%	0.13%	0.03%	0.01%	98%	96,015.00
Percentages of Workers	89.92%		2.57%		5.21%		0.40%		1.86%		0.04%		100.00%	
2011 Hours Total	4,220,297.90	114,553.30	111,156.70	6,573.40	269,046.70	2,293.40	15,512.40	735.40	87,880.30	7,638.00	653.00	104.30	4,740,927	Hours
Percentages of Hours	87.26%	2.37%	2.30%	0.14%	5.56%	0.05%	0.32%	0.02%	1.82%	0.16%	0.01%	0.00%	98%	9,577,371.30
Percentages of Hours	89.63%		2.43%		5.61%		0.34%		1.97%		0.02%		100.00%	
2012 Q TOTAL	46,520.00	1,359.00	1,339.00	19.00	2,524.00	34.00	195.00	7.00	743.00	79.00	30.00	6.00	52,033	Workers
Percentages of Workers	88.01%	2.57%	2.53%	0.04%	4.78%	0.06%	0.37%	0.01%	1.41%	0.15%	0.06%	0.01%	98.44%	104,888.00
Percentages of Workers	90.59%		2.57%		4.84%		0.38%		1.56%		0.07%		100.00%	
2012 Hours Total	4,342,786.90	112,855.30	103,977.20	5,189.20	266,633.10	2,291.80	19,406.50	1,828.90	76,224.60	9,400.40	2,170.70	247.00	4,857,327	Hours
Percentages of Hours	87.86%	2.28%	2.10%	0.10%	5.39%	0.05%	0.39%	0.04%	1.54%	0.19%	0.04%	0.00%	98%	9,800,278.20
Percentages of Hours	90.14%		2.21%		5.44%		0.43%		1.73%		0.05%		100.00%	
2013 Q TOTAL	42,455.00	1,223.00	1,320.00	13.00	2,330.00	34.00	156.00	14.00	748.00	63.00	50.00	5.00	47,602	Workers
Percentages of Workers	87.69%	2.53%	2.73%	0.03%	4.81%	0.07%	0.33%	0.03%	1.55%	0.13%	0.10%	0.01%	98.32%	96,015.00
Percentages of Workers	90.22%		2.75%		4.88%		0.36%		1.68%		0.11%		100.00%	
2013 Hours Total	3,925,021.40	119,266.00	95,910.60	6,121.50	258,089.60	3,430.00	16,392.70	2,146.40	77,442.60	7,260.20	4,777.90	155.10	4,435,311	Hours
Percentages of Hours	86.84%	2.64%	2.21%	0.14%	5.71%	0.08%	0.36%	0.05%	1.71%	0.16%	0.11%	0.00%	98.02%	8,955,325.20
Percentages of Hours	89.48%		2.35%		5.79%		0.42%		1.87%		0.11%		100.00%	
2014 Q TOTAL	47,662.00	1,521.00	1,967.00	20.00	2,891.00	60.00	171.00	17.00	711.00	59.00	110.00	6.00	54,425	Workers
Percentages of Workers	66.35%	2.76%	3.56%	0.04%	5.24%	0.11%	0.31%	0.03%	1.29%	0.11%	0.20%	0.01%	98.60%	109,620.00
Percentages of Workers	85.11%		3.60%		5.35%		0.34%		1.40%		0.21%		100.00%	
2014 Hours Total	4,718,629.40	136,386.20	184,655.10	11,428.00	363,520.10	6,770.00	14,967.00	2,951.40	73,058.70	6,360.10	15,207.80	87.00	5,454,601	Hours
Percentages of Hours	85.24%	2.46%	3.34%	0.21%	6.57%	0.12%	0.27%	0.05%	1.32%	0.15%	0.27%	0.00%	98.25%	10,990,620.80
Percentages of Hours	87.70%		3.54%		6.69%		0.32%		1.47%		0.28%		100.00%	

TOTALS 2009-2014	Caucasian		African American		Hispanic		Asian		Native American		2 Races or more		Total Non Native	TSTW
	214,759.00	6411	7478	95	13430	202	887	74	3668	301	227	21	248,584	491,137
Total Percentages of Workers Averages	85.92%	2.62%	3.21%	0.06%	5.99%	0.08%	0.38%	0.03%	1.47%	0.11%	0.10%	0.01%	98.41%	
Total Percentage of Workers 2009-2014	88.43%		3.21%		6.23%		0.43%		1.62%		0.08%			
TOTAL TSTW HOURS	22,383,986.20	624,374.90	730,867.00	42,626.50	1,757,704.40	24,222.90	90,437.00	11,507.90	394,287.30	38,546.20	24,258.50	858.00	25,690,843.30	51,814,520.10
Total Percentages of Hours Averages	511.46%	14.58%	17.57%	1.18%	41.82%	0.54%	2.03%	0.25%	9.16%	0.86%	0.52%	0.03%	98.24%	
Total Percentage of Hours 2009-2014	87.67%		3.12%		7.06%		0.38%		1.67%		0.09%			

Chapter 9.2 Chart WisDOT MRA 2009-2014

WisDOT Minority Report Analysis 2009-2014

Male	Female	Male	Female	Male	Female	Male	Female	Male	Female		Participaption
Head Count 2009											
4,529.00	157.00	244.00	17.00	457.00	6.00	24.00	5.00	66.00	5.00	5,510.00	1.29%
								1.20%	0.09%		
Hours Worked 2009											Hours Worked
784,155.40	25,838.10	38,449.20	4,052.50	84,813.90	841.50	2,633.80	246.00	14,871.90	1,001.50	956,903.80	1.66%
								1.55%	0.10%		
Head Count 2010											Head Count
8,432.00	245.00	384.00	19.00	757.00	13.00	37.00	9.00	143.00	9.00	10,048.00	1.51%
								1.42%	0.09%		
Hours Worked 2010											Hours Worked
2,185,057.10	58,055.30	96,397.90	4,646.30	260,693.30	4,274.50	10,696.30	325.80	32,345.80	2,472.30	2,654,964.60	1.31%
								1.22%	0.09%		
Head Count 2011											Head Count
11,016.00	364.00	384.00	20.00	774.00	9.00	36.00	2.00	217.00	21.00	12,843.00	1.85%
								1.69%	0.16%		
Hours Worked 2011											Hours Worked
4,238,610.10	114,950.40	1,111,766.10	6,573.30	270,251.90	2,293.10	15,539.50	735.30	88,256.00	7,637.80	5,856,613.50	1.64%
								1.51%	0.13%		
Head Count 2012											Head Count
11,411.00	342.00	342.00	14.00	731.00	8.00	44.00	3.00	187.00	23.00	13,105.00	1.60%
								1.43%	0.18%		
Hours Worked 2012											Hours Worked
4,345,260.40	112,854.70	104,034.90	5,189.00	266,632.90	2,231.80	19,406.00	1,828.80	73,224.20	9,400.00	4,940,063.70	1.67%
								1.48%	0.19%		
Head Count 2013											Head Count
10,985.00	358.00	403.00	19.00	723.00	6.00	40.00	4.00	209.00	20.00	12,767.00	1.79%
								1.64%	0.16%		
Hours Worked 2013											Hours Worked
3,921,300.60	119,265.70	99,546.00	5,968.40	258,007.40	3,429.80	16,392.50	2,146.30	7,742.20	7,259.80	4,441,058.70	0.34%
								0.17%	0.16%		
Head Count 2014											Head Count
11,422.00	378.00	518.00	31.00	760.00	15.00	38.00	4.00	185.00	19.00	13,370.00	1.53%
								1.38%	0.14%		
Hours Worked 2014											Hours Worked
4,610,025.00	132,248.60	171,806.20	9,317.40	330,169.00	6,769.60	14,966.80	2,951.30	72,976.00	8,359.80	5,359,589.70	1.52%
57,795.00	1,844.00	2,275.00	120.00	4,202.00	57.00	219.00	27.00			67,643.00	Total Head count
	20,647,621.40		1,657,747.20		1,490,408.70		87,868.40	1.36%	0.16%	24,209,193.00	

	Male	Female		
Total Native American Hours	289,416.10	36,131.20	325,547.30	1.34%
People on the project	1,007.00	97.00	1,104.00	Total Tribal
Hours Per person Male & Female	287.40	372.49	294.88	Total Per Tribal
Tenative 32 wks const per year	32	32	32	
Hours available per person in 32 week Const	8.98	11.64	9.21	Hrs Available per wk

Chapter 10.1 Chart WisDOT 2015 Regional Report

Information received from the CRCS System from Labor Compliance

Total from 2015Regional Report for Wisconsin

Minorties	Caucasian		African American		Hispanic		Asian		Native American		2 Races or more		Total Non Native		Total
Gender	Male	Female	Male	Female	Male	Female	Male	Female	Male	Female	Male	Female	Male	Female	Workers
Workers															
Q1	3,280	73	163	4	231	5	5	0	36	1	12	0	55,632	1,677	58,023
Q2	13,236	418	563	23	873	9	67	9	173	15	90	10			
Q3	23,373	776	1023	47	1618	18	119	15	327	26	174	18			
Q4	9,555	293	448	17	695	6	49	5	124	12	58	5			
2015 Q TOTAL	49,444	1,560	2,197	17	3,417	38	240	29	660	54	334	33			
Percentages of Workers	85.21%	2.69%	3.79%	0.03%	5.89%	0.07%	0.41%	0.05%	1.14%	0.09%	0.58%	0.06%	98.77%		
Percentages of Workers	87.90%		3.82%		5.95%		0.46%		1.23%		0.63%				
Hours Worked	Male	Female	Male	Female	Male	Female	Male	Female	Male	Female	Male	Female	Male	Female	Hours
Q1	152,419.10	3,327.80	8,344.70	326.00	13,611.60	133.9	331.40	0	796.30	0.00	836.50	0.00	4,687,507.10	141,882.40	4,897,733.10
Q2	1,491,067.70	45,928.60	51,959.80	2,432.10	111,058.10	807.2	5,091.10	635.3	22,650.80	2,418.30	8,895.80	1,164.10			
Q3	1,687,810.30	56,990.10	63,250.50	2,809.70	127,921.70	567.9	7,036.20	556.5	27,717.30	2,779.60	12,737.20	1,482.40			
Q4	839,718.80	22,830.50	31,486.90	979.20	65,948.00	499.6	3,938.80	169.8	11,092.30	889.00	4,042.90	241.70			
2015 Hours Total	4,171,015.90	129,077.00	155,041.90	6,547.00	318,539.40	2,008.60	16,397.50	1,361.60	62,256.70	6,086.90	26,512.40	2,888.20			
Percentages of Hours	85.16%	2.64%	3.17%	0.13%	6.50%	0.04%	0.33%	0.03%	1.27%	0.12%	0.54%	0.06%	98.00%		
Percentages of Hours	87.80%		3.30%		6.54%		0.36%		1.40%		0.60%		100.00%		

Chapter 11.1 Chart WisDOT 2016 Regional Report

Information received from the CRCS System from Labor Compliance

Total from 2016Regional Reportfor Wisconsin															
Minorties	Caucasian		African American		Hispanic		Asian		Native American		2 Races or more		Total Non Native		Total
Gender	Male	Female	Male	Female	Male	Female	Male	Female	Male	Female	Male	Female	Male	Female	Workers
Workers															
Q1	2,379	59	159	4	212	5	4	0	23	1	10	0	47,274	1,436	49,287
Q2	9,038	290	500	23	762	5	52	6	106	10	48	7			
Q3	23,373	776	1023	47	1618	18	119	15	327	26	174	18			
Q4	6,766	208	403	16	574	6	32	3	75	9	28	4			
2016Q TOTAL	41,556	1,333	2,085	16	3,166	34	207	24	531	46	260	29			
Percentages of Workers	84.31%	2.70%	4.23%	0.03%	6.42%	0.07%	0.42%	0.05%	1.08%	0.09%	0.53%	0.06%	98.83%		
Percentages of Workers	87.02%		4.26%		6.49%		0.47%		1.17%		0.59%				
Hours Worked	Male	Female	Male	Female	Male	Female	Male	Female	Male	Female	Male	Female	Male	Female	Hours
Q1	117,662.20	3,151.50	8,152.90	326.00	13,003.80	133.9	324.10	0	398.80	0.00	827.50	0.00	3,991,733.00	121,767.20	4,165,183.80
Q2	1,068,426.80	33,627.00	47,058.20	2,432.10	100,054.40	754.90	3,052.10	510.30	12,064.70	1,235.50	6,710.80	907.80			
Q3	1,687,810.30	56,990.10	63,250.50	2,809.70	127,921.70	567.9	7,036.20	556.5	27,717.30	2,779.60	12,737.20	1,482.40			
Q4	632,258.50	15,794.90	29,479.60	918.90	59,705.60	499.6	3,202.50	93.3	6,850.20	597.50	3,058.10	210.40			
2016 Hours Total	3,506,157.80	109,563.50	147,941.20	6,486.70	300,685.50	1,956.30	13,614.90	1,160.10	47,071.00	4,612.60	23,333.60	2,600.60			
Percentages of Hours	84.18%	2.63%	3.55%	0.16%	7.22%	0.05%	0.33%	0.03%	1.13%	0.11%	0.56%	0.06%	98.14%		
Percentages of Hours	86.81%		3.71%		7.27%		0.35%		1.24%		0.62%		100.00%		

Chapter 12.1 Chart WisDOT 2017 Regional Report

Information received from the CRCS System from Labor Compliance

Total from 2017 Regional Reportfor Wisconsin

Minorties	Caucasian		African American		Hispanic		Asian		Native American		2 Races or more		Total Non Native		Total
Gender	Male	Female	Male	Female	Male	Female	Male	Female	Male	Female	Male	Female	Male	Female	Workers
Workers															
Q1	1,904	36	68	3	95	0	3	1	19	0	13	2	53,558	3,886	59,040
Q2	32,453	2655	68	42	95	0	3	1	1007	151	13	2			
Q3	10,268	573	0	0	0	0	0	0	183	30	0	0			
Q4	8,575	616	0	0	0	0	0	0	181	25	0	0			17,879
2017 Q TOTAL	53,200	3,880	136	0	190	0	6	2	1,390	206	26	4			
Percentages of Workers	90.11%	6.57%	0.23%	0.00%	0.32%	0.00%	0.01%	0.00%	2.35%	0.35%	0.04%	0.01%	97.30%		
Percentages of Workers	96.68%		0.23%		0.32%		0.01%		2.70%		0.05%				
Hours Worked	Male	Female	Male	Female	Male	Female	Male	Female	Male	Female	Male	Female	Male	Female	Hours
Q1	159,213.00	3,278.40	7,071.40	677.50	8,284.10	0	202.50	278.5	1,800.40	0.00	1,448.60	104.60	3,858,479.40	250,518.10	4,234,258.00
Q2	264,195.80	58,479.40	103,235.30	5,963.10	303,502.60	1686.8	53,571.60	8468.4	47,042.00	6,779.50	26,019.80	5,961.30			
Q3	1,306,193.00	94,603.00	0.00	0.00	0.00	0	0.00	0	30,295.30	4,406.30	0.00	0.00			
Q4	1,623,624.60	70,960.10	322.80	0.00	1,478.30	0	116.00	57	31,579.00	3,358.00	0.00	0.00			208,218.00
2017 Hours Total	3,353,226.40	227,320.90	110,629.50	6,640.60	313,265.00	1,686.80	53,890.10	8,803.90	110,716.70	14,543.80	27,468.40	6,065.90			
Percentages of Hours	79.19%	5.37%	2.61%	0.16%	7.40%	0.04%	1.27%	0.21%	2.61%	0.34%	0.65%	0.14%	96.25%		
Percentages of Hours	84.56%		2.77%		7.44%		1.48%		2.96%		0.79%		100.00%		

Appendix D

Influences Discussed in Chapter 18: Influences of the WTBA Surrounding the TERO/IP or the NAHP
(January to November 2019)

WisDOT APPARENT BID RESULTS FOR THE LETTING OF
January 15, 2019

January 15 2019		
Bid Amount	**Contractor**	**Address City and State**
$791,587.35	ZENITH TECH., INC.	Waukesha, WI 53187
$1,487,766.55	JAMES PETERSON SONS, INC.	Medford, WI 54451-0120
$13,958,011.50	ZENITH TECH., INC.	Waukesha, WI 53187
$3,432,809.95	LUNDA CONSTRUCTION	Black River Falls, WI 54615
$1,412,653.33	ZENITH TECH., INC.	Waukesha, WI 53187
$16,822,050.04	ZIGNEGO COMPANY, INC.	Waukesha, WI 53186
$764,794.11	LUNDA CONSTRUCTION	Black River Falls, WI 54615-
$560,802.17	JAMES PETERSON SONS, INC.	Medford, WI 54451-0120
$4,539,097.96	NORTHEAST ASPHALT, INC	Greenville, WI 54942)
$2,561,886.71	NORTHEAST ASPHALT, INC	Greenville, WI 54942
$1,270,870.12	AMERICAN ASPHALT OF WI	Mosinee, WI 54455
$137,809,890.42	**Total Projects let for January**	
$47,602,329.79	**Board of Directors of WTBA Companies awarded Projects**	

AWARDED		Bid but NOT AWARDED
$1,270,870.12	AMERICAN ASPHALT OF WI	$0.00
$2,048,568.72	JAMES PETERSON SONS, INC.	$21,560,232.44
$4,197,604.06	LUNDA CONSTRUCTION-	$12,894,436.66
$7,100,984.67	NORTHEAST ASPHALT, INC	$2,142,980.00
$0.00	PAYNE AND DOLAN, INC-	$16,895,171.77
$2,204,240.68	ZENITH TECH., INC. -	$19,729,188.95
$16,822,050.04	ZIGNEGO COMPANY, INC.	$16,985,550.81
Awarded	**Percentage awarded to WTBA**	**Bid On but not awarded**
$33,644,318.29	37%	$90,207,560.63

Total **$137,809,890.42** attempting to bid on projects by the Construction Companies directly associated with the WTBA. On just **January 15, 2019**, the WTBA Board received the amount of **$47,602,329.79** Awarded Projects by WisDOT.

WisDOT APPARENT BID RESULTS FOR THE LETTING OF February 12, 2019

February 12, 2019		
Bid Amount	**Contractor**	**Address City and State**
$1,129,657.51	**JAMES PETERSON SONS, INC.**	Medford, WI 54451-0120
$5,838,016.82	**ZENITH TECH., INC**	Waukesha, WI 53187
$2,289,162.88	**NORTHEAST ASPHALT, INC**	Greenville, WI 54942
$1,531,536.89	**AMERICAN ASPHALT OF WI**	Mosinee, WI 54455
$1,774,422.42	**ZENITH TECH., INC.-**	Waukesha, WI 53187-
$1,344,244.67	**LUNDA CONSTRUCTION-**	Black River Falls, WI 54615-
$41,209,385.48	**Total Projects let for February**	
$13,907,041.19	**Board of Directors Of WTBA Companies awarded Projects**	

AWARDED		Bid but NOT AWARDED
$2,802,407.01	AMERICAN ASPHALT OF WI	$0.0
$0.00	INTEG GRADING and EXC INC.-	$3,106,340.?
$3,178,226.23	JAMES PETERSON SONS, INC.	$21,560,232.4
$5,541,848.73	LUNDA CONSTRUCTION-	$24,198,097.4
$0.00	MEGA RENTALS, INC.-	$2,798,740.8
$9,390,147.55	NORTHEAST ASPHALT, INC	$3,754,612.8
$0.00	PAYNE AND DOLAN, INC-	$16,895,171.?
$9,386,502.17	ZENITH TECH., INC. -	$22,083,415.?
$5,541,848.73	ZIGNEGO COMPANY, INC.	$23,113,293.?

Awarded	Percentage awarded to WTBA	Bid On but not awarded
$35,840,980.42	31%	$117,509,904.9

Total **$41,209,385.48** attempting to bid on projects by the Construction Companies directly associated with the WTBA. On just **February 12, 2019**, the WTBA Board received the amount of **$13,907,041.19** Awarded Projects by WisDOT.

WisDOT APPARENT BID RESULTS FOR THE LETTING OF
March 12, 2019

March 12, 2019		
Bid Amount	**Contractor**	**Address City and State**
$3,970,008.10	JAMES PETERSON SONS, INC.	Medford, WI 54451-0120
$2,428,775.64	PAYNE AND DOLAN, INC	Waukesha, WI 53187-0781
$16,913,376.34	JAMES PETERSON SONS, INC.	Medford, WI 54451-0120
$1,836,026.18	ZENITH TECH., INC.	Waukesha, WI 53187
$403,617.88	LUNDA CONSTRUCTION	Black River Falls, WI 54615
$3,751,362.08	NORTHEAST ASPHALT, INC	Greenville, WI 54942
$2,327,330.72	JAMES PETERSON SONS, INC.	Medford, WI 54451-0120
$3,063,832.63	MUSSON BROS., INC.	Rhinelander, WI 54501
$1,141,365.88	AMERICAN ASPHALT OF WI	Mosinee, WI 54455
$3,569,722.52	NORTHEAST ASPHALT, INC	Greenville, WI 54942
$136,865,534.48	**Total Projects let for March**	
$43,375,426.07	**Board of Directors of WTBA Companies awarded Projects**	

AWARDED		Bid but NOT AWARDED
$3,943,772.89	AMERICAN ASPHALT OF WI	$0.00
$0.00	INTEG GRADING and EXC INC.-	$3,106,340.54
$26,388,941.39	JAMES PETERSON SONS, INC.	$21,560,232.44
$5,945,466.61	LUNDA CONSTRUCTION-	$24,198,097.40
$0.00	MEGA RENTALS, INC.-	$2,798,740.84
$0.00	MUSSON BROS., INC.-	$5,282,556.78
$16,711,232.15	NORTHEAST ASPHALT, INC	$4,329,279.92
$2,428,775.64	PAYNE AND DOLAN, INC-	$21,931,099.55
$11,222,528.35	ZENITH TECH., INC. -	$28,193,892.75
$5,541,848.73	ZIGNEGO COMPANY, INC.	$93,843,161.48

Awarded	Percentage awarded to WTBA	Bid On but not awarded
$108,023,546.18	53%	$205,243,401.70

Total $136,865,534.48 attempting to bid on projects by the Construction Companies directly associated with the WTBA. On just **March 12, 2019**, WTBA Board received the amount of **$43,375,426.07** Awarded Projects by WisDOT.

WisDOT APPARENT BID RESULTS FOR THE LETTING OF
April 09, 2019

April 09, 2019		
Bid Amount	**Contractor**	**Address City and State**
$11,934,442.30	PAYNE AND DOLAN, INC	Waukesha, WI 53187-0781
$347,177.44	ZENITH TECH., INC.	Waukesha, WI 53187-
$381,103.00	LUNDA CONSTRUCTION	Black River Falls, WI 54615
$3,311,038.99	ZENITH TECH., INC.	Waukesha, WI 53187
$747,587.30	PAYNE AND DOLAN, INC	Waukesha, WI 53187-0781
$3,311,038.99	ZENITH TECH., INC.	Waukesha, WI 53187
$598,767.61	PAYNE AND DOLAN, INC	Waukesha, WI 53187-0781
$3,894,169.20	NORTHEAST ASPHALT, INC	Greenville, WI 54942
$2,053,316.84	NORTHEAST ASPHALT, INC	Greenville, WI 54942
$776,348.53	LUNDA CONSTRUCTION	Black River Falls, WI 54615
$495,427.65	NORTHEAST ASPHALT, INC	Greenville, WI 54942
$569,024.34	AMERICAN ASPHALT OF WI	Mosinee, WI 54455
$5,406,759.51	JAMES PETERSON SONS, INC.	Medford, WI 54451-0120
$837,144.53	NORTHEAST ASPHALT, INC	Greenville, WI 54942
$80,384,185.17	**Total projects let for April**	
$34,663,346.23	**Board of Directors Of WTBA Companies awarded Projects**	

AWARDED		Bid but NOT AWARDED
$4,512,797.23	AMERICAN ASPHALT OF WI	$0.00
$0.00	INTEG GRADING and EXC INC.-	$6,417,901.99
$31,795,700.90	JAMES PETERSON SONS, INC.	$27,978,134.43
$7,102,918.14	LUNDA CONSTRUCTION-	$26,225,843.18
$0.00	MEGA RENTALS, INC.-	$2,798,740.84
$0.00	MUSSON BROS., INC.-	$5,282,556.78
$23,991,290.37	NORTHEAST ASPHALT, INC	$7,771,821.54
$15,709,572.85	PAYNE AND DOLAN, INC-	$40,952,453.19
$18,191,783.77	ZENITH TECH., INC. -	$30,944,529.20
$5,541,848.73	ZIGNEGO COMPANY, INC.	$109,010,161.48

Awarded	Percentage awarded to WTBA	Bid On but not awarded
$106,845,911.99	42%	$257,382,142.0

Total **$80,384,185.17** attempting to bid on projects by
the Construction Companies directly associated with the
WTBA. On just **April 09, 2019**, the WTBA Board received the
amount of **$34,663,346.23** Awarded Projects by WisDOT.

WisDOT APPARENT BID RESULTS FOR THE LETTING OF
May 12, 2019

May 12, 2019		
Bid Amount	**Contractor**	**Address City and State**
$2,334,600.72	PAYNE AND DOLAN, INC	Waukesha, WI 53187-0781
$1,522,687.44	LUNDA CONSTRUCTION	Black River Falls, WI 54615
$657,400.44	PAYNE AND DOLAN, INC	Waukesha, WI 53187-0781
$2,717,625.18	NORTHEAST ASPHALT, INC	Greenville, WI 54942
$2,397,293.64	NORTHEAST ASPHALT, INC	Greenville, WI 54942
$1,824,519.04	NORTHEAST ASPHALT, INC	Greenville, WI 54942
$1,686,152.96	NORTHEAST ASPHALT, INC	Greenville, WI 54942
$1,577,359.23	NORTHEAST ASPHALT, INC	Greenville, WI
$1,024,432.70	NORTHEAST ASPHALT, INC	Greenville, WI 54942
$2,848,424.64	ZENITH TECH., INC.	Waukesha, WI 53187-
$1,127,735.09	NORTHEAST ASPHALT, INC	Greenville, WI 54942
$583,962.54	ZENITH TECH., INC.	Waukesha, WI 53187-
$548,226.07	NORTHEAST ASPHALT, INC	Greenville, WI 54942
$1,749,059.63	AMERICAN ASPHALT OF WI	Mosinee, WI 54455-
$1,152,393.75	LUNDA CONSTRUCTION	Black River Falls, WI 54615
$1,649,182.10	NORTHEAST ASPHALT, INC	Greenville, WI 54942
$4,321,955.59	AMERICAN ASPHALT OF WI-	Mosinee, WI 54455-
$1,230,256.10	AMERICAN ASPHALT OF WI-	Mosinee, WI 54455-
$56,381,127.05	Total projects let for May	
$33,633,639.75	Board of Directors of WTBA Companies awarded Projects	

AWARDED		Bid but NOT AWARDED
$11,814,068.55	AMERICAN ASPHALT OF WI	$586,841.35
$0.00	INTEG GRADING and EXC INC.-	$6,417,901.99
$31,795,700.90	JAMES PETERSON SONS, INC.	$27,978,134.43
$9,777,999.33	LUNDA CONSTRUCTION-	$27,765,475.17
$0.00	MEGA RENTALS, INC.-	$2,798,740.84
$0.00	MUSSON BROS., INC.-	$8,081,297.62
$38,543,816.38	NORTHEAST ASPHALT, INC	$9,786,617.44
$18,701,574.01	PAYNE AND DOLAN, INC-	$51,559,463.79
$21,040,208.41	ZENITH TECH., INC. -	$35,917,950.90
$3,763,701.80	ZIGNEGO COMPANY, INC.	$110,579,260.67

Awarded	Percentage awarded to WTBA	Bid On but not awarded
$138,117,442.27	49%	$281,471,684.20

Total **$56,381,127.05** attempting to bid on projects by the Construction Companies directly associated with the WTBA. On just **May 12, 2019**, the WTBA Board received the amount of **$33,633,639.75** Awarded Projects by WisDOT.

WisDOT APPARENT BID RESULTS FOR THE LETTING OF
June 11, 2019

June 11, 2019		
Bid Amount	**Contractor**	**Address City and State**
$6,185,627.55	**ZENITH TECH., INC.**	Waukesha, WI 53187-
$1,379,979.97	**PAYNE AND DOLAN, INC**	Waukesha, WI 53187-0781
$1,459,174.21	**ZENITH TECH., INC.**	Waukesha, WI 53187-
$26,552,594.84	**Total projects let for May**	
$9,024,781.73	**Board of Directors of WTBA Companies awarded Projects**	
AWARDED		**Bid but NOT AWARDED**
$2,717,625.18	AMERICAN ASPHALT OF WI	$586,841.35
$0.00	INTEG GRADING and EXC INC.-	$6,417,901.99
$31,795,700.90	JAMES PETERSON SONS, INC.	$27,978,134.43
$9,777,999.33	LUNDA CONSTRUCTION-	$34,441,833.07
$0.00	MEGA RENTALS, INC.-	$2,798,740.84
$0.00	MUSSON BROS., INC.-	$8,081,297.62
$38,543,816.38	NORTHEAST ASPHALT, INC	$9,786,617.44
$20,081,553.98	PAYNE AND DOLAN, INC-	$51,559,463.79
$28,685,010.17	ZENITH TECH., INC. -	$35,917,950.90
$3,763,701.80	ZIGNEGO COMPANY, INC.	$120,348,204.88
Awarded	**Percentage awarded to WTBA**	**Bid On but not awarded**
$135,365,407.74	**45%**	$297,916,986.

Total **$26,552,594.84** attempting to bid on projects by the Construction Companies directly associated with the WTBA. On just **June 11, 2019**, the WTBA Board received the amount of **$9,024,781.73** Awarded Projects by WisDOT.

WisDOT APPARENT BID RESULTS FOR THE LETTING OF July 09, 2019

January 09, 2018		
Bid Amount	**Contractor**	**Address City and State**
$2,337,607.64	ZENITH TECH., INC.	Waukesha, WI 53187
$1,023,009.41	LUNDA CONSTRUCTION	Black River Falls, WI 54615
$1,466,022.28	LUNDA CONSTRUCTION-	Black River Falls, WI 54615-
$453,743.48	JAMES PETERSON SONS, INC.-	Medford, WI 54451-0120-
$118,152,127.99	January Total projects let for 2018	
$5,280,382.81	Board of Directors of WTBA Companies awarded Projects	

AWARDED		Bid but NOT AWARDED
$453,743.48	JAMES PETERSON SONS, INC.	$42,492,059.63
$2,942,775.17	LUNDA CONSTRUCTION-	$50,012,346.68
$0.00	MICHELS CORPORATION-	$646,768.06
$0.00	MUSSON BROS., INC.-	$6,929,506.05
$0.00	PARISI CONSTRUCTION CO INC.	$2,222,616.01
$2,337,607.64	ZENITH TECH., INC. -	$6,690,243.43
$0.00	ZIGNEGO COMPANY, INC.	$34,759,914.56

Awarded	Percentage of projects awarded	Bid On but not awarded
$5,734,126.29	4%	$143,753,454.42

Total **$367,670,063.71** attempting to bid on projects by the Construction Companies directly associated with the WTBA. On just **July 09, 2019**, the WTBA Board received the amount of **$16,007,745.67** Awarded Projects by WisDOT.

WisDOT APPARENT BID RESULTS FOR THE LETTING OF
August 13, 2019

August 13, 2019		
Bid Amount	**Contractor**	**Address City and State**
$860,050.25	**ZENITH TECH., INC.**	Waukesha, WI 53187-
$2,271,593.20	**LUNDA CONSTRUCTION COMPANY**	Black River Falls, WI 5461₹
$10,018,451.19	**ZIGNEGO COMPANY, INC.**	Waukesha, WI 53186
$21,813,451.16	**PAYNE AND DOLAN, INC**	Waukesha, WI 53187-0781
$4,264,390.64	**MUSSON BROS., INC.**	Rhinelander, WI 54501-
$2,433,667.29	**AMERICAN ASPHALT OF WI**	Mosinee, WI 54455-
$867,273.70	**NORTHEAST ASPHALT, INC**	Greenville, WI 54942
$110,020,091.33	**Total projects let for August**	
$42,528,877.43	**Board of Directors of WTBA Companies awarded Projects**	

AWARDED		Bid but NOT AWARDED
$6,434,900.89	AMERICAN ASPHALT OF WI	$1,488,504.55
$0.00	Edgerton Contractors, Inc.	$18,034,338.54
$38,543,816.38	INTEG GRADING and EXC INC.-	$10,688,498.95
$46,519,838.15	JAMES PETERSON SONS, INC.	$53,339,382.03
$12,049,592.53	LUNDA CONSTRUCTION-	$168,651,104.56
$0.00	MEGA RENTALS, INC.-	$3,922,663.31
$4,264,390.64	MUSSON BROS., INC.-	$9,080,982.62
$39,411,090.08	NORTHEAST ASPHALT, INC	$9,786,617.44
$41,895,005.14	PAYNE AND DOLAN, INC-	$51,559,463.79
$0.00	Rock Road Companies	$31,533,335.48
$29,545,060.42	ZENITH TECH., INC. -	$162,719,712.34
$13,782,152.99	ZIGNEGO COMPANY, INC.	$189,848,012.65

Awarded	**Percentage awarded to WTBA**	**Bid On but not awarded**
$232,445,847.22	**33%**	**$710,652,616.26**

Total **$110,020,091.33** attempting to bid on projects by the
Construction Companies directly associated with the WTBA.
On just **August 13, 2019**, the WTBA Board of Directors
received the amount of **$42,528,877.43** Awarded Projects by
WisDOT.

WisDOT APPARENT BID RESULTS FOR THE LETTING OF September 10, 2019

September 10, 2019		
Amount	**Contractor**	**Address City and State**
$3,319,099.56	**ZIGNEGO COMPANY, INC.**	Waukesha, WI 53186
$9,361,606.48	**ZIGNEGO COMPANY, INC.**	Waukesha, WI 53186
$24,873,411.99	**Total projects let for Sept**	
$12,680,706.04	**Board of Directors of WTBA Companies awarded Projects**	

ARDED		**Bid but NOT AWARDED**
$6,434,900.89	AMERICAN ASPHALT OF WI	$960,772.94
$0.00	Edgerton Contractors, Inc.	$18,034,338.54
$38,543,816.38	INTEG GRADING and EXC INC.-	$10,688,498.95
$46,519,838.15	JAMES PETERSON SONS, INC.	$53,339,382.03
$12,049,592.53	LUNDA CONSTRUCTION-	$172,856,799.34
$0.00	MEGA RENTALS, INC.-	$6,171,053.51
	MICHELS CORPORATION	
$4,264,390.64	MUSSON BROS., INC.-	$9,080,982.62
$39,411,090.08	NORTHEAST ASPHALT, INC	$9,786,617.44
$41,895,005.14	PAYNE AND DOLAN, INC-	$52,824,260.84
$0.00	Rock Road Companies	$31,533,335.48
$29,545,060.42	ZENITH TECH., INC. -	$167,193,536.26
$26,462,859.03	ZIGNEGO COMPANY, INC.	$189,848,012.65

Awarded	**Percentage awarded to WTBA**	**Bid On but not awarded**
$245,126,553.26	34%	$722,317,590.60

Total **$24,873,411.99** attempting to bid on projects by the Construction Companies directly associated with the WTBA. On just **September 10, 2019**, the WTBA Board of Directors received the amount of **$12,680,706.04** Awarded Projects by WisDOT.

WisDOT APPARENT BID RESULTS FOR THE LETTING OF
November 12, 2019

November 12, 2019		
Bid Amount	**Contractor**	**Address City and State**
$2,495,178.79	**ROCK ROAD COMPANIES, INC.**	
$6,086,766.38	**LUNDA CONSTRUCTION CO**	Black River Falls, WI 54615
$1,116,980.42	**PAYNE AND DOLAN, INC**	Waukesha, WI 53187-0781
$8,421,896.79	**PAYNE AND DOLAN, INC**	Waukesha, WI 53187-0781
$4,993,894.39	**ROCK ROAD COMPANIES, INC.**	
$1,620,287.16	**ZENITH TECH., INC.-**	Waukesha, WI 53187-
$1,425,824.34	**PAYNE AND DOLAN, INC**	Waukesha, WI 53187-0781
$10,284,006.15	**JAMES PETERSON SONS, INC.**	Medford, WI 54451-0120
$1,716,236.29	**LUNDA CONSTRUCTION Co**	Black River Falls, WI 54615
$3,795,992.46	**AMERICAN ASPHALT OF WI**	Mosinee, WI 54455-
$1,842,449.82	**ZENITH TECH., INC.-**	Waukesha, WI 53187-
$102,997,209.75	**Total projects let for November**	
$43,799,512.99	**Board of Directors of WTBA Companies awarded Projects**	

AWARDED		Bid but NOT AWARDED
$10,230,893.35	AMERICAN ASPHALT OF WI	$960,772.94
$0.00	Edgerton Contractors, Inc.	$18,034,338.54
$38,543,816.38	INTEG GRADING and EXC INC.-	$25,124,485.12
$56,803,844.30	JAMES PETERSON SONS, INC.	$87,339,030.20
$19,852,595.20	LUNDA CONSTRUCTION-	$180,348,180.82
$0.00	MEGA RENTALS, INC.-	$6,171,053.51
$0.00	MICHELS CORPORATION	$10,295,660.13
$4,264,390.64	MUSSON BROS., INC.-	$9,080,982.62
$39,411,090.08	NORTHEAST ASPHALT, INC	$9,786,617.44
$52,859,706.69	PAYNE AND DOLAN, INC-	$58,134,178.85
$60,348,779.87	Rock Road Companies	$31,533,335.48
$33,007,797.40	ZENITH TECH., INC. -	$179,983,124.18
$26,462,859.03	ZIGNEGO COMPANY, INC.	$189,848,012.65

Awarded	Percentage awarded to WTBA	Bid On but not awarded
$341,785,772.94	**42%**	$806,639,772.4

Total **$102,997,209.75** attempting to bid on projects by the Construction Companies directly associated with the WTBA. On just **November 12, 2019**, the WTBA Board of Directors received the amount of **$43,799,512.99** Awarded Projects by WisDOT.

<u>*Chapter 18 Influences of the WTBA surrounding the TERO/IP or the NAHP (January to December 2018)*</u>

WisDOT APPARENT BID RESULTS FOR THE LETTING OF
January 09, 2018

January 09, 2018		
Bid Amount	**Contractor**	**Address City and State**
$2,337,607.64	ZENITH TECH., INC.	Waukesha, WI 53187
$1,023,009.41	LUNDA CONSTRUCTION	Black River Falls, WI 54615
$1,466,022.28	LUNDA CONSTRUCTION-	Black River Falls, WI 54615-
$453,743.48	JAMES PETERSON SONS, INC.-	Medford, WI 54451-0120-
$118,152,127.99	**January Total projects let for 2018**	
$5,280,382.81	**Board of Directors of WTBA Companies awarded Projects**	
AWARDED		**Bid but NOT AWARDED**
$453,743.48	JAMES PETERSON SONS, INC.	$42,492,059.63
$2,942,775.17	LUNDA CONSTRUCTION-	$50,012,346.68
$0.00	MICHELS CORPORATION-	$646,768.06
$0.00	MUSSON BROS., INC.-	$6,929,506.05
$0.00	PARISI CONSTRUCTION CO INC.	$2,222,616.01
$2,337,607.64	ZENITH TECH., INC. -	$6,690,243.43
$0.00	ZIGNEGO COMPANY, INC.	$34,759,914.56
Awarded	**Percentage of projects awarded**	**Bid On but not awarded**
$5,734,126.29	4%	$143,753,454.42
February 13 2018		
Bid Amount	**Contractor**	**Address City and State**
$3,998,162.45	EDGERTON CONTRACTORS, INC.-	Oak Creek, WI-
$1,413,201.90	PAYNE AND DOLAN, INC-	Waukesha, WI 53187-0781
$9,283,447.92	MUSSON BROS., INC.-	Rhinelander, WI 54501-
$3,885,375.52	LUNDA CONSTRUCTION	Black River Falls, WI 54615
$14,472,290.75	ZIGNEGO COMPANY, INC.	Waukesha, WI 53186

Total **$118,152,127.99** attempting to bid on projects by the Construction Companies directly associated with the WTBA. On just **January 09, 2018**, the WTBA Board of Directors received the amount of **$5,280,382.81** Awarded Projects by WisDOT.

WisDOT APPARENT BID RESULTS FOR THE LETTING OF
February 13, 2018

February 13, 2018		
Bid Amount	**Contractor**	**Address City and State**
$3,998,162.45	**EDGERTON CONTRACTORS, INC.-**	Oak Creek, WI-
$1,413,201.90	**PAYNE AND DOLAN, INC-**	Waukesha, WI 53187-0781
$9,283,447.92	**MUSSON BROS., INC.-**	Rhinelander, WI 54501-
$3,885,375.52	**LUNDA CONSTRUCTION**	Black River Falls, WI 54615
$14,472,290.75	**ZIGNEGO COMPANY, INC.**	Waukesha, WI 53186
$121,083,239.17	**February Total projects let for 2018**	
$33,052,478.54	**Board of Directors of WTBA Companies awarded Projects**	
AWARDED		**Bid but NOT AWARDED**
$3,998,162.45	Edgerton Contractors, Inc.	$0.00
$0.00	INTEG GRADING and EXC INC.-	$4,162,602.33
$453,743.48	JAMES PETERSON SONS, INC.	$59,373,631.18
$6,828,150.69	LUNDA CONSTRUCTION-	$60,729,227.25
$0.00	MICHELS CORPORATION-	$26,760,628.41
$9,283,447.92	MUSSON BROS., INC.-	$12,659,753.68
$0.00	PARISI Construction CO Inc-	$8,099,069.47
$1,413,201.90	PAYNE AND DOLAN, INC-	$4,279,640.98
$2,337,607.64	ZENITH TECH., INC. -	$18,953,455.87
$14,472,290.75	ZIGNEGO COMPANY, INC.	$34,759,914.56
Awarded	**Percentage of projects awarded**	**Bid On but not awarded**
$38,786,604.83	17%	$229,777,923.73

Total $121,083,239.17 attempting to bid on projects by the Construction Companies directly associated with the WTBA. On just **February 13, 2018**, the WTBA Board of Directors received the amount of **$33,052,478.54** Awarded Projects by WisDOT.

WisDOT APPARENT BID RESULTS FOR THE LETTING OF
March 13, 2018

March 13, 2018		
Bid Amount	**Contractor**	**Address City and State**
$2,866,393.51	**INTEG GRADING and EXC INC.**	Schofield, WI 54476-0138
$3,630,964.18	**Rock Road Companies**	Janesville, WI
$2,101,074.76	**LUNDA CONSTRUCTION**	Black River Falls, WI 54615
$6,666,919.20	**LUNDA CONSTRUCTION**	Black River Falls, WI 54615
$1,780,057.70	**LUNDA CONSTRUCTION**	Black River Falls, WI 54615
$1,742,922.06	**ZIGNEGO COMPANY, INC.-**	Waukesha, WI 53186
$5,995,953.31	**PAYNE AND DOLAN, INC**	Waukesha, WI 53187-0781
$41,111,995.06	**MICHELS CORPORATION-**	Waukesha, WI
$158,094,067.15	**March Total projects let for 2018**	
$65,896,279.78	**Board of Directors of WTBA Companies awarded Projects**	

AWARDED		**Bid but NOT AWARDED**
$0.00	AMERICAN ASPHALT OF WI	$3,421,118.70
$3,998,162.45	Edgerton Contractors, Inc.	$0.00
$2,866,393.51	INTEG GRADING and EXC INC.-	$4,162,602.33
$453,743.48	JAMES PETERSON SONS, INC.	$63,805,810.12
$17,376,202.35	LUNDA CONSTRUCTION-	$69,022,447.76
$41,111,995.06	MICHELS CORPORATION-	$34,745,534.96
$9,283,447.92	MUSSON BROS., INC.-	$14,957,289.02
$0.00	PARISI Construction CO Inc-	$11,103,625.03
$1,413,201.90	PAYNE AND DOLAN, INC-	$11,027,999.98
$3,630,964.18	Rock Road Companies	$10,152,134.28
$2,337,607.64	ZENITH TECH., INC. -	$41,208,692.54
$16,215,212.81	ZIGNEGO COMPANY, INC.	$54,495,110.08

Awarded	**Percentage of projects awarded**	**Bid On but not awarded**
$98,686,931.30	31%	$318,102,364.80

Total **$158,094,067.15** attempting to bid on projects by the Construction Companies directly associated with the WTBA. On just **March 13, 2018**, the WTBA Board of Directors received the amount of **$65,896,279.78** Awarded Projects by WisDOT.

WisDOT APPARENT BID RESULTS FOR THE LETTING OF
April 10, 2018

April 10, 2018		
Bid Amount	**Contractor**	**Address City and State**
$547,415.67	**MICHELS CORPORATION**	Waukesha, WI-
$640,411.83	**LUNDA CONSTRUCTION**	Black River Falls, WI 54615
$6,615,632.92	**ZENITH TECH., INC.-**	Waukesha, WI 53187-
$423,222.76	**ZIGNEGO COMPANY, INC.**	Waukesha, WI 53186
$1,808,139.68	**LUNDA CONSTRUCTION**	Black River Falls, WI 54615
$1,621,868.78	**PAYNE AND DOLAN, INC-**	Waukesha, WI 53187-0781
$1,832,014.75	**MEGA RENTALS, INC.-**	Madison, WI-
$2,688,005.50	**MUSSON BROS., INC.**	Rhinelander, WI 54501-
$54,519,107.68	**April Total projects let for 2018**	
$16,176,711.89	**Board of Directors of WTBA Companies awarded Projects**	

AWARDED		**Bid but NOT AWARDED**
$0.00	AMERICAN ASPHALT OF WI	$3,421,118.70
$3,998,162.45	Edgerton Contractors, Inc.	$0.00
$2,866,393.51	INTEG GRADING and EXC INC.-	$8,632,799.04
$453,743.48	JAMES PETERSON SONS, INC.	$74,304,960.51
$19,824,753.86	LUNDA CONSTRUCTION-	$79,739,518.19
$1,832,014.75	MEGA RENTALS, INC.-	$432,184.20
$41,111,995.06	MICHELS CORPORATION-	$35,094,343.83
$11,971,453.42	MUSSON BROS., INC.-	$17,935,629.50
$0.00	PARISI Construction CO Inc-	$11,103,625.03
$1,413,201.90	PAYNE AND DOLAN, INC-	$11,027,999.98
$3,630,964.18	Rock Road Companies	$10,152,134.28
$8,953,240.56	ZENITH TECH., INC. -	$48,656,815.35
$16,638,435.57	ZIGNEGO COMPANY, INC.	$55,943,631.98
Awarded	**Percentage of projects awarded**	**Bid On but not awarded**
$112,694,358.74	32%	**$356,444,760.59**

Total **$54,519,107.68** attempting to bid on projects by
the Construction Companies directly associated with the
WTBA. On just **April 10, 2018**, the WTBA Board of Directors
received the amount of **$16,176,711.89** Awarded Projects by
WisDOT.

WisDOT APPARENT BID RESULTS FOR THE LETTING OF
May 08, 2018

	May 08, 2018	
Bid Amount	**Contractor**	**Address City and State**
$2,293,615.25	ZIGNEGO COMPANY, INC.	Waukesha, WI 53186
$11,077,680.83	PAYNE AND DOLAN, INC	Medford, WI 54451-0120-
$1,916,389.28	LUNDA CONSTRUCTION	Black River Falls, WI 54615
$2,896,370.44	JAMES PETERSON SONS, INC.	Medford, WI 54451-0120-
$6,335,704.25	MICHELS CORPORATION	Waukesha, WI
$3,522,990.04	ASPHALT OF WI	Mosinee, WI 54455-
$3,219,183.82	ASPHALT OF WI	Mosinee, WI 54455-
$1,084,540.94	ASPHALT OF WI	Mosinee, WI 54455-
$4,030,754.85	ASPHALT OF WI	Mosinee, WI 54455-
$15,265,934.53	JAMES PETERSON SONS, INC.	Medford, WI 54451-0120
$3,348,345.42	ASPHALT OF WI	Mosinee, WI 54455-
$139,463,984.76	**May Total projects let for 2018**	
$54,991,509.65	**Board of Directors of WTBA Companies awarded Projects**	

WARDED		Bid but NOT AWARDED
$15,205,815.07	AMERICAN ASPHALT OF WI	$6,769,464.12
$3,998,162.45	Edgerton Contractors, Inc.	$16,587,334.00
$2,866,393.51	INTEG GRADING and EXC INC.-	$24,170,821.44
$18,616,048.45	JAMES PETERSON SONS, INC.	$91,015,689.37
$21,741,143.14	LUNDA CONSTRUCTION-	$79,739,518.19
$1,832,014.75	MEGA RENTALS, INC.-	$432,184.20
$47,447,699.31	MICHELS CORPORATION-	$35,094,343.83
$11,971,453.42	MUSSON BROS., INC.-	$36,260,262.85
$0.00	PARISI Construction CO Inc-	$11,103,625.03
$12,490,882.73	PAYNE AND DOLAN, INC-	$11,027,999.98
$3,630,964.18	Rock Road Companies	$10,152,134.28
$8,953,240.56	ZENITH TECH., INC. -	$56,887,261.49
$18,932,050.82	ZIGNEGO COMPANY, INC.	$64,369,154.08

Awarded	Percentage of projects awarded	Bid On but not awarded
$167,685,868.39	38%	$443,609,792.86

Total **$139,463,984.76** attempting to bid on projects by the Construction Companies directly associated with the WTBA. On just **May 10, 2018**, the WTBA Board of Directors received the amount of **$54,991,509.65** Awarded Projects by WisDOT.

WisDOT APPARENT BID RESULTS FOR THE LETTING OF
May 22, 2018

May 22, 2018		
Bid Amount	**Contractor**	**Address City and State**
$168,872,899.28	**MICHELS CORPORATION**	Waukesha, WI
$80,026,047.53	**MICHELS CORPORATION**	Waukesha, WI
$331,597,600.84	**May Total projects let for 2018**	
$248,898,946.81	**Board of Directors of WTBA Companies awarded Projects**	
AWARDED		**Bid but NOT AWARDED**
$15,205,815.07	AMERICAN ASPHALT OF WI	$6,769,464.12
$3,998,162.45	Edgerton Contractors, Inc.	$16,587,334.00
$2,866,393.51	INTEG GRADING and EXC INC.-	$24,170,821.44
$18,616,048.45	JAMES PETERSON SONS, INC.	$91,015,689.37
$21,741,143.14	LUNDA CONSTRUCTION-	$79,739,518.19
$1,832,014.75	MEGA RENTALS, INC.-	$1,280,716.16
$296,346,646.12	MICHELS CORPORATION-	$35,094,343.83
$11,971,453.42	MUSSON BROS., INC.-	$36,260,262.85
$0.00	PARISI Construction CO Inc-	$11,103,625.03
$12,490,882.73	PAYNE AND DOLAN, INC-	$11,027,999.98
$3,630,964.18	Rock Road Companies	$10,152,134.28
$8,953,240.56	ZENITH TECH., INC. -	$56,887,261.49
$18,932,050.82	ZIGNEGO COMPANY, INC.	$146,219,276.15
Awarded	**Percentage of projects awarded**	**Bid On but not awarded**
$416,584,815.20	**79%**	**$526,308,446.89**

Total **$331,597,600.84** attempting to bid on projects by
the Construction Companies directly associated with the
WTBA. On just **May 22, 2018**, the WTBA Board of Directors
received the amount of **$248,898,946.81** Awarded Projects
by WisDOT.

WisDOT APPARENT BID RESULTS FOR THE LETTING OF
June 12, 2018

June 12, 2018		
Bid Amount	**Contractor**	**Address City and State**
$33,685,010.40	ROCK ROAD COMPANIES, INC	Janesville, WI
$16,302,799.12	JAMES PETERSON SONS, INC.-	Medford, WI 54451-0120-
$8,964,539.53	ZIGNEGO COMPANY, INC.	Waukesha, WI 53186
$6,739,172.67	ZIGNEGO COMPANY, INC.	Waukesha, WI 53186
$2,954,292.27	ASPHALT OF WI-	Mosinee, WI 54455-
$1,009,795.72	LUNDA CONSTRUCTION	Black River Falls, WI 54615
$162,985,514.43	June Total projects let for 2018	
$69,655,609.71	Board of Directors of WTBA Companies awarded Projects	

AWARDED		Bid but NOT AWARDED
$18,160,107.34	AMERICAN ASPHALT OF WI	$6,769,464.12
$3,998,162.45	Edgerton Contractors, Inc.	$16,587,334.00
$2,866,393.51	INTEG GRADING and EXC INC.-	$24,170,821.44
$34,918,847.57	JAMES PETERSON SONS, INC.	$137,530,161.10
$21,741,143.14	LUNDA CONSTRUCTION-	$79,739,518.19
$1,832,014.75	MEGA RENTALS, INC.-	$1,280,716.16
$296,346,646.12	MICHELS CORPORATION-	$35,094,343.83
$11,971,453.42	MUSSON BROS., INC.-	$36,260,262.85
$0.00	PARISI Construction CO Inc-	$11,103,625.03
$12,490,882.73	PAYNE AND DOLAN, INC-	$11,027,999.98
$37,315,974.58	Rock Road Companies	$10,152,134.28
$8,953,240.56	ZENITH TECH., INC. -	$60,716,871.52
$34,635,763.02	ZIGNEGO COMPANY, INC.	$146,219,276.15

Awarded	Percentage of projects awarded	Bid On but not awarded
$485,230,629.19	84%	$576,652,528.65

Total **$162,985,514.43** attempting to bid on projects by the Construction Companies directly associated with the WTBA. On just **June 12, 2018,** the WTBA Board of Directors received the amount of **$69,655,609.71** Awarded Projects by WisDOT.

WisDOT APPARENT BID RESULTS FOR THE LETTING OF
July 10, 2018

Bid Amount	Contractor	Address City and State
July 10, 2018		
$16,814,507.71	ZIGNEGO COMPANY, INC.	Waukesha, WI 53186
$2,034,128.57	INTEG GRADING and EXC INC.-	Schofield, WI 54476-0138-
$2,887,993.23	PAYNE AND DOLAN, INC-	
$4,118,523.82	PAYNE AND DOLAN, INC-	Waukesha, WI 53187-0781
$44,184,486.26	ZIGNEGO COMPANY, INC.	Waukesha, WI 53186
$144,424,427.86	July Total projects let for 2018	
$70,039,639.59	Board of Directors of WTBA Companies awarded Projects	

AWARDED		Bid but NOT AWARDED
$18,160,107.34	AMERICAN ASPHALT OF WI	$6,769,464.12
$3,998,162.45	Edgerton Contractors, Inc.	$16,587,334.00
$4,900,522.08	INTEG GRADING and EXC INC.-	$50,717,302.42
$34,918,847.57	JAMES PETERSON SONS, INC.	$156,737,641.97
$21,741,143.14	LUNDA CONSTRUCTION-	$79,739,518.19
$1,832,014.75	MEGA RENTALS, INC.-	$1,280,716.16
$296,346,646.12	MICHELS CORPORATION-	$35,094,343.83
$11,971,453.42	MUSSON BROS., INC.-	$36,260,262.85
$0.00	PARISI Construction CO Inc-	$11,103,625.03
$19,497,399.78	PAYNE AND DOLAN, INC-	$13,228,453.13
$37,315,974.58	Rock Road Companies	$10,152,134.28
$8,953,240.56	ZENITH TECH., INC. -	$61,099,347.37
$95,634,756.99	ZIGNEGO COMPANY, INC.	$154,593,696.73

Awarded	Percentage of projects awarded	Bid On but not awarded
$555,270,268.78	88%	$633,363,840.08

Total **$144,424,427.86** attempting to bid on projects by the Construction Companies directly associated with the WTBA. On just **July 10, 2018**, the WTBA Board of Directors received the amount of **$70,039,639.59** Awarded Projects by WisDOT.

WisDOT APPARENT BID RESULTS FOR THE LETTING OF
July 24, 2018

July 24, 2018		
$209,960,876.71	**July Total projects let for 2018**	
$0.00	**Board of Directors of WTBA Companies awarded Projects**	
AWARDED		**Bid but NOT AWARDED**
$18,160,107.34	AMERICAN ASPHALT OF WI	$6,769,464.12
$3,998,162.45	Edgerton Contractors, Inc.	$16,587,334.00
$4,900,522.08	INTEG GRADING and EXC INC.-	$50,717,302.42
$34,918,847.57	JAMES PETERSON SONS, INC.	$156,737,641.97
$21,741,143.14	LUNDA CONSTRUCTION-	$79,739,518.19
$1,832,014.75	MEGA RENTALS, INC.-	$1,280,716.16
$296,346,646.12	MICHELS CORPORATION-	$245,055,220.54
$11,971,453.42	MUSSON BROS., INC.-	$36,260,262.85
$0.00	PARISI Construction CO Inc-	$11,103,625.03
$19,497,399.78	PAYNE AND DOLAN, INC-	$13,228,453.13
$37,315,974.58	Rock Road Companies	$10,152,134.28
$8,953,240.56	ZENITH TECH., INC. -	$61,099,347.37
$95,634,756.99	ZIGNEGO COMPANY, INC.	$154,593,696.73
Awarded	**Percentage of projects awarded**	**Bid On but not awarded**
$555,270,268.78	66%	**$843,324,716.79**

Total **$209,960,876.71** attempting to bid on projects by the Construction Companies directly associated with the WTBA. On just **July 24, 2018**, the WTBA Board of Directors received the amount of **$0.00** Awarded Projects by WisDOT.

WisDOT APPARENT BID RESULTS FOR THE LETTING OF
August 14, 2018

August 14, 2018		
Bid Amount	**Contractor**	**Address City and State**
$12,863,221.33	**ZIGNEGO COMPANY, INC.**	Waukesha, WI 53186
$4,740,427.18	**ZENITH TECH., INC.-**	
$55,507,474.24	**August Total projects let for 2018**	
$17,603,648.51	**Board of Directors of WTBA Companies awarded Projects**	
AWARDED		**Bid but NOT AWARDED**
$18,160,107.34	AMERICAN ASPHALT OF WI	$6,769,464.12
$3,998,162.45	Edgerton Contractors, Inc.	$16,587,334.00
$4,900,522.08	INTEG GRADING and EXC INC.-	$64,389,062.89
$34,918,847.57	JAMES PETERSON SONS, INC.	$170,044,383.21
$21,741,143.14	LUNDA CONSTRUCTION-	$84,770,928.50
$1,832,014.75	MEGA RENTALS, INC.-	$1,280,716.16
$296,346,646.12	MICHELS CORPORATION-	$245,055,220.54
$11,971,453.42	MUSSON BROS., INC.-	$36,260,262.85
$0.00	PARISI Construction CO Inc-	$11,103,625.03
$19,497,399.78	PAYNE AND DOLAN, INC-	$15,065,579.22
$37,315,974.58	Rock Road Companies	$10,152,134.28
$13,693,667.74	ZENITH TECH., INC. -	$65,156,134.99
$108,497,978.32	ZIGNEGO COMPANY, INC.	$154,593,696.73
Awarded	**Percentage of projects awarded**	**Bid On but not awarded**
$572,873,917.29	65%	**$881,228,542.52**

Total **$55,507,474.24** attempting to bid on projects by the Construction Companies directly associated with the WTBA. On just **August 14, 2018**, the WTBA Board of Directors received the amount of **$17,603,648.51** Awarded Projects by WisDOT

WisDOT APPARENT BID RESULTS FOR THE LETTING OF
September 11, 2018

September 11, 2018		
Bid Amount	**Contractor**	**Address City and State**
$1,653,503.66	**ZENITH TECH., INC.**	Waukesha, WI 53187
$17,243,719.84	**ZIGNEGO COMPANY, INC.**	Waukesha, WI 53186
$1,567,196.56	**ZENITH TECH., INC.**	Waukesha, WI 53187
$8,406,765.29	**ZIGNEGO COMPANY, INC.**	Waukesha, WI 53186
$3,684,300.68	**ROCK ROAD COMPANIES, INC**	Janesville, WI
$57,441,258.17	**September Total projects let for 2018**	
$32,555,486.03	**Board of Directors of WTBA Companies awarded Projects**	

AWARDED		Bid but NOT AWARDED
$18,160,107.34	AMERICAN ASPHALT OF WI	$6,769,464.12
$3,998,162.45	Edgerton Contractors, Inc.	$16,587,334.00
$4,900,522.08	INTEG GRADING and EXC INC.-	$64,389,062.89
$34,918,847.57	JAMES PETERSON SONS, INC.	$170,044,383.21
$21,741,143.14	LUNDA CONSTRUCTION-	$88,752,006.54
$1,832,014.75	MEGA RENTALS, INC.-	$1,280,716.16
$296,346,646.12	MICHELS CORPORATION-	$245,055,220.54
$11,971,453.42	MUSSON BROS., INC.-	$36,260,262.85
$0.00	PARISI Construction CO Inc-	$11,103,625.03
$19,497,399.78	PAYNE AND DOLAN, INC-	$18,965,079.17
$41,000,275.26	Rock Road Companies	$10,152,134.28
$16,914,367.96	ZENITH TECH., INC. -	$82,161,329.14
$134,148,463.45	ZIGNEGO COMPANY, INC.	$154,593,696.73

Awarded	Percentage of projects awarded	Bid On but not awarded
$605,429,403.32	67%	$906,114,314.66

Total **$57,441,258.17** attempting to bid on 2018 projects by the Construction Companies directly associated with the WTBA. On just **September 11, 2018**, the WTBA Board of Directors received the amount of **$32,555,486.03** Awarded Projects by WisDOT

WisDOT APPARENT BID RESULTS FOR THE LETTING OF
November 13, 2018

November 13 2018		
Bid Amount	**Contractor**	**Address City and State**
$873,139.47	**JAMES PETERSON SONS, INC.**	Medford, WI 54451-0120
$16,230,006.16	**MICHELS CORPORATION**	Waukesha, WI
$33,477,552.68	**INTEG GRADING and EXC INC.**	Schofield, WI 54476-0138
$972,003.80	**LUNDA CONSTRUCTION**	Black River Falls, WI 54615
$1,969,648.57	**JAMES PETERSON SONS, INC.**	Medford, WI 54451-0120
$14,918,859.31	**MICHELS CORPORATION**	Waukesha, WI
$4,508,842.51	**LUNDA CONSTRUCTION**	Black River Falls, WI 54615
$17,057,384.08	**JAMES PETERSON SONS, INC.**	Medford, WI 54451-0120
$251,812,476.69	**November Total projects let for 2018**	
$90,007,436.58	**Board of Directors of WTBA Companies awarded Projects**	

AWARDED		Bid but NOT AWARDED
$18,160,107.34	AMERICAN ASPHALT OF WI	$6,769,464.12
$3,998,162.45	Edgerton Contractors, Inc.	$16,587,334.00
$38,378,074.76	INTEG GRADING and EXC INC.-	$82,029,492.71
$54,819,019.69	JAMES PETERSON SONS, INC.	$237,737,222.96
$27,221,989.45	LUNDA CONSTRUCTION-	$93,651,253.12
$1,832,014.75	MEGA RENTALS, INC.-	$5,977,254.66
$327,495,511.59	MICHELS CORPORATION-	$251,273,155.15
$11,971,453.42	MUSSON BROS., INC.-	$40,956,801.35
$0.00	PARISI Construction CO Inc-	$11,103,625.03
$19,497,399.78	PAYNE AND DOLAN, INC-	$18,965,079.17
$41,000,275.26	Rock Road Companies	$27,670,666.02
$16,914,367.96	ZENITH TECH., INC. -	$92,696,342.02
$134,148,463.45	ZIGNEGO COMPANY, INC.	$187,198,202.96
Awarded	**Percentage of projects awarded**	**Bid On but not awarded**
$695,436,839.90	**65%**	**$1,072,615,893.27**

Total **$251,812,476.69** attempting to bid on projects by the
Construction Companies directly associated with the WTBA.
On just **November 13, 2018**, the WTBA Board of Directors
received the amount of **$90,007,436.58** Awarded Projects by
WisDOT.

WisDOT APPARENT BID RESULTS FOR THE LETTING OF
December 11, 2018

December 11 2018		
Bid Amount	**Contractor**	**Address City and State**
$6,042,795.35	**PAYNE AND DOLAN, INC-**	Waukesha, WI 53187-0781-
$5,328,097.76	**ZIGNEGO COMPANY, INC.**	Waukesha, WI 53186
$1,791,592.49	**ZENITH TECH., INC.-**	Waukesha, WI 53187-
$103,228,531.74	**December Total projects let for 2018**	
$13,162,485.60	**Board of Directors of WTBA Companies awarded Projects**	
AWARDED		**Bid but NOT AWARDED**
$18,160,107.34	AMERICAN ASPHALT OF WI	$6,769,464.12
$3,998,162.45	Edgerton Contractors, Inc.	$16,587,334.00
$38,378,074.76	INTEG GRADING and EXC INC.-	$86,411,911.78
$54,819,019.69	JAMES PETERSON SONS, INC.	$306,870,469.26
$27,221,989.45	LUNDA CONSTRUCTION-	$96,007,603.89
$1,832,014.75	MEGA RENTALS, INC.-	$5,977,254.66
$327,495,511.59	MICHELS CORPORATION-	$251,273,155.15
$11,971,453.42	MUSSON BROS., INC.-	$47,736,100.99
$0.00	PARISI Construction CO Inc-	$12,354,656.65
$25,540,195.13	PAYNE AND DOLAN, INC-	$18,965,079.17
$41,000,275.26	Rock Road Companies	$27,670,666.02
$18,705,960.45	ZENITH TECH., INC. -	$94,176,049.84
$139,476,561.21	ZIGNEGO COMPANY, INC.	$188,746,895.62
Awarded	**Percentage of projects awarded**	**Bid On but not awarded**
$708,599,325.50	61%	**$1,159,546,641.15**

Total **$1,159,546,641.15** attempting to bid on projects by the Construction Companies directly associated with the WTBA. On just **December 11, 2018**, the WTBA Board of Directors received the amount of **$708,599,325.50** Awarded Projects by WisDOT to the Wisconsin Transportation Builders Association (WTBA averaged 61% for December 2018.

Chapter 18 Influences of the WTBA surrounding the TERO/IP or the NAHP (January to December 2017)

WisDOT APPARENT BID RESULTS FOR THE LETTING OF
January 10, 2017

January 10, 2017		
Bid Amount	**Contractor**	**Address City and State**
$1,394,291.19	**ROCK ROAD COMPANIES, INC.**	Janesville, WI
$1,087,028.70	**ROCK ROAD COMPANIES, INC.**	Janesville, WI
$561,529.18	**JAMES PETERSON SONS, INC.**	Medford, WI 54451-0120
$1,272,007.31	**LUNDA CONSTRUCTION**	Black River Falls, WI 54615-
$77,587,099.18	**January Total projects let for 2017**	
$4,314,856.38	**Board of Directors of WTBA for 2017**	
AWARDED		**Bid but NOT AWARDED**
$0.00	INTEG GRADING and EXC INC.-	$11,986,090.71
$561,529.18	JAMES PETERSON SONS, INC.	$24,909,687.90
$1,272,007.31	LUNDA CONSTRUCTION-	$2,816,920.82
$0.00	MICHELS CORPORATION-	$15,032,513.81
$0.00	MUSSON BROS., INC.-	$12,535,470.74
$0.00	PAYNE AND DOLAN, INC-	$1,489,198.18
$2,481,319.89	Rock Road Companies	$0.00
$0.00	TRIERWEILER CONST and SUPPLY COMP	$5,617,174.20
$0.00	ZENITH TECH., INC. -	$9,782,969.90
Awarded	**Percentage of projects awarded**	**Bid On but not awarded**
$4,314,856.38	**5%**	**$84,170,026.26**

Total $77,587,099.18 attempting to bid on projects by the
Construction Companies directly associated with the WTBA.
On just **January 10, 2017**, the WTBA Board of Directors
received the amount of **$4,314,856.38** Awarded Projects by
WisDOT.

WisDOT APPARENT BID RESULTS FOR THE LETTING OF
February 14, 2017

February 14, 2017		
Bid Amount	**Contractor**	**Address City and State**
$800,772.99	**MICHELS CORPORATION**	Waukesha, WI
$743,716.65	**ZENITH TECH., INC.**	Waukesha, WI 53187
22,149,075.18	**February Total projects let for 2017**	
1,544,489.64	**Board of Directors of WTBA for 2017**	
AWARDED		**Bid but NOT AWARDED**
$0.00	INTEG GRADING and EXC INC.-	$11,986,090.71
$561,529.18	JAMES PETERSON SONS, INC.	$24,909,687.90
$1,272,007.31	LUNDA CONSTRUCTION-	$14,678,138.76
$0.00	MEGA RENTALS, INC.-	$499,702.86
$800,772.99	MICHELS CORPORATION-	$15,032,513.81
$0.00	MUSSON BROS., INC.-	$12,535,470.74
$0.00	PARISI Construction CO Inc-	$393,092.47
$0.00	PAYNE AND DOLAN, INC-	$1,489,198.18
$2,481,319.89	Rock Road Companies	$0.00
$0.00	TRIERWEILER CONST and SUPPLY COMP	$5,617,174.20
$743,716.65	ZENITH TECH., INC. -	$17,633,542.17
Awarded	**Percentage awarded to WTBA**	**Bid On but not awarded**
$5,859,346.02	6%	**$104,774,611.80**

Total $22,149,075.18 attempting to bid on projects by the Construction Companies directly associated with the WTBA. On just **February 14, 2017**, the WTBA Board of Directors received the amount of **$1,544,489.64** Awarded Projects by WisDOT.

WisDOT APPARENT BID RESULTS FOR THE LETTING OF
March 14, 2017

March 14, 2017		
Bid Amount	**Contractor**	**Address City and State**
$2,223,626.99	**ROCK ROAD COMPANIES, INC**	Janesville, WI
$797,547.87	**ZENITH TECH., INC.**	Waukesha, WI 53187
$2,701,542.23	**MICHELS CORPORATION**	Waukesha, WI
$8,057,969.18	**LUNDA CONSTRUCTION**	Black River Falls, WI 54615
$4,651,821.75	**MICHELS CORPORATION**	Waukesha, WI
$5,079,408.04	**MUSSON BROS., INC.**	Rhinelander, WI 54501-
$1,868,434.40	**JAMES PETERSON SONS, INC.**	Medford, WI 54451-0120
$247,955,431.61	**March Total projects let for 2017**	
$25,380,350.46	**Board of Directors of WTBA for 2017**	
AWARDED		**Bid but NOT AWARDED**
$0.00	Edgerton Contractors, Inc.	$11,177,696.45
$0.00	INTEG GRADING and EXC INC.-	$11,986,090.71
$2,429,963.58	JAMES PETERSON SONS, INC.	$84,334,332.33
$1,272,007.31	LUNDA CONSTRUCTION-	$18,949,064.75
$0.00	MEGA RENTALS, INC.-	$499,702.86
$8,154,136.97	MICHELS CORPORATION-	$60,254,193.29
$0.00	MUSSON BROS., INC.-	$52,257,002.36
$0.00	PARISI Construction CO Inc-	$393,092.47
$0.00	PAYNE AND DOLAN, INC-	$5,520,855.96
$4,704,946.88	Rock Road Companies	$25,543,653.17
$0.00	TRIERWEILER CONST and SUPPLY COMP	$9,628,121.56
$1,541,264.52	ZENITH TECH., INC. -	$30,857,471.45
$0.00	ZIGNEGO COMPANY, INC.	$15,948,415.59
Awarded	**Percentage awarded to WTBA**	**Bid On but not awarded**
$18,102,319.26	**6%**	**$327,349,692.95**

Total **$247,955,431.61** attempting to bid on projects by the
Construction Companies directly associated with the WTBA.
On just **March 14, 2017**, the WTBA Board of Directors
received the amount of **$25,380,350.46** Awarded Projects by
WisDOT.

WisDOT APPARENT BID RESULTS FOR THE LETTING OF
April 11, 2017

April 11, 2017		
Bid Amount	**Contractor**	**Address City and State**
$2,297,946.47	ZENITH TECH., INC.	Waukesha, WI 53187
$1,197,577.17	PAYNE AND DOLAN, INC	Waukesha, WI 53187-0781-
$387,243.10	ZENITH TECH., INC.	Waukesha, WI 53187
$885,618.24	MICHELS CORPORATION	Waukesha, WI
$5,203,597.23	ZIGNEGO COMPANY, INC.	Waukesha, WI 53186-
$6,128,869.94	PAYNE AND DOLAN, INC	Waukesha, WI 53187-0781-
$9,559,766.72	PAYNE AND DOLAN, INC	Waukesha, WI 53187-0781-
$1,948,016.12	LUNDA CONSTRUCTION	Black River Falls, WI 54615
$1,394,893.80	LUNDA CONSTRUCTION	Black River Falls, WI 54615
$992,007.90	ZENITH TECH., INC.	Waukesha, WI 53187
$2,338,762.88	AMERICAN ASPHALT OF WISCONSIN	Mosinee, WI 54455-
$671,240.36	ZENITH TECH., INC.	Waukesha, WI 53187
$911,247.83	LUNDA CONSTRUCTION	Black River Falls, WI 54615
$2,028,028.28	JAMES PETERSON SONS, INC.	Medford, WI 54451-0120
$8,966,365.53	ZIGNEGO COMPANY, INC.	
$171,101,027.90	April Total projects let for 2017	
$44,911,181.57	Board of Directors of WTBA for 2017	

AWARDED		Bid but NOT AWARDED
$0.00	Edgerton Contractors, Inc.	$11,177,696.45
$0.00	INTEG GRADING and EXC INC.-	$14,423,187.49
$4,457,991.86	JAMES PETERSON SONS, INC.	$84,334,332.33
$5,526,165.06	LUNDA CONSTRUCTION-	$28,826,382.22
$0.00	MEGA RENTALS, INC.-	$3,185,731.98
$9,039,755.21	MICHELS CORPORATION-	$79,917,169.86
$0.00	MUSSON BROS., INC.-	$78,641,589.41
$330,315.85	PARISI Construction CO Inc-	$1,882,012.32
$16,886,213.83	PAYNE AND DOLAN, INC-	$7,127,732.19
$4,704,946.88	Rock Road Companies	$25,543,653.17
$0.00	TRIERWEILER CONST and SUPPLY COMP	$18,774,527.35
$5,889,702.35	ZENITH TECH., INC. -	$42,532,826.33
$14,169,962.76	ZIGNEGO COMPANY, INC.	$15,948,415.59
Awarded	**Percentage awarded to WTBA**	**Bid On but not awarded**
$63,343,816.68	15%	$412,315,256.69

Total $171,101,027.90 attempting to bid on projects by the Construction Companies directly associated with the WTBA. On just **April 11, 2017**, the WTBA Board of Directors received the amount of **$44,911,181.57** Awarded Projects by WisDOT.

WisDOT APPARENT BID RESULTS FOR THE LETTING OF
May 09, 2017

Bid Amount	Contractor	Address City and State
	May 09, 2017	
$12,651,921.99	ROCK ROAD COMPANIES, INC	Janesville, WI
$996,572.96	ROCK ROAD COMPANIES, INC	Janesville, WI
$2,900,000.00	ZIGNEGO COMPANY, INC.	Waukesha, WI 53186-
$3,403,713.24	ZENITH TECH., INC.	Waukesha, WI 53187
$12,280,740.05	ZIGNEGO COMPANY, INC.	Waukesha, WI 53186-
$4,027,202.00	LUNDA CONSTRUCTION	Black River Falls, WI 54615
$1,393,032.71	ROCK ROAD COMPANIES, INC	Janesville, WI
$3,747,126.28	MICHELS CORPORATION	Waukesha, WI
$372,981.77	MICHELS CORPORATION	Waukesha, WI
$3,498,557.24	MICHELS CORPORATION	Waukesha, WI
$626,370.14	MEGA RENTALS, INC.	Madison, WI 53708 -
$5,187,383.01	JAMES PETERSON SONS, INC.	Medford, WI 54451-0120
$1,131,425.01	AMERICAN ASPHALT OF WISCONSIN	Mosinee, WI 54455-
$1,124,755.18	AMERICAN ASPHALT OF WISCONSIN	Mosinee, WI 54455-
$1,632,718.63	AMERICAN ASPHALT OF WISCONSIN	Mosinee, WI 54455-
$2,343,987.91	PAYNE AND DOLAN, INC	Waukesha, WI 53187-0781-
$646,334.96	LUNDA CONSTRUCTION	Black River Falls, WI 54615
$1,075,926.05	LUNDA CONSTRUCTION	Black River Falls, WI 54615
$143,352,550.27	May Total projects let for 2017	
$59,040,749.13	Board of Directors of WTBA for 2017	
$6,227,661.70	AMERICAN ASPHALT OF WI	$2,829,751.33
$0.00	Edgerton Contractors, Inc.	$27,418,131.52
$0.00	INTEG GRADING and EXC INC.-	$19,720,275.06
$9,645,374.87	JAMES PETERSON SONS, INC.	$88,658,499.70
$11,275,628.07	LUNDA CONSTRUCTION-	$29,869,060.45
$626,370.14	MEGA RENTALS, INC.-	$3,185,731.98
$16,658,420.50	MICHELS CORPORATION-	$90,983,553.17
$0.00	MUSSON BROS., INC.-	$85,502,850.67
$330,315.85	PARISI Construction CO Inc-	$1,882,012.32
$16,886,213.83	PAYNE AND DOLAN, INC-	$29,136,178.83
$4,704,946.88	Rock Road Companies	$25,543,653.17
$0.00	TRIERWEILER CONST and SUPPLY COMP	$23,233,931.22
$5,889,702.35	ZENITH TECH., INC. -	$42,532,826.33
$14,169,962.76	ZIGNEGO COMPANY, INC.	$20,171,415.59
Awarded	**Percentage awarded to WTBA**	**Bid On but not awarded**
$86,414,596.95	18%	$490,667,871.34

Total **$143,352,550.27** attempting to bid on projects by the Construction Companies directly associated with the WTBA. On just **May 09, 2017**, the WTBA Board of Directors received the amount of **$59,040,749.13** Awarded Projects by WisDOT.

WisDOT APPARENT BID RESULTS FOR THE LETTING OF
June 13, 2017

June 13, 2017		
Bid Amount	**Contractor**	**Address City and State**
$780,731.48	LUNDA CONSTRUCTION	Black River Falls, WI 54615
$1,882,239.14	ZENITH TECH., INC.	Waukesha, WI 53187
$15,211,339.33	ZENITH TECH., INC.	Waukesha, WI 53187
$3,233,961.50	AMERICAN ASPHALT OF WISCONSIN	Mosinee, WI 54455
$414,123.63	LUNDA CONSTRUCTION	Black River Falls, WI 54615
$422,731.44	LUNDA CONSTRUCTION	Black River Falls, WI 54615
$4,165,758.37	ZENITH TECH., INC.	Waukesha, WI 53187
$1,543,852.84	PAYNE AND DOLAN, INC	Waukesha, WI 53187-0781-
$14,171,144.57	MICHELS CORPORATION	Waukesha, WI
$1,626,279.06	AMERICAN ASPHALT OF WISCONSIN	Mosinee, WI 54455-
$487,528.88	LUNDA CONSTRUCTION	Black River Falls, WI 54615
$1,491,168.85	ZENITH TECH., INC.	Waukesha, WI 53187
$880,441.84	LUNDA CONSTRUCTION	Black River Falls, WI 54615
$210,181,089.59	**June Total projects let for 2017**	
$46,311,300.93	**Board of Directors of WTBA for 2017**	
$11,087,902.26	AMERICAN ASPHALT OF WI	$7,689,991.89
$0.00	Edgerton Contractors, Inc.	$38,862,562.17
$0.00	INTEG GRADING and EXC INC.-	$61,745,934.81
$9,645,374.87	JAMES PETERSON SONS, INC.	$96,232,038.26
$14,261,185.34	LUNDA CONSTRUCTION-	$29,869,060.45
$626,370.14	MEGA RENTALS, INC.-	$3,185,731.98
$16,658,420.50	MICHELS CORPORATION-	$126,437,485.63
$0.00	MUSSON BROS., INC.-	$92,463,667.78
$330,315.85	PARISI Construction CO Inc-	$1,882,012.32
$18,430,066.67	PAYNE AND DOLAN, INC-	$31,824,255.79
$4,704,946.88	Rock Road Companies	$27,798,052.89
$0.00	TRIERWEILER CONST and SUPPLY COMP	$23,233,931.22
$28,640,208.04	ZENITH TECH., INC. -	$78,381,811.74
$14,169,962.76	ZIGNEGO COMPANY, INC.	$27,788,306.75
Awarded	**Percentage of projects awarded**	**Bid On but not awarded**
$118,554,753.31	18%	$647,394,843.68

Total **$210,181,089.59** attempting to bid on projects by the Construction Companies directly associated with the WTBA. On just **June 13, 2017**, the WTBA Board of Directors received the amount of **$46,311,300.93** Awarded Projects by WisDOT.

WisDOT APPARENT BID RESULTS FOR THE LETTING OF
July 11, 2017

	July 11, 2017	
Bid Amount	**Contractor**	**Address City and State**
$54,483,394.79	**ROCK ROAD COMPANIES, INC**	Janesville, WI
$29,601,639.85	**INTEG GRADING and EXC INC.-**	Schofield, WI 54476-0138-
$1,083,669.51	**ZENITH TECH., INC.**	Waukesha, WI 53187
$739,809.76	**JAMES PETERSON SONS, INC.**	Medford, WI 54451-0120
$558,646.16	**INTEG GRADING and EXC INC.**	Schofield, WI 54476-0138-
$219,733,097.70	**July Total projects let for 2017**	
$86,467,160.07	**Board of Directors of WTBA for 2017**	
$11,087,902.26	AMERICAN ASPHALT OF WI	$7,689,991.89
$0.00	Edgerton Contractors, Inc.	$38,862,562.17
$29,601,639.85	INTEG GRADING and EXC INC.-	$62,368,526.47
$10,385,184.63	JAMES PETERSON SONS, INC.	$159,123,768.38
$14,261,185.34	LUNDA CONSTRUCTION-	$33,291,425.15
$626,370.14	MEGA RENTALS, INC.-	$3,185,731.98
$16,658,420.50	MICHELS CORPORATION-	$126,437,485.63
$0.00	MUSSON BROS., INC.-	$93,850,037.40
$330,315.85	PARISI Construction CO Inc-	$1,882,012.32
$18,430,066.67	PAYNE AND DOLAN, INC-	$31,824,255.79
$59,188,341.67	Rock Road Companies	$27,798,052.89
$0.00	TRIERWEILER CONST and SUPPLY COMP	$23,233,931.22
$29,723,877.55	ZENITH TECH., INC. -	$143,324,693.27
$14,169,962.76	ZIGNEGO COMPANY, INC.	$27,788,306.75
Awarded	**Percentage of projects awarded**	**Bid On but not awarded**
$204,463,267.22	**26%**	**$780,660,781.31**

Total **$219,733,097.70** attempting to bid on projects by the Construction Companies directly associated with the WTBA. On just **July 11, 2017**, the WTBA Board of Directors received the amount of **$86,467,160.07** Awarded Projects by WisDOT.

WisDOT APPARENT BID RESULTS FOR THE LETTING OF
August 08, 2017

August 08, 2017		
Bid Amount	**Contractor**	**Address City and State**
$48,779,509.06	ROCK ROAD COMPANIES, INC	Janesville, WI
$2,521,426.72	LUNDA CONSTRUCTION	Black River Falls, WI 54615
$50,398,861.10	INTEG GRADING and EXC INC.-	Schofield, WI 54476-0138-
$11,413,727.07	LUNDA CONSTRUCTION	Black River Falls, WI 54615
$289,814,094.74	August Total projects let for 2017	
$113,113,523.95	Board of Directors of WTBA for 2017	
$11,087,902.26	AMERICAN ASPHALT OF WI	$7,689,991.89
$0.00	Edgerton Contractors, Inc.	$90,486,410.79
$80,000,500.95	INTEG GRADING and EXC INC.-	$62,368,526.47
$10,385,184.63	JAMES PETERSON SONS, INC.	$268,008,189.18
$28,196,339.13	LUNDA CONSTRUCTION-	$33,291,425.15
$626,370.14	MEGA RENTALS, INC.-	$3,185,731.98
$16,658,420.50	MICHELS CORPORATION-	$126,437,485.63
$0.00	MUSSON BROS., INC.-	$93,850,037.40
$330,315.85	PARISI Construction CO Inc-	$1,882,012.32
$18,430,066.67	PAYNE AND DOLAN, INC-	$31,824,255.79
$107,967,850.73	Rock Road Companies	$27,798,052.89
$0.00	TRIERWEILER CONST and SUPPLY COMP	$23,233,931.22
$29,723,877.55	ZENITH TECH., INC. -	$158,725,167.90
$14,169,962.76	ZIGNEGO COMPANY, INC.	$27,788,306.75
Awarded	**Percentage of projects awarded**	**Bid On but not awarded**
$317,576,791.17	33%	$956,569,525.36

Total $34,980,016.20 attempting to bid on projects by the Construction Companies directly associated with the WTBA. On just **August 08, 2017**, the WTBA Board of Directors received the amount of **$155,498,211.40** Awarded Projects by WisDOT.

WisDOT APPARENT BID RESULTS FOR THE LETTING OF September 12, 2017

Bid Amount	Contractor	Address City and State
	September 12, 2017	
$21,999,240.60	**MUSSON BROS., INC.**	Rhinelander, WI 54501-
$16,175,537.94	**ZENITH TECH., INC.**	Waukesha, WI 53187
$155,498,211.40	**September Total projects let for 2017**	
$34,980,016.20	**Board of Directors of WTBA for 2017**	
$11,087,902.26	AMERICAN ASPHALT OF WI	$7,689,991.89
$0.00	Edgerton Contractors, Inc.	$90,486,410.79
$80,000,500.95	INTEG GRADING and EXC INC.-	$62,368,526.47
$10,385,184.63	JAMES PETERSON SONS, INC.	$268,008,189.18
$28,196,339.13	LUNDA CONSTRUCTION-	$33,291,425.15
$626,370.14	MEGA RENTALS, INC.-	$3,185,731.98
$16,658,420.50	MICHELS CORPORATION-	$126,437,485.63
$21,999,240.60	MUSSON BROS., INC.-	$93,850,037.40
$330,315.85	PARISI Construction CO Inc-	$1,882,012.32
$18,430,066.67	PAYNE AND DOLAN, INC-	$31,824,255.79
$107,967,850.73	Rock Road Companies	$27,798,052.89
$0.00	TRIERWEILER CONST and SUPPLY COMP	$23,233,931.22
$45,899,415.49	ZENITH TECH., INC. -	$158,725,167.90
$14,169,962.76	ZIGNEGO COMPANY, INC.	$27,788,306.75
Awarded	Percentage of projects awarded	Bid On but not awarded
$355,751,569.71	37%	**$956,569,525.36**

Total **$155,498,211.40** attempting to bid on 2017 projects by the Construction Companies directly associated with the WTBA. On just **September 12, 2017**, the WTBA Board of Directors received the amount of **$34,980,016.20** Awarded Projects by WisDOT.

WisDOT APPARENT BID RESULTS FOR THE LETTING OF
November 14, 2017

	November 14, 2017	
Bid Amount	**Contractor**	**Address City and State**
$808,569.78	LUNDA CONSTRUCTION	Black River Falls, WI 54615
$6,668,938.06	PAYNE AND DOLAN, INC	Waukesha, WI 53187-0781-
$5,184,178.62	MICHELS CORPORATION	Waukesha, WI
$3,126,755.79	MICHELS CORPORATION	Waukesha, WI
$1,365,021.10	ZENITH TECH., INC.	Waukesha, WI 53187
$1,213,350.00	ZENITH TECH., INC.	Waukesha, WI 53187
$28,000,000.00	ZIGNEGO COMPANY, INC.	Waukesha, WI 53186-
$5,082,783.55	ZIGNEGO COMPANY, INC.	Waukesha, WI 53186-
$3,032,810.41	PAYNE AND DOLAN, INC	Waukesha, WI 53187-0781-
$269,269.86	LUNDA CONSTRUCTION	Black River Falls, WI 54615
$19,875,713.66	LUNDA CONSTRUCTION	Black River Falls, WI 54615
$1,234,571.11	MICHELS CORPORATION	Waukesha, WI
$6,130,132.77	JAMES PETERSON SONS, INC.	Medford, WI 54451-0120
$370,399.85	ZENITH TECH., INC.	Waukesha, WI 53187-
$1,639,576.10	JAMES PETERSON SONS, INC.	Medford, WI 54451-0120
$241,867,552.87	November Total projects let for 2017	
$84,002,070.66	Board of Directors of WTBA for 2017	
$11,087,902.26	AMERICAN ASPHALT OF WI	$7,689,991.89
$0.00	Edgerton Contractors, Inc.	$108,141,774.87
$80,000,500.95	INTEG GRADING and EXC INC.-	$62,368,526.47
$18,154,893.50	JAMES PETERSON SONS, INC.	$285,885,807.02
$49,149,892.43	LUNDA CONSTRUCTION-	$42,211,087.12
$626,370.14	MEGA RENTALS, INC.-	$3,185,731.98
$26,203,926.02	MICHELS CORPORATION-	$153,624,707.47
$21,999,240.60	MUSSON BROS., INC.-	$103,154,715.39
$330,315.85	PARISI Construction CO Inc-	$6,067,852.22
$28,131,815.14	PAYNE AND DOLAN, INC-	$33,093,508.84
$107,967,850.73	Rock Road Companies	$27,798,052.89
$0.00	TRIERWEILER CONST and SUPPLY COMP	$23,233,931.22
$48,848,186.44	ZENITH TECH., INC. -	$218,123,968.75
$47,252,746.31	ZIGNEGO COMPANY, INC.	$39,855,351.44
Awarded	**Percentage of projects awarded**	**Bid On but not awarded**
$439,753,640.37	39%	$1,114,435,007.57

Total **$241,867,552.87** attempting to bid on projects by the
Construction Companies directly associated with the WTBA.
On just **November 14, 2017,** the WTBA Board of Directors
received the amount of **$84,002,070.66** Awarded Projects
by WisDOT.

WisDOT APPARENT BID RESULTS FOR THE LETTING OF
December 12, 2017

	December 12, 2017	
Bid Amount	**Contractor**	**Address City and State**
$21,341,320.44	ROCK ROAD COMPANIES, INC	Janesville, WI
$580,618.37	ZENITH TECH., INC.	Waukesha, WI 53187
$13,110,202.02	ZIGNEGO COMPANY, INC.	Waukesha, WI 53186-
$6,859,758.09	ZIGNEGO COMPANY, INC.	Waukesha, WI 53186-
$4,873,718.61	ZENITH TECH., INC.	Waukesha, WI 53187
$7,397,696.21	AMERICAN ASPHALT OF WISCONSIN	Mosinee, WI 54455-
$882,943.00	JAMES PETERSON SONS, INC.	Medford, WI 54451-0120
$283,814,853.89	December Total projects let for 2017	
$55,046,256.74	Board of Directors of WTBA for 2017	
AWARDED		**Bid but NOT AWARDED**
$18,485,598.47	AMERICAN ASPHALT OF WI	$7,689,991.89
$0.00	Edgerton Contractors, Inc.	$108,141,774.87
$80,000,500.95	INTEG GRADING and EXC INC.-	$62,368,526.47
$19,037,836.50	JAMES PETERSON SONS, INC.	$381,039,931.65
$49,149,892.43	LUNDA CONSTRUCTION-	$59,195,357.11
$626,370.14	MEGA RENTALS, INC.-	$3,185,731.98
$26,203,926.02	MICHELS CORPORATION-	$195,344,039.27
$21,999,240.60	MUSSON BROS., INC.-	$124,900,687.77
$330,315.85	PARISI Construction CO Inc-	$6,067,852.22
$28,131,815.14	PAYNE AND DOLAN, INC-	$53,875,374.28
$129,309,171.17	Rock Road Companies	$27,798,052.89
$0.00	TRIERWEILER CONST and SUPPLY COMP	$23,233,931.22
$54,302,523.42	ZENITH TECH., INC. -	$227,618,806.82
$67,222,706.42	ZIGNEGO COMPANY, INC.	$62,743,546.28
Awarded	**Percentage of projects awarded**	**Bid On but not awarded**
$494,799,897.11	37%	$1,343,203,604.72

Total **$283,814,853.89** attempting to bid on projects by the Construction Companies directly associated with the WTBA. On just **December 12, 2017**, the WTBA Board of Directors received the amount of **$55,046,256.74** Awarded Projects by WisDOT to the Wisconsin Transportation Builders Association (WTBA averaged 37% for December 2017).

Appendix E

Acronyms

- *African American Chamber of Commerce (AACC)*

- *Bad River Band of Lake Superior Chippewa (BRB)*

- *Bureau of Aeronautics (BOA)*

- *Bureau of Indian Affairs (BIA)*

- *Civil Rights and Compliance Systems (CRCS)*

- *Civil Rights and Labor offices (CRLO)*

- *Construction Industry (CI)*

- *Construction and Materials Manual (CMM)*

- *Construction Unions (CU)*

- *Dept. of Defense (DOD)*

- *Department of Workforce Development (DWD)*

- *Disadvantaged Business Enterprises (DBE)*

- *Division of Transportation System Development Administration (DTSD)*

- *Eleven Federally recognized Tribes of Wisconsin (TRIBES)*

- *Executive Order #39 (EO#39)*

- *Federal Aviation Administration (FAA)*

- *Federal Highways Adminstration (FHWA)*

- *Federal Motor Carrier Safety Administration (FMCSA)*

- *Federal Railroad Administration (FRA)*

- *Federal Transit Administration (FTA)*

- *Federally Recognized Tribes (TRIBES)*

- *Forest County Potawatomi (FCP)*

- *Great Lakes Inter-tribal Committee (GLITC)*

- *Ho Chunk Nation (HCN)*

- *Indian Preference Coordinator (IPC)*

- *Indian Preference laws (IP)*

- *Indian Reservation Roadways (IRR)*

- *Inter-governmental Agreement Opportunities (IGA)*

- *Inter-tribal Tribal Task Force (ITTF)*

- *Lac Courte Oreilles Band of Lake Superior Chippewa (LCO)*

- *Lac Du Flambeau (LDF)*

- *Local 139 Operating Engineers (Local 139OE)*

- *Menominee Indian Tribe of Wisconsin (MITW)*

- *Michigan Tribal Technical Assistance Program (MTTAP)*

- *Memorandum of Agreements (MOA)*

- *Memorandums of Understandings (MOU)*

- *National Association of Minority Contractors (NAMC)*

- *National Highway Traffic Safety Administration (NHTSA)*

- *Native American Hiring Provision (NAHP)*

- *Native American Labor Development Committee (NALDC)*

- *Occupational Safety and Health Administration (OSHA)*

- *Office of Business Opportunity and Equity Compliance (OBOEC)*

- *Office of General Council (OGC)*

- *Oneida Nation of Wisconsin (ONW)*

- *Partnership Agreement (PA)*

- *Red Cliff Band of Lake Superior Chippewa (RCLSC)*

- *Sokaogon Chippewa Community Mole Lake Band of Lake Superior Chippewa (SCC)*

- *Standardized Special Provision (STSP)*

- *Statewide Native American Labor Database (SNALDB)*

- *Stockbridge-Munsee Band of Mohican Indians (SMBM)*

- *St. Croix Chippewa Indians of Wisconsin (SCCIW)*

- *Transportation Advisory Committee (TRANS-AC)*
  Tribal Employment Rights Ordinances (TERO)

- *Tribal Labor Advisory Committee (TLAC)*

- *Tribal Skilled Trades Workers (TSTW)*

- *Wisconsin Department of Administration (WDOA)*

- *Wisconsin Department of Transportation (WisDOT)*

- *Wisconsin Department of Transportation Tribal Affairs representative (WisDOT TA)*

- *Wisconsin Division Federal Highway Administration (WDFHWA)*

- *Wisconsin Transportation Builders Association (WTBA) TLAC coordinator is working on an Awards Program.*

About Atmosphere Press

Founded in 2015, Atmosphere Press was built on the principles of Honesty, Transparency, Professionalism, Kindness, and Making Your Book Awesome. As an ethical and author-friendly hybrid press, we stay true to that founding mission today.

If you're a reader, enter our giveaway for a free book here:

SCAN TO ENTER
BOOK GIVEAWAY

If you're a writer, submit your manuscript for consideration here:

SCAN TO SUBMIT
MANUSCRIPT

And always feel free to visit Atmosphere Press and our authors online at atmospherepress.com. See you there soon!

About the Author

TRAVIS WALLENFANG grew up in the construction industry as General Laborer, worked up to be a Pre-apprentice for Carpentry and Millwrighting, then went on to receive an Associates in Drafting & Design and a Bachelor of Construction Management. He attained a position as Field Engineer contracted to work for WisDOT on megaprojects from the cities of Howard, Green Bay, Appleton, and Oshkosh, Wisconsin, until transitioning to the Position of Indian Preference Coordinator with the Oneida Nation for almost nine years. During that time, Travis worked diligently to attain his Jurisprudence of Indian Law from University of Tulsa, Oklahoma, to have the ability to understand and interpret Tribal Laws, Executive Orders, Memorandums of Agreements & Understandings, Legal opinions, Native American Hiring Provisions and Partnership Agreements. While working as TLAC Representative for six years, he was awarded Excellent in Action two years in a row from Wisconsin Department of Transportation for his hard work done to enhance and fortify the 2018 Partnership Agreements and the Native American Hiring Provision.